Ireland is increasingly recognized as a crucial element in early modern British political and cultural history. Christopher Highley's book explores the ways in which writers responded to the decade-long struggle of a coalition of groups in Ireland against English oppression. Exploring a range of literary representations from Shakespeare and Spenser to contemporaries like John Hooker, John Derricke, and George Peele, Highley traces the emergence of an ideologically diverse discourse on Ireland. This book complicates our understanding of the effect upon Spenser's work and cultural identity of his sojourn in Ireland, while also arguing that the Irish crisis constitutes a provocative yet long-overlooked subtext in the work of Shakespeare and his fellow dramatists. At the end of the sixteenth century, Ireland proved to be a central if problematic element in the imaginative formation of a national and poetic English self.

Cambridge Studies in Renaissance Literature and Culture 23

Shakespeare, Spenser, and the crisis in Ireland

Cambridge Studies in Renaissance Literature and Culture

General editor
STEPHEN ORGEL
Jackson Eli Reynolds Professor of Humanities, Stanford University

Editorial board
Anne Barton, *University of Cambridge*
Jonathan Dollimore, *University of Sussex*
Marjorie Garber, *Harvard University*
Jonathan Goldberg, *Duke University*
Nancy Vickers, *University of Southern California*

Since the 1970s there has been a broad and vital reinterpretation of the nature of literary texts, a move away from formalism to a sense of literature as an aspect of social, economic, political, and cultural history. While the earliest New Historicist work was criticized for a narrow and anecdotal view of history, it also served as an important stimulus for post-structuralist, feminist, Marxist, and psychoanalytical work, which in turn has increasingly informed and redirected it. Recent writing on the nature of representation, the historical construction of gender, and of the concept of identity itself, on theatre as a political and economic phenomenon and on the ideologies of art generally, reveals the breadth of the field. Cambridge Studies in Renaissance Literature and Culture is designed to offer historically oriented studies of Renaissance literature and theatre which make use of the insights afforded by theoretical perspectives. The view of history envisioned is above all a view of our own history, a reading of the Renaissance for and from our own time.

Recent titles include

The marketplace of print: pamphlets and the public sphere in early modern England
ALEXANDRA HALASZ, Dartmouth College

Courtly letters in the age of Henry VIII: literary culture and the arts of deceit
SETH LERER, Stanford University

The culture of slander in early modern England
M. LINDSAY KAPLAN, Georgetown University

Narrative and meaning in early modern England: Browne's skull and other histories
HOWARD MARCHITELLO, Texas A & M University

The homoerotics of early modern drama
MARIO DIGANGI, Indiana University

A complete list of books in the series is given at the end of the volume

Shakespeare, Spenser, and the crisis in Ireland

Christopher Highley
The Ohio State University

CAMBRIDGE
UNIVERSITY PRESS

PUBLISHED BY THE PRESS SYNDICATE OF THE UNIVERSITY OF CAMBRIDGE
The Pitt Building, Trumpington Street, Cambridge CB2 1RP, United Kingdom

CAMBRIDGE UNIVERSITY PRESS
The Edinburgh Building, Cambridge CB2 2RU, United Kingdom
40 West 20th Street, New York, NY 10011–4211, USA
10 Stamford Road, Oakleigh, Melbourne 3166, Australia

First published 1997

Printed in the United Kingdom at the University Press, Cambridge

Typeset in Times 10/12 pt [CE]

A catalogue record for this book is available from the British Library

Library of Congress cataloguing in publication data
Highley, Christopher.
Shakespeare, Spenser, and the crisis in Ireland / Christopher Highley.
  p.   cm. – (Cambridge studies in Renaissance literature and culture; 23)
Includes bibliographical references and index.
ISBN 0 521 58199 0 (hardback)
1. Shakespeare, William, 1564–1616 – Histories. 2. English literature –
Early modern, 1500–1700 – History and criticism. 3. Shakespeare, William,
1564–1616 – Knowledge – Ireland. 4. Historical drama, English – History and
criticism. 5. Spenser, Edmund, 1552?–1599 – Knowledge – Ireland.
6. Ireland – History – 1558–1603 – Historiography. 7. British – Ireland –
History – 16th century. 8. Ireland – In literature. 9. Renaissance – England.
PR2982.H48   1997
820.9′32415–dc21   96-40360 CIP

ISBN 0 521 58199 0 hardback

For Susie

Contents

Illustrations

Acknowledgements

Many people's generosity has helped me with this book. I am very grateful to Stephen Orgel for continual interest, advice, and friendship over many years. I am also indebted to John N. King, who carefully read the entire book, and commented in constructive detail on each chapter. For advice and for reading various sections, I give special thanks to Morris Beja, Alan Brown, David Frantz, Nick Howe, Lisa Kiser, Lisa Klein, Ruth Lindeborg, Caroline McManus, John Norman, Terence Odlin, Thomas Olsen, Phoebe Spinrad, and Luke Wilson. I am grateful to my other colleagues at the Ohio State University Department of English for their friendship and enthusiasm. At an earlier stage, David Riggs and Ronald Rebholtz offered encouragement and valuable guidance. I thank Ron especially for giving me a place to read and write in my last year at Stanford. Alan Sinfield also lent good advice from afar.

Shorter versions of chapters 1 and 4 have appeared previously in *Spenser Studies* and *Renaissance Drama*; I am grateful to A.M.S. Press and to Northwestern University Press for permission to reprint those materials.

I thank my parents, Frank and Stella Highley, for support during my graduate-school years, and my parents-in-law, Jane and Robert Kneedler, for all their kindness and encouragement over the years. I must also mention my two extraordinary children, Alexander and Gregory, and my greatest inspiration, Susan Kneedler. Her influence on this book's ideas and expression, as well as on my life, has been profound and constantly generous. I dedicate this book to her.

Introduction: Elizabeth's other isle

In the reign of James I, Sir Thomas Wilson, the Keeper of the Records at Whitehall, claimed to have discovered in the State Paper Office, "more ado with Ireland than all the world beside."[1] The massive archive of Irish materials was initially built up in the 1580s and 1590s when English efforts to reform, settle, and reconquer Ireland necessitated an increasing volume of correspondence between the court and the Irish administration. Yet this official collection of letters, manuscript tracts, surveys, and maps – large as it is – constitutes only a fraction of the Elizabethan discourse about Ireland, where intractable conflicts provoked debate in "literary" works, including epic poems, public plays and court masques, as well as in more ephemeral material like ballads, proverbs, jokes, and graffiti. The following study does not attempt a comprehensive survey of these multiple voices but focuses mainly upon the canonical figures of Spenser and Shakespeare, examining how their works both shaped and were in turn shaped by the larger English discourse about Ireland. Writing from, respectively, within and without Ireland, and from distinct cultural and institutional locations, Spenser and Shakespeare take up the vexed issue of English interference in Ireland, elaborating imaginary solutions to what the English continue to think of as the Irish "problem." Because my study is about English representations of Ireland, I inevitably explore English perspectives that see the war as an Irish "crisis" caused by Irish "rebels." English "perception" itself, though, is a large part of the "problem," part of the legerdemain of imperialist enterprises. We must always be aware that within their own culture, the Irish who resisted English domination were not "rebels" but freedom-fighters or "men in Action."[2] My own descriptive use of English epithets, far from endorsing their Anglocentric assumptions, seeks to understand the prejudices behind them.

The texts I examine belong to a roughly twenty-year period from 1580 to 1603, a period that spans the rebellions of the Earl of Desmond in the south and the Earl of Tyrone in the north of Ireland. Tyrone's rebellion, spreading eventually into a nation-wide war against English rule, finally

1

elevated Elizabeth's "other isle" to new and urgent prominence in the minds of her government and subjects alike. During the 1580s English foreign and military policy was mainly oriented toward the Low Countries and France, as the Spanish-led Catholic League threatened to extend Philip II's hegemony throughout Europe. But by the early 1590s the escalating crisis to the west diverted ever more attention and resources away from the continental conflict to Ireland.[3] At the end of the Nine Years War in Ireland, the Privy Council blamed England's involvement there rather than in Europe for virtually bankrupting the nation.[4] Elizabeth's troubles in Ireland, moreover, intensified at a time when the site of Anglo-Spanish conflict was shifting from land to sea; while England turned increasingly to sea-borne raids against the Spanish main and Spanish shipping, Spain – now recovered from the defeat of its armada in 1588 – turned again to a strategy of maritime invasion. The renewed Spanish designs on Elizabeth's territory now aimed as much at Ireland as at England.[5]

The fin-de-siècle political and military crisis in Ireland overlay a long-standing and deep-seated English preoccupation with their oldest "colony." Ireland assumed a crucial symbolic place in the formation of emergent English notions of nationhood, empire, and cultural self-understanding – a place that has been inadequately addressed in recent accounts of the ligatures between national self-fashioning and colonial expansion in early modern Britain.[6] Transcending specific political exigencies, Ireland's importance in the English imagination illustrates the anthropological insight "that what is *socially* peripheral is so frequently *symbolically* central."[7]

But if Ireland's centrality to imaginative formations of Englishness in the sixteenth century was assured, Ireland's constitutional and strategic position within the English/British polity was less certain. The crucial political Act was Henry VIII's declaration of 1541 that he was no longer lord but king of Ireland. Claiming dominion over his new kingdom, Henry denied the counter-claims of popes and Irish high-kings while at the same time initiating efforts to extend English law, land tenure, and custom throughout the whole island, and to transform all the inhabitants into his loyal subjects.[8] Far from clarifying Ireland's geopolitical status, Henry's bid at reform and incorporation only added to a sense of ambiguity and conceptual indeterminacy. As Karl S. Bottigheimer argues, Ireland had become both a kingdom in its own right – a discrete administrative entity with claims to autonomy – and a colony of England – the site of outside interference, exploitation, and domination.[9] If Ireland were a colony, how would it be classified: as the vestige of an ancient British empire, as the edge of a new westward-looking empire, or as the would-be northern outpost of an expanding Spanish empire?

Ireland's geopolitical identity could prove confusing but it was also essential in defining and authorizing English self-perceptions.[10] Thus, accounts of Ireland's violence-torn and decentralized polity – a land of "more than 60 countries, called regions . . . where reigneth more than 60 chief captains, whereof some calleth themselves kings" – highlighted the imagined internal unification of England under a single sovereign power.[11] Henry VIII's willingness to acknowledge all the inhabitants of Ireland as his liege subjects with the same rights as his English ones, did not, however, prevent the construction of the "meer" or "wild" Irish in strongly pejorative terms. Negative images of the Gaelic inhabitants of Ireland as idle, libidinous, violent, and godless – in short, as uncivilized "barbarians" – begin in late Medieval works by writers like Gerald of Wales.[12] These perceptions of the Irish varied in intensity until the sixteenth century when, as part of the expansion of English rule and the attempted transformation of the indigenous culture, such prejudices were articulated with renewed vigor. In the Medieval period, the Irish (whatever their diverse regional or dynastic affiliations) were viewed by outsiders (and often viewed themselves) as a single *gens* or people, just as the English, Welsh, Scottish, or Normans were perceived as *gentes* or "communities of common descent . . . identifiable by origin, blood, descent and character."[13] But in the Renaissance's emergent discourses of race and ethnicity, the inhabitants of Ireland were reconceptualized as "a race apart." As a genealogically integrated group, occupying a bounded space, and displaying common linguistic and cultural traits, the Irish were not only constructed as different from but also as socially inferior to the English.[14]

Stereotypical and derogatory images of the Irish were certainly the products of "the ignorant prejudice of metropolitan Englishmen," but they were also fabricated in Ireland from within the Old English colonial community.[15] "Old English" was the sixteenth-century appellation for the descendants of the Anglo-Norman families who had conquered and settled Ireland in the twelfth century.[16] As the representatives of the English crown and the guardians of English law, institutions, and "civility," "the English born in Ireland" – as they called themselves throughout the Medieval period – had continuously and vigorously asserted their English identity and their superiority to the "meer" Irish.[17] But assimilation into the native culture through intermarriage and fostering so mixed the groups that, by the mid-sixteenth century, many Old English families had virtually merged with their Gaelic neighbors.[18] On the other hand, the Old English who resisted Gaelicization (a group mainly confined to the "civil" Pale and port towns) molded a communal identity that felt closely linked to England but that was also inflected by its roots in Ireland. Partly motivating this process of collective self-fashioning was the effort to retain the confidence of the crown – a confidence essential to Old English maintenance of their historic position as Ireland's governing elite.[19]

The supremacy of the Old English was challenged by newcomers from England – the cadre of administrators, churchmen, soldiers, planters, and settlers – who arrived in increasing numbers during the sixteenth century and who became known collectively as the "New English."[20] Disillusioned with traditional attempts at reform and embracing a more radical vision of social transformation, many of the newcomers saw the Old English as the major impediment to the crown's goals in Ireland; beginning in the 1570s with the appointment of militant Protestant governors, the New English increasingly excluded the Old English from positions of influence – treatment that could be justified on the grounds of the Catholic sympathies of many in the Pale community.

As a New English émigré, Edmund Spenser was personally invested both in discrediting the Old English and in shaping perceptions of Ireland's various ethnic groups and alignments. As I shall argue, his work insists upon the complexities and interconnections, slippery and palpably constructed, of the collective identities of the Gaelic Irish, and the Old, and New, English. In delineating Spenser's own project of cultural self-fashioning in Ireland, I envisage him as more detached from and critical of the dominant power structures in Elizabethan society than is usually acknowledged. Recent attempts to revise Spenser's reputation as "Elizabeth's arse-kissing poet" – while helpful in demystifying the cult of the "prince of poets" – do not adequately relate the countercurrents in Spenser's work to his complex material and cultural circumstances in Ireland.[21] In paying renewed attention to the Irish underpinnings of the conflicted and sometimes oppositional modality of Spenser's social and political analysis, I adopt "a model of Elizabethan culture that recognizes the room for artistic maneuver between the two extremes of total affirmation of royal mythology and all-out, open subversion."[22]

Chapter 1 argues that Spenser's experiences in Ireland – a place seen as a wild backwater by sixteenth-century observers and modern critics alike – represents less an exile from the centers of power, than an opportunity for a man of modest beginnings to fashion more flexibly his social and cultural identity. Spenser negotiates the handicap of distance by cultivating substitute networks of patronage in Ireland from English centers of influence and by fabricating in his poetry alternative Irish courts that place him at the center of his own structures of power. In the other chapter devoted to Spenser (5), I develop the notion that Ireland gave him a critical distance upon England and especially upon the queen's contested role in Irish affairs. As a reaction to the deepening crisis of the 1590s, Spenser's agenda increasingly conflicts with the queen's, as he comes to imagine Ireland as a female-free zone, the site of a New English homosocial community.

II

Whereas the two installments of *The Faerie Queene* (1590, 1595) and other poems by Spenser (his prose dialogue on Ireland was not published until 1633) offered English audiences a diffuse and often cryptic perspective on Ireland, there was little else published in the crisis decade of the 1590s that directly confronted the Irish "problem." Yet these were years when public interest in Ireland was at its height and when *manuscript* descriptions, plans, and other materials about the colony were produced in abundance. Public discussion about Ireland was, if not officially prohibited, extremely sensitive; the subject of Ireland represented a marginal, "grey," area included under the rubric of "matters of later yeeres that concern the State," and an area which writers in the public domain approached with extreme caution.[23] The simultaneous paucity of printed materials dealing openly with Ireland in the 1590s, as well as the dearth of evidence that works were ever censored or suppressed, suggest a situation in which writers and authorities observed a tacit code that broadly determined which subjects required more tactful and indirect means of communication.[24] The one major treatise about Ireland published in the 1590s, Richard Beacon's *Solon his Follie, or A Politique Discourse, Touching the Reformation of common-weales conquered, declined or corrupted* (1594), may well have owed its appearance in print to its non-provocative (and non-specific) title, and to the fact that it was printed at Oxford where the writ of the London Stationers and the ecclesiastical licensing authorities did not run.

I would suggest that a growing fascination with England's troubles in Ireland was satisfied less by printed materials than by the public stage. As recent New Historicist work has shown, the Elizabethan theater, as an institution of indeterminate ideological complexion, was continually negotiating its role and power with the authorities of court, church, and city. Enjoying a peculiar license within the cultural world of early modern London, the stage had greater latitude than the printing press, in part because dramatic performance was more difficult to police than the printed word.[25] Although new playscripts were supposedly scrutinized by the Master of the Revels, such oversight could not restrict subsequent public performances to what had originally been licensed. The "fixed" texts of Renaissance plays constructed by modern scholarship provide little sense of the "open," adaptable nature of the script in performance.

Shakespeare critic Peter Thomson sums up received opinion when he expresses his surprise, "that no one wrote about the Irish troubles for the English stage – for so long has Ireland been a blind spot for English playwrights."[26] The blindness, though, is less the dramatists' than many critics'. In fact, as J. O. Bartley observes, Irish characters appeared in masques for Edward VI; in 1553 William Baldwin's (lost) *Irisshe Playe of the State of Ireland* entertained the court; in 1577 the Earl of Warwick's men staged a court performance of the *Irish Knight* (also lost); at the Rose amphitheater in the 1590s, playgoers could see a daringly uncamouflaged rendering of Shane O'Neill's rebellion and death.[27] In discussing Ireland explicitly, the anonymous *Captain Thomas Stukeley*, as I argue in chapter 4, was an anomaly among Elizabethan plays; most plays deployed strategies that disguised their engagement with Ireland. My understanding of these enabling strategies, or "strategies of indirection" as Annabel Patterson calls them, owes much to recently reinvigorated approaches to topical meaning in Renaissance drama and, especially, to Leah Marcus's version of "local reading."[28] For Marcus, "local reading" does not involve recreating the idiosyncratic perspective of particular Renaissance spectators or readers, but of registering the unstable and changing range of topical meanings that theatrical performances and dramatic texts could suggest. Renaissance drama speaks about and to its historical moment in elusive, equivocal, and highly mediated ways. Because public discussion had to be elliptical, Renaissance discourse turns into "combat," an elaborate game of engagement and "cover-up."

When describing, let alone challenging, the controversial subject of English involvement in Ireland, Shakespeare and other writers both in and out of the theater worked out strategies of temporal displacement and spatial transcoding.[29] The slide in signification which allowed other "dark corners" of the British Isles to refer to Ireland was made possible by the fact that the English discourse about Ireland was part of a broader discursive ensemble about the nation's boundaries and borderlands. In the public imagination, Ireland, Scotland, and Wales were inextricably intertwined and could even be constructed as a single territorial and economic zone, with a common linguistic and cultural heritage. Stereotypes and prejudices about the Irish had a certain cross-cultural currency making them readily transferrable to the Welsh and Scots. In chapters 3 and 4 I argue that England's nearer western neighbor, its history, people, and landscape, provided writers with a screen for obliquely registering and imaginatively negotiating the current crisis in Ireland. Writers turned to present-day Wales as an ideal submissive colony, an image of their hopes for Ireland, and therefore they also looked to England's past subjugation of Wales as a precedent for the re-conquest of Ireland. Scotland too could be imaginatively aligned with Ireland and Wales; but Scotland, having emerged as an independent kingdom within the British Isles, represented in political terms a different case from Wales and was thus not as useful to English observers in thinking about Ireland. With the transformation in 1603 of the Scot, James VI, into the British James I, and with the prospect of union between the two kingdoms, writers and public alike became as preoccupied with Scotland as they had earlier been with Ireland. Xenophobic English Protestants had long raised misgivings about a Stuart succession, but the collective attention of the nation was not turned decisively northwards until the death of Elizabeth and the accession of James – events that coincided with the nominal end of the Irish crisis and that are therefore beyond the scope of this study.[30]

My attention to the British dimension of Anglo-Irish relations counteracts a tendency among critics to invoke English activities in the New World as the primary explanatory context for the English presence in Ireland. Drawing upon a few contemporary comparisons, critics have been quick to liken Irishmen to Indians and to assimilate English discourse on Ireland to an over-totalized and speciously unified "discourse of colonialism" that functioned mainly in the domain of America.[31] As Meredith Anne Skura argues, such approaches are anachronistic in their assumptions about the formation and evolution of "colonialist discourse." Even at the time of *The Tempest* in 1611–12, England had barely established its first overseas colonies; earlier attempts at "western planting" like Ralegh's Roanoke enterprise in the 1580s had failed. Moreover, in the early seventeenth century, "colonialist discourse" was neither uniform nor coherent, but a diverse array of images and texts, including eclectic collections of travel narratives and exotic wonders.[32] In the 1580s and 1590s, British adventurers like Humphrey Gilbert and intellectuals like John Dee dreamed of recreating the ancient British Empire of a legendary Arthurian past, but in reality only Spain could boast of huge and wealthy overseas dominions.[33] In practical terms, the English were restricted to disrupting and exploiting Spain's imperial ambitions by plundering Spanish treasure ships or, as Richard Hakluyt proposed, by arming Spain's Indian enemies and thus "troubl[ing] the kinge of Spaine more in those partes [Nova hispania], then he hath or can trouble us in Ireland."[34]

Given the embryonic and uncertain nature of England's aspirations in the New World between 1580 and 1602, public conversation about

Ireland took its bearings predominantly from the history of English expansionism and conquest within not without the British Isles. Yet, while I explore the English "problem" with Ireland in terms of a dynamic of "internal colonialism," I do not claim that the centrifugal momentum carrying English domination from the nation's core to its semi-periphery, or the accompanying consolidation of state power, were in any way linear or uncontested processes. On the contrary, I see the period in question as one of intense English anxiety about the security of the nation as well as the loyalties of supposedly friendly neighbors in Wales and Scotland.[35]

III

The attention given to the work of Shakespeare in this study is not meant to suggest that he achieved a privileged or transcendent perspective on Irish affairs; indeed, my discussion of George Peele's *Edward I* in chapter 3, and my examination of plays by other dramatists throughout, demonstrate how Shakespeare's interest in Ireland was not unique. Present-day cultural politics demand that Shakespeare be foregrounded in a study that raises still-crucial issues of national myth-making, Othering, and the arts of resistance. In spite of calls for a decentering of Shakespeare that would allow us to extend the canon of early modern writing, Shakespeare's works continue to be a highly charged locus in current struggles over the meaning of the past, the relation of cultural production to structures of authority, and the role of culture in the formation of personal and collective identities. Nevertheless, the "Bard" (a moniker that, ironically, appropriates Celtic resonances for an artist who has become a veritable icon of Englishness) merits a central place in this study because of the remarkably sustained and provocative tenor of his analysis of Anglo-Irish affairs, an analysis that spans nearly a decade and provides a bridge between his first and second cycles of English histories.

The Shakespeare plays that I study – *2 Henry VI*, *1 Henry IV*, and *Henry V* – continually illustrate one of my guiding themes: that discourse about Ireland in the late sixteenth century was not only far from monolithic or ideologically coherent, but also unpredictably challenging. Even texts lacking the dialogic and interrogative impulses of Shakespeare's plays – texts that are usually seen as constructing Ireland in official or normative ways – can be made to disclose ideological faultlines and moments of dissidence. I approach all texts not as stable and unified inscriptions of ideology but as sites of possible conflict between various and competing meanings and agendas. Accordingly, part of my project is

to push back "the limits of what was 'thinkable'" during the later
sixteenth century about the "problems" of Ireland and English expansionism.[36] My position is thus opposed to a dominant "common sense"
belief about early modern English perceptions of Ireland and its peoples.
As Philip Edwards writes, "Elizabethan intellectuals" showed an "inability to contemplate, even as a thesis to be disproved, that the Irish
might have a case for resistance, an inability, even as a dialectical
exercise, to put themselves in the Irishman's position and look at the
conflict from his point of view."[37] Edwards's homogeneous category of
"Elizabethan intellectuals," in eliding the range of geographic,
institutional, and ideological positions from which Shakespeare, Spenser,
Peele, Ralegh, and others spoke, flattens out the multiplicity of discourse
on Ireland. I contend that among the available perspectives on Ireland
were indeed angles that could foster, however tentatively, an imaginative
empathy with the Irish victims of English power, and that could
also destabilize prejudicial constructions of Ireland and its "wild"
inhabitants.

IV

The veiled dispute about Ireland that engaged Spenser, Shakespeare, and
their contemporaries, had its formative stage during the twelfth-century
Anglo-Norman conquest of Ireland. The most detailed and influential
account of that conquest is the *Expugnatio Hibernica* by Gerald of
Wales, who, as the blood-relation of some of the major settler families,
visited Ireland four times.[38] The *Expugnatio*, which dates from around
1189, was widely available during Medieval times in Latin manuscript
copies, but did not appear in a complete English translation until 1587,
when it was published as part of the expanded second edition of
Holinshed's *Chronicles*.[39]

The *Expugnatio* serves this study as a foundational text in the
sixteenth-century discourse about Ireland; according to the Old English
writer Geoffrey Keating, Gerald was "the bull of the herd for" all later
writers of "the false history of Ireland."[40] But the *Expugnatio* is also
crucial because, along with the other texts that comprised Holinshed's
Irish Chronicle, it offered Spenser, Shakespeare, and their contemporaries
an unrivaled aperture onto Ireland, its history, peoples, and present
condition. Moreover, the 1587 edition of Holinshed's Irish volume is a
singular textual intersection of the conflicting perspectives of late
Elizabethan representations of Ireland. Annabel Patterson's claim that
Holinshed's *Chronicles* as a whole is no "tool of hegemony" but a deeply
provocative work, grounded upon principles of multivocality and

inclusiveness, is especially true of the section on Ireland.[41] In addition to John Hooker's translation of the *Expugnatio*, the Irish section also includes: Richard Stanihurst's "A Plaine and Perfect Description of Ireland"; Stanihurst's history of the country from its mythical origins to the death of Henry VIII; and Hooker's own continuation of this history (the "Supplie of this Irish Chronicle") up to the deputyship of Sir John Perrot in 1584.

In the early seventeenth century, the militant New English author, Barnabe Rich, clearly had Holinshed's compilation in mind when he invoked the names of Gerald and Stanihurst to complain that Ireland was "in nothing more unfortunate than in this: that the history of the country was never undertaken to be truly set forth but by papists."[42] Stanihurst, a member of an influential Catholic family of the Pale, had in fact fled Ireland before the second edition of the *Chronicles* appeared. His "Description," moreover, was based largely upon the manuscripts and published history of his mentor, the Jesuit Edmund Campion, who – as Rich also observes – suffered a traitor's death at Tyburn in 1582.[43] In terms of their religious and cultural backgrounds, Gerald, Stanihurst, and Campion were strange textual bedfellows for the staunchly Protestant Hooker, who, in addition to writing Protestant propaganda, had served in Ireland as an outspoken member of parliament.[44]

Holinshed's compilation of these diverse voices must have made it difficult for readers to envision Ireland as a unified and homogeneous entity. Stanihurst's "Description," which revolves around the integrity and loyalty to the crown of the Old English community, showcases Ireland as a land of abundant resources and natural wonders with a rich intellectual heritage. Although Stanihurst omits Gaelic learning from praise and censures the "meere Irish" as a "rude people," he ultimately sees the Gaelic population as redeemable through education and religious reform: "they lacke universities," he argues, "they want instructors, they are destitute of teachers, they are without preachers." To expect civility in a people lacking these sources of enlightenment is the same as expecting "a créeple that lacketh both his legs to run, or one to pipe or whistle a galiard that wanteth his upper lip."[45]

John Hooker's contributions to Holinshed's Irish volume form an often jarring counter-vision to Stanihurst's. Hooker struggles in his "Supplie" with the very possibility of writing a history of Ireland according to humanist principles. The edifying function of humanist historiography seems drastically at odds with the spectacle of "actions of bloud, murther, and lothsome outrages; which to anie good reader are greevous and irksome to be read and considered, much more for anie man to pen and set downe in writing."[46] Faced with this contradiction,

Hooker's attempt to master Ireland textually, "to reduce [it] into an historie," takes the form of supposing a providential design in which God punishes the wicked and rewards the virtuous. But, as the narrative unfolds through a depressing sequence of setbacks for the first conquerors and their heirs, Hooker is disillusioned by his design. The colonists' intermittent successes are continually undercut by the larger recursive pattern in which brief periods of peace alternate with longer periods of rebellion. While Hooker's main animus is against the original Gaelic Irish, he is also nervous about Old English loyalties. Moreover, Hooker's view of the Irish as irredeemably malevolent contrasts with Stanihurst's more conciliatory outlook. Hooker stresses that only coercion, not kindness, can control this "wicked, effrenated, barbarous, and unfaithfull nation," while his narrative resounds with accounts of Irish resistance and exhortations for vengeance.[47]

The tensions in Holinshed between Stanihurst's "Description" and Hooker's "Supplie" on the one hand are compounded by the implicit ideological friction between the latter text and Hooker's own translation of Gerald's *Expugnatio*. For Hooker, one of the attractions of Gerald's work was its rehearsal of the English monarchy's "Five-Fold Right" to Ireland, despite the "Right's" inclusion of *Laudabiliter* – the papal grant of the lordship of Ireland to Henry II and his heirs. Whereas the anti-Catholic Hooker records *Laudabiliter* with an uneasy silence, in other places he tries to make Gerald's text more compatible with his own ideological agenda through combining notes and marginal glosses into a system of editorial and exegetical controls.[48] Thus, when Gerald mentions Thomas à Becket, Hooker adds a note denouncing the martyr as "a froward and obstinat traitor," then refuses to print Gerald's praise of Thomas's saintliness.[49]

Although Hooker tries to redeem Gerald as "a noble man by birth . . .brought up in learning . . . [and] a man of the clergie," he finally cannot reconcile the disjunctions between Gerald's elevation of papal over secular authority with his own absolute insistence upon obedience to the monarch.[50] By including Gerald's text alongside his own narratives, Hooker, instead of reinforcing his vision of the Irish conflict and its solutions, seems inadvertently to have complicated and clouded that vision. At moments, Gerald's essentialism and cultural chauvinism complement Hooker's, but at others Gerald implicitly calls into question the entire "colonial" enterprise in Ireland and levels national differences between English and Irish. Thus, in a chapter explaining "whie this conquest could not nor had his full perfection," Gerald argues that in God's eyes both English and Irish "were sinfull people and merited not anie favour . . . but deserved to be severelie punished."[51] From a theological perspective, the conquest of Ireland becomes an unholy instance of Christian-on-Christian violence – "these cruell and bloudie conquests" – and a distraction from the exercise of legitimate religious violence against the infidels.[52] My book, by exploring such evidence as Gerald's troubled ambivalence about Anglo-Norman designs in Ireland, reveals what most past criticism has either ignored or denied, that even the most apparently reactionary and essentialist representations of Ireland and the Irish could create counter-meanings and even inspire radical insights.

1 Spenser's Irish courts

So ships he to the wolvish westerne ile,
Among the savage Kernes in sad exile.

Joseph Hall, *Virgidemiarum*, Satire Five

By the late 1590s, Joseph Hall's satirical portrait of the young English gentleman, down on his luck and seeking refuge in Ireland, was something of a commonplace. For the "threedbare malecontent" of Hall's poem who has sold his lands and whose creditors are closing in, Ireland represents a convenient if dangerous hiding place.[1] Stereotypes aside, many Englishmen who shipped to Ireland in the sixteenth century did indeed look upon their sojourn as a form of exile. When in 1582 the courtier and poet Barnabe Googe accepted the position of Provost Marshal of Connaught at an annual salary of £40, he informed his patron, Lord Burghley, that he had done so through "mere carefulness of my poor estate" – an estate which included "a wife and a great sort of children."[2] Googe saw his service in Ireland as a temporary expedient for managing a financial crisis. But it was also a painful expedient: "I shall ffor thys wynter tyme have ffull experryens off the purgatory off Saynt Patryck," he complained; "I hear lyve amongste a sort off Scythians, wantynge the comffort off mye Contrey, mye poor wyff and chyldren."[3] Googe remained in Ireland only until his fortunes changed in England upon the death of his stepmother in 1587 when he received his inheritance.

Although only a short-term resident, Googe belongs to an expatriate group of English writers, poets, translators, intellectuals, and humanists who in the mid to late sixteenth century secured positions in the administrative and military hierarchies of colonial Ireland. Edmund Spenser, the best-known member of this cadre, arrived in Ireland in 1580 as chief secretary to the new deputy, Lord Grey de Wilton; but when, after a little over two years in the post, Grey resigned and returned to England, Spenser – now set up by his patron with land, property, and offices – remained in Ireland.[4] That Ireland represented a viable, even

13

attractive, long-term option for Spenser but not for Googe, is explained by the two men's different social positions, resources, and expectations. Whereas Googe – the son of a middle-ranking royal officer – was a gentleman by birth, with a powerful patron at court, and a prospective legacy, Spenser – the son of a London merchant – was a gentleman only by virtue of his education and, like the many other university-educated men of non-gentle stock, was forced to compete for scarce offices at court, in noblemen's houses, and in the civil service. For the likes of Spenser as well as for the younger sons of gentry families, prospects in Ireland for employment, self-advancement, and for land – that indispensable marker of gentility – were irresistible. Potential English investors in the first Munster plantation were lured by the promise "that a gentleman undertaker could expect to rise ultimately to baronial wealth – to become the 'chief lord of a great seignory'."[5] Unlike England where the codes governing rank and status were more rigidly enforced, Ireland offered English émigrés an environment conducive to the active fashioning and manipulation of their social and cultural identities. For instance, the absence of "heralds' visitations to establish standards" of gentility in Munster meant that "gentlemen there were self-appointed." In Munster, a man was a gentleman if he was recognized as such by his peers.[6]

To claim that Spenser's nearly twenty-year association with Ireland represented a bitter exile and that, like Shakespeare's Bolingbroke, he trod "the stranger paths of banishment" (1.3.143) as an alienated intellectual, hardly does justice to the shifting and complex ways in which he appears to have experienced and recorded his place there. Certainly, Spenser's acquisition of offices, grants, and land in Ireland – as well as the accompanying professional and social prestige – could never fully erase a sense of displacement from the undisputed focus of political and cultural activity. For "Gentlemen of limited means [like Spenser] ... the royal Court was the acknowledged center of the realm, and such environments as the Inns of Court, the universities, London business and professional circles, the counter, even the English-occupied areas of the Low Countries and Ireland, were satellites to it."[7] But feelings of displacement in Ireland were also interwoven for Spenser with ones of opportunity. As Richard Rambuss astutely observes: the "possibility for parlaying the condition of exile into one of (relative) empowerment is to see the distance of exile as opening up a space for saying what cannot be said elsewhere, nearer to the centers of power ... Exile thus construed is enabling."[8] Recent criticism, in fact, has become increasingly sensitive to the contours and nuances of Spenser's Irish "exile," and to the ways in which both in his life and his writing he engaged in "home-making" projects.[9] Building on this work, I examine Spenser's exploration of his uncertain situation vis-à-vis the cultural center and his negotiation of a place in Ireland that registers both a sense of isolation and a contradictory sense of authority that isolation confers. Spenser constructs in his poetry alternative structures of power and patronage – alternative courts, in fact – that reflect in often unexpected ways his complex immersion in Irish culture.

Spenser's disabling distance from the royal court was not ameliorated by the existence of more accessible satellite courts within Ireland. Throughout the Tudor period the headquarters of the English viceroy in Dublin signally failed to perform the kinds of cultural functions that might sustain a "courtly society" in the town. "The Irish monarch's proxies, the viceroys," writes Ciaran Brady, failed

> to establish an Irish court within the new kingdom which might have served both as a symbol and a practical instrument of the reformist intent of government. Early suggestions that special viceregal palaces should be established as centre points in each of the provinces were not pursued, and throughout the century the viceroys' residences at Kilmainham and at Dublin Castle continued to serve only the most basic functions of providing board and lodging for the governors' household and retinue.[10]

For Spenser's Irish courts, then, we must look not to the political landscape of sixteenth-century Ireland but to the poetry that is inspired and powerfully informed by that landscape. I turn first not to the familiar court settings of *The Faerie Queene*'s later books – the books most often related to Irish contexts – but to the marginal and obscure court of Merlin in Book Three, a book that Spenser may not have begun in Ireland but one that he probably revised and completed there.[11]

I

Criticism of Merlin usually glosses the magician and his "looking glasse" (3.2.18) as embodying Spenser's claims about the status of the artist and his creations. Thus William Blackburn argues that in Spenser's romance and chronicle sources "Merlin is a prophet, a magician, an artificer; he is all those things in *The Faerie Queene*, but he is also something more: a figure for the poet, and so of central importance to the treatment of art in the entire poem."[12] If Merlin is a generic poet-surrogate, I would also argue that his appearance is a nexus for the anxieties and desires surrounding Spenser's predicament in Ireland. This claim hinges upon the similar geopolitical locations of Merlin and Spenser on the fringes of their respective realms. Merlin resides at an unspecified distance from the court of his nominal overlord, the Welsh king Ryence.[13] When

Ryence's daughter Britomart and her nurse set out in search of the magician,

> To *Maridunum*, that is now by chaunge
> Of name *Cayr-Merdin* cald, they tooke their way:
> There the wise *Merlin* whylome wont (they say)
> To make his wonne, low underneath the ground,
> In a deepe delve, farre from the vew of day,
> That of no living wight he mote be found,
> When so he counseld with his sprights encompast round.
>
> And if thou ever happen that same way
> To travell, goe to see that dreadfull place:
> It is an hideous hollow cave (they say)
> Under a rocke that lyes a little space
> From the swift *Barry*, tombling downe apace,
> Emongst the woodie hilles of *Dynevowre*
>
> (3.3.7–8)[14]

Typed as wild and sinister, Merlin's environment, like many a landscape in *The Faerie Queene*, evokes the uncharted, dangerous spaces of Gaelic Ireland beyond the Pale of Dublin and the "civil" walled towns – spaces that Spenser himself traversed on his campaigns with Grey and on his Kilcolman estate. Strikingly, Merlin's inhospitable surroundings and his distance from Ryence's court are not presented as a disadvantage; on the contrary, his "hideous hollow cave" constitutes the locus of real power in the realm. "With his sprights encompast round" like attentive courtiers, Merlin presides over an alternative and far more powerful court than Ryence's. In fact, the "looking glasse" that reveals to Britomart the image of her destined spouse, thus prompting her to seek Merlin's help, had originally been fashioned as an instrument to secure her father's political and military hegemony:

> It was a famous Present for a Prince,
> And worthy worke of infinite reward,
> That treasons could bewray, and foes convince.
>
> (3.2.21)

With its panopticon-like powers to foresee and disarm both the internal threat of treason and the external threat of foreign invasion – "What ever foe had wrought, or frend had faynd, / Therein discovered was" (3.2.19) – Merlin's glass is an object of political and military fantasy, one especially meaningful in the tense socio-political climate of the late 1580s. More tellingly, Ryence's reliance upon the "glasse" for his political survival reveals an arrangement in which a subject not only willingly serves but actually maintains in power a weaker monarch:

Huge hostes of men he could alone dismay,
And hostes of men of meanest things could frame,
When so him list his enemies to fray.

(3.3.12)

With the power to conjure his own army and to disperse his enemies at
will, Merlin is a version of the overmighty subject – both the maker of
kings and their potential undoer. In the episode's redistribution of power
between ruler and subject, then, Spenser imaginatively reconstructs his
own position on the margins of the Elizabethan state in Ireland into a
privileged site of vision and power.

In the role reversals of Merlin and Ryence, Spenser also sheds his
accustomed stance of needy petitioner, exchanging its frustrations for a
condition of mastery and independence. Yet even as Spenser appears to
stand above the exigencies of the patronage system, he uses the Merlin
episode to advertise his utility to political authority and to lodge large
claims about the place of poetry in the state – claims that depend on a
perception of Merlin's "glasse" and Spenser's epic as homologous
artifacts. *The Faerie Queene* like the "glasse" is conceived as a container
of cautionary wisdom, offering images of the nation's friends and foes
and relentlessly unmasking the evil that lurks beneath feigned shows of
goodness in figures like Archimago and Duessa. Furthermore, by helping
to "fashion a gentleman or noble person in vertuous and gentle discipline" the poem serves a complementary function to Merlin's "glasse" in
securing political stability. For while the "glasse" alerts loyal subjects to
the forces of disorder, Spenser's poem helps to construct those subjects in
the first place. Merlin's gift of the "glasse" to Ryence thus constitutes an
instructive analogue to Spenser's own act of royal gift-giving. The
presentation to the queen of Spenser's own "fair mirrhour" is enacted in
two ways (2.0.4). The poem is textually remitted to Elizabeth via its
dedication. But as Spenser later recounts in the loosely autobiographical
Colin Clouts Come Home Againe, the queen also receives the poem in a
physical sense when Colin visits the English court with the first installment of the epic. By equating his poem with Merlin's "glasse," Spenser
appears to be insisting that the power of his creation lies as much in its
physicality, its existence as an actual book, as it does in its status as an
abstract linguistic construct. Valorizing *The Faerie Queene* as artifact,
Spenser thus elevates it to the same level as other books sacred to the
Protestant state like the Bible and Foxe's *Acts and Monuments*. Gift-
giving and service, of course, call for gifts and favors in return. When
Spenser describes the "glasse" as a "worthy worke of infinite reward" he
means both the "reward" reaped by its grateful owner and the "reward"
due to its maker.

II

In so far as Merlin uses his magic to legitimate the authority of both Ryence and the Tudor dynasty, Spenser's act of covert identification can be seen as an essentially conservative gesture, a coded reassurance to the Elizabethan regime of his unswerving loyalty. Yet the fact that Merlin is more powerful than his ruler carries with it a latent threat of political opposition, a threat accentuated in the poem by the shadowy, undomesticated existence of Merlin and the dubious sources of his powers. Throughout, Merlin is associated with a mixture of the demonic and beneficent forces that inform his genesis: "begonne / By false illusion of a guilefull Spright, / On a faire Ladie Nonne" (3.3.13). The demonic overtones of Merlin's power are reinforced by the description of his servants as "Feends." They are a conscript workforce of carnivorous demons, kept under control only by fear of their master, and would "devowre" any traveller unfortunate enough to stray into their "balefull Bowre" (3.3.8).[15]

The implications of Spenser's personal investment in Merlin are further complicated and darkened when we consider the magician's reputation in late Elizabethan culture. In short, Merlin – like the power of prophecy he personified – was a deeply suspect figure for a Protestant audience. Although his prophecies were occasionally deployed in support of reformed religion and Tudor orthodoxy, the "Anglican establishment" denounced Merlin and his prophecies as Catholic propaganda that encouraged religious and political instability. Edwin Sandys, the Archbishop of York, warned that papists had "books of Merlin and other fantastical spirits, full of doubtful sayings and deceitful dreams . . . all tending to this end, that alteration is near, that the state will not long continue, that religion cannot endure long."[16]

Howard Dobin has recently related Spenser's choice of Merlin as the prophet of the Tudor regime to the Elizabethan state's own periodic use of "unofficial, even illicit forms of power" – forms that included "the dubious popular vernacular of marginal practices such as astrology and prophecy."[17] An important example and analogue to Merlin is the government's vexed relation to John Dee – the astrologer, mathematician, imperial propagandist, and Elizabethan intellectual – whose alleged powers of prognostication and casting horoscopes made him both threatening and useful; although his unlicensed powers were publicly denounced he still enjoyed the favor of prominent noblemen, even the attentions of the queen herself.[18] Spenser's attraction to Merlin in *The Faerie Queene* is intimately bound up with the magician's transgressive reputation in the culture. Poised in the poem between loyalty and opposition, between inclusion in the political community and an uneasy separation from it, Merlin figures Spenser's own liminal position both inside and outside an official order. The Merlin episode thus affords another aperture on what Louis Montrose terms Spenser's "equivocal" relationship with political authority as invested in the queen and her court. Focusing on the "Aprill" eclogue of *The Shepheardes Calender*, Montrose finds this equivocation in the "interplay between submission and resistance to the project of royal celebration" – an interplay that turns on Spenser's simultaneous assertion of the monarch's glory and his own determining power in formulating the representations through which that glory is manifested.[19]

If Spenser can be seen as already developing an "equivocal," conflicted relationship to the political center in *The Shepheardes Calender*, his later removal to Ireland, and his various posts in a state apparatus that was functionally semi-autonomous from the larger power structures of England, could only have heightened a sense of divided loyalties. Contributing to the blurring of loyalties and identities was Spenser's unavoidable contact with the rich indigenous culture of Gaelic Ireland – a culture in which the figure of Merlin also had a revered place. Merlin's importance to the Irish may strike us as odd since he is a figure usually associated with Welsh cultural identity and a messianic belief in the return of an ancient hero who would rid Wales of foreign intruders. Moreover, if we examine Merlin's career in Geoffrey of Monmouth's *Historia Regum Britanniae* – an important source for Spenser and the work most influential in fixing Merlin's image for English readers – the magician is actually shown assisting in the oppression of the Irish.[20] In the *Historia*, Merlin both suggests and makes possible the transportation of the "Giants' Ring" from "Mount Killaraus in Ireland" to the burial place of the British heroes. Utherpendragon, the British king's brother, invades Ireland with fifteen thousand men, defeats the Irish king and his army, and – with Merlin's help – conveys the magical stone pillars to England.[21] This inaugural act in the English expropriation of Irish culture foreshadows the total conquest of Ireland by Arthur later in the narrative.[22]

Geoffrey's anti-Irish Merlin, however, can be distinguished from the Merlin of a different legendary tradition. As John Hooker explains in the glosses to Gerald of Wales's *Expugnatio Hibernica*, there were in fact two Merlins: "both were prophesiers: the one was named *Merlinus Calidonius*, or *Sylvestris* . . . he was borne in the marches of Scotland . . . in the time of king Arthur . . . The other Merlin was before this man and in the time of Vortiger . . . and he was named *Ambrosius Merlinus*."[23] Far from showing disdain for the Irish as does Geoffrey's *Ambrosius Merlinus*,

Gerald's *Merlinus Calidonius* is, along with "Bracton, Patrike, and Columkill," one of "The foure Irish prophets" whom the people of Ireland hold in "great veneration and credit . . . [and] whose books and prophesies they have among themselves in their owne language." What this Merlin and his brethren foresee, according to Gerald, is that Ireland "shall be assailed with often warres, the strifes shall be continuall, and the slaughters great. But yet they doo not assure nor warrant anie perfect or full conquest unto the English nation not much before dooms daie."[24] These were sentiments more likely to embolden the subject peoples of Ireland than they were to reassure their would-be conquerors.

The possibility that this "other" Merlin – *Merlinus Calidonius* – and his association with Ireland inform Spenser's treatment, makes the poet's choice of Merlin as a figure on which to project his own anxieties and desires even more intriguing and provocative.[25] Viewed in the context of Spenser's Irish experiences and his relation to Gaelic culture, the Merlin episode takes on a new layer of suggestiveness. Specifically, Merlin's prophetic powers now evoke the ancient druids of Ireland and – by extension – the genealogical and poetic pursuits of their heirs, the present-day bards.[26] In his notes to the first printed edition of Spenser's *A View of the State of Ireland* (1633), Sir James Ware defined the Irish bards as "rayling Rimer[s]" but he also mentioned their larger professional reputation for having *"knowledge of things to come."*[27]

III

Building upon my recovery of Merlin's Irish subtext, I want to suggest that bardic culture comes to offer Spenser a home or court of sorts – a space for the construction of new cultural identities and imaginative possibilities. This seemingly unlikely hypothesis diverges from W. B. Yeats's classic claim that "When Spenser wrote of Ireland he wrote as an official, and out of thoughts and emotions that had been organized by the State."[28] Complicating this "official" side with its doctrinaire conclusions were conflicting impulses that can be felt throughout Spenser's corpus in equivocations and doubts about New English designs in Ireland and as moments of near-sympathy with Gaelic culture.[29] In the following sections, I pursue this "unofficial," fugitive side of Spenser's interest in the proscribed figure of the bard, by working outward from key passages of *A View of the Present State of Ireland* into the poetry, specifically *The Faerie Queene*'s dedicatory sonnet to Ormond and, more centrally, *Colin Clouts Come Home Again*. What we discover is Spenser's subtle and evolving awareness of the strategic possibilities of the bard and bardic practice for his own poetic and cultural identities. And in engaging with the symbolic possibilities of the bard, Spenser ventures into other courts: settings, like Merlin's cave, that serve to redefine his cultural position as well as his relation to the queen and a court-identified English polity.

Whereas the Welsh bards of the late sixteenth century enjoyed the patronage of an Anglicized gentry and were officially recognized at periodic eisteddfods, their Irish counterparts were feared rather than celebrated.[30] Bards, brehons, chroniclers, and other learned groups were routinely denounced in accounts of the Irish "problem" written by New English settlers and officials.[31] In Thomas Gainsford's *The True Exemplary, and Remarkable History of the Earle of Tirone* (London, 1619), the "Bards and Rimers" who "by many superstitious presages" had successfully "animated" Tyrone against English rule are considered the agents of both political and domestic disorder. For Gainsford, the bards and their associates are

the very bane and confusion of *Ireland*, living in such obscenity and filthinesse, that no Gentlewoman thinketh herselfe happy without them, and supposeth it no disgrace even to bee prostituted unto them . . . So that (in my conscience) the most of the rebells and strumpets amongst them, are the bastards of these rogues and vagabonds: and all the treasons, which have turmoiled our Nation, have received life and originall from their imposturing and perswasions. (26–27)

According to Sir John Perrot, Lord Deputy of Ireland from 1584 to 1588, the solution to the subversions of the bards and other "undesirables" was clear:

all Brehons, Carraghes, Bardes and Rymers, that infect the people, Friars, Monkes, Jesuites, Pardoners, Nunns, and such like, that openly seeke the maintenance of Papacy, a Traytrous kinde of people . . . [should] be executed by Marshall Law, and their favourers and maintainers by due course of law, to be tryed and executed as in cases of Treason.[32]

When in Spenser's *A View of Ireland* Irenius adds his voice to this anti-poetic discourse by urging the immediate suppression of "the evill Custome" of Gaelic poetry, the text fulfills what is almost a requirement of the genre of the Irish essay.[33] Critics have long accepted Irenius' harsh conclusion as Spenser's final word on the bards, but in so doing they have overlooked the nuances of Irenius' full analysis. Only superficially does Spenser's attitude to bardic culture resemble that of either Gainsford or Perrot.[34]

The bards are first mentioned in *A View* when Irenius defends them and their associates, the Irish chroniclers, against the charges of his intolerant, Anglocentric friend Eudoxus. Adopting an antiquarian perspective, Irenius recuperates the bards and chroniclers as legitimate sources of knowledge about the past – provided that they are treated with adequate caution as well as studied alongside other authorities and forms of evidence:

> Besides the Bardes and Irishe Cronicles them selves, though through desyre of pleasinge perhapps too much and ignorance of arte and pure learninge, they have clouded the truth of those tymes, yett there appearethe amongst them some reliques of the true antiquitie, though disguised, which a well eyde man may happelye discover and fynde out. (52)[35]

Irenius' condescension, his confidence in his own culture's superior intellect and perception, do not damp his sense of the bards' work as of great anthropological value.

Not only have critics overlooked Irenius' grudging defense of bardic art, but they have also underestimated the complexity of his final condemnation. For Irenius concedes that the poets' professional task of "sett[ing] forth the prayses and disprayses of men" and of melding impressionable young minds is admirable, at least in theory. Many of the bards' praises are even deemed suitable by Irenius for "men of best desert" (94, 97). What Irenius distrusts is the bards' habit of picking "for the most parte," the unsuitable heroes of traitors and rebels (95–96). Yet even that qualification – "for the most parte" – militates against the usual classification of Irenius as the monolithic and authoritarian thinker in the dialogue. Especially in the first half of *A View* where the focus is on Irish ethnography, Irenius routinely lays out in sympathetic detail the indigenous cultural practices that he will ultimately proscribe. For example, the Gaelic practice of tanistry by which a sept elected its new chief emerges in Irenius' scrupulous account as eminently fair and rational (10–12). As an alternative to the English system of primogeniture, tanistry ensures that leadership of the clan passes not automatically to the present chief's eldest son but to the best contender in terms of age, strength, and experience. Tanistry thus eliminates the possibility of an immature, weak, or otherwise unsuitable heir. If Irenius' strategy of disavowing the customs he scrutinizes offers a kind of artificial closure, it cannot negate and make unsaid the more sympathetic elements of his foregoing analyses.

Irenius confirms his more-than-censorious fascination with native culture when he tells Eudoxus how he has had "dyverse" bardic poems translated, one of which he summarizes in detail (97–98). Roland M. Smith has noted the similarity in tone between this poem celebrating the life of an Irish chief – a "wicked outlawe" whose "musicke was not the harpe nor layes of love, but the cryes of people, and Clashinge of armor" – and the poetry of Tadhg Dall Ó Huiginn (1550–91), a contemporary of

Spenser's, and one of the best-remembered bards of the period.[36] But the poem referred to by Irenius is representative neither of Ó Huiginn's individual corpus nor of the "diversity" of bardic verse in circulation during the later sixteenth century. While Smith claims that Ó Huiginn's poems "often advocate unrelenting war against the 'foreigner'," T. J. Dunne by contrast sees in Ó Huiginn's verse an example of a "bardic pragmatism" that was more concerned with establishing a lord's lineage, rights, and duties than with fomenting anti-English sentiment.[37] Dunne acknowledges that some of Ó Huiginn's compositions indeed advocate "resistance to the newcomers and the need to present a united front against them," but "most . . . were conventional and made no mention of the growing threat from the new and more intractable colonialism."[38]

In fact, most bardic verse, instead of inciting violence and rebellion, was laudatory, "written to establish the ancestry and rights of the patron, to celebrate his battles in defense of these rights, and the fulfillment of his social obligations – not least his hospitality to the poets."[39] When the patron was perceived as failing in these obligations, the aggrieved bard could turn from eulogy to his other staple genre of satire. The Gaelic lords, observed the Palesman Richard Stanihurst, "esteem their poets, who write Irish learnedly and pen their sonnets heroical, for the which they are bountifully rewarded; if not they send out libels in dispraise, whereof the lords and gentlemen stand in great awe."[40] That it was ungrateful Gaelic lords rather than English "newcomers" who were the main targets of bardic satire reflects the fact that Gaelic verse was most often local rather than national or "racial" in outlook. In addition to preserving his personal and professional reputation, the bard's major task was to defend his chief's rights against regional threats.[41]

IV

The praises and dispraises of the bards, however, were not reserved only for the Gaelic elite. Thomas Butler, the tenth Earl of Ormond and Ossory, as well as speaking fluent Gaelic and countenancing Brehon law in his territories, cultivated the style and discharged the traditional responsibilities of the Old English chief. And as did many Old English noblemen in sixteenth-century Ireland – whether enemies or friends of the crown, whether modest landowners like Spenser's neighbor Lord Roche or the greatest of magnates – Ormond received in return for his patronage and protection the traditional encomiums of the bards.[42]

The Butlers – "ancient English gentlemen" according to Richard Stanihurst – were one of the Anglo-Norman families that had established themselves in Ireland during Henry II's reign. Many of the descendents of these twelfth-century conquerors had since cast off their allegiance to the crown; but Ormond, unlike his family's historic rivals in southern Ireland, the Desmond Fitzgeralds, remained steadfastly loyal to the Tudor regime.[43] Educated at the Protestant court of Edward VI, and a cousin and favorite of Elizabeth, Ormond seemed to many at court – especially the Cecil faction – a reliable representative of royal power in Ireland. As a way of symbolically asserting his loyal Englishness, Ormond is reputed to have worn his George medallion at all times; and in a move designed to consolidate his standing in the English peerage, Ormond in 1582 married the Englishwoman, Elizabeth Sheffield, the daughter of John, second Baron Sheffield.[44]

Despite his credentials, Ormond was for many in the New English community no trueborn Englishman and hence automatically suspect.[45] Resentment of Ormond's status as Ireland's most powerful subject compounded anxieties aroused by his ambivalent ethnic identity. As lord deputy, Sir Henry Sidney accused Ormond of frustrating reform efforts by advocating leniency toward the rebels, as well as of putting the security of his own estates before his military responsibilities. And in the turbulent 1590s, Ormond was accused by his enemies of conspiring with Hugh O'Neill, Earl of Tyrone, and of planning to divide the country between themselves after securing an alliance through the intermarriage of their children.[46]

Underlying these allegations against Ormond were anxieties about a figure who had negotiated a cultural position at the intersection of English and Gaelic spheres, thus making his "true attachments [often difficult] to discern."[47] One sign of this uncertain, slippery identity – his support for the disruptive practice of bardic rhyming – was used against Ormond by his enemies. Their charges may, to some extent, have been justified. James Carney – the modern editor of *Poems on the Butlers* – sees in a poem written to honor Ormond "the implication . . . that Ormond encouraged the poets against his sovereign's wishes" when in 1585 he failed to carry through a commission from "Elizabeth to execute martial law in the counties of Kilkenny and Tipperary [against] all 'idle men, vagabonds, sturdy beggars, harpers, rymers and bards'."[48]

Although we know little about Ormond's relations with Spenser, Roland M. Smith has proposed that Ormond acted as a special channel through which Spenser acquired his knowledge of bardic poetry and the Gaelic learned tradition. Spenser "may have been aided by one of the MacClancys . . . who were brehons to the Earl of Ormond . . . whose 'brave mansione' at Carrick was not far from Kilcolman."[49] If geographic proximity brought Spenser into Ormond's orbit, so too did their shared status as "undertakers" in the Munster plantation scheme;

Ormond's seignory was one of the largest, Spenser's at approximately 3,000 acres one of the smallest. The likeliest point of contact between the two men was the provincial council of Munster and its headquarters in Limerick.[50] As deputy clerk and later clerk of the council from about 1583, Spenser would have developed a working relationship with Ormond, who was not only the leading landowner and power broker in southern Ireland but was also appointed the governor of Munster in 1583.[51] Ormond was ideally placed, then, to promote Spenser's career within the Irish bureaucracy and to help his fellow undertaker secure his estate against the claims of local rivals like Lord Roche.[52]

Spenser's most overt bid for the protection and patronage of Ormond appears in the dedicatory sonnet appended, along with sixteen others, to the first installment of *The Faerie Queene*.[53] Here Spenser fuses the conventional posture of needy supplicant with the figure of the tenant offering produce to his lord. Thus Spenser asks that the "noble Lord" receive his poetic offering, "the wilde fruit, which salvage soyl hath bred." Set in what has become a war-ravaged wasteland covered by "brutish barbarisme," Ormond's "brave mansione" is held up as an outpost of civility and learning, a last *"Parnassus"* and singular *"Helicone"* in the "wasted soyl" of Ireland where the "sweete Muses" and "faire Graces" can find shelter. Spenser portrays Ormond as the benevolent purveyor of "goodly bountie and true honour." And like the patron–householder in Jonson's "To Penshurst" – a poem with which Spenser's sonnet is generically affiliated – this "lord dwells." Spenser's pose is designed to win an invitation to come inside, a chance to exchange the "barren field" for the nurturing surroundings of Ormond's "brave mansione." Unlike the corresponding sonnet to Grey which attempts to repay his former employer for favors past, the Ormond sonnet constitutes an act of investment that carries with it the expectation that the recipient will be equally generous in return.

Figuring himself as the outsider at Ormond's door, Spenser is also exploiting his would-be protector's reputation as patron of bards. Spenser subtly dons the mantle of the unaccommodated bard – the kind of bard, in fact, who was in greatest danger from the rigors of martial law in the province. To have any chance of survival, the bard needed "to be able to give [the English authorities] a patron's name [and] to be accounted part of the retinue of a specific lord."[54] Spenser, moreover, was not the only petitioner to seek Ormond's support at this time. In *A Scourge for Rebels* (1584), the soldier of fortune and hack writer Thomas Churchyard sought to ingratiate himself with "mine auncient friende the worthye earle of Ormounde" (B2ʳ).[55] Churchyard proposed to write further about Ormond as part of his effort "to purchase noble friends, whose power may further my good fortune here" (C3ᵛ). And in the 1567 dedication to Ormond of *Horace His Arte of Poetrie, Pistles, and Satyrs Englished*, the translator Thomas Drant speaks of Horace – and by implication of himself – as a kind of unhoused bard in search of a patron: "masterles to gadde abroade at wyde adventure" (iv).

As secretary to Lord Grey, Spenser paid at least two visits to Ormond's Kilkenny residence in 1580 and 1581. On the first of these, Ormond himself was absent but had instructed his wife to "make good cheer for the Lord Deputy and that he may be supplied on his way to Limerick."[56] Spenser likewise encounters a reassuring female presence in the sonnet's "brave mansione" where the "sweete Muses," along with the "faire Graces many one. / And gentle Nymphes, delights of learned wits" amount to a kind of female salon. Chief among the mansion's female occupants would have been Ormond's wife and daughter (two more Elizabeths in Spenser's life in addition to his sovereign, his mother, and his wife). Spenser's allusive gesture to them in the sonnet echoes the bardic convention of acknowledging the patron's wife and her own considerable influence in controlling patronage. In "Taghaim Tomas" (c.1588) – one of the few extant bardic poems addressed to Ormond – the earl's English wife is the focus of praise in the final three stanzas.[57]

Through deploying tropes of exile and domestication and in envisaging Ormond's residence as a partly feminized space, the sonnet to Ormond in effect resolves the predicament imagined in *The Teares of the Muses* – a poem that appeared in the *Complaints* volume of 1591, the year after the first installment of *The Faerie Queene*.[58] Whereas the sonnet shows the Muses and Graces finding "harbour" in the earl's mansion, *Teares* portrays a similar sisterly community being banished, "From our owne native heritage exilde," in the words of the Muse Terpsichore (line 341). Forced to "beg" (line 407) to survive, the Muses and the Graces,

> Walk through the world of every one revilde.
>
> Nor anie one doth care to call us in,
> Or once vouchsafeth us to entertaine,
> Unlesse some one perhaps of gentle kin
> For pitties sake compassion our paine,
> And yeeld us some reliefe in this distresse:
> Yet to be so reliev'd is wretchednesse.
>
> So wander we all carefull comfortlesse,
> Yet none doth care to comfort us at all.
>
> (lines 342–50)

Figured as a "crew" of mobile, wandering, and begging women, the Muses are assimilated to a discourse of vagrancy that emphasized the collective, mob-like aspects of "masterless" behavior.[59] At the same time, images of vagrancy are complicated by a nexus of specifically Irish resonances. As each of the seven Muses speaks her lament, a collective female voice emerges. This voice, which passes from speaker to speaker in a ritual of female bonding, is characterized as much by the women's "troublous noyse" – their "wayling," "exceeding mone," "lowd laments," "shrieks and cries and dreery yells" (lines 30, 18, 416–18, 538) – as it is by their actual words. The noise of women that fills the poem enacts the Muses' vision of a world that has abandoned true poetry and learned poets for the "scoffing Scurrilitie" and "rymes of shameles ribaudrie" of "base-borne men" (lines 211–19). Gathered to grieve the demise not just of true poetry but of a noble, heroic culture in general, the Muses take on the appearance of mourning Irish women.[60] The noise generated by mourners at Gaelic funerals was a manifestation of what English commentators like Spenser and Barnabe Rich derisively labelled "the Irishe Hubbubb."[61] Among the Irish, wrote William Camden, "When the soul is once departed they mourn by the claping of hands, and hideous howlings" – a practice for which female relatives were especially responsible. In the late eighteenth century the practice continued: "both men and women, particularly the latter," wrote one observer, "are hired to cry, that is to howl the corps to the grave, which they do in a most horrid manner."[62] By transferring this "barbarous" noise to the mythopoetic figures of inspiration and graceful expression, Spenser underscores the utter alienation of the Muses from English culture. The Muses' despair ineluctably evokes Spenser's own.

In other ways, too, the tropes of Irishness permeate *Teares*, complicating the construction of the Muses. For example, the Muse of Pastoral, Euterpe, asserts that the Muses' enemy "Ignorance," "fed with furies milke,"

> And gathering unto him a ragged rout
> Of *Faunes* and *Satyres*, hath our dwellings raced
> And our chast bowers, in which all vertue rained,
> With brutishnesse and beastlie filth hath stained.

(lines 259, 261; 267–70)

In the historical/Irish allegory of *The Faerie Queene*, "*Faunes* and *Satyres*" invariably figure either the Gaelic or "degenerate" Old English inhabitants of Ireland. Through the assault of the "*Faunes* and *Satyres*" here upon the Muses' "pleasant groves, which planted were with paines" (line 277) and their transformation of this cultivated landscape "into wildernesse" (line 287), Spenser reinscribes the Muses as versions of the English planters whose mission was to convert wilderness into habitable and productive land. Euterpe's vision of a landscape devastated by

rebellion looks forward presciently to the wasting of the English settlement in Munster, including Spenser's own estate at Kilcolman, in 1598.[63]
But whereas *Teares* reduces a once orderly and fruitful landscape to a
barren "wildernesse," the Ormond sonnet allows Spenser to eke out of
the "salvage soyl" of a hard land a "wilde fruit" whose very ambivalence
suggests the same paradoxical blend of civility and incivility, Englishness
and Irishness that inheres in the patron to whom it is offered.

Although Spenser's only recorded visits are to Ormond's castle at
Kilkenny, the "brave mansione" of the sonnet more readily suggests
Ormond's other residence at Carrick. When in *Colin Clout* Spenser
compliments Lady Ormond as one of Queen Elizabeth's attendants he
refers to her as the Nymph "of the famous Shure" (line 526), thus
associating her with the Carrick-on-Suir residence. Begun in 1568, the
Carrick country house was designed, as Ciaran Brady has observed, as a
symbolic reflection of Ormond's nearly unassailable position in Ireland.
"Opulent, unembattled and modern, [Carrick was] an emblem of the
manner in which the earl planned to exert his authority" – an authority
that rested upon his favored status at the English court.[64] In copying the
style of an English Tudor manor, the Carrick house "was unique in
Ireland." Ormond, for instance, had

> decorated the long gallery-hall on the first floor with stucco medallions showing
> busts of his kinswoman, Queen Elizabeth, whom he hoped to entertain there. . .
> The rest of the house followed the same pretensions to comfort and style: it was
> constructed of stone and brick, with brick gables and chimneys, and interior
> partition walls of lath and plaster. There were good stairs, large mullioned
> windows, a liberal supply of privies and extensive offices round a large cobbled
> court.[65]

Ormond's Carrick residence, in other words, was designed to imitate the
English country house both in its appearance and in its function of
extending hospitality and patronage.[66] Spenser's sonnet, though, constructs Ormond's "brave mansione" in even more grandiose terms,
imagining it as a sort of national, humanist court, a place to which
writers and intellectuals like Spenser would naturally gravitate.[67] This
particular construction of Ormond's residence can be seen as answering
an unfulfilled need of Spenser's and like-minded New English émigrés for
a center of cultural activity in Ireland.

V

In his search for a humanist court in Ireland – an alternative institutional
center of cultural privilege to the English court – Spenser was not alone.
This same desire is also implicit in Lodowick Bryskett's *A Discourse of*

Civill Life, a work dedicated to his patron Lord Grey.[68] Describing his translation of Cinthio's treatise "as a thing rare in [this barbarous countrie of Ireland], where almost no trace of learning is to be seene, and where the documents of Philosophie are most needfull, because they are so geason [scarce]," Bryskett grafts the works of classical antiquity onto the English language in an alien soil, thus contributing to a New English cultural project of which Spenser's poetry and prose are key products.[69] A major part of that project was finding a stable and reliable site – both geographical and political – around which to organize cultural work. In the narrative frame of Bryskett's translation, a site of sorts is offered in his own "little cottage which I had newly built neare unto Dublin." It is here that Bryskett, Spenser, and other statesmen, soldiers, and churchmen assembled to discuss such conventional humanist topics as education, gentlemanly self-fashioning, and the relative merits of political engagement and withdrawal.[70] Modelled on the kind of learned and witty humanist exchange in texts like Castiglione's *The Book of the Courtier*, Bryskett's dialogue significantly shifts the location from a palace to the obscure and marginal surroundings of his cottage.[71] Through its ironic incongruity, the cottage-setting of Bryskett's *conversazione* highlights the absence of a more distinguished institutional site for New English cultural work in Ireland.

As Spenser imagines this kind of artistic–philosophical milieu in Ormond's "brave mansione," he strategically extends his own patronage network by turning to Irish-based support at a time when English court-based ones were rapidly disappearing. Sidney, Leicester, and Walsingham – patrons from earlier in Spenser's career – were all dead by mid-1590. Further catastrophe was to follow just three years after the first installment of *The Faerie Queene*, when Lord Grey – the man who had been instrumental in promoting Spenser's Irish career and whom Spenser addressed in another dedicatory sonnet as "the pillor of my life, / And Patrone of my Muses pupillage" – also died.[72] Moreover, Spenser's embrace of Sir Walter Ralegh as a new benefactor in *Colin Clout* was problematic; although Ralegh's imprisonment and subsequent banishment from court came in 1592 after his secret marriage to Elizabeth Throckmorton, and after Spenser's dedication of *Colin Clout* and the composition of *The Faerie Queene*'s dedicatory sonnet, by even 1589–91 Ralegh was a dubious figure on which to rely.[73]

VI

The bardic overtones informing Spenser's sonnet to Ormond emerge more diffusely in *Colin Clouts Come Home Againe*, a poem that bears the dedication date of December 27, 1591 but which was not published until 1595.[74] Yet the bardic overtones of *Colin Clout* are more far-reaching and potentially more radical in terms of their implications for Spenser's poetic and cultural identity. By setting *Colin Clout* in Ireland and by specifically drawing upon the topography of his Munster estate and its environs, Spenser reinvests the traditional figures and topoi of pastoral with unusual local and topical resonances, while adding a new and provocative twist to the poetic persona he had introduced over a decade earlier in *The Shepheardes Calender*.[75]

From the poem's opening, the shepherd–piper Colin – who entertains and instructs his assembled companions with music, song, and narrative – appears distinctly bard-like:

> Charming his oaten pipe unto his peres,
> The shepheard swaines that did about him play:
> Who all the while with greedie listfull eares,
> Did stand astonisht at his curious skill,
> Like hartlesse deare, dismayd with thunders sound.

(lines 5–9)

Performing for an enthusiastic group-audience, Colin recalls Irenius' account in *A View* of how the bard's verses "are taken upp with a generall applause, and usuallie sounge at all feastes and metinges, by certaine other persons whose proper function that is, which also receyve for the same greate rewardes, and reputacion besides." The division of poetic labor that Irenius notes between composer and singer is extended in Thomas Smith's 1561 tract on the learned classes of Ireland into a tripartite division among the bard who composes the rhyme, the Rakry who delivers it, and the Harper who accompanies the Rakry.[76] Calling on his pipe and "sleepie *Muse* [to] awake" so that he may deliver the "song" of his adventures at Cynthia's court, Colin simultaneously embodies all three roles of creator, singer, and musician: he becomes, as it were, a composite bardic artist (line 48).[77]

Colin's "charming" with his pipe implies both "playing" and "enchanting."[78] The poet–piper's ability to hypnotize his listeners and to transform his physical surroundings alludes to the Renaissance Ur-poet and archetype of poetic power, Orpheus. But Colin is an Irish Orpheus and in the poem's Irish setting the image of a poet-figure magically "charming" his audience ineluctably evokes the Gaelic belief in the strange efficacy of words. This belief was manifested in the idea that bardic satire, powerful in its ability publicly to shame its victims, could also inflict psychological and physical injury.[79] The belief that in Ireland a man could be "rhymed to death" was made notorious by Philip Sidney at the close of his *Apology for Poetry* as an example of the affective power of verse, a power that Sidney and other humanists promoted, albeit in restrained terms.[80] We could easily dismiss Sidney's reference to the deadly potency of Irish bards as purely fanciful – part of his final, playful warning to the enemies of poetry; but if, like Sidney, Spenser ultimately stopped short of granting the poet a power over life and death, he assumed nevertheless that his own words were capable of powerfully molding individual identity – of "fashion[ing] a gentleman or noble person in vertuous and gentle discipline."

To explain Spenser's attraction to a bardic persona in *Colin Clout* we need to turn to the material circumstances out of which the poem grew and which the poem itself commemorates. Colin's trip to England in the company of "the shepheard of the Ocean" parallels Spenser's visit in 1589 to oversee the printing of the first installment of *The Faerie Queene*. For his poetic services in dedicating the work to Elizabeth – and, if we are to believe *Colin Clout*, of reading part of his epic to her – Spenser was awarded an annual pension of £50.[81] In Ireland, where prices were significantly lower than in England, £50 was a considerable sum. Robert Payne, an estate manager near Spenser in Munster and the author of an early promotional pamphlet for the plantation, assured prospective English settlers that they "may keepe a better house in Ireland for L.li. [£50] a yeare, then in England for CC.li [£200] a yeare."[82]

The evidence suggests that when completing the first part of *The Faerie Queene* and during his trip to England, Spenser was keeping his options open in the search for patronage and advancement. As the dedicatory sonnets to Ormond, Ralegh, and Norris – which date from the same period as *Colin Clout* – indicate, Spenser sought to strengthen his alliances in Ireland as a way of furthering his career within the colonial administration. Spenser's ambitions in Ireland did not mean that he relinquished his hopes for sustenance at the English court; given the opportunity, he might have abandoned or subordinated his Irish commitments. In spite of the relative generosity and value of the queen's pension, then, Spenser seems to have remained unsatisfied. His goals – and the role of his poetry in promoting them – have recently been illuminated by Richard Rambuss. Focusing on Spenser's earliest bid for public attention in *The Shepheardes Calender*, Rambuss argues that Spenser advertises his skills as a secretary – literally someone skilled at keeping secrets – as a way of advancing his own career not as a poet only but as a civil servant, perhaps even as a member of the queen's own cabinet.[83] These same ambitions, for professional advancement through secretarial or office-holding responsibilities, were undoubtedly part of the mix of motives informing Spenser's trip to England and his presentation of his epic to Elizabeth.

If Spenser was dissatisfied after the award of his pension in February 1591, so too were those contemporaries who "continued to lament the poet's poverty, and to complain (on his behalf) of what they evidently perceived to be a want of proper recognition and respect for him, and, by extension, for poetry itself."[84] For one observer, Spenser's residence in Ireland represented a form of exile that injured the poet as well as his admirers. In a commendatory sonnet to the *Amoretti and Epithalamion* volume (1595), Geoffrey Whitney Senior complained that while Spenser's "Muse in forraine landes doth stay, / invention weepes, and pens are cast aside." Invoking Spenser as England's model Poet, Whitney urges him, "hie thee home, that art our perfect guide" (lines 598–99).

But as Colin/Spenser discovers in *Colin Clout*, despite the queen's hospitality there is no "home" for him at the English court. In a starkly physical image of his rejection and maltreatment there, Colin recalls how he was "shouldred . . . [and] out of doore quite shit" (line 709). Similarly, the qualities of "Truth and simple honestie" that Colin embodies are said to "wander up and down" at court, "despys'd of all" (lines 727–28).[85] Evident here is the trope of Irish wandering that informs *The Teares of the Muses*. But if Spenser invests Colin and his fellow shepherds with these "Irish" traits, he purges them of their usual moral stigma. Idleness, the negative correlative and moral consequence of Irish wandering, is displaced from Colin and the shepherds onto the courtiers whom Colin encounters at Cynthia's court. This jaded group exhibits both the specific taint of Gaelic idleness and the more general moral degeneracy, marked especially by what Colin depicts as effeminacy, for which Irenius attacks the Old English in *A View*. Cynthia's courtiers, says Colin,

> do most-what fare amis,
> And yet their owne misfaring will not see:
> For either they be puffed up with pride,
> Or fraught with envie that their galls do swell,
> Or they their dayes to ydlenesse divide,
> Or drownded lie in pleasures wastefull well,
> In which like Moldwarps nousling still they lurke,
> Unmyndfull of chiefe parts of manlinesse.
>
> (lines 757–64)

In contrast to these "degenerates," Colin's choices figure him as morally upright, tough, and stereotypically masculine. He abandons the blandishments of a court ruled by a woman and dominated by foppish men for the harsh but implicitly masculinizing environment of Ireland, "Where cold and care and penury do dwell" (line 657).

Given Spenser's own embittered sense of exclusion and maltreatment at court, there was much about the bard that, at least subliminally, would have attracted him. Unlike the under-supported or unrecognized poets whom Colin encounters at Cynthia's court, the Irish bards traditionally received generous remuneration for their services in the form of land, cattle, jewels, and other valuables. Within Gaelic culture, moreover, the bard was a prestigious, even sacred, figure, credited with impressive rhetorical powers. In short, bards enjoyed the kind of reputation and remuneration in their culture that Spenser continually sought but never received in his.[86] But perhaps the most significant aspect of the bard's allure to the career-conscious Spenser was the fact that a chief's official bard or "ollamh flatha" was, to borrow Rambuss's phrase, "doubly-employed," fulfilling various diplomatic and political duties for his chief in addition to his usual poetic ones.[87] In the Irish lordship system, ollamhs were secretaries, messengers, and ambassadors for their chiefs, and in their poems depicted themselves as the privileged confidants of their masters, sitting at his elbow and sharing his cup and secrets. In another self-promoting trope, the ollamh figured himself as his chief's mistress and bedfellow.[88]

VII

While Spenser's refashioning of his poetic alter-ego in *Colin Clout* can be seen as a response to his sense of exclusion and underappreciation in England, the appropriation of a bardic persona also represents part of a larger effort by Spenser to reconceive his cultural identity. That reconceptualization involves shifting his emotional center from England to Ireland, thinking of himself as more fully grounded in his adopted homeland, and of reconciling himself and his fellow settlers to a life away from their ancestral home.[89]

Between the dedication of *Colin Clout* in December, 1591, and its eventual publication in 1595, Spenser probably circulated the manuscript among his acquaintances in Ireland. "Some parcels" of *The Faerie Queene*, as Bryskett's *Discourse* informs us, had circulated in like manner.[90] In *Colin Clout*, Spenser challenges the poem's first readers by inviting a local, coterie audience to recognize itself in the various shepherds who engage Colin during his narrative. Spenser had used a similar strategy in *The Shepheardes Calender*; as E. K.'s gloss on the "September" eclogue explains: "by the names of other shepheardes, [the author] covereth the persons of divers other his familiar freendes and best acquayntaunce" (164). Lodowick Bryskett has been identified in *Colin Clout* as the shepherd Thestylis – a sobriquet confirmed by his elegy for Sir Philip Sidney: *The Mourning Muse of Thestylis* – while Arthur Hyde, Spenser's Munster neighbor and fellow undertaker has been linked with Cuddy (the river Funcheon with which Cuddy is associated, flowed through Hyde's estates). The presence of Hobbinol – Spenser's pseudonym in *The Shepheardes Calender* for his Cambridge friend and mentor Gabriel Harvey – would appear to resist this kind of local placement, since Harvey, as far as we know, never visited Ireland.[91] By including him as Colin's first and principal interlocutor in the poem, Spenser can be seen imaginatively transferring what was undoubtedly one of his most cherished friendships from England to Ireland. The latter country, transformed into the locus of an ideal and inclusive coterie of friends, no longer supplements but supplants England as the main source of Spenser's emotional and intellectual sustenance.

However appealing the poem's first readers may have found the use of pastoral names, far more suggestive for our purposes is the description of Colin and his companions, as "the shepheards nation" (line 17) – a designation that imputes to them a kind of tribal unity and celebrates for Spenser's assorted readership of friends, neighbors, and fellow settlers a positive image of collective identity based upon mutual loyalty and movement away from the old country to the new. Spenser's evocation of a cohesive group of shepherds/settlers helps offset the hardships of life in Ireland that Colin enumerates so graphically in the poem (lines 312–19); but this ideal community also serves as a way of imaginatively healing the endemic strife and divisions afflicting the New English population of Munster. Since the plantation's inception in the late 1580s, the undertakers had been in open conflict both with each other and with the local Old English elite over the distribution and ownership of land.[92] As one weary observer remarked: "So many causeless contentions happen between the undertakers, striving who shall have most when much less were sufficient."[93] William Herbert, Spenser's Munster neighbor and the author of a Latin treatise on the colony – *Croftus sive de Hibernia Liber* (c.1591) – complained to Burghley in October 1588 that "Our pretence in the enterprise of plantation was to establish in these parts piety, justice, 'inhabitation,' and civility, with comfort and good example to the parts adjacent. Our drift now is, being here possessed of land, to extort, make the state of things turbulent and live by prey and by pay."[94] In the group of shepherds that eagerly interrogates Colin we can see Spenser constructing the sort of unified and supportive "imagined community" that he hoped would emerge both locally amongst the settlers in Munster and, perhaps, nationally amongst the New English population in Ireland as a whole.[95]

Colin's vision of an Irish-based community reaches beyond the New English constituency in Ireland to embrace loyalist elements among the Old English as well. At Cynthia's court, Colin finds Ormond's wife –

transplanted from her "brave mansione" at Carrick – and Frances Howard, daughter of Charles Howard, the Earl of Nottingham and Lord High Admiral, and the wife of the Earl of Kildare.[96] The encounter reminds Colin of the place he has left and leads him to "claim" the two women (who bear the names of sea-nymphs) as members of a symbolic Irish family:

> [*Galathea*/Lady Kildare] there then waited upon *Cynthia*,
> Yet there is not her won, but here with us
> About the borders of our rich *Coshma*,
> . . . Ne lesse praisworthie faire *Neaera* [Lady Ormond] is,
> *Neaera* ours, not theirs, though there she be.
>
> (lines 520–25)

While the insistent tone of Colin's "ours, not theirs" implies almost a rivalry between Ireland and England, the presence at Cynthia's court of the two women establishes them as cross-over figures between two geographic and cultural spheres and thus as important mediators for Spenser between England and Ireland.

If Spenser is not prepared in *Colin Clout* to sever completely his ties with England and the English court he is at least willing to envisage a group identity and kinship system based in Ireland – one that elevates local ties to the point where they supersede the more distant and merely inherited bonds of English nationality. Because the patriotism of the settlers was a matter of memory rather than of propinquity, the greatest threat that *Colin Clout* poses to England's continued influence in Ireland is a transference of ties of affection and "blood" among the settlers from their shared English ancestry to that of their shared Irish locale. Recounting his sea-crossing from Ireland to England, Colin speaks fondly of "that land our mother" which he is leaving (line 226). The true motherland, whose influence is felt even when its citizens are far away, is now not England but Ireland.[97] When Colin comes home again, he comes home to Ireland.

In the new motherland, Colin compensates for his earlier rejection from Cynthia's court by imagining himself as the consummate insider, the high-priest and door-keeper of the court of Cupid. Through an elaborate neo-platonic allegory, Spenser fantasizes a role for himself as guardian of a community of true believers and the scourge of its enemies. He, not they, can create the chosen and the rejected, the "at home" and the exiled, those

> outlawes . . . [who Cupid's] lore do disobay.
> For their desire is base, and doth not merit,
> The name of love, but of disloyall lust:

Ne mongst true lovers they shall place inherit,
But as Exuls out of his court be thrust.

(lines 890–94)

Colin's nomination of Cupid as his "dread Lord" and "the greatest of
the Gods" (lines 793, 799) helps bind together the "shepheards nation,"
setting it in opposition to Cynthia's deviant courtiers who "prophane"
Cupid's "mightie mysteries" (lines 785, 788). The "poore shepheards'"
faithful dedication to Cupid, by contrast, invests them with an ennobling
moral authority.

Possessed with a "celestiall rage" (line 823), Colin functions as inter-
mediary between heaven and earth by revealing the mysteries of Cupid
and delivering a long neo-platonic account of creation. Colin speaks here
with the authority of those original, mythical poets whom George
Puttenham describes in his *Arte of English Poesie* (1589) as *"the first
priests, the first prophets, the first Legislators and politicians in the
world."*[98] In Ireland the venerable powers mentioned by Puttenham were
still residually associated with the ollamhs or fileads, those poets who sat
at the top of the bardic hierarchy. Colin's vatic performance as the Priest
of Love signals his movement up the hierarchy of bardic orders, from a
kind of wandering bard on his trip to England, to an ollamh, the modern
descendent of the ancient druids and seers of Celtic society.[99] In this act
of poetic metamorphosis, Spenser imaginatively bypasses the need for
patrons and their meager support; he stages his own self-promotion, the
ability to propel himself without benefactors from a lowly, obscure status
to the position of moral leader and spokesman of his community.
Moreover, Colin's inclusion of himself as a privileged insider in Cupid's
court is framed by that other court: the assembly of shepherds listening
to Colin composes a kind of outdoor rural congregation of which Colin
is the undisputed center. The poem dramatizes Spenser's Irish court, a
court in which he is neither servant nor dependent but the presiding
authority.[100]

VIII

Spenser's appropriation of a bardic persona in *Colin Clout* intimates to
readers his increasingly strained relationship with England and its queen.
In one way, the poem's startling juxtaposition of high-flown praise of
Elizabeth with attacks on her courtiers interfuses the encomiastic and
satirical strands of bardic verse, channelling these Irish poetic energies
into the service of an English and monarchical agenda. Spenser's fellow-
undertaker, William Herbert, imagined a similar process of cultural
transformation and renewal, one that would transmute the disruptive

songs of "the windy and lying poets" of Ireland into "sacred hymns . . . songs in the Irish language which will encourage [the natives] to virtue and entice them to moderation and tranquility of spirit."[101]

In another way, though, Spenser's adoption of a bardic persona embodies a symbolic violation of the apartheid-like laws established for the Munster plantation and, thus, an implied gesture of defiance to English-based authority. For one of the Articles of Plantation required undertakers to employ only English-born families on their estates and prohibited all intercourse between the English planters and "rhymers, bards, harpers or such idle persons."[102] But in *Colin Clout*, just as in the actual history of the plantation, pure and self-contained ethnic categories cannot be sustained. From the beginning of the enterprise, the settlers ignored the government's fantasy of segregation by employing Irish tenants and servants instead of the English-born families they had agreed to bring over. The settlers perforce interacted with the Gaelic people and their culture, even patronizing "Irish music and provid[ing] patronage in their houses for harpists." By the early seventeenth century, the main landowner in Munster, Richard Boyle, "had come to appreciate . . . that a landowner in Ireland was at a distinct disadvantage in dealing with his neighbours and tenants if he was not conversant in their language."[103]

The darker side of Colin's bard-like stance is closely interwoven with the poem's oppositional energies generally, energies that arise from the deeply ambiguous praise of the queen and her court. As Thomas H. Cain notes in relation to the growing pessimism of *The Faerie Queene*'s later books: "signs of tension in encomium are already apparent in 'Colin Clouts Come Home Againe' (1591), where excited and vatic praises of Cynthia conflict with a stubbornly satirical picture of her court."[104] If Colin's disenchantment with English court culture is profound, his gushing descriptions of the queen – who seems to rise above the corruption around her – is finally compromised by the introduction of the private, local figure of Rosalind. Colin's devotion to Rosalind displaces and absorbs devotion to Cynthia – the devotion that Colin had earlier proclaimed as unique and inviolate. This abrupt and unexpected transference of loyalty is hardly the gesture of an eternally grateful and singleminded worshipper.[105]

In substituting Rosalind for Cynthia, Spenser both dismisses the queen and confronts his ambivalent feelings toward her, since Rosalind both is and is not a figure for Elizabeth. Colin's companions accuse Rosalind of cruelty for not returning his love, but Colin himself, through remarks which are at once self-deprecating and self-protective, clears her of all such imputations. Colin's complaint of the "long affliction which I have endured" (line 944) is the furthest Spenser can go in revealing personal

grievance toward the queen. More strenuously to protest his disappoint-
ment or directly to blame Rosalind/Elizabeth would be foolhardy,
perhaps dangerous. Colin's friend Lucid, in fact, by adducing the
cautionary parable of Stesichorus, makes shockingly clear how the
writer's relationship to female authority is circumscribed by fears of
transgression and punishment:

> And well I wote, that oft I heard it spoken,
> How one that fairest *Helene* did revile:
> Through judgement of the Gods to been ywroken
> Lost both his eyes and so remaynd long while,
> Till he recanted had his wicked rimes,
> And made amends to her with treble praise.

(lines 919–24)

If Spenser, unlike the unnamed Stesichorus, wisely stopped short of
slandering his Helen, he was still capable of registering in more elusive
ways what David Norbrook has called his "suppressed discontent with
the Virgin Queen."[106] Moreover, when *Colin Clout* was eventually
published in a volume of belated elegies for Sir Philip Sidney in 1595, the
context emphasized the poem's elegiac rather than eulogistic strands. By
including *Colin Clout* in the *Astrophel* volume, Spenser presented his
poem as part of a collective lament for a heroic male figure whose
advocacy of militant Protestantism and an interventionist foreign policy
had brought him into frequent conflict with the queen.

IX

Less well known than the English settlers' reliance upon Gaelic tenants
and servants in the Munster plantation was the controversial practice of
employing kerns or Gaelic foot soldiers to fill up English regiments, a
tactic made necessary by the chronic lack of money and properly trained
English soldiers.[107] In a related move, the English authorities would
sometimes turn to the bards for propaganda against rebellious Gaelic
chiefs.[108] English attempts to harness bardic powers for their own
purposes are evident in a statute of Edward VI ordering that "no poet or
any other person hereafter shall make or compose any poems or anything
which is called 'auran' to any person, except to the king, on pain of
forfeiting all his goods, and imprisonment." Although no bardic poem in
praise of Edward survives, there is one extant poem from c.1588–89 in
praise of Elizabeth I.[109] "Loyalist" bardic poetry, however, was not
directed only toward English monarchs. In the early years of the
seventeenth century, Sir George Carew, the lord president of Munster,
and Lord Deputy Mountjoy, sought to exploit the Gaelic community's

well-known fear of bardic satire by hiring "a renegade Irish satirist, Angus O'Daly, the Red Bard, or Angus of the Satires, to travel up and down the four provinces of the island, satirizing the ancient Irish families and clans (chiefly on the grounds of poverty and inhospitality)".[110] Whatever short-term advantages it may have offered, the English strategy of cultural appropriation in the military and political affairs of early modern Ireland often proved hazardous and even self-defeating. Hired kerns would desert the English ranks, taking their weapons with them, and "loyal" bards were notoriously unreliable.[111] Embodying a similar instability, Spenser's appropriation of a bardic persona in the Ormond sonnet and in *Colin Clout* – while from one perspective marking him as Elizabeth's loyal Irish bard – represents him from another perspective as an estranged and deracinated figure, one engaged in the construction of alternative non-monarchical centers of power. Even as the Spenser of *A View* advocated the brutal suppression of Irish "barbarism" and the radical reorganization of Gaelic culture, he actually plundered that culture as a means of empowering and recreating himself. The act of cultural self-fashioning, conducted at a distance from the English court and in a country that lacked established mechanisms for determining and policing social identity, inevitably fostered in Spenser a sense of autonomy from the structures of authority in Elizabethan England.

2   Reversing the conquest: deputies, rebels, and Shakespeare's *2 Henry VI*

Midway through the first part of Shakespeare's *Henry VI*, "English John Talbot," that "terror" of the French and embodiment of patriotic heroism, finds himself and his soldiers cut off from reinforcements and surrounded by enemies before Bordeaux. "O negligent and heedless discipline!," he exclaims:

> How are we parked and bounded in a pale,
> A little herd of England's timorous deer
> Mazed with a yelping kennel of French curs!
>
> (4.2.44–47).[1]

Undeterred, Talbot fights on against the odds until, spiritually broken by the death of his son, he finally expires, the symbol of a vanishing chivalry (4.7.30–32). As part of the play's evocation of the vicissitudes of English militarism in France, Talbot's fatal isolation at Bordeaux has been expertly related by Leah Marcus to the involvement of Protestant Englishmen in the French wars of religion of the early 1590s, the years to which Shakespeare's first tetralogy belongs.[2] In flocking to assist the beleaguered regime of Henri IV, English volunteers were defending a foreign prince against Catholic insurgency, rather than securing their nation's sovereign territories. Yet as recently as 1559, land in France had been under English control. In that year, Elizabeth had agreed to return the Pale of Calais to the French, thus giving up the final piece of a Medieval empire that at its height under Henry V had covered much of France. Although Elizabeth continued to style herself queen of England, Ireland, and France, the last claim was more symbolic than substantive, a nostalgic glance toward a glorious national past.[3]

In fact, after 1559 Ireland remained the only overseas territory to which the English monarch could realistically claim sovereignty. And it is Ireland with its vexed identity – part colony, part kingdom, in part the residue of an old empire, in part the cusp of a new westward-looking one – that also overshadows Talbot's poignant words in *Henry VI*. Talbot's brand of embattled Englishness, "parked and bounded in a pale,"

conjures up the quintessential predicament of the front-line conqueror–
colonist who starts out as the representative of a central home authority,
but ends up finally abandoned by and alienated from that authority. In
early Anglo-Irish relations, this pattern found its analogue in figures like
Maurice Fitzgerald, the Anglo-Norman *conquistador* whose forays into
Ireland eventually lost the backing of his overlord, Henry II. The result,
according to the account in Gerald's *Expugnatio Hibernica*, was a sense
of cultural disorientation: "Whie then doo we tarie?," Fitzgerald asks his
followers at the siege of Dublin in 1170,

and wherefore doo we so linger? Is there anie hope of releefe from home? No, no,
the matter is otherwise, and we in woorse case. For as we be odious and hatefull
to the Irishmen, even so we now are reputed: for Irishmen are become hatefull to
our owne nation and countrie, and so are we odious both to the one and to the
other.[4]

If Talbot shares with Fitzgerald the problem of how to survive in an
uncertain middle position in between metropolis and colony, he also
shares a direct connection to Ireland, since the historical John Talbot,
Earl of Shrewsbury, had served as Lieutenant there for Henry V and VI
on three occasions.[5] This service earned him the additional titles, "Great
Earl of Washford [and] Waterford" (4.7.63).

When Shakespeare surveyed the reign of Henry VI, he looked back to
a moment that was widely considered to be the beginning of England's
current and unresolved troubles in Ireland. Never simply an inward-
looking conflict, the English Civil Wars of the fifteenth century had
repercussions throughout the British Isles, precipitating – in the reigns of
Richard II and Henry VI most notably – a decisive rupture in the English
control of Ireland.[6] In the early seventeenth century, Fynes Moryson
summed up a historiographical consensus: "from the first Conquest of
Ireland, to the following warres betweene the Houses of Yorke and
Lancaster in England . . . I find very rare mention of any seditions in
Ulster . . . [or] of great forces or summes of mony sent out of England
into Ireland." But when "the English Irish" (or Old English, the
mainstay of English rule in Ireland), left Ireland to participate in
England's civil strife, then,

the meere Irish boldly rushed into the possessions, which the other had left void
in Ireland. And from that time . . . seditions and murthers grew more frequent,
the authority of the English kings became lesse esteemed of the Irish, then in
former times, and the English Pale had sometimes larger, sometimes straighter
limits, according to the divers successes of the Irish affaires at divers times.[7]

As a critical turning point in the history of Anglo-Irish relations, then,
Henry VI's reign stood as a resonant setting in which Shakespeare could

reflect upon the current political realities of Ireland, realities that *1 Henry VI* refracts through the parallel dilemmas of governing France. While *1 Henry VI* traces the decay of England's French empire, *2 Henry VI* adjusts the geographic focus of dynastic and national politics by introducing an important British dimension. After the loss of France in Part One, Ireland emerges directly as a key locus in the continuing power struggles of Part Two. Centering on *2 Henry VI*, this chapter aims to recover the diffuse Irish subtext of Shakespeare's earliest analysis of what has been too narrowly conceived as "English" history. Working back and forth between *2 Henry VI* and its dense political and textual milieu, I focus upon two ostensibly antithetical figures in the political landscape of the early 1590s: the English viceroy and Irish rebel. I argue that Shakespeare weaves into the play a provocative and deeply conflicted analysis of the threats and stereotypes associated with Ireland, and that the figures of viceroy and rebel turn out to be curiously interconnected, the joint bearers of English anxieties about colonial rule and domestic security.

I

In the first part of *Henry VI*, Talbot's troubles and the loss of England's French empire are blamed not upon the nation's military commanders or soldiers, nor upon the strength and cunning of the French, but upon the "worthless emulation" among court factions in England and the king's regents in France. Their responsibility is emphasized at the play's opening when Henry V's funeral rites are interrupted by messengers announcing the loss of England's French territories: "Amongst the soldiers this is muttered," declares the first messenger to the assembled court,

> That here you maintain several factions
> And, whilst a field should be dispatched and fought,
> You are disputing of your generals.

> (1.1.70–73)

Subsequent events confirm the soldiers' diagnosis: aristocratic "dissension" pervades the play, most notably in the rivalry between the Duke of Gloucester and the Bishop of Winchester for control of the king, and in the struggle between Richard Plantagenet and the Duke of Somerset for the succession. Yet the "factious emulations" that galvanize domestic politics arouse greatest alarm when played out on French soil: "Remember where we are," Henry VI warns the squabbling supporters of York and Somerset during his coronation in Paris:

In France, amongst a fickle wavering nation;
If they perceive dissension in our looks
And that within ourselves we disagree,
How will their grudging stomachs be provoked
To wilful disobedience and rebel!

                                                    (4.1.137–42)

But York and Somerset ignore Henry's warning; their "worthless emulation," in fact, is directly responsible for the death of Talbot who expects
but never receives their help at Bordeaux (4.4.21).

That internal discord within the conqueror community inevitably
gives comfort and strength to the conquered was a maxim well known
to the rulers of Tudor Ireland. And in the later sixteenth century,
divisions in the form of an aggressive factionalism were threatening the
consolidation of English power throughout the island. Faction, as
Thomas Wilson recognized, was intrinsic to the operation of power in
the Tudor state. And the tentacles of factionalism at the English court
reached deep into Irish affairs, with domestic factions fighting over
offices in Ireland, including the supreme position of lord deputy.[8] Once
appointed, the deputy dispensed patronage to secure his interests
against rival New and Old English groupings on the Dublin administration and throughout the country. But contrary factions both in
England and Ireland frequently derailed the deputy's program and
undermined his authority; even those governors "with best credit and
countenance," lamented Sir Henry Wallop in 1585, were "erased and
disgraced within six or eight months by reason of . . . the information
of this nation."[9]

If *1 Henry VI* delineates through Talbot's fate the dangers and
constraints imposed upon Ireland's proxy rulers by "factious emulations," *2 Henry VI* explores in the Duke of York's career a different set
of powers and risks associated with the Irish deputyship. When, in Part
Two, news arrives at court that "Th'uncivil kerns of Ireland are in arms /
And temper clay with blood of Englishmen" (3.1.310–11), Cardinal
Winchester and the Duke of Suffolk, as part of a plan to remove their
rival, Richard Plantagenet, the Duke of York, from court, urge him to
suppress the rebellion with an army that they will supply.[10] Winchester
and Suffolk equate service in Ireland with exile and political oblivion.[11]
But York sees the Irish post as an opening in his scheme to outmaneuver
his rivals. As a permanent offstage location, a land literally outside the
space of representation, Ireland confers a temporary invisibility upon
York which his enemies wrongly assume to be disempowering.[12] Later,
alone on stage, York articulates the plan that will place him on the
English throne:

'Twas men I lacked, and you [Winchester and Suffolk]
                    will give them me:
I take it kindly, yet be well assured
You put sharp weapons in a madman's hands.
Whiles I in Ireland nurse a mighty band,
I will stir up in England some black storm
Shall blow ten thousand souls to heaven, or hell.

                                                    (3.1.345–350)

York's exploitation of his Irish commission taps into an enduring unease among England's rulers in the later sixteenth century that the office of lord deputy provided ambitious aristocrats with the chance to build a rival power-base to that of the monarch. Remote from the metropolis and in control of his own army, the deputy was always in danger of being perceived as an autonomous and potentially disruptive figure.[13] As the alternative title of "Vice-Roy" implied, the deputy was literally *in loco* the queen and the *de facto* ruler of a separate country with its own privy council, parliament, and provincial presidencies. In the opinion of Fynes Moryson (secretary to Elizabeth's last deputy, Lord Mountjoy), the scope of the deputy's power was "litle differing from Regall": he could, for example, pardon traitors, dispose of their lands, and make appointments to important offices of state.[14] When Moryson proposed extending the deputy's term of office, he acknowledged that "it may prove dangerous to give a great man the absolute Commaunde of a kingdome for many years." However, Moryson reassured his readers:

the State may allwayes be confident of a lord Deputy, whose faythfullnes and endes free from ambition, are well knowne to them. And lett him be never so fitt to imbrace newe and dangerous Counsells, yet if he have a good estate of landes in England there is no danger of his attempts. For a wise man would not change that Certayne estate for any hopes of Ireland.[15]

Yet even the crown's apparently wisest and most loyal Irish deputies were not beyond suspicion. Sir Henry Sidney, for example, who served three terms in office (1566–67, 1568–71, 1575–78), is often considered one of Elizabeth's most successful Irish viceroys. Yet in a group of documents that retrospectively defended the policies and reputation of Sidney after his final recall, the statesman's relation to his monarch is presented as at best uneasy and at worst incipiently rebellious. The most notable of these texts is John Derricke's *The Image of Irelande, with a Discoverie of Woodkarne* (1581), which although dedicated to Sir Philip Sidney, is organized around and pays tribute to the achievements of the poet's father.[16] *The Image* is a strange, polysemous work that interweaves rambling verse with moralistic glosses, prose prefaces, and twelve illustrative woodcuts. Together the text and illustrations vindicate Henry

Sidney's deputyship and present a narrative of English triumphalism in which Gaelic barbarism is first opened to a "civil" gaze (an optical maneuver promised in the subtitle, *A Discoverie of Woodkarne*) and then roundly exorcised. The first woodcut shows a Gaelic chieftain defiantly arming for battle; then succeeding cuts depict a rebel raid on a village, and a feast at which the spoils of the raid are enjoyed. In the fourth cut, though, rebel aggression is checked by the counterattack of English soldiers. Images of a victorious and disciplined English army, of severed rebel-heads, and of defeated and contrite Irish leaders then dominate the sequence (figure 1). The eleventh and penultimate cut directly echoes the first: what we now see, though, is no self-possessed rebel chieftain but the figure of the isolated and disarmed chieftain, Rory Og O'More, "a gross and corpulent man, lapped in a mantle," who looks out disconsolately at the reader (figure 2).[17] In the text's concluding woodcut, Sir Henry Sidney holds outdoor court and receives the submissions of a group of kneeling rebel leaders.

That final image of Sir Henry Sidney, adorned with the trappings of his office, surrounded by his gentlemen officers, and enthroned beneath an ornate canopy, is both a reassuring and a deeply troubling one. "Loe where he sittes," reads the caption, "in honours seate, most comely to be seene, / As worthy is to represent the person of a Queene." But if Sidney here "represents" the queen, he also brings into focus the representational problem confronting Derricke of how to commemorate Sidney without implicitly detracting from the authority of his mistress. The text, in fact, far from resolving this tension seems to derive much of its appeal from exploiting the opposition between monarch and deputy. Hence, Sidney's association with traditional royal symbols and rituals tends to constitute him not so much as the queen's factor but as her rival. Verbal and visual references to Sidney's "progresses" through Ireland, for example, transfer to him a peculiarly Elizabethan cultural practice. Indeed, an observer in 1599 argued that the "roads and journeys" undertaken by deputies into the north of Ireland were self-promoting exercises, intended "not judicially to advance the service, but ambitiously to get themselves a name."[18] There is also a revealing slippage in the poem around the figure of the lion, a distinctly royal beast. At first the lion as royal symbol figures "her noble grace" the queen, but the recognition that the animal's male violence is invested in *"Sidney's* hand" compromises the queen's status as the unrivalled source of authority.[19]

The wavering loyalties of *The Image* resonate with the insistent undercurrent of royal disapproval in Sir Henry Sidney's own memoir of his Irish service.[20] Addressed to Sir Francis Walsingham and intended as a self-defense against his detractors both at court and in Ireland, Sidney's

1 Woodcut showing English soldiers returning to camp with the scalps of Irish kerns. From John Derricke's *The Image of Irelande* (1581).

2 Woodcut of the rebel chief Rory Og O'More. From John Derricke's *The Image of Irelande* (1581).

narrative proclaims his successes, castigates the Earl of Ormond and other rivals, and bemoans his lack of recognition and reward from the queen. The devastating financial "charges" incurred by Sidney echo as a refrain throughout his memoir's "tragicall discourse"; he claimed, for example, to have "retorned from each of those three Deputacions three thousand poundes worse then I went." The post had thus been "a miserable thraldom" for Sidney, who complained bitterly that "he would rather be steward of Kenilworth [the seat of his patron, the Earl of Leicester] than viceroy of Ireland."[21]

Even as Sidney thanks the queen for favors past and defends her prerogative in Ireland – a prerogative that he claims his antiquarian researches have shown to be more ancient than formerly thought – he is compelled to express resentment at her treatment of him.[22] A tone of bitterness toward the queen pervades especially the final pages of the memoir:

I could not obtayne at any time a letter from her majesty of thanks for this service . . . I saw the Queene make so little account of my service in killing that pernicious rebell [Rory Og], and was contented to be persuaded that there was no more difficultie to kill such a rogue as he was, then to kill mad George the sweeper of the Queen's court . . . It greeved me not a little that Her Majesty rejected those bills which I sent to be allowed to be made lawes . . .

Notwithstanding all these my paynfull services, I was accompted *servus inutilis*.[23]

Derricke's work and Sidney's memoir, far from constructing a clear opposition between the English and their Irish adversaries, delineate an unstable triangular grouping of monarch, deputy, and rebel. And the deputy, instead of standing firmly with his monarch, is poised precariously between the camps of monarch and rebel, a wavering and uncertain figure. In his memoir, Sidney appears to have recognized the dangerous constructions to which his (private) recollections were open, constructions against which he needed to guard himself. Hence, he includes a disarmingly harmless self-portrait: "fifty-four yeres of age, toothlesse and trembling, being five thousand pounds in debt." The prospect of such a man mounting any kind of threat to the queen was no doubt intended to strike Walsingham and other readers as ludicrous.[24]

II

In Shakespeare's *2 Henry VI*, however, the threat to the English monarch from his Irish viceregent is far from ludicrous. When we next hear of York, who had originally left for Ireland with "a band of [English] men / Collected choicely, from each county some," he has returned home, as the messenger announces, with an Irish force: "a puissant and a mighty power / Of galloglasses and stout kerns" (3.1.312–13; 4.9.25–26). Back in England and offering feigned loyalty to the king on condition that his rival, the Duke of Somerset, be imprisoned, York orders his Irish army to disperse: "Meet me tomorrow in Saint George's Field, / You shall have pay and everything you wish" (5.1.46–47). The pointed irony of Irish soldiers assembling at a place named after England's patron saint is compounded by the alarming prospect of an unpaid and unsatisfied foreign army wandering about London, with the openness of York's "everything" being especially worrisome. Later, when York discovers that Somerset is still free, he finally confronts Henry, openly claims the crown, and prepares for war.

In dramatizing York's return with an army of Irishmen, Shakespeare telescopes, rearranges, and embellishes the details of his two main sources, Hall and Holinshed, neither of which presents the threat to Henry's crown as coming directly from Ireland. In both chronicles, after York returns from Ireland he bides his time before eventually raising an army of "Marchemen" in the Welsh borders.[25] The effect of Shakespeare's changes is to make Ireland central to the inception and staging of rebellion within England. But what would incline Shakespeare to foreground Ireland in this way, and, moreover, how might audiences have responded to the unusual appearance of what the Folio stage direction refers to as "Yorke, and his Army of Irish, with Drum and Colours" (5.1)?

York's arrival with his "Army of Irish" crystallizes a larger centripetal movement in the first two parts of *Henry VI*, whereby the nation's geographical margins are seen as encroaching upon and contaminating the core. After the disintegration of England's French empire beginning in *1 Henry VI*, the centrifugal, expansionist thrust of English power initiated under Henry V is arrested and reversed. The pattern culminates in the siege of London by Jack Cade's force of Kentishmen – an assault that the Duke of Buckingham imagines as prefiguring the complete inversion of English overseas domination:

> Methinks already in this civil broil
> I see [the French] lording it in London streets,
> Crying "Villiago!" unto all they meet.
>
> (4.8.41–43)

If this nightmare of collapsing boundaries evokes the continuing threat in the early 1590s of a Spanish invasion, then York's reappearance at the head of "a mighty power / Of galloglasses and stout kerns" raises anxieties about Ireland as the staging post of disruption within England.

Ireland had long figured in the English imagination not so much as an autonomous and self-contained problem but as a threat to England's own territorial and dynastic integrity. As the contemporary proverb put it: "He that will England winne, Must with Ireland first beginne."[26] Ambitious lord deputies were not the only potential bearers of the threat from Ireland. In Henry VII's reign, the uprisings of the Yorkist pretenders Perkin Warbeck and Lambert Simnel had both originated and found their major support in Ireland.[27] Throughout the sixteenth century, Ireland afforded a potential base for foreign military operations against the British mainland. At mid-century a French-led attack from Ireland seemed imminent as Henri II armed and intrigued with Irish "malcontents." Then, under Elizabeth, the Spanish appeared set to seize Ireland as Irish exiles urged Philip to invade England from Ireland – a plan that was nearly adopted by the Armada commanders in 1588.[28] In common parlance, Ireland was England's "postern" (a term applied to Scotland earlier in Elizabeth's reign) – a narrow but vulnerable rear entry.[29]

The spectacle of "galloglasses and stout kerns" on English soil in *2 Henry VI*, although brief, seems calculated – like other images and rumors of a reversed conquest – to foment anti-Irish sentiment and so to justify English aggression as necessary for the containment of the Irish and the protection of England's national integrity.[30] Throughout the sixteenth century, observers claimed that an "invasion" from Ireland was already underway – an invasion not of soldiers but of beggars and masterless men.[31] A Welshman reported in 1528 that "20,000 Irishmen had entered Pembrokeshire in the past twelve months . . . and had practically overrun the county," while the antiquarian Richard Carew, discussing the underclass of his home county in *The Survey of Cornwall* (1602), described Ireland as "the nursery, which sendeth over yearly, yea and daily, whole shiploads of these crooked slips." "Many good statutes have been enacted for redress of these abuses," he continued, but after a short time the "law is forgotten, the care abandoned, and those vermin swarm again in every corner."[32]

The staged appearance of a band of Irish soldiers under an English general would have provoked hostilities and fears in Shakespeare's audience, but a sense too that the dangerous Other was also a danger from within. A similar kind of encounter with the Irish Other had occurred when Shane O'Neill visited Elizabeth's court in 1562 "with an escort of gallowglass, armed with battle-axes, bare-headed, with flowing curls, yellow shirts dyed with saffron . . . large sleeves, short tunics and rough cloaks." William Camden recalled that "the English followed [them] with as much wonderment as if they had come from China or

America."[33] Whether on the stage or the streets of early modern London, the Gaelic Irishman (actual or impersonated) aroused a volatile mix of emotions in English spectators whose ethnic prejudices would at the very least have been complicated by directly encountering "galloglasses and stout kerns."[34]

These same figures appear in *Macbeth*, where, as a shadowy, symbolic presence they serve in a small but significant way to mark Macbeth's lapse from national savior at the play's opening to national scourge at its end; whether they actually appeared on stage in early performances is unclear from the text.[35] Macbeth's early identity as self-sufficient warrior is achieved in part against the "skipping kerns" whom he fights and scatters at the outset; later, as the tyrant of Dunsinane, Macbeth's degeneration and dependency are registered by the fact that he now relies on these same kerns for his own defense.[36]

Macduff's outburst against Macbeth's "hired" kerns reminds us that outsiders perceived these Gaelic warriors as lacking any fixed loyalties. This mobility may have made them difficult figures to classify but it also lent them a certain attraction, especially if they could be employed to serve English militarism.[37] Thus, Richard Stanihurst relates approvingly Henry VIII's use of "an armie of Irishmen" against the French in 1544.

In the siege of Bullongne, [the Irishmen] stood the armie in verie good sted . . . If they tooke any Frenchman prisoner, lest they should be accounted covetous, in snatching with them his entier bodie, his onelie ransome should bee no more but his head. The French with this strange kind of warfaring astonished, sent an ambassador to king Henrie, to learne whether he brought men with him or divels, that could neither be woone with rewards, nor pacified by pitie: which when the king had turned to a jeast, the Frenchmen ever after, if they could take anie of the Irish scatering from the companie, used first to cut off their genitals, and after to torment them with as great and as lingering paine as they could devise.[38]

If Henry VIII's Irish warriors proved utterly confusing to French categories and practices, the gallowglass in particular proved no less so to English ones. From one perspective, in fact, York's gallowglasses were no alien Others but the spectators' own distant relatives. The gallowglass, claims Irenius in *A View of the Present State of Ireland,* was "auncyente Englishe, [for *Gallogla* signifies an Englishe] servitor or yeoman." And in his notes to Gerald's *Expugnatio Hibernica*, John Hooker glossed "galloglasse" as one "who was first brought into this land by the Englishmen, and thereof taketh his name. For Galloglas is to saie, an English yeoman or servant."[39] In the figure of the gallowglass, then, easy oppositions between self and Other, English and Irish break down; Spenser's *View* and related ethnographic texts construct England's relation to Ireland in terms not of some absolute difference (a "radical alterity") but of dialectical interconnections. Accordingly, Ireland could be seen as the origin or "home" of English culture, and as a site that preserved what was now old or lost to England.[40]

III

2 Henry VI's specter of a reversed conquest, of the contamination of England by the material and semiotic traces of Irishness, is present not only in York's Irish army. As part of his plan to return from Ireland and seize the crown, York reveals that he has "seduced a headstrong Kentishman, / John Cade of Ashford, / To make commotion, as full well he can" in England. Cade's task is to stir disaffection among the commons and generally to set the stage for York's return; but Cade also prefigures the subsequent appearance of the kern and gallowglass by carrying, in his own person, the displaced rebelliousness of the Gaelic warrior (3.1.356–58). Cade, in fact, internalizes the threat from Ireland that is later externalized by York and his Irish force. Suggestively, York's reappearance comes immediately after the death of Cade, thus signalling how the Irish threat is subliminally transferred from one man to the other. Since Cade and York are never on stage together, the perception that they represent each other's alter-egos was possibly reinforced in performance by dramatic doubling.[41]

In a passage that, notably, has no basis in any of Shakespeare's sources, York recalls how he first met Cade on a previous visit to Ireland:

> In Ireland have I seen this stubborn Cade
> Oppose himself against a troop of kerns
> And fought so long till that his thighs with darts
> Were almost like a sharp-quilled porpentine;
>
> . . .
>
> Full often, like a shag-haired crafty kern,
> Hath he conversed with the enemy
> And, undiscovered, come to me again
> And given me notice of their villanies.
> This devil here shall be my substitute.

> (3.1.360–71)

Alternately fighting and infiltrating the enemy, Cade represents a form of tactical Gaelicization to which the crown forces routinely resorted in their undercover operations. During the Desmond wars of the early 1580s, for example, one Captain Dowdall acquired crucial intelligence through the efforts of "a notable spiall, named Richard mac James," who "drawing himselfe to the companies of the rebels, and lieng among them in their cabins where they laie in the woods, he fell in companie, and then entered into a great familiaritie of one which was a messenger from the Desmonds." The messenger, mistaking mac James for a fellow rebel, revealed the planned movements of Sir John of Desmond, a plan that mac James then relayed to his superiors, enabling them to trap and kill the rebel chief.[42]

The ease with which Cade, like mac James, crosses boundaries to mingle with the enemy suggests his essentially mobile or theatrical self. Indeed, York's description figures Cade as a strangely mongrel figure who hovers among the ontological realms of the human, the animal ("porpentine"), and the demonic ("this devil"). But York's account also insinuates that Cade's duplicitous intimacy with the kerns ineluctably taints him with the very Irishness he is ostensibly fighting against. This deeper symbolic association between Cade and the kerns is implicit in York's image of the wounded Cade "caper[ing] upright, like a wild Morisco, / Shaking the bloody darts as he his bells" (3.1.365–66). Etymologically, the "wild Morisco" links Cade to the North African moors as well as to English morris dancers, but the dance has Irish resonances as well. One English observer described the maneuvers of Irish troops as being more like "a morris dance, by their tripping after their bagpipes, than any soldier-like exercise."[43] Cade's morris, like the Gaelic jig or hay – a dance of "mad and wild changes" – is a fitting emblem for English prejudices about Irish disorder.[44]

While York's image of the "Morisco" reverberates with cruel laughter at Cade's grotesque contortions, it also empowers Cade. For Cade's gestures also constitute a kind of victorious war dance, a defiant assertion of his extraordinary physical endurance – and especially his insensitivity to pain. This trait was part of an English mythology of Gaelic character; for better or worse, the Irish, like all "primitive" peoples, were thought to have cruder physical sensations than the more delicate members of the English governing classes.[45] "Say [Cade] be taken, racked, and tortured," York adds, "I know no pain they can inflict upon him / Will make him say I moved him to those arms" (3.1.376–78).

In fashioning Cade as a quasi-Irishman, Shakespeare again embellishes on his sources, none of which mention Cade's service in Ireland but several of which allude tantalizingly to his Irish birth: "his name was John Cade, or (of some) John Mend-all [an Irishman as Polychronicon saith]."[46] Once Cade enters the play in 4.2, however, neither his putative Irish origins nor his Irish service under York are mentioned again. The genealogy that he now fabricates connects him to John Mortimer, the long-lost grandson of Edmund Mortimer, and "rightful heir unto the crown" (4.2.110). Cade's new identity as royal pretender links him to the last of the Yorkist pretenders – Perkin Warbeck and Lambert Simnel –

whose rebellions had also been nurtured in Ireland.[47] Masquerading as John Mortimer, moreover, Cade claims "cousinage," as Holinshed puts it, "to diverse noble houses" in Ireland, the name of Mortimer having long been associated with Ireland and the position of lord deputy.

Although Cade's self-fashioning now revolves ominously around his impersonation of a dead man, his symbolic affiliation with the kerns remains a vestigial if muted component of his identity until the end of his brief and turbulent career. Thus, when Lord Clifford assures Cade's wavering supporters that their leader

> hath no home, no place to fly to;
> Nor knows he how to live but by the spoil,
> Unless by robbing of your friends and us

he employs the same terms of opprobrium used to constitute the Irish rebels as "outlaws" who rejected a settled life for a wandering and marauding existence (4.8.35–37). Once Cade is abandoned by his followers, his struggle for survival revives memories of the Irish context that introduced him. Forced into hiding in the woods, the fugitive Cade now resembles the folkloric wodwose or wild man, a mythic analogue to the Irish kern, while his scrawny body and grinding hunger are reminiscent of the many Irish starved into submission by the scorched earth and crop destruction policies of the English government.[48] Spenser apparently witnessed the consequences of Lord Grey's famine policy upon the Munster rebels in the early 1580s; in *A View*, Irenius recollects in an account tinged with revulsion and pity the plight of the victims who "out of everie Corner of the woodes and glennes . . . came crepinge forth upon theire handes, for theire legges could not beare them, they looked Anotomies of death, they spake like ghostes cryinge out of theire graves."[49]

What, ultimately, is the import of this "Irishing" of Cade? As critics have recognized, Shakespeare's portrait of Cade as "a cruel, barbaric lout," radically distorts earlier chronicle accounts of him. In Hall's chronicle, Shakespeare's main source for Cade's rebellion, Cade is "a young man of goodly stature and pregnant wit," and accorded respect, while in Stow's *Annales of England* (1592) he is admired for restraint and for the legitimate demands he presents to an overbearing and intransigent aristocracy.[50] To complete his demonization, Shakespeare's Cade gives off echoes of other popular rebellions, particularly the fourteenth-century Peasants' Revolt. Cade's tantalizing links with the kerns and Irish rebelliousness thus add another layer to his thoroughly stigmatized image. As the intersection of plebeian violence and Irish incivility, Cade is constituted as a double threat, bodying forth the tendency of official discourse to bracket various "deviant" populations by constructing a composite symbolic Other. As Alan Sinfield and Jonathan Dollimore observe, the

ideological containment [of the Irish] was continuous with the handling of the disaffected lower-class outgroup (a proclamation of 1594 dealt together with vagabonds who begged "upon pretense of service in the wars without relief" and "men of Ireland that have these late years unnaturally served as rebels against her majesty's forces beyond the seas").[51]

Unofficial popular texts were often complicit with official discourse in constructing the Irish and the domestic poor as a composite enemy. In the rogue pamphlets of Thomas Dekker, for instance, the Irish are repeatedly invoked as an alien subgroup within a broader symbolic constituency of disenfranchised and masterless people. Dekker's *Lanthorne and Candle-light* (1608) constructs a revealing relation among social groups in the context of Henry VI's reign. The narrator-cum-ethnographer, having pursued his subjects to Deerhurst Fair in Gloucestershire, remarks that,

you shall see [there] more rogues than ever were whipped at a cart's arse through London and more beggars than ever came dropping out of Ireland. If you look upon them you would think you lived in Henry VI's time, and that Jack Cade and his rebellious ragamuffins were there mustering. Dunkirk cannot show such sharks. The wild Irish are but flocks of wild geese to them. And these swarms of locusts come to this lousy fair from all parts of the land within an hundred miles' compass.[52]

If, in his "Irishing" of Cade, Shakespeare seems no less shameless than Dekker in playing upon the anti-Irish prejudices of his audience, he is also willing, unlike Dekker, faintly to unsettle those prejudices. Cade's death-scene, especially, invites a complex range of responses. This final appearance has frequently caused problems for critics who, committed to a view of Cade as irredeemably bad, feel obliged to celebrate his death at the hands of "Alexander Iden, an Esquire of Kent," as emblematic of a victory for property rights and an upwardly mobile gentry over the anarchic lower orders. To be sure, Cade's ultimate defeat and abjection would be greeted by some sections of an audience, whether Renaissance or modern, with delight. But the play stages Cade's end in such a way that this approval is by no means assured. When Cade enters at 4.10 he is for the first and only time in the play alone on stage and divested of the rebel crew whose presence has previously defined him. If only for a moment, we glimpse Cade not as the demagogic leader but as a starkly isolated and suffering individual against whom the complete power of the state is now ranged. Tellingly, Cade neither despairs nor capitulates but remains unrepentant and defiant. In his duel with Iden, Cade sounds a positively heroic note: "Iden, farewell, and be proud of thy victory," says Cade after receiving his death blow, "Tell Kent from me she hath lost her best man, and exhort all the world to be cowards; for I, that never feared any, am vanquished by famine, not by valour" (4.10.65–68). This is not the kind of "last dying speech" we have been led to expect from a renegade; by proclaiming himself "unconquered" even in death, Cade recalls the noble heroes like Talbot in *1 Henry VI* who die upholding an ideal of empire. I am not suggesting that Shakespeare ultimately redeems or rehabilitates Cade; rather, through Cade's memorable death-scene, Shakespeare makes it possible for the demonized outsider's audacity and courage in resisting state power to elicit grudging recognition, even muted admiration from an audience. Cade's remarkable final performance, then, possesses a certain subversive undercurrent that destabilizes state power at the precise moment when that power appears total and unfaltering.

In fact, even the most Anglocentric and "reactionary" representations of the Irish in this period could potentially call forth multiple and divergent responses – ones, perhaps, neither foreseen nor intended by the work's producers. John Derricke's *The Image of Irelande*, for example, is usually treated complacently as a storehouse of anti-Irish prejudices and stereotypes. Yet the depiction of Rory Og (as Derricke calls him), the work's central Irish rebel who shares with Cade a similar representational genesis and instability, problematizes these assumptions and demonstrates a dialogic impulse in the text. Derricke provides in the first two sections of *The Image* (subtitled "A Notable Discovery most lively describing the state and condition of the Wilde men in Ireland, properly called Woodkarne") what is perhaps the most detailed, eccentric, and vicious portrait of the kern in the Tudor period. These opening sections are related by an omniscient, self-conscious and deeply sarcastic editor/ narrator, but in the third section this narrative voice is literally shunted to the side into the marginal glosses by the first-person narrative of Rory Og himself. Rory's narrative is conceived as a confession, a self-abasement and self-denunciation in the mode of the fictional autobiographies of notorious rebels and fallen rulers in *The Mirror for Magistrates* (1559), which numbers Jack Cade among its ghostly speakers.[53] Like the Cade of *The Mirror*, but unlike Shakespeare's defiant Cade, Rory Og testifies meekly and remorsefully to his own guilt: he rehearses his rebellious career, acknowledges the righteousness of Sir Henry Sidney and the queen, and anticipates his own impending death.

On the surface, Derricke's anti-Irish agenda appears to be well served by the spectacle of Rory indicting himself, lauding his adversaries, and warning others to avoid his fate. But there are dangers as well as advantages to the rhetorical device of allowing "the enemy" to speak directly. The dialogic format invites readers to apprehend Rory not as the stereotypical Irish rebel the text has been relentlessly inventing to this point, but as a speaking subject capable of arousing sympathy through relating common experiences of pain and remorse. Whereas the third-person narration had succeeded in distancing and demonizing Rory, Og's own voice helps to humanize him, transforming him from enemy to victim. This transformation is also produced in the interplay between Rory's narrative and the glosses of the authoritative editor/narrator. Many of the glosses simply echo or summarize Rory's remarks, thus rhetorically reinforcing his defeat and humiliation. But other glosses are opinionated and judgmental, attempting to control the reader's response. When Rory curses himself, for instance, the marginal gloss reads: "Where Rory bid the three curses light upon him, I wish him for every one twenty (saving my charity)." The comment is darkly humorous but it also makes the editor appear inhumanly callous.[54]

Derricke's Rory Og, like Shakespeare's Cade, is not guaranteed sympathy from an audience but he does have the potential to call forth a complex mixture of responses as opposed to simple loathing. Derricke seems aware that his own representational strategies may, by stimulating unforeseen responses, work against his expressed goal of arousing only "pleasure and delight" in his readers. At the conclusion of Og's narrative, Derricke relates that he had originally intended to "adjoin the lives of many [Irish rebels]" to Rory's. But perhaps sensing the inherent risks of granting rebels their own voices, he reconsiders this plan, anxious lest "I might seem to prosecute an endless work, making a volume greater than grateful and more painful than pleasant . . . And thus I breviated my former intent."[55] Was Derricke afraid that readers would tire of the work's length and repetitions, or did he sense the dangerous ideological effects of witnessing a procession of speaking traitors?

In place of multiple rebel self-portraits, Derricke offers only two brief first-person narratives. In the first, *"Thirlaugh Leonaugh* the great ONEALE of Ireland" recounts his vow of submission to the queen demanded by Sir Henry Sidney; in the second, the ghost of Rory Og recounts a death that is imagined to have befallen him since the composition of his first narrative.[56] Rory's second appearance, though, is even more uncertain than the first in its ideological effects. Whereas Rory had earlier appeared as "a gross corpulent man, lapped in a mantle, overwhelmed with misery," he is now

a monstrous devil, a trunkless head and a headless body living, the one hid in some mixen and dunghill but the other exalted, yea mounted upon a pole, a proper sight, God wot, to behold, vaunting itself on the highest top of the Castle of Dublin, uttering in plain Irish the things that ensue.[57]

This ghostly and ghastly spectacle of Rory's talking head resonates with accompanying woodcuts depicting severed and spiked rebels' heads, and functions as an emblematic warning of the fate awaiting England's enemies. In Ireland, such displays of state violence, both real and represented, were designed to instill terror in all who opposed English power: Sir Humphrey Gilbert's practice of lining the path to his tent with the heads of rebels being perhaps the most notorious.[58] But just how compatible were such displays with Derricke's desire to arouse "pleasure and delight [in] the well disposed reader"?[59] Surely not all readers of *The Image* were disposed to read it according to the author's cues. Both in the sixteenth century and since, there were other less complacent and compliant ways of responding to the violence that the state inflicts upon its "outlaws."

Similarly, in *2 Henry VI* the spectacle of Cade's severed head is a complex moment that refuses any single, predictable reaction. Here, our response to Cade is influenced by our response to his killer, the hypocritical and self-seeking Alexander Iden. Iden enters the play denouncing the court and extolling the life of the country gentleman, but after killing Cade and presenting the rebel's head at court, he abandons his idealism, accepts a knighthood, "a thousand marks," and a place in the royal entourage (4.10.14–21, 5.1.79). The conflict between Iden – the state's representative – and the outlaw Cade is hardly one between pure and impure motives. Iden's scalping of Cade, while ostensibly done for patriotic reasons, results in his own self-betrayal.

IV

In the politically charged atmosphere of the public theater of the early 1590s, the Irish intrigues of York and Cade in Shakespeare's play were suspiciously evocative of a contemporary set of events that centered upon the figure of the ex-Irish lord deputy, Sir John Perrot. Perrot had received the post in 1582, according to Sir Robert Naunton, for one of two reasons: "for a kind of haughtiness of spirit and repugnancy in counsels, or . . . as the fittest person then to bridle the insolency of the Irish" – in other words, his posting was either a way of disposing of him or of rewarding him.[60] Perrot served for four years before being driven out (so he claimed) by his enemies on the Dublin Council and in the Old English community. Opposed to Perrot's sweeping reform proposals, these enemies, led by Adam Loftus, the Lord Chancellor of Ireland and

Archbishop of Dublin, complained to the queen and urged his recall. To discredit Perrot they charged him with favoring Gaelic chieftains over various Old and New English interest groups and of using "a more absolute Authority then [the deputy] had usually exercised".[61] Spenser, who thought Perrot had undermined the achievements of Lord Grey – Perrot's predecessor – echoed these allegations in *A View*. Perrot, Spenser alleged,

did treade downe and disgrace all the Englishe, and sett upp and countenance the Irish all that he could, whether thinckinge thereby to make them more tractable and buxome to his goverment, wherein he thought much amisse, or privilie plottinge some other purposes of his owne, as it partlie afterwardes appeared.[62]

Perrot's headstrong reputation and his advocacy of a stronger mandate and greater independence from the crown only fuelled suspicions about him. In his policy papers, he urged the greater centralization of power in the hands of the lord deputy, and the repeal of legislation that made decisions of the Irish parliament contingent upon the approval of the English parliament. If Perrot had been successful in loosening metropolitan control over the New English leadership in Ireland, his Old English opponents would have had their authority drastically curtailed.[63]

Perrot's departure from Ireland, however, did not silence his critics. In 1590, possibly at the instigation of Loftus's patron at court, Sir Christopher Hatton, he was arrested on a charge of treason and later committed to the Tower.[64] Perrot's indictment in the King's Bench-Bar, Westminster, stated:

That the last of January 1587, in the 30th year of the queen's majesty, [Perrot] . . . falsely and traiterously, &c. did imagine in his heart to deprive, depose, and disinherit the queen's most excellent majesty from the royal seat, to take her life away, to make slaughter in her realm, to raise Rebellion in England and Ireland; and that he did procure a foreign power [Spain] to invade the two realms.[65]

In return for assisting the Spanish, Perrot, claimed the prosecution, would rule Wales, "as the princes of Germany have their dukedoms, that is *jure regio*, to be a prince and lord himself, and not to depend on any other."[66]

The Perrot scandal constitutes a crucial but overlooked element of the political landscape in which *2 Henry VI* was written and first performed.[67] Indeed, this long-running affair which came to a head in spring 1592 lends a distinct topical coloring to York's ambitions in the play. Drawing upon an intoxicating mixture of allegations, rumors, and half-truths, Shakespeare constructs a loose structural parallel between York's rebellion and the traitorous plot ascribed to Perrot. This method of insinuating topical meaning by manipulating chronicle sources means that the parallel is not sustained or complete but comes into focus only in a partial and fragmentary way. Such an oblique form of allusion gives Shakespeare an invaluable claim to political innocence; perceived topicality in the text can be attributed by its author to coincidence or to an unforeseen pattern of historical repetition.[68]

The details of Perrot's prosecution also illuminate Shakespeare's "Irishing" of Jack Cade. In *2 Henry VI* York's exploitation of Cade resonates suggestively with one of the most damaging and widely known accusations Perrot faced at his trial: that he had "procured and animated" the "notorious false Traitor" O'Rourke, "to move and stir up Rebellion in Ireland."[69] Sir Brian O'Rourke, Perrot's alleged accomplice, was the Gaelic chieftain of Connaught, who had himself stood trial for treason the year before.[70] When, in early 1591, O'Rourke left Ireland in search of Scottish support he was arrested and handed over to the English by James VI. O'Rourke was tried in London, found guilty, and – in keeping with grim ritual – hanged, drawn, and quartered at Tyburn. Londoners' fascination with O'Rourke's fate is reflected in the 1592 edition of John Stow's *Annales of England*. As a continuation of his *Summarie of Englyshe Chronicles*, the *Annales* provided readers with a remarkably up-to-date account of local and national events, including generous helpings of Irish news. Bearing the dedication date of "this 26. of May," the 1592 edition culminates with O'Rourke's trial and execution, the lengthy story of which crowds out other competing accounts of trials and executions.[71]

What makes that story particularly memorable is O'Rourke's public show of resistance at the gallows. Not for O'Rourke the conventional "last dying speech" in which the condemned man confessed his crimes, acknowledged he was receiving his just deserts, and extolled the monarch's justice. Instead, a defiant O'Rourke refused to admit his treasons or to ask the queen's forgiveness; and when the Archbishop of Cashell stepped forward with "counsaile," O'Rourke spurned him, saying Cashell "had more neede to looke to himselfe, and that he was neither heere nor there."[72] O'Rourke's unbending resistance to the apparatus of power, then, provides an instructive analogue to the way in which Cade – the accomplice of another traitorous Irish deputy – meets his own end in *2 Henry VI*.

To understand how the Perrot–O'Rourke subtext functions in *2 Henry VI*, we need to enlist other works that engaged with Perrot's predicament as a window onto the vexed issues of service, loyalty, and rebellion. Barnabe Rich's novella of 1592, *Busiranus*, obliquely defends Perrot against charges of treason and attacks Loftus, his main acccuser. That same year, Robert Greene's pamphlet, *Greenes Groats-worth of Witte*, used the coded language of the beast fable to allude, sympathetically, to Perrot's difficulties since leaving Ireland.[73] Barnabe Rich was himself the victim of Loftus's animosity and thus had sound reasons to satirize him, but Greene, like Shakespeare, had no personal stake in Irish affairs.[74] Evidently, then, Perrot's case attracted broad interest. But if Rich and Greene side with Perrot, Shakespeare seems implicitly to lend his support to the enemies of the former lord deputy. The prosecution charged that Perrot had imagined treason "in his heart," "which imagination was in itself High-Treason, albeit the same proceeded not to any overt fact."[75] York's rebellion in *2 Henry VI* effectively transforms this imagination of treason – the intention to rebel – into "overt fact" by bringing to frighteningly dramatic fulfillment the alleged plot of Perrot and his accomplices against Elizabeth. As a displaced realization of Perrot's thwarted designs, then, York's rebellion could be seen as giving shape and substance to the charges against Perrot.

This conclusion, though, is complicated by the fact that Perrot's "presence" in *2 Henry VI* is not tied solely to the traitorous career of the Duke of York. The play offers not a single but a dual and conflicted perspective on the issue of traitorous deputies. Thus, if the topical implications of the York plot (as both a narrative and a political scheme) point accusingly at Perrot, and mark him as a genuine threat, the plot of the Duke of Gloucester and his tragic downfall in the play turn the finger away from Perrot, and portray him as the victim of his enemies' malice and the scapegoat who must rid the community of internecine conflict. At his trial, Perrot steadfastly maintained his innocence and, judging from early seventeenth-century accounts of Perrot's downfall, suspicions existed that the charges against him were groundless. Sir Robert Naunton concluded his brief "Life" of Perrot confident of "the innocency of his intentions, exempt and clear from the guilt of treason and disloyalty."[76]

Like York – and like Perrot – the Duke of Gloucester, as Lord Protector of England, is an example in the play of a powerful surrogate ruler. Gloucester's enemies, envious of his influence over the king, his popularity with the common people, and his status as next in line to the throne, arraign him on false charges of treason and eventually murder him. Shakespeare, in charting the path that leads to Gloucester's destruction, recapitulates the sequence of events that helped to produce so many "traitors" in early modern England. Gloucester's fate represents, in effect, an object lesson in the politics and psychology of accusations of treason – a lesson that contemporary audiences were invited to apply not only to Perrot but to the numerous noble "traitors" who had met their ends in a cultural climate suffused with "a conspiratorial psychology," the tendency, that is, to see treason and subversive plotting in every corner.[77] At his trial, Perrot was positioned as the latest figure in a long and invidious line of traitors. Lord Anderson summed up the prosecution's case by stating that "he himself had been at the arraignment of divers [traitors], as namely of Babington, Abington, with others; adding, that the Treasons of Sir John Perrot far surpassed them all, most wickedly conspiring her majesty's death and deprivation, and invasion of this realm by foreign enemies."[78]

In *2 Henry VI*, Gloucester's enemies make their initial move against his wife, Eleanor Cobham, first inciting her to acts of illegal conjuring and political prophecy and then arresting her in the act. Although innocent of any wrongdoing himself, Gloucester is tainted through association with his wife. Having thus aroused suspicion about Gloucester, his enemies exploit all the strategies of incrimination that the state mobilized to discredit and convict "traitors." "I shall not want false witness to condemn me / Nor store of treasons to augment my guilt," says Gloucester to his accusers, fully familiar with how convictions for treason were usually secured (3.1.178–79). At Perrot's trial, one of the key pieces of evidence was a set of letters he had purportedly written to Elizabeth's foreign enemies, but which were more likely forged by his enemies.

Before Gloucester's trial can take place he is murdered by hired assassins; the discovery of his body on the day appointed for his trial forms an ironic commentary on the status of Tudor treason trials as empty rituals inevitably resulting in the judicial "murder" of the accused. Like many alleged traitors of the Tudor state, Gloucester dies in mysterious circumstances before the law has taken its course. His death mimics, if it does not directly mirror, Perrot's fate of dying in the Tower of an unspecified sickness before his execution could be carried out. But in the play, the mystery of Gloucester's death is solved by the public inspection of his corpse:

> His eye-balls further out than when he lived,
> Staring full ghastly like a strangled man;
> His hair upreared, his nostrils stretched with struggling.
>
> (3.2.169–71)

Gloucester's body speaks not only against the cover-up of his own murder but against the sham official accounts that failed to explain the sudden and unexplained deaths in custody of convicted traitors. The legal proceedings against Gloucester – like many of those against alleged traitors to the Tudor state – invoke as a legitimating pretext the security of monarch and nation against subversion. Yet far from serving a patriotic or popular cause, Gloucester's downfall only benefits self-seeking aristocrats while hurting the common people by removing their only ally at court, their sole defender against a rapacious nobility. Only through the urging of an enraged commons is Gloucester's death investigated, and Suffolk – the man chiefly responsible for the murder – banished.

The entire "discourse of treason" in Tudor England was aimed at convincing subjects that their communities, their nation, and their queen were under threat from shadowy "jesuitical" and other rebel forces whose defeat required a unity of purpose and the consent of the governed to the dictates of their governors.[79] In a central way, *2 Henry VI* gains energy from inciting anxiety about such threats, from cultivating a kind of pathology of national emergency. But the play's treatment of Gloucester also places the "discourse of treason" under strain, prodding spectators into penetrating official appeals to national security and the safety of the monarch that were routinely used to manufacture the "reality" of treason. The play's participation in the circulation and interrogation of "official" constructions of treason intersects with other texts emanating from different cultural locations, including recusant responses to government propaganda that were illegally imported into England or printed on secret domestic presses. In one of these works, Richard Verstegan's *An Advertisement Written to a Secretarie of my L. Treasurers of Ingland* (Antwerp, 1592), William Cecil and his supporters were accused of transforming England into Turkey in their search for seminary priests, of "feigning terrours and troubles at home" and of whipping up fear of an "imaginarie invasion" (9, 63). And in an account of the state's manufacturing of traitors that parallels the fate of Gloucester, Robert Southwell exposed in his *An Humble Supplication to Her Majestie* (1595) the framing of the "traitors" Babington and Ballard and their subsequent stage-managed trials. Southwell identified Walsingham as the master-magician orchestrating these "buggish and terrible shewes;" like Gloucester's enemies in *2 Henry VI*, the English spy-master stood only to further his own factional interests.[80]

2 Henry VI thus eschews a single authoritative perspective on the Perrot affair in favor of overlapping interpretive frameworks that can accommodate the interests of different sections of an audience – including commoners and nobles, Perrot's detractors and his defenders. Moreover, while state propaganda collapsed in the figure of Perrot the jarring categories of deputy and rebel, the play unsettles audience certainties about where guilt and culpability lie, prompting in the process a potentially sympathetic rethinking of rebel stereotypes.[81]

V

In the midst of growing public concern about the security of Ireland, and capitalizing on the high-profile trials of O'Rourke and Perrot, Shakespeare encodes in *2 Henry VI* a nuanced analysis of Ireland's role in domestic English politics and of the problems of ruling an overseas territory – an analysis that entails a subtle reimagining of the assumptions and stereotypes regarding rebels and deputies. As resistance to English rule in Ireland intensified during the 1590s and as more men and resources were committed there, the financing of the wars increasingly preoccupied the court. "The Irish action," wrote Sir Robert Naunton, "we may call a malady and a consumption of [Elizabeth's] times, for it accompanied her to her end, and it was of so profuse and vast expense that it drew near a distemperature of state and passion in herself." Indeed, so intense was Elizabeth's anxiety about this "unthrifty and inauspicious war," Naunton claims, that it "did much disturb and mislead her judgment."[82] In another retrospective on the queen's reign, John Clapham reported that in order not "to overburden her subjects who had granted her many subsidies and lent her great sums of money, she was contented to sell some of her own lands and jewels to support the charge of the Irish war."[83] Notwithstanding such personal "sacrifices" by Elizabeth, the financial burden of the Irish campaign was spread well beyond the nation's wealthy elite. The economic costs of English militarism in Ireland are central to Shakespeare's evolving analysis of Anglo-Irish relations in *Richard II* (c.1595–97).[84] Whereas in Holinshed, Richard's unpopular tax policies are unrelated to his designs in Ireland, in the play Richard pointedly finances his Irish campaign with "burthenous taxations" on the commons (a repeated cause for complaint [2.1.259–61; 1.4.42–52, 61–62; 2.2.128–30]), and with the property he has illegally seized from Gaunt.[85]

Shakespeare's interest in Richard II's "unlucky Irish wars" and the financial hardships they impose provides a cautionary example, a veiled warning, to the rulers of Elizabethan England of the dangers of embroilment in Ireland.[86] As in *2 Henry VI*, Ireland is an absent presence in the dramatic action of *Richard II*, an offstage locus that helps to determine the outcome of the power struggle between Richard and Bolingbroke. In a move that neither Elizabeth nor James ever contemplated, King Richard goes in person to Ireland (1.4.38–52). (The next monarch to do the same was James II). According to historian John Hayward in 1599, Richard had "deliberated whether [to] . . . undertake the warre in person, or commit it to commanders of lower degree":

Some perswaded him that wholly to subdue Ireland stoode neither with pollicie, nor yet almost with possibilitie. For if it were fully and quietly possessed, some governour might hap to growe to that greatnesse, as to make himselfe absolute lord thereof, and therefore it was better to hold it certaine by weake enemies, then suspected by mightie friendes.[87]

In avoiding the hazards of appointing an Irish viceroy, however, Richard falls prey to a greater risk. His absence from England opens the realm to Bolingbroke who now returns from exile with "three thousand men of war" (2.1.286). Shakespeare rearranges the chronology of events in his sources to make the opportunistic Bolingbroke a master of timing, the antithesis of the unsynchronized Richard who arrives back from Ireland "One day too late," the day after his Welsh army has dispersed (3.2.67). During his sojourn "far off" in Ireland, the king is cut off from the court; news of Bolingbroke's invasion is sent to Richard, "But none returns" (2.2.80, 2.2.123). Ireland is thus figured as the land beyond both communication and representation, and it is here, fittingly, that Richard suffers a symbolic death: " 'Tis thought the king is dead," the Welsh Captain tells Salisbury (2.4.7).[88] Richard's seclusion in Ireland metaphorically suggests just how out of touch he is with the needs of his English subjects and how, unlike the highly visible and popular Bolingbroke, he has failed to use spectacle and the privileged visibility of his office to help secure his authority with the commons.

In *Richard II*, then, Shakespeare depicts Ireland as an expensive and dangerous distraction to England's rulers – an idea surely not lost upon the queen and her government at a moment when English control in Ireland looked increasingly fragile. The play offers no excuse for Richard's expedition, no sense that it is needed to secure the "scept'red isle" itself (2.1.40). Richard never explains what he sees as Ireland's importance for England, nor does he justify risking his own person in the expedition. Holinshed's Irish Chronicle, by contrast, justifies the king's mission on the grounds that it is to avenge the murder of his kinsman and heir, the lord deputy Roger Mortimer.[89] But Shakespeare omits this mitigating motive from the play, and instead depicts Richard as undertaking a quasi-exotic hunting trip to

> supplant those rough rug-headed kerns,
> Which live like venom where no venom else,
> But only they, have privilege to live.
>
> (2.1.156–58)

On his return to England, Richard describes his late "wand'ring with the Antipodes," an image culled from the discourse of the fabulous and one which further undermines the legitimacy of his expedition (3.2.49). In sum, Shakespeare presents Richard's Irish sojourn as one more of the king's "fierce blaze of riot[s]" and a prelude to his wanton self-destruction (2.1.33). Removing any sense of legitimacy or justice from the king's Irish mission, *Richard II* arouses suspicions that Elizabeth's own adventures in Ireland were equally unnecessary and irresponsible.

The introduction of the Welsh as the loyal friends of the king in *Richard II* prepares us for their more prominent role in *1 Henry IV*. As the second tetralogy unfolds and as Shakespeare develops a more sustained interest in the relations between England and Ireland, Wales and the Welsh emerge as a central symbolic idiom through which politically sensitive material can be obliquely explored. To understand the utility and nuances of this idiom, I turn next to the ways in which Wales was inscribed in the cultural imagination of England in the sixteenth century. Before returning to Shakespeare in chapter 4, I chart a course through other more marginal texts, texts that have not before been recognized as part of the multifaceted Elizabethan discourse of Ireland.

3 Ireland, Wales, and the representation of England's borderlands

What little attention has been given to the impact of Ireland and Irish affairs upon the Elizabethan theater has usually stopped at noting allusions and tracing the emergence of the comic Irishman as a stock dramatic character.[1] My argument, by contrast, is the larger one that Ireland – as the locus of recurrent political crises and a testing ground for categories of national identity in the 1590s – represented a compelling, if always displaced and elusive, subtext for a politically engaged public theater. In later chapters I return to Shakespeare's complex and evolving relation to the subtext of Ireland; in this chapter I want to explore further the representational strategies developed by writers both in and out of the theater for handling the "problem" of Ireland in ways that preserved the fictional distance required by the spoken and unspoken rules of censorship surrounding the performance and publication of texts.[2] Specifically, I examine how *within* the British mainland, Ireland was discursively mapped in the context of a larger set of discourses about England's Celtic borderlands, discourses that made particular use of the fraught connections between Ireland and Wales. Although my discussion of Welsh materials may seem like a detour, a swerving away from the central focus on Ireland, the texts I traverse invariably point through Wales to Ireland, albeit an Ireland that often takes the form of a powerfully felt absent presence. By foregrounding two non-canonical works, David Powel's chronicle *The Historie of Cambria now called Wales* (1584) and George Peele's play *Edward I* (c.1590), I mean, first, to recover largely ignored works for a new cultural history of early modern Britain, and, second, to delineate the full breadth of the discursive field to which the canonical works of Shakespeare and Spenser belong. Attending to the overlapping constructions of Ireland and Wales will also help to disclose the countercurrents, contradictions, and faultlines in contemporary discourses of England's borderlands.[3] Far from being ideologically monolithic, those discourses could interrupt and contest the hegemonic construction of Ireland and its inhabitants thus promoting critical reflection upon, if not outright rejection of, the imperatives of

English expansionism, conquest, and colonization within the borders of the British Isles.

I

To emphasize the coupling of Ireland and Wales may seem counter-intuitive, an odd variation of the more familiar coupling of Ireland and Scotland. Indeed, in pre- and early modern theories of racial origin, it was a commonplace that the peoples of Ireland and Scotland derived from the same stock. "The Scots and Irish are all one people . . . mixed of the Scithian and Spanish blood," claimed William Harrison, Edmund Spenser, and countless other commentators.[4] For the English observer John Dymmok in 1600, the consanguinity of Irish and Scots could also be inferred from the fact that in Ireland "the wilde Scottes" lived alongside the "English Irish, meer Irish, [and] degenerate English."[5] Yet an exclusive focus on the genealogical and spatial proximity of Irish and Scots obscures a widespread English impulse to see connections between all its borderlands, and to merge Ireland, Scotland, and Wales into a single territorial and ethnographic zone, with common linguistic and cultural ties, and with a shared hostility toward the English. Such an impulse went back at least to the twelfth century when writers like William of Malmesbury and Gerald of Wales seized upon the distinct agricultural, military, and sexual practices of Britain's border peoples to construct a stereotype of the Celt and Celtic culture that persisted with little modification into the sixteenth century and beyond. Historian John Gillingham argues that William of Malmesbury's "revival of Greco-Roman modes of perception resulted in the Christian view of the world, one which divided men and women into two basic groups – Christian and non-Christian – being decisively supplemented by a non-religious system of classification, one which divided men and women into the civilized and the barbarians. In the course of British history this was to be the great divide, the creation of an imperialist English culture."[6]

With the Reformation in England, perceived religious differences reinforced the conflation of Ireland, Scotland, and Wales as "dark corners" of the British Isles. Despite the official conversion of Scotland to a more thorough brand of Calvinism than Elizabeth Tudor herself was willing to support in England, many of her countrymen before 1587 continued to identify Scotland with Mary Stuart, a militant Catholic and a claimant to the English throne. For English Protestants, Wales also represented an intractable locus of Catholicism, a *pays de mission* as late as the period of the Puritan Commonwealth."[7] In Wales, unlike in Ireland, the alleged "blind ignorance" and "grosse superstition" of the people never fuelled active resistance to English authority and institu-tions.[8] But the incompleteness of the Reformation in Wales was still troubling enough to elicit the concern and surveillance of Puritan zealots like John Penry (the author of treatises on the religious backwardness of Wales) as well as of the Anglican establishment.[9]

However, even as English observers mapped the Celtic borderlands as an almost homogeneous cultural territory, they could also draw on perspectives that imposed important distinctions both within and between the various outlying parts of the British Isles. No distinction was more central to English typologies than that between Highland and Lowland Scotland. While Highland Scotland, along with the Anglo-Scottish marches, and the Western Isles were thoroughly Gaelic and oriented toward Ireland, Lowland Scotland was non-Gaelic, Protestant, and oriented toward England. Lowland Scotland had more in common culturally and economically with England than with Ireland, and after the victory of the Protestant Congregation party over the Catholic and Francophile establishment in 1559 and the early 1560s, the Scottish state was by-and-large friendly to England, and – in some accounts – even a client state of her southern neighbor.[10]

The Anglo-Protestant orientation of the Scottish lowlands did not diminish an awareness both north and south of the Tweed that Scotland, unlike Wales and Ireland, was an independent kingdom. Although Scot-land had been the target of Anglo-Norman *conquistadores* and English kings since the late eleventh century, in the following two centuries English "relationships with Scotland were those between two kingdoms, whereas Wales and Ireland were clearly regarded as part of the king of England's dominions."[11] English rulers did exercise suzerainty over Scot-land at various times before the reign of Henry VIII, but the Scots always repulsed efforts at more complete domination.[12] Partly in response to a history of English aggression and claims to overlordship, the Scots had developed political and cultural institutions commensurate with their perception of themselves as an independent people.[13]

Like the Scots, the Welsh had forged a distinct cultural identity through generations of strife with Anglo-Norman and English invaders; yet unlike Scotland, Wales had ultimately failed to resist the encroach-ment of English power. Following its military subjugation by Edward I in the late thirteenth century, Wales was "annexed and united . . . unto the Crown of [England], as a Member of the same Body."[14] By the time of the formal Act of Union of 1536 – an Act engineered with the help of the Anglican Welsh gentry whose cooperation generally was crucial in securing English hegemony in Wales – the country was virtually a province of the English state.[15] It was only logical then, that for English writers in the later sixteenth century, the conquered and incorporated Wales rather than the independent Scotland represented the more appropriate precedent for exploring the aspirations and anxieties about current English efforts to subdue Ireland.

In offering writers an expedient means of obliquely engaging the subject of Ireland, Wales operated in two main ways. For some observers, a post-conquest, post-Union Wales furnished a counterexample or model colony for a recalcitrant Ireland. Other observers, though, focused on the condition of Wales before the Union, on the history of Anglo-Welsh conflict, and on the process of conquest as a precedent to guide and justify the subjugation of Ireland. Convinced that the Welsh were once "as far from conformity and civility as these mere Irish now," Elizabethan commentators – echoing the recommendations of Gerald's *Expugnatio Hibernica* – urged that the policies and tactics once used against the Welsh be applied to the rebellious Irish.[16] As Sir Henry Sidney's secretary William Gerard punningly assured the Privy Council upon his master's transfer from Wales to Ireland: "A better president [precedent] . . . colde not be founde then to imitate the course that reformed Walles."[17]

II

As England's "good" colony that set off and compensated for the "bad" colony of Ireland, post-conquest Wales was figured in strongly idealizing terms designed to vindicate the wisdom and blessings of English expansionism. Among the poems, topographies, family histories, and legal texts written by Englishmen and by Welsh gentlemen like Sir John Wynn and George Owen, no document was more central to this discourse than the text of Henry VIII's Act of Union.[18] Declaring that "The Dominion Principality and Country of Wales justly and righteously is, and ever hath been incorporated annexed united and subject to and under the Imperial Crown of this Realm, as a very Member and Joint of the same," the Act rewrote history as myth by suppressing Wales's claim to independence and its historic struggle against English domination.[19] And as an expression of the king's "singular Zeal Love and Favour . . . towards his subjects of his said Dominion of WALES" – a love which included bestowing upon them the laws and "natural Mother Tongue" of England – the Act helped to institutionalize the self-serving myth of the Tudors' "benevolent paternalism" toward the Welsh.[20]

Official recognition of the good order established in Wales by the Union was summed up by Sir Henry Sidney, who, as chief governor of both Wales and Ireland, enjoyed a special perspective: "a better people to governe," Sidney wrote of his Welsh wards, "or better subjects to their sovereign Europe holdeth not."[21] Just as Sidney's praise of the Welsh expresses implicit disdain for his other wards, the Irish, so Thomas Churchyard's celebration of Wales in his poetic tour book, *The Worthines of Wales* (1587), is in part inspired by his contempt for the Irish. A veteran of the Irish wars and a prolific writer on Irish affairs, Churchyard turns to Wales at the opening of his work after declaring that "Ireland growes nought, the people ware unkynd" (14).[22] His vision of Wales as a flourishing and obedient colony that positively embraces its dependence on England throws into relief and implicitly compensates for what he sees as the barrenness, ingratitude, and disobedience of England's other western neighbor. While the Irish treat strangers with unkindness, the Welsh acknowledge English visitors with warmth and deference:

let the meanest of the Court come downe to that countrey, he shalbe so saluted, halsed and made of, as though he were some Lords sonne of that soyle, and further the plain people thinks it debt and duetie, to follow a strangers Stirrop (being out of the way) to bring him where he wisheth. ("The Epistle Dedicatorie," 5–6)

The work's dedication assures the queeen of the "curtesie, loyalty, and naturall kindnes" of her Welsh subjects: "your highnes is no soner named among [the Welsh], but such a generall reioysing doth arise . . . it proceeds of such an affectionate favour" (5).[23] The Welsh people, it seemed, had so completely internalized their subordination as to consider themselves the privileged recipients of English rule. Churchyard thus holds up the disposition of the Welsh as living proof of the benevolent efficacy of English sovereign power.

Churchyard underscores his view of Wales's political and social stability by setting the present against a turbulent past, before the "tyme that rule and lawe came here" (14). The many ruined castles that dot the landscape are physical reminders of this past and a testimony to the success of England's rulers in abolishing the power of local overlords (86–87). The Welsh landscape, then, is realized by Churchyard in richly historical terms, as a kind of living museum or memory theater; to journey through it is to travel back into the past – both the recent conflict-torn past of the fifteenth century, and the deeper mythical past of Arthurian legend (29–31).

III

While Churchyard evokes a disorderly and violent past in order to highlight contemporary peace and prosperity, other writers foregrounded the bitter struggle between Wales and England that had led to the construction of those castles in the first place. David Powel's *The Historie of Cambria now called Wales* (1584) offered sixteenth-century English readers a unique chronicle account of that historic Anglo-Welsh struggle.[24] In a virtually compulsory genuflection, Powel pays tribute in his prefatory address "To the Reader" to the wonder of the Tudor Union: "now the countrie of Wales . . . is in as good order for quietnes and obedience as anie countrie in Europe." Yet the prolonged story of Welsh suffering and English injustice that unfolds across the course of some four hundred pages overwhelms and marginalizes the significance and benefits of the Union.

In the preface, Powel also lays out the work's complex auspices and transmission. *The Historie* was begun by "Caradoc of Lancarvan" "in the Brytish language above two hundreth yeares past" (facsimile title page), and thereafter "yearelie augmented" by the "Beirdh" (bards) (To the Reader).[25] The work was then "translated into English, and partlie augmented" in the sixteenth century by "Humffrey Lhoyd" (1527–68) before Powel himself "Corrected, augmented, and continued [the text] out of Records and best approoved Authors" and published it for the first time (title page). Powel acknowledges not only the various historical layers within the text, but also the collective nature of his own enterprise – one that collated the findings of other histories, and that was indebted to the help of friends and patrons like John Stow and William Cecil who had supplied materials and allowed him access to archives. Powel extends the act of collaboration even to the reader, whose "helping hand" he requests in "the perfecting of this worke" (To the Reader).

But for all these gestures of acknowledgement and dependency, Powel is not merely passing on other men's views. His "corrections and additions, founded as they were on independent research, made the 'Historie' practically a new work."[26] And in the preface, Powel underscores his personal commitment to the book's thesis: England's historically brutal treatment of the Welsh people and their native rulers. Powel reveals his reluctance to undertake the project when first requested by his employer, Sir Henry Sidney, but two factors finally prompt him to agree: his conviction that the deeds of the Welsh people lie obscured and unwritten, and his desire to answer and redress the

slanderous report of such writers, as in their bookes do inforce everie thing that is done by the Welshmen to their discredit, leaving out all the causes and circumstances of the same: which doo most commonlie not onelie elevate or dissemble all the injuries and wrongs offered and done to the Welshmen, but also conceale or deface all the actes worthie of commendation atchieved by them. Search the common Chronicles touching the Welshmen, and commonlie thou shalt find that the King sendeth some noble man or other with an armie to Wales, to withstand the rebellious attempts, the proud stomachs, the presumptuous pride, stirre, trouble and rebellion of the fierce, unquiet, craking, fickle and unconstant Welshmen, and no open fact laid downe to charge them withall, why warre should be levied against them. (To the Reader)

Here Powel confronts an Anglocentric historiographic tradition that had consistently misrepresented the Welsh and resorted to a standard rhetoric of abuse; in challenging the veracity and completeness of this dominant discourse he becomes an advocate for the Welsh people's own views, allowing this Other of the English state to speak directly and powerfully. One way is by reprinting a series of letters and petitions in which leading Welshmen defend their ancient rights and privileges and set out their grievances against the English. In order to illuminate "the causes and circumstances" of Anglo-Welsh conflict in the reign of Edward I, for instance, Powel gives both Latin and English versions of a letter from Lluellen ap Gruffyth to the Archbishop of Canterbury, in which the Welsh prince makes an impassioned but highly reasonable appeal for the church to intervene on the side of the Welsh against the violent impositions of the English.

In the narrative of *The Historie of Cambria*, Lluellen ap Gruffyth, as the last in a line of native Welsh kings and princes that stretches back to the era of Cadwallader in the seventh century, is a pivotal figure (1–6, 16). Lluellen's defeat by Edward I marks the end of Welsh self-rule and the transference of the title Prince of Wales to the English king's eldest son. But Lluellen's end does not mean an end to the Welsh people's hostility to English domination; in fact, despite the "many good lawes" enacted by Edward I, "he could never winne the good will of the common people of the countrie to accept him for their Prince" (376). Along with Edward I's reign, Powel identifies Henry IV's as a time of intensified struggle, focusing again upon "causes and circumstances" to explain and justify the rebellion of the Welsh leader, Owen Glendower. Whereas English chroniclers portrayed Glendower as an unfathomable and ambitious traitor, Powel takes a more balanced approach, probing the social and psychological basis of Glendower's actions and, in particular, the unjustified seizure of a piece of common ground by his English neighbor, Lord Gray of Ruthyn (386). Although Powel censures Glendower for later pressing his cause too far out of a misplaced faith in prophecies, the real villain remains Henry IV, "a manifest oppressor," who, "for the offense of one man and his complices," persecutes an entire nation with "lawes both unreasonable and unconcionable (such as no prince among the heathen ever offered to his subjects)" (387–88). In closing this denunciation, Powel protests against the thoughtless denigration of the Welsh as barbarians: "Let anie indifferent man therefore judge and consider whether this extremitie of law, where justice it selfe is meere injurie and crueltie, be not a cause and matter sufficient to withdraw anie people from civilitie to barbarisme" (387–88).

That the conquerors themselves might be responsible for instilling barbarism in a subject people is one of *The Historie of Cambria*'s most provocative insights – and one, moreover, that also appears in contemporary discourse on Ireland. Thus, in John Hooker's influential translation of Gerald's *Expugnatio Hibernica* (1587), the dominant construction of the Irish as a barbarous "race apart," a "wicked and perverse generation, constant alwaies in that they be alwaies inconstant," is fissured by episodes that document an alternative etiology of Irish barbarism.[27] For instance, in an account of Prince John's arrival at Waterford with an entourage including Gerald himself, we learn that the local Irish chiefs at first welcomed them:

But our new men and Normans, who had not before beene in those parties, making small account of [the Irish], did not onelie mocke them, and laugh them to scorne for the manner of their apparell, as also for their long beards and great glibs, which they did then weare and use according to the usage of their countrie: but also they did hardlie deale and ill intreat manie of them.[28]

This display of cultural chauvinism by the "new men and Normans" immediately alienates the chiefs, prompting them "to stand and joine togither against the English nation, and to their uttermost to adventure their lives, and to stand to the defense of their countrie and libertie." Although Gerald's primary aim in this passage is to discredit the "new men" – the latest wave of Norman colonizers whom he sees as morally and practically unfit to carry forward the work of the first wave of Cambro-Norman adventurers – it also reconceives of Irish rebellion in terms not of a mysterious and intrinsic "racial" impulse but of a reaction against unjustified maltreatment by boorish outsiders. The chapter of the *Expugnatio* in which this account appears catalogues the outrages of these "new men": their confiscation of the lands of loyal chiefs, their drunkenness and self-indulgence, and their disregard for the Anglo-Norman mission generally. The government of a "rude and barbarous" land is now entrusted to "such as be not onelie rude and barbarous, but also lewd and evill disposed."[29] Gerald's treatment of this encounter hardly dilutes the *Expugnatio*'s anti-Gaelic thrust, but it does complicate the colonial picture by implicating the conquerors themselves (or at least one faction among them) in the problem of barbarism. By inverting the norms of barbarism and civility, and by showing how conquest and colonization actively engender native intransigence and resistance, the

text articulates a central faultline in the dominant discourse of colonialism – a faultline that Powel and others opened even further.

By making available an extended critique of English expansionism
generally and of the English monarchy's arrogant and brutal treatment
of the Welsh in particular, *The Historie of Cambria* put in circulation a
set of meanings and values whose oppositional resonances were perhaps
unforeseen by both Powel, an Oxford-educated Protestant cleric, and
the English officials associated with the project. The likes of Henry
Sidney and William Cecil may have regarded *The Historie* as a pleasant
curiosity composed by a proudly patriotic Welshman – an eccentric
example of the antiquarian enterprise that engaged the interests of many
among the intellectual and political elites of England and Wales. Other
readers, however, may not have been willing or able to assimilate and so
efface the political ramifications of Powel's work quite as smoothly. The
"indifferent man," whom Powel invokes as a kind of ideal reader, might
well have viewed the work's retelling of Anglo-Welsh conflict not as a
dead letter, the matter of antiquarian researches, but as a lively image
and window onto present political realities. This "man" was certainly
encouraged to do so by Powel's own theoretical and universal claims. In
the preface, where Powel's own voice is heard loudest and clearest,
he discards the single instance of Welsh oppression to invoke absolute
and general principles about the privileges of all subject peoples: "by the
law of Nature it is lawfull for all men to withstand force by force" (To
the Reader) – a sentiment that obviously strains official injunctions
"against Disobedience and Wilfull Rebellion" to their breaking-point,
and which propels *The Historie* into the discourse of Tudor resistance
theory.[30]

The "indifferent" reader of Powel's *Historie* might easily extrapolate
from England's past conflict with Wales to the present conflict with
Ireland. Powel's work was in fact linked to Ireland through the patronage
of the Sidney family. Sir Henry Sidney, the chronicle's sponsor, had
served as chief governor of both countries, while his son, Sir Philip, was
the book's dedicatee. Moreover, as Powel was getting *The Historie* into
print, Sir Henry was maneuvering (unsuccessfully) to secure the post of
Irish lord deputy for his talented but under-employed son. At the very
least, then, Powel may have wanted his account of England's maltreatment of the Welsh to warn England's governors how *not* to handle the
Irish.[31] For other readers, the example of Wales in Powel's work could
stimulate a critical reassessment of English efforts to impose their laws,
customs, and will upon the peoples of Ireland. As a dissident account of
English state-building on the margins of the nation, *The Historie of
Cambria* helps to fashion a counter-discourse that draws attention to

competing forms of colonialism, scrambles the opposition between "civil" Englishmen and "barbarous" Celts, and even casts doubt on England's supposedly self-evident "right" to dominate her immediate neighbors.

IV

The subject of England's historical struggle with Wales also found its way onto the public stage of the 1590s where it offered dramatists and playgoers a way of indirectly confronting the ongoing extension of English power in Ireland. Shakespeare's *1 Henry IV* (the focus of my next chapter) and George Peele's *Edward I* both use past Anglo-Welsh conflict as a screen onto which misgivings, anxieties, and fantasies about the English presence in Ireland are projected and interrogated. A third play, now lost, *The Famous Wars of Henry I and the Prince of Wales*, was performed by the Admiral's Men in 1598, and may also have belonged to this group.[32] Henry I, as the English king credited by Gerald with "the final subjugation of Wales," offered much to interest English audiences. He twice led armies into Wales, although his overlordship relied less on war than on the threat of force and on the distribution of patronage to native magnates, one of whom, Gruffud ap Cynan of Gwynedd, is probably the Prince of Wales of the play's title. An influential and resilient local power-broker, Gruffud was the subject both of Henry's force and favor (hence, perhaps, the play's alternative title of *The Welshman's Prize*).[33]

In *Edward I*, George Peele selected a reign that both Anglo-Norman/ English and Welsh chroniclers recognized as a crucial chapter in the extension and consolidation of "English" sovereign power throughout the British Isles.[34] Edward was widely acknowledged as the most territorially ambitious monarch since the Norman Conquest: "Through his conquest of Wales and his exercise of direct and superior lordship over Scotland [Edward] came closest to making English overlordship effective throughout most of Britain. During the last fifteen years of his reign the prospect of a single over-kingdom of Britain – under the ultimate judicial, legislative, fiscal and administrative control of Westminster – seemed about to materialize."[35] Given these aspirations and achievements, Edward I came to represent the historical model *par excellence* of how the Elizabethans could master Ireland: "the only way to regain and recover the entire dominion of this cursed land," wrote an exasperated English observer in 1599, "is to proceed as King Edward I did, after long wars (and extreme losses) with the Welshmen, for the subduing of Wales."[36]

V

As the king's principal adversary in Peele's *Edward I*, Lluellen is prominently identified in upper-case print on the title page of the 1593 first quarto:

> THE
> Famous Chronicle of king Edward
> the first, sirnamed Edward Longshankes,
> with his returne from the holy land.
> ALSO THE LIFE OF LLEUELLEN
> rebell in Wales.
> Lastly, the sinking of Queene Elinor, who sunck
> at Charingcrosse, and rose againe at Potters-
> hith, now named Queenehith.[37]

This menu of dramatic highlights is an index to the hybrid and often randomly connected events taken up in the play. In *Edward I*, Peele grafts onto a loose historical framework diverse popular materials drawn from ballads, May day plays, and folk tradition.[38] The result is a work that unsettles any fixed perspective on the protagonists or action. Lluellen, for example, appears as both a serious political figure, the determined and articulate representative of his country's cause, and as an ardent lover whose political acumen is clouded by infatuation for his fiancée Elinor. Lluellen's "seriousness" as a political figure is most compromised when he "plays" Robin Hood and abandons the world of political and military maneuvering to revel as a lord of misrule in the greenwood. Such promiscuous mingling of the materials of history, comedy, romance, and popular balladry has traditionally led critics to designate *Edward I* a "historical romance" or "comical history," a kind of history play defined as "immature" or "prototypical" when compared to the "serious" and "authentic" treatment of historical causation and process offered by Shakespeare's history plays.[39]

In defending non-canonical drama like *Edward I* from charges of aesthetic and moral debasement, Simon Shepherd argues that "When modern commentators write of the incoherence of Elizabethan playtexts they are repeating the discourse of control spoken by the City authorities," as well as the aesthetic discourse of humanists like Sir Philip Sidney, who, attacking the indecorum of contemporary theatrical practice, remarked that "'all their plays be neither right tragedies nor right comedies, mingling kings and clowns, not because the matter so carrieth it, but thrust in the clown by head and shoulders to play part in majestical matters with neither decency nor discretion'." Shepherd

concludes that "the urgency behind strictures on form" articulated by
Sidney and anti-theatricalists, "derived from a political fear that the
disordered work played to a large audience might open the gaps for
'crooked subjects,' and fail to create the truth-effect [the notion that
truth is unitary and fixed] which would give authority to examples of
necessary obedience."[40]

In *Edward I*, the formal disjunctions and heterogeneity of the playtext
that earlier critics saw as signs of artistic incoherence or textual corruption can be recuperated as part of a deliberate dramatic strategy. I would
argue that the play's "diffusion of history ... by the elements of
romance and folklore" is a precondition at a time of dramatic censorship
for engaging with "intractable political themes."[41] Generic and formal
"incoherence" thus function as a means of negotiating political constraints; formal choices prove inseparable from political meanings and
requirements.

VI

In *Edward I*, Welsh resistance to English domination finds its fullest
justification in Lluellen's opening speech to his supporters: "Followe the
man that meanes to make you great," he urges them,

> Follow Lluellen rightfull prince of Wales,
> Sprong from the loines of great Cadwallader.
> Discended from the loines of Trojan Brute,
> And though the traiterous Saxons, Normans, Danes,
> Have pent the true remanes of glorious Troy,
> Within the westerne mountaines of this Ile,
> Yet have we hope to clime these stonie pales,
> When Londoners as Romains earst amazde,
> Shall trembling crie Lluellens at the gate.
>
> (81)

While Lluellen's rousing account of Welsh victimization may stir sympathies in an English audience, the prospect of an attack upon London
quickly clouds those positive feelings. Similarly, Lluellen's call for
vengeance – "With bloud of thousands [of English] guiltlesse of this rage"
(93) – after the English kidnap his fiancée, the French princess Elinor de
Montfort, compromises the moral probity of the Welshman's cause (93).
Yet in the event, Welsh threats turn out to be threats only; far from
becoming merciless invaders themselves, the Welsh are forced to defend
their homeland – where the bulk of the play is set – from the English. At
the same time, the specter of Celtic barbarism evoked by Lluellen's talk of
Welsh atrocities is displaced from the Welsh to Edward's royal family,

and especially the Spanish queen Elinor of Castile, whose demand that all women cut off their right breasts in recognition of her power, conjures an image of Scythian barbarism (130–33).

Apart from these two early threats of violence, Peele's Lluellen has little in common with the Lluellen of the English chronicles where he is either given little attention or slighted in stereotypical terms. As William Tydeman has shown, Peele's version of the Welsh prince "generally ignores material inimical to Llewellyn's good reputation and nobleness of character, and emphasizes such grudging sorts of praise as [Holinshed] spares Edward's antagonist." Peele, for instance, omits the "political arguments for Edward's detention of Eleanor de Montfort" that appear in Holinshed, an omission that "has the effect of rendering the king's conduct unacceptably high-handed, and thus the prince's ardent desire to have her returned more reasonable." Furthermore, Peele draws on the positive description of Lluellen in Robert Fabyan's chronicle while pointedly ignoring the accompanying negative one.[42]

Edward I's undeniable admiration for Lluellen and the Welsh struggle for independence also surfaces in the fate of Lluellen's brother and chief confederate, David of Brecknock. Near the end of the play, with Welsh resistance crushed, the brothers' destinies coalesce: David is "drawne on a hurdle" across the stage with other captured Welshmen, while Lluellen's head is paraded on the end of a spear (159).[43] Even as this spectacle of broken and mutilated Welsh bodies attests to the final, uncompromising triumph of English power, the rebels are further humiliated by the friar, Hugh ap David, a former ally of Lluellen and David who has now defected to the English. Referring back to an earlier prophecy that Lluellen would eventually triumph and reach great heights, the renegade friar jokes that the prophecy has now been realized in a perverse way:

> Said [the prophet] not oft and sung it to,
> Lluellen after much adoe,
> Should in spite heave up his chin,
> And be the highest of his kinne:
> And see aloft Lluellens head,
> Empalled with a crowne of lead.
>
> (160)

It is surely a tribute to David's dignified resilience that in the face of this mockery and with the gallows beckoning he is able to protest unrepentently: "I goe where my starre leads me, and die in my countreis just cause and quarrell" (159). Indeed, David has pursued his nation's "just cause and quarrell" with courageous integrity throughout the play, beginning with his dangerous role as spy at the English court, where – feigning loyalty to Edward – he sits on the king's council and passes information back to the Welsh (98–99). Later, in David's most impressive contribution to the Welsh cause, he pretends to be taken prisoner by and is then ransomed from the Welsh – a stratagem devised with Lluellen and designed to win the release of Lluellen's fiancée. David instructs his Welsh "captors" to exchange him for Elinor,

> and when you parle on the walles,
> Make shew of monstrous tirannie you intend,
> To execute on me, as on the man,
> That shamefullie rebels gainst kin and kinde.

(99–100)

Exploiting as it does Edward's reputation for "ruthe and pittie," the brothers' stratagem works and the prisoners are exchanged, but only after David is tortured before the English onlookers: "Meredeth stabs [David] into the armes and shoulders," "He showes [David] hote Pinsers," "He cuts his nose" (102–3).[44] David's stoical self-sacrifice – and the stage directions suggest these are real not feigned wounds – is not born of self-interest or even of family loyalty but of a belief that the Welsh cause depends on the crucial political union of Lluellen and his French princess (82).

Whether through design or accident, *Edward I*'s restrained, even respectful, treatment of the leading Welsh "rebels" and their "countreis just cause and quarrell" would likely have stirred up thoughts in some playgoers of contemporary Irish "rebels" and the nature of their "cause and quarrell." When the play was written and first performed c.1590, its "application" to events in Ireland may not have been as clear as during later performances. Between August 29, 1595, and July 6, 1596, Philip Henslowe "records fourteen performances of a play called *longshanckes* . . . which is almost certainly Peele's *Edward I*."[45] By 1595–96, Irish affairs were demanding more attention from English audiences as tensions mounted between the proxy government and native groups. Furthermore, the publication of a second edition of *Edward I* in August, 1599, may have been planned to capitalize on the widespread interest aroused by the latest, contemporaneous initiative to subdue Ireland. On March 27, the populist and controversial Earl of Essex left for Ireland with an army of unprecedented size, only to return unexpectedly and against orders on September 28. As we will see in chapter 6, to this same six-month window the composition of the Folio version of *Henry V* can also be assigned.

One detail prompting theater audiences and readers to see the play as in dialogue with the unfolding situation in Ireland is the scene in which Lluellen and his followers assume the identity of Robin Hood and his merry men – the kind of scene, that is, seized upon by critics as undercutting the play's political seriousness. The legend of Robin Hood was a malleable one in the Renaissance, with Robin's status and symbolic meaning varying across discourses. For poet William Warner, Robin was a popular hero, the nostalgic embodiment of a vanished pastoral England; but for the Elizabethan authorities, the name of Robin Hood was synonymous with rebel and outlaw.[46] And to no group was the name of Robin Hood attached more often in the sixteenth century than to the rebellious Irish.[47]

The greenwood scenes of *Edward I* represent an uneasy hiatus in the play's political narrative. As Robin Hood, Lluellen tries to inspire a festive spirit among his followers – "How well they coucht in forrest green, / Frolike and livelie withouten teene" (116) – but political and military exigences remain close to the surface. In the forest, Meredith warns "beware of spies" (117), and Lluellen uses the sojourn to regroup his forces, lift morale, and raise revenues for the impending war against Edward (116, 138); also, while in disguise Lluellen is confronted and nearly killed by his royal adversary (140–41). This scene of hand-to-hand combat between Edward and Luellen transforms England's war against the Welsh into an intensely personal attack and augurs the impending defeat of the Welsh cause. Eventually, when "The King hath Lluellen downe, and David hath Mortimer [Edward's ally] downe," Edward and David release their opponents in exchange for their friends' lives (140).[48] As the English pair exit, the Welsh brothers "prepare to strengthen [them] selves against the last threatnings" (141). But from this point on, the Welsh are increasingly helpless against superior English force. In a subsequent brief scene, Mortimer enters, "pursuing of the Rebels," and ordering his soldiers to "Follow, pursue, spare not the proudest he, / That havocks Englands sacred roialty" (147). Afterwards, we witness Lluellen and David in desperate retreat, then the spectacle of ignominious defeat: the hurdle and the severed head.

VII

Even as *Edward I* traces the inexorable suppression of Welsh resistance through cumulative scenes of violence and punishment, the play examines a different form of "conquest" – or at least a different relation between England and Wales that depends on a language not of the sword but of negotiation and accommodation (101). After the two sides exchange David and Elinor, Peele inserts a remarkable dialogue between the king (Longshanks) and an anonymous Welsh foot soldier:

LONG   How say you Welshmen, will you leave your armes,
         And be true liegemen unto Edwards crowne?

SOLDIER If Edward pardon surely what is past,
         Upon conditions we are all content.

LONG   Belike you will condition with us then.

SOLDIER Speciall conditions for our safetie first,
         And for our countrie Cambrias common good,
         T'avoide th'efusion of our guiltie bloud.

LONG   Go to, say on.

SOLDIER First for our followers, and our selves and all,
         We aske a pardon in the Princes word,
         Then for this Lords possession in his love:
         But for our Countrie cheefe these boones we beg,
         And Englands promise princely to thy Wailes,
         That none be Cambrias prince to governe us,
         But he that is a Welshman borne in Wales.
         Graunt this and sweare it on thy knightly sword,
         And have thy man, and us, and all in peace.

                                                    (105)

Edward agrees to the soldier's conditions and immediately puts in
motion his "secrete" purpose to have the pregnant queen deliver their
child in Wales. Although the queen resents being carried "into his ruder
part of wales," Edward's ruse works (109). After the birth, four Welsh
barons visit the English camp as the representatives of "The poore
countrey of *Cambria*" on whose behalf they offer "most zealous duetie
and affection" to their new ruler (128).

What are we to make of the fact that it is an ordinary soldier, never
heard from nor mentioned again, who intervenes in the wrangling
between Lluellen and Edward and who initiates negotiations with
Edward while simultaneously overruling Lluellen's objections to them?
As a representative of "the popular voice," the soldier's articulate and
patriotically disinterested involvement imputes to the commons a meaningful and constructive role in the political process – a role that helps to
move their antagonistic superiors beyond a destructive impasse. The
Welsh soldier's proposal for a negotiated settlement "upon conditions"
offers a compromise solution to the conflict which proves acceptable to
both sides. Under the terms of the proposal, England's ultimate overlordship of Wales would still permit Welsh autonomy through a principle of
home rule. In short, to quote Mortimer, the truce would ensure "Wales
happines [and] Englands glorie" (106).

The visible token of this settlement is the "mantle of frize" presented
to the new-born prince by the representatives of the Welsh people.
Edward accepts the garment of rough cloth, promising that his son
will wear it at his christening as a symbol of his initiation into and

identification with Welsh culture (128–29). But the mantle immediately becomes a point of controversy between Edward and the queen, whose "Spanish pride" scorns the garment as socially "low," fit to serve only as "a goodly warme Christemas coate" – a reaction that risks alienating the Welsh commons (130). Though the dispute is a seemingly minor one in the play's dramatic economy, the "mantle of frize" resonates powerfully with contemporary fear and fascination about the Irish mantle. Spenser's description in *A View* of this curiously over-determined and multi-functional artifact is perhaps the most notorious of many accounts that virtually fixate upon it.[49]

Edward's "gift" of his new-born heir to the Welsh and their reciprocal gift of the mantle have implications for the play's imagining of colonial relations. As an act of cross-cultural rapprochement, the exchange of gifts adumbrates a form of domination based upon conciliation and cooperation rather than upon the violent imposition of a conqueror's will. By dramatizing the alternative approaches of conciliation and conquest to English mastery in Wales, *Edward I* also holds up for scrutiny the competing approaches for the English subjugation of Ireland. In "Sword, Word and Strategy in the Reformation in Ireland," Brendan Bradshaw identifies coercion and persuasion as the two poles of a spectrum of strategies for which the metropolitan government, the New English, and the Old English communities argued in attempting to subdue and "civilize" Gaelic Ireland.[50] Advocates of persuasion maintained that they could reform the Gaels by deploying the mechanisms of English government, especially parliamentary authority and common law, and by winning the consent of the Irish masses through preaching and education. In practice, "conciliatory measures" included the policy of surrender and re-grant whereby local chiefs would exchange their traditional titles and forms of land tenure for English ones; the appointment of governors and provincial presidents from within the Old English elite; and the use of pacts to win the cooperation of Gaelic chiefs.[51] Supporters of coercion argued, on the other hand, that reformation first required the violent suppression of the state's enemies. Yet advocates of coercion were not necessarily united over questions about the kind or degree of force to be used or when force was appropriate in the "civilizing" process. Thus, the various New English administrators, planters, soldiers, and churchmen who backed coercion did so with different understandings of what constituted force and with varying goals, emphases, and caveats. Some pushed for an immediate and total war while others thought of force as a carefully calibrated component of an overall strategy. The persuasive policy with its basis in what Ciaran Brady calls "reform thought" was advanced principally by the Old

English elite of the Pale and, in one form or another, had been a guiding principle of government policy in Ireland since the 1540s. By the early 1590s, however, the more strident advocates of an all-out policy of coercion were now in the ascendancy and the "reformers" increasingly discredited.[52]

Edward I does not promote any particular colonial policy but lays out the alternatives of accommodation and coercion as general strategies, inviting audiences to weigh the consequences and moral force of each. Edward's willingness to create a "native" Prince of Wales inspires widespread loyalty among the local people: at the ceremonial bestowing of the mantle "The whole countrey of Cambria round about . . . both men and women in their best array" assemble, while "the men and women of Snowdone" – the mountain base of Lluellen's rebellion – offer generous provisions to the king (129). In contrast to the evident satisfaction of the Welsh people and their barons with the policy of accommodation, Lluellen and David remain unreconciled. Pursued and finally killed after the settlement is reached, the brothers and their fate suggest how coercion starts cycles of violence in which killing provokes retaliation and more killing. Even the sponsors of force in Ireland were capable of discerning the underlying, long-term consequences of violence: "And sure I am," declared Lord Deputy Fitzwilliam, "by many woful experiences that the Irish after blood and murder is drawn and done upon them will never be reconciled, and will revenge with blood if they may. Neither will they trust any that hath so dealt with them."[53]

This sense of violence as endlessly self-perpetuating is vividly inscribed at the conclusion of the playtext of *Edward I*. Peele, after earlier portraying the murder of Lluellen and displaying his severed head, now shows us the king unexpectedly proclaiming, "Againe Lluellen he rebels in Wales" (169). According to the play's modern editor, the "confusion and inconsistency" that characterize the playtext's final moments, simply "defy explanation," thus betraying "an unusually corrupt text."[54] However we explain these anomolies – as the result of a process of textual revision, as the outcome of copyists' and compositors' errors, or as Peele's intentionally confusing "hodgepodge" – we should also consider how this ending was registered by readers of the early quartos. Perhaps the ghostly reemergence of Lluellen suggested, albeit in a non-realistic mode, the "miraculous powers of renewal, even resurrection" of the Welsh rebels, as well as the interminable and irrepressible nature of organized violence.[55] Also embedded in the "confused" ending may be a recognition of the malleability of dramatic scripts in performance: on the public stage, *Edward I* was not a fixed and unitary object but an "unstable, infinitely revisable script" with at least two very different endings.[56]

Finally, then, *Edward I* stands as a remarkably open-ended and provocative interrogation of England's relationship with its closest neighbors – one that treats Celtic figures and claims to autonomy with an unusual sympathy. By reanimating an earlier phase of English expansionism, Peele's work, like Powel's, prompts audiences to reflect critically upon current expansionist efforts in Ireland. And, in forging a larger discourse about England's domination of the British Isles, both works complicate the contemporary conversation about Ireland, generating oppositional insights that contest prejudices about England's self-evident cultural superiority over and right to "own" Ireland. Before the seventeenth century there was no place in either print or public performance for the open and coherent repudiation of English designs in Ireland, but there was room for the airing of moral uncertainties and for the weighing of various *forms* of colonization. To different degrees and with their own particular emphases, Powel's *Historie*, by exposing English barbarism and injustice, and Peele's *Edward I*, by lauding Edward's creative receptivity, suggest that conciliation, accommodation, or what others considered a "benevolent" colonialism, represented the best way forward for all parties. Whereas in Gerald's *Expugnatio*, the ridicule and intimidation of the Irish by Prince John's entourage of "new men" proves disastrous for Anglo-Irish relations, Edward I's willingness to have his son born in Wales and clad in the symbolic "mantle of frize" helps him win the hearts and minds of the Welsh people, if not of their leaders.

4   The Tyrone rebellion and the gendering of colonial resistance in *1 Henry IV*

When, at the beginning of the fourteenth century, the King of Scotland's brother, Edward Bruce, was crowned King of Ireland, "there was in prospect something very like a pan-Celtic alliance against the English" in which Scots, Irish, and Welsh would join forces around "their 'common national ancestry,' their 'common language' and their 'common custom'."[1] Edward Bruce died in 1318, effectively ending hopes of an alliance at this time, but English anxieties about a coalition among Irish, Welsh, Scots, and other "outlandish" peoples remained a vestigial part of the national psyche.[2] These anxieties surfaced again early in the fifteenth century when Owen Glendower sought Scottish support for his anti-English rebellion, thus infusing it with an air of "racial conflict."[3] By the later sixteenth century, fears of anti-English collusion focused upon the Scots–Irish mercenaries and Redshanks ("Scottish Irishmen") who assisted their rebellious kinsmen in the north of Ireland. The English authorities also suspected that the rebellion in Ireland was fuelling broader structures of anti-English collaboration. Fears that Welsh malcontents were in league with Irish rebels were based in part on English awareness of the residual popularity of Catholicism in Wales and the conviction that Catholics would naturally support fellow Catholics. During an invasion alarm in 1594, the president of the council in the Marches of Wales was instructed to keep all "the more dangerous recusants . . . at least twelve miles from the coast," to prevent them from giving assistance to a Spanish force, while in 1597 a Spanish observer, anticipating an invasion through Wales, claimed that at Milford Haven "There are many Catholics and the people are naturally enemies of the English and do not speak their language."[4]

Alarm over Welsh–Irish collusion was also registered by a group of Welsh gentry who in January 1599 informed the Privy Council of the local popularity of the rebellious Earl of Tyrone and of a sympathetic bond between the subject people of Wales and Ireland. "No Welshmen," they warned "should be used in service against the Irishmen, because they were not to be trusted." The local people had allegedly proclaimed

Tyrone prince of Wales and king of Ireland. He now "had in his service 500 Welshmen" and "friends in Wales that looked for him, as he was both favourable and bountiful to Welshmen." Furthermore, Tyrone's Welsh friends had made the intriguing assertion that their Irish hero was "descended of Owyne Clyne Dore, who had interest both in Ireland and Wales . . . [and] that there was a prophecy the Earl of Tyrone should prevail against the English nation."[5]

This alleged claim of consanguinity between Owyne Clyne Dore (a variant spelling of Owen Glendower) and the Earl of Tyrone reinforces the perception that Tyrone was in compelling ways Glendower's modern political and cultural heir. When John Hayward composed the two parts of his *The Life and Raigne of King Henrie IIII* which covered the first four years of the king's reign, he was certainly thinking of Glendower as Tyrone's precursor and of Henry's wars against the Welsh as foreshadowing the Earl of Essex's imminent wars against the Irish.[6] Similarly, in *1 Henry IV*, I shall argue, Shakespeare takes advantage of perceived resemblances and connections between the rebellions of Glendower and Tyrone, weaving into the fabric of the play a displaced representation of Tyrone's resistance to English authority in Ireland.

1 Henry IV represents an intensification as well as a reorientation in Shakespeare's engagement with Anglo-Irish affairs. Whereas in the first two parts of *Henry VI*, Ireland gains Shakespeare's attention mainly as a factor in aristocratic power struggles and as a point of origin for disruption within England, in *1 Henry IV* it is the specter of rebellion within Ireland that haunts the action and calls forth an extended, if always oblique, consideration of the unrest's sources, dynamics, and solutions. In reengaging with the problem of Ireland, the play works at a topical level, encoding and exploring various historical figures, events, and patterns; yet the dramatic aperture also opens out to map local concerns onto perennial sources of English anxiety in Ireland, especially anxieties of gender.

I

Written and first performed between August 1596 and February 25, 1598 (when it was entered in the Stationers' Register), *1 Henry IV* coincides with a critical new phase in Elizabeth's Irish wars when reports of the imminent collapse of English rule were becoming more frequent and alarming.[7] In February 1597, for example, Maurice Kyffin reported that the army was in a state of disarray, and the country approaching anarchy: "our soldiers die wretchedly in the open streets and highways; the native subjects spoiled and brought to extreme beggary; no service in war performed; no military discipline or civil justice exercised; briefly, the whole kingdom ruined and foraged."[8] That a lingering crisis had now become an emergency is conveyed in the frantic endorsement on a packet of letters from the Irish Privy Council to the queen dated September 25, 1596: "Deliver these in haste, haste. Haste, post haste, for life, life. For Her Majesty's most special affaires." With the proliferation of news-letters and the circulation of political gossip, a general – though not necessarily accurate – awareness of events and conditions in Ireland spread beyond the council chamber to a much broader audience.[9]

1 Henry IV, then, coincides with a nation-wide intensification of Irish resistance to English rule. After the suppression of the Earl of Desmond's Munster rebellion in the early 1580s, opposition to plantation schemes and the extension of English influence beyond the Pale had been local and uncoordinated.[10] English control in Ulster, traditionally the most intractable province, had depended since 1567 upon the cooperation of Hugh O'Neill (Baron Dungannon) whom the government installed as its native representative, and whom in 1585 it created second Earl of Tyrone in recognition of his service.[11] But Tyrone's loyalty became increasingly dubious over the next decade, and in 1595 he provocatively accepted the outlawed Gaelic title of The O'Neill. At first, Tyrone drifted into indirect opposition to the English by supporting the disturbances of his kinsmen and allies; only following his first direct attack upon crown forces was he declared a traitor in June 1595. Although Tyrone was to reassert his loyalty and receive a temporary pardon a year later, he had now set upon a course of galvanizing and transforming Irish resistance into a nation-alist struggle for independence.[12] Under Tyrone's leadership, the Ulster Irish were no longer a primitive fighting-force but a well-trained and well-equipped army.[13] Ironically, their proficiency was due in part to Sir John Perrot's earlier policy of training the natives in the use of modern firearms; ever since, as William Camden pointed out, the Irish had "exercised the English . . . with a more difficult war."[14]

If Tyrone, "the arch-traitor," seemed to some observers to be single-handedly confounding English authority, he was in fact the leader of a diffuse coalition of families, factions, and groups including Scots, Welsh, and Spaniards. At the core of this coalition was a "developing confed-eracy of the Ulster lords," "the Maguires, O'Donnells, and O'Neills" – related families that gave the alliance "the quality of a family compact."[15] The English worked relentlessly to unravel this and other hostile groupings by fostering competition among and within the clans and septs. Spenser recalled how the English themselves had originally "set up" Tyrone, "then called Baron of Dongannon," to "beard" his rival and predecessor "Turlagh Lenagh." But the plan backfired when

Tyrone turned the power invested in him by Elizabeth against the English.[16] Unlike his predecessors, Tyrone largely succeeded in foiling the English strategy of divide and conquer, and through cultivating connections with other families was able to establish a nearly unified front of opposition: "All Ulster," declared an English tract of 1598, "is now joined together in Rebellion against the Quene, saving the Countie of Louth . . . all the Captens of Countries are bound to the Earle of Tyrone, either by Affinitie or Consanguinitie or duetie."[17] During negotiations with Tyrone in December 1597, an English delegation was astonished by his effrontery in pushing demands on behalf of other septs and Gaelic leaders. Thomas Jones, the English recorder of the interviews, saw in Tyrone's audacity an attempt by the "crafty traitor" to enlarge his constituency by adopting the grievances of groups he had previously ignored: "His demand made now for the Moores and Connors, and for Edmund Gerald [Kavanagh], of whom he made no mention in his treaty with Sir John Norreys, may induce us to think that, the longer he is suffered, the further will he extend his power." Even more alarming to the English delegation was Tyrone's demand for "liberty of religion . . . for all the Catholics of the land," a claim he made, according to Jones, in order "to become popular amongst this idolatrous people."[18] By the end of 1597, then, the English faced in Tyrone a rebel leader of national standing whose aspirations appeared disturbingly similar to those of his precursor, Glendower, some two centuries earlier.

II

The rebel alliance of *1 Henry IV* can be seen as reconfiguring the coalition of factions and families ranged against the English in Ireland. When Edmund Mortimer, Earl of March, marries Glendower's daughter, he completes a triangular alliance that through the marriage of Mortimer's sister to Hotspur also includes the powerful Percy family. To the king, Mortimer's marriage into a rebellious Welsh family is a provocative crossing of cultural and dynastic boundaries – and one that equips his rival and the legitimate heir to the throne with a power base; to the rebels, on the other hand, Mortimer's marriage represents an invaluable exogamic alliance that unites the north of the realm (the Percy base) with both the west and Wales in a bond of blood against the king. The rebels further strengthen their alliance by drawing in the Scots – the Percys' erstwhile rivals in the north – and a dissident group of clergy led by the Archbishop of York. United against the king by the end of Act One, then, is a heterogeneous rebel confederacy that magnifies the threat from the Celtic borderlands by compounding it with the threat of a factious nobility under Percy leadership.[19]

Although Glendower is the member of this confederacy whose actions most insistently suggest Tyrone's activities in Ireland, Mortimer also triggers a cluster of topical resonances about Tyrone and the politics of English–Irish conflict. In fact, in the early seventeenth century, Mortimer was invoked by Sir John Davies as an equivalent figure to Tyrone from England's own past:

> when England was full of tenants-at-will our barons were then like the mere Irish lords, and were able to raise armies against the crown; and as this man [Tyrone] was O'Neal in Ulster, so the Earl of Warwick was O'Nevill in Yorkshire, and the Bishopric and Mortimer was the like in the Marches of Wales.[20]

Mortimer, in his obscure capitulation to Glendower, embodies the oldest and most pervasive of English anxieties about contact with the Irish: like those Anglo-Norman and English settlers who had abandoned past loyalties and assimilated themselves to Gaelic culture, Mortimer "goes native." Moreover, in marrying Glendower's daughter and embracing her tongue, Mortimer violates the most charged and repeated of government injunctions in medieval and early modern Ireland against cultural mixing (3.1.201–2).[21]

In late sixteenth-century Ireland, Mortimer's lapse from "civility" was most recognizable in the Old English population – that former "store of gentlemen, and other warlike people" – which through intermarriage and promiscuous contact had "degenerated and growen almost mere Irishe, yea and more malycious to the Englishe then the verye Irishe them selfes." As Spenser's Irenius explains, many Old English families in order to mark their irreversible detachment from their English ancestry and to proclaim their new-found identities, had "quite shaken off theire Englishe names and putt on Irishe, that they might be altogeather Irishe." Significantly, among the families that had "degendred from their antient dignities," Spenser includes "the great Mortymer, who forgettinge how great he was once in England, or English at all, is now become the most barborous of them all, and is called *Macnemarra*."[22] In the Glendower–Mortimer bond, then, Shakespeare gives shape to the possibility of a much-feared collusion between England's Gaelic and Old English enemies in Ireland. Appealing for support from all available quarters, Tyrone had persuaded the Old English "'gentlemen of Munster' to join the Ulster confederacy and to 'make war with us'."[23]

With the major influx into Ireland of English settlers and soldiers in the sixteenth century, the Old English were not alone in running the risk of "degeneration." Officers and soldiers in the queen's pay regularly deserted to the enemy and "converted into Irish." One renegade Englishman, a Captain Tyrell, after defecting to Tyrone, married a native woman and helped train Irishmen in the use of firearms.[24] The miserable fighting conditions alone might explain this pattern of desertion, but it is also conceivable that some men were motivated by a quasi-utopian hope that Gaelic society afforded a better alternative to their present predicament. The tempting "libertie" from "harde [restraintes]" that Spenser thought the Old English had discovered in Ireland was a powerful pull on the loyalties of men who had little personal stake in the work of conquest.[25]

There was, finally, another, less clear-cut, form of "going native" to which Mortimer's defection also gestures and that is exemplified in the figure of Captain Thomas Lee, an English "soldier of fortune" and a cousin of the queen's Champion at the Tilt, Sir Henry Lee.[26] The profound ambiguities in Lee's role as Captain General of the Irish kern are vividly captured in his full-length portrait by Marcus Gheeraerts (1594; figure 3). Lee poses confidently amid a rough mountainous landscape, at his back a dark and forbidding "fastness" of forest. From the waist up, Lee is all English: he wears an open-necked shirt beneath a military style tunic and carries a round shield slung across his back, a conical helmet, sword, and a modern snap-haunce pistol. But from the thighs down Lee is unclad and barefooted, suggesting, along with the native spear he is clutching, the style of the Irish kern.[27] The portrait captures Lee's fascination with his liminal position on the cusp of two worlds – half-in and half-out – of native society – a position that allowed him to act as a government go-between with the Earl of Tyrone. Lee's "long familiarity and affection to the Earl" (supposedly, they were regular bedfellows) assisted his efforts but also led to accusations that the two were conspiring against the queen.[28] In short, the figure of Lee provides a bridge from the kind of total defection represented by Mortimer to the more provisional type of crossing-over embodied by Cade in *2 Henry VI*, who as York's messenger and spy in Ireland exhibits a curiously energetic mobility between the opposing camps of colonizer and native.[29]

III

Although Tyrone was declared a traitor in 1595, English opinion about him remained divided. In 1596 Sir John Norris maintained "that Tyrone had not in the past intended to rebel and did not now."[30] Reporting to Burghley on Tyrone's grateful acceptance of a pardon in July that year, Sir Geoffrey Fenton thought the earl should be "cherished and borne up

3   Captain Thomas Lee by Marcus Gheeraerts, the Younger, 1594.

in his well doings." Despite his recent offenses, Tyrone might still be "secured" as an ally "by time and good usage."[31] After visiting the earl in August, Captain Thomas Lee counselled likewise that Tyrone not be abandoned by the English. Tyrone, "this honourable man," was caught in a dilemma between the "damnable crew" urging him to rebel and the English, of whose intentions, should he submit, Tyrone was understandably suspicious. If he were only given certain guarantees, Lee argued, Tyrone would eagerly "perform his duty to Her Majesty."[32] In the eyes of other officials, though, Tyrone had shown himself an unredeemable enemy to whom truces and pardons were only a way of gaining time and consolidating his power. Looking back to 1596, William Camden summed up their impatience with Tyrone's strategy thus: "I am weary of running over the particular clokes of his dissimulation. In a word, when any danger threatened him from the English, hee then both in countenance and words bare such a feigned shew of submission, and pretending such penitency for his faults, that he deluded them till the opportunity of prosecuting him was lost."[33]

With the appointment of Thomas, Lord Burgh, as deputy in the summer of 1597, Tyrone's committed enemies finally found a determined and vociferous advocate. Dropping the traditional titles of respect with which Tyrone had been addressed, Burgh applied to his adversary a series of evocative epithets, including the Running Beast, the Great Bear, the Northern Lucifer, and Beelzebub – epithets that suggest a menacing blend of elusiveness, boldness, and inscrutable evil.[34] The rhetorical effect of Burgh's vitriol was to inflate the image of Tyrone, transforming him from just one more in a series of rebellious Gaelic chiefs into something of a mythical entity, more animal or demon than mortal man.

Much like Tyrone between 1596 and 1597, Glendower in *1 Henry IV* is marked by a studied ambiguity in the descriptions that precede his appearance at 3.1. In the play's opening scene, Westmorland calls Glendower "irregular and wild," characterizing him as an uncivilized outlaw whose "rude hands" have defeated and captured "the noble Mortimer" at their confrontation in the Welsh borderlands (1.1.38–41). The king adds a sinister note to this formidable image by ascribing Glendower's strength not to physical valor but to witchcraft. Henry's reference to "that great magician, damned Glendower" (1.3.83), resonates suggestively with Tyrone's reputation as "the Great Divill."[35] In the subsequent exchange, Hotspur disputes the claim that his brother-in-law Mortimer willingly submitted to Glendower; Hotspur offers an account of the confrontation that seeks to reestablish his kinsman's slighted loyalty and courage against his "valiant combatant," "great Glendower" (1.3.107, 101). Hotspur's recollection of the honorable "hand to hand" combat between the two men and their gentlemanly "agreement" to interrupt it for occasional respites, evinces a respect – even an admiration – for Glendower that Westmorland and the king both withhold (1.3.93–112).

Glendower continues to excite conflicting perspectives during his only appearance where he turns out to bear little resemblance either to the play's earlier descriptions of him or to those in Shakespeare's main sources. Whereas in Holinshed the alliance between Mortimer, Glendower, and the Percys is sealed "by their deputies in the house of the archdeacon of Bangor," Shakespeare brings the rebel leaders together at an unspecified location in Wales.[36] By making their meeting a direct, personal affair Shakespeare invests the rebel alliance with the air of a family compact; Hotspur and Glendower address each other as "cousin" while Mortimer calls Glendower "father" (3.1.3, 6, 142). At home in his own sequestered, private realm we see the ostensibly "irregular and wild" Glendower in the "civilized" role of courteous host. Although taunted by Hotspur about his supposed magical powers, Glendower remains restrained, and when he is dismissed by Hotspur as a barbarous Welsh-speaker he recalls his proficiency in English and musical composition. When the two argue over how the realm should be divided it is Glendower who shows the greater courtesy by graciously yielding (3.1.131).

The play's shifting, dizzying perspectives on Glendower dramatize the complex and conflicting feelings swirling about Tyrone in even his most resolute antagonists.[37] Those uncertain feelings were only compounded by Tyrone's anomalous cultural identity. When Glendower first informs Hotspur of his education in England – "I can speak English, lord, as well as you; / For I was trained up in the English court" (3.1.117–18) – the play's first audiences could have recalled that Tyrone too was popularly reputed "well brought up, partlie in the Court of Ingl[and]."[38] Both Glendower and Tyrone had experienced the "civilizing" effect of court culture and had initially served their English masters: Glendower as a member of Henry Bolingbroke's retinue, Tyrone as a protégé of Sir Henry Sidney and Elizabeth. For both men, though, familiarity with English ways had only bred a latent resentment, and upon their strategic reinsertion into their respective home cultures they had eventually shaken off the yoke of English servitude.[39]

Tyrone's humanist education and familiarity with "civilized" ways made him a difficult figure for the English to classify and thus to handle both in person and figuratively. Whereas his enemies might denigrate him as a "base wood kern" or "the generation of a blacksmith," such language concealed an uneasy knowledge that the earl was at best the equivocal Other of English "civility."[40] Like Glendower in 3.1, Tyrone could impressively regale his English guests. During a visit to "the arch-rebel" in October 1599, Sir John Harington discovered "far greater respect . . . than I expected." He found Tyrone's sons dressed "in English cloths like a nobleman's sons" and learning "the English tongue," and when he presented them with his "English translation of 'Ariosto,'" Tyrone requested that they "read all the book over to him."[41]

IV

In the process of domesticating Glendower and so revising his fearful reputation, Shakespeare makes the chieftain an object of ridicule. Falstaff's satirical vignette of Glendower mastering the forces of Hell lays the ground for Hotspur's thorough demystification of the Welsh-man's prodigious self-image and magical pretensions (2.4.326). Glendo-wer's repeated insistence upon his own terribleness simply cannot withstand the sardonic wit of the pragmatist Hotspur, whose exposure of Glendower as a hoax is all the more devastating precisely because they are allies and because of Hotspur's earlier defense of Glendower to Henry (1.3.93–112). At the same time, Glendower's image as formidable warrior–wizard is also undermined through figurative and literal associ-ation with the female. In response to Glendower's boast of literary accomplishments, Hotspur speaks dismissively of "mincing poetry," thereby characterizing it in terms of a woman's small and delicate steps (1.3.129). Hotspur's complaints about Glendower's garrulousness – "He held me last night at least nine hours" – and his comparison of Glendower to "a railing wife," further diminish the Welshman's status through association with traits stereotyped as feminine (3.1.151, 155). For a warrior chieftain, Glendower is also surprisingly at ease in the company of women, offering first to break the news of the men's departure to their wives, and then to accompany the women to the rendezvous (3.1.89–92). More striking, Shakespeare focuses exclusively upon Glendower's relationship with his daughter while omitting any reference to his son.[42] As a result Glendower appears a fussing, over-protective parent – "I am afraid my daughter will run mad, / So much she doteth on her Mortimer" (3.1.140–41).

Shakespeare's strategy of effeminizing Glendower helps to manage the pervasive English recognition of Tyrone's enviable toughness and virility: "He is the best man of war of his nation, having had his education in our discipline, and being naturally valiant," opined Sir George Carew.[43] According to Fynes Moryson, Tyrone "was of a meane stature, but a strong body, able to indure labors, watching, and hard fare."[44] Tyrone

himself only epitomized what observers considered the impressive yet
disturbing hyper-masculinity of all Irish men, whom Spenser's Irenius
describes as "very valyante and hardye, for the most parte great endurors
of the could, labour hunger and all hardnesse, verie active, and stronge of
hand, verye swifte of foote, verie vigillante and circumspecte in theire
enterprises, very presente in perills, verie great scorners of death."[45] For
Richard Stanihurst, the free-wheeling Irish horsemen were "like arrant
knights of the round table," while their immediate inferiors in the order of
Gaelic warriors, the gallowglasses, were "grim of countenance, tall of
stature, big of lim, burlie of bodie, well and stronglie timbered."[46] Similar
perceptions of bodily strength and military prowess extended to the male
inhabitants of England's other frontier regions. "The inhabitants on both
sides" of the Anglo-Scottish border, wrote William Camden, "as bor-
derers in all other parts, are a military kind of men, nimble, wilie, always
in readiness for any service."[47] In *1 Henry IV*, it is "brave Archibald, /
That ever-valiant and approvèd Scot" and not Glendower who gains and
keeps English respect for Celtic toughness (1.1.53–54). Although defeated
and captured at the battle of Shrewsbury, Archibald is applauded by Hal
as a model of valor, and released – "ransomeless and free" – in recognition of his future dependability and usefulness to the English crown
(5.5.27–31). Shakespeare's choice of Archibald as the recuperable Celt no
doubt reflects the basically amicable state of Anglo-Scottish relations in
the late sixteenth century, but it also suggests an English readiness to
recruit the talents of all bordering peoples.

Anxious tributes to the hyper-masculinity of Gaelic and especially
Irish men again suggest just how slippery and contradictory were the
constructs of the "civil" and "uncivil." For if the "uncivil" implied a
degenerate barbarism to be shunned, it also implied a collection of
mostly physical attributes that were fully consistent with the ideals of
English chivalry – hence Stanihurst's comparison of the Irish horsemen
with King Arthur's knights. Similarly, if the "uncivilized" connoted
vitality and "hardness," the "civilized" could suggest an undesirable
passivity and "softness," the very qualities that Hotspur rails against in
the foppish messenger sent by the king to demand his prisoners
(1.3.29–69). English accounts of the toughness of Irish men, then, were
bound up with considerable nostalgia for the kind of raw physical
courage that Englishmen themselves had once supposedly possessed.
Reflecting on this decline, Stephen Gosson remarked how Englishmen
had exchanged their former masculine exercises of "shooting and
darting, running and wrestling" for the emasculating arts of "banquet-
ting, playing, pyping, and dauncing, and all such delightes as may winne
us to pleasure, or rocke us in sleepe."[48]

Shakespeare's strategy of establishing Glendower's reputation as a formidable rebel before domesticating and feminizing him, I submit, works to disarm the threat of the rebellious Celtic chieftain and of the Earl of Tyrone in particular. But the play's displacement of current Irish threats and its performance of a kind of ameliorative "social *work*" does not end here.[49] After his humiliation by Hotspur, Glendower is not seen again. His disarming seems complete when, discouraged by unfavorable prophecies, he fails to appear for the crucial battle (4.1.125–27; 4.4.16–18). Following Samuel Daniel's account, Shakespeare evacuates the Welsh altogether from the battle of Shrewsbury, thus emphasizing Glendower's absence; in Holinshed, Welsh soldiers, but not Glendower himself, are present (3:25). Ascribing Glendower's absence to adverse prophecies is Shakespeare's invention and it has the effect of nullifying Glendower's alleged "magic" by transforming it from a potential source of opposition into a rationale for inaction.[50] For the Irish rebels, prophecies like the one that claimed "a boat of two tons shall one day carry away all Englishmen from Ireland," were an obvious source of encouragement in their struggle. Glendower's prophecies, conversely, predict the failure of his cause and thus legitimate his disengagement from the impending conflict.[51]

Glendower's individual fate extends to the rebel alliance as a whole, for it dissolves before its full military potential can be tested. After a planning session marked by personal rivalries and arguments over the distribution of land, the coalition unravels internally and spontaneously as if in confirmation of the continuing trust placed by the English in the policy of undermining the cohesion of the Irish confederacy. Despite Tyrone's acknowledged success at uniting the native community, his opponents were confident that "many [Irish families], which now shadow themselves under the cloak of Tyrone's villainies, will yield great means, and plot good courses for Tyrone's ruin and overthrow, if they might see Her Majesty fully resolved to prosecute war against them."[52]

In the deterioration of Glendower from a principal scourge of the English to charlatan and palpable absence – and in the parallel fate of the alliance generally – the play can be seen as disempowering the figure of the Celtic chieftain by literally wishing him away. Theatrical magic thus assuages English anxieties about Glendower's modern counterparts in Ireland.

V

1 Henry IV was not the only play of these years to trade in wish-fulfillments about quelling rebellion in Ireland. Whereas the Irish crisis is

registered indirectly in Shakespeare's play, it is presented in the anonymous *The History of the Life and Death of Captain Thomas Stukeley* with
a directness unique in Elizabethan drama.[53] First performed by the
Admiral's Men in 1596, *Stukeley* relates the swashbuckling career of the
eponymous renegade whose travels take him first to Ireland at the time
of Shane O'Neill's revolt in the 1560s.[54] Stukeley joins the "Irish
expedition" after abandoning his father, his new wife, his creditors, and
his studies at the Inns of Court in search of wealth and honor. His
powerful blend of wayward, aggressive Englishness and sexual potency
undoubtedly attracted many of the Inns' students in the audience, some
of whom, like John Donne, would be drawn to the prospects of
advancement that the enterprise in Ireland seemed to promise.[55]

Before Stukeley arrives in Ireland we see O'Neill and his allies
besieging the English garrison in Dundalk (D2^v-D4^r) – a scene, curiously,
that the first edition of the play prints in two parallel versions, one in
verse and one in prose. While this duplication may indicate the revision
of an original text, it also delineates different dramatic strategies for
handling the Irish threat through either fear or ridicule. In the first
version of the scene, O'Neill and his compatriots speak the Queen's
English, are familiar with the identities of the English commanders, talk
about cutting English throats, and are generally presented as confident
and menacing. In the second version, by contrast, the Irishmen speak in
"funny" Gaelic dialects with "third", for example, becoming "turd" (line
962). This second version also renders O'Neill less threatening than the
first by adding ridicule of him by his associates, as well as comic appeals
by both master and men to Saint Patrick.[56]

After Stukeley and his soldiers rout the Irish, a repentant O'Neill
prepares to submit to the deputy and beg the queen's pardon – gestures
that implausibly suggest that "breaking military resistance is tantamount
to obtaining loyalty."[57] However, the prospect of a pardoned O'Neill
who is free to rebel again is prevented by his murder at the hands of his
former allies, the Scotsmen, Alexander Oge and MacGilliam Buske (E4^v-
F1^r). Their revenge-killing of O'Neill for his murder of a kinsman enacts
the same fantasy of an unstable rebel alliance violently destroying itself
that we find in *1 Henry IV*. When the Scots hold Shane's severed head
aloft and dispatch it to the English deputy, some playgoers must have felt
a vicarious satisfaction at the thought of Hugh O'Neill – Shane's blood
relative and political successor – suffering a similar fate (F1^v).

Yet if *Stukeley* offers an illusory solution to the menace of Shane
O'Neill and his heirs, it is less sanguine about other problems besetting
English rule in Ireland. The play, for example, has no answer to the
dangerous activities of "the townsmen" of Dundalk – the Old English

citizens who act as spies for the rebels whom they "love . . . better then us Englishmen" (line 997). Moreover, the English garrison is wracked by the kind of internal dissension that precipitates the downfall of the rebel alliance. Thus, when Stukeley discovers that the governor of Dundalk is his old rival, Captain Herbert, he challenges him to fight and a scuffle breaks out (E2ᵛ). Bloodshed is averted, but later Herbert teaches Stukeley the "discipline of warre" by shutting the gates and forcing him to spend the night beyond the walls (line 1229). Stukeley's position outside Dundalk symbolically aligns him with the Irish rebels, who a few scenes earlier had huddled there under cover of darkness. Here, then, the line between rebel and rebel-slayer has all but disappeared. Ultimately, Stukeley's defeat of the rebels is further compromised by the realization that the suppressor of rebels is destined to become an "Irish" rebel himself, the papally appointed "Marquesse of Ireland" (line 2429) and the leader of Catholic insurgents against Elizabeth's other island.[58]

VI

Like *Stukeley*, *1 Henry IV* struggles to contain the multiple dangers of Ireland. Thus, even as Glendower is feminized to help drain away the threat of Tyrone's hyper-masculinity, the Irish menace is relocated in the different feminine form of the play's Welshwomen. Although Glendower's daughter is the only Welshwoman to appear on stage, she is not the only one mentioned; Mortimer falls into her hands after coming perilously close to other, more menacing, women of Wales. In the opening scene, Westmorland reports how:

> the noble Mortimer,
> Leading the men of Herefordshire to fight
> Against the irregular and wild Glendower,
> Was by the rude hands of that Welshman taken,
> A thousand of his people butcherèd –
> Upon whose dead corpse there was such misuse,
> Such beastly shameless transformation
> By those Welshwomen done as may not be
> Without much shame retold or spoken of.
>
>   (1.1.38–46)

When this incident is first broached in Holinshed's *Chronicles*, Abraham Fleming is just as reticent as Westmorland, refusing to give details of the atrocity committed by Welshwomen against Englishmen lest readers' "honest eares" and "continent toongs" be scandalized (3:20).[59] However, three years further into the narrative, Fleming gives a freer account:

The dead bodies of the Englishmen, being above a thousand lieng upon the ground imbrued in their owne bloud, was a sight (a man would thinke) greevous to looke upon, and so farre from exciting and stirring up affections of crueltie; that it should rather have mooved the beholders to commiseration and mercie: yet did the women of Wales cut off their privities, and put one part thereof into the mouthes of everie dead man, in such sort that the cullions [testicles] hoong downe to their chins; and not so contented, they did cut off their noses and thrust them into their tailes as they laie on the ground mangled and defaced. (3:34)

The Welshwomen's "transformation" of their victims turns the male English body into a text upon which relations of power and gender are symbolically contested.[60] First, the dead soldier is castrated and his "privities" stuffed in his mouth; then his nose – a surrogate phallus – is cut off and stuffed in his anus. At the simplest level, by cutting and transposing the soldiers' noses and "privities" the Welshwomen attack and invert an "official" or classical version of the body as a hierarchically organized and inviolately whole entity. The women effectively transform this version into an antithetical grotesque body in which the mouth and anus are the prominent parts and the lower regions are conflated with the higher.[61] And since grotesque imagery was central to the subversive discourse of early modern carnival, the women's "creation" of this indecorous body signals their rejection of the oppressive ideologies of class and nation.

The Welshwomen's independent "fiercenesse and barbarisme" links them to other "deviant" female groups like the frenzied Maenads of antiquity who withheld their sexuality from men and adopted an active, defiant virginity.[62] Although Fleming's account is silent about the Welshwomen's marital or sexual condition, their atrocity is striking in that it takes the form of a perverse necrophilic rape in which only men suffer penetration and defilement. The women, as the active participants, overturn the normative sex–gender system by assuming the kind of sexual dominance that the culture reserved for men. The gagging of the soldiers with their own "privities" is also a telling gesture of female insubordination that symbolically transfers to men the stipulation of silence enjoined by patriarchy upon women. At the same time, the Welshwomen's acts graphically evoke and reject attempts to impose the English language upon the people of the Celtic borderlands.[63] But perhaps the most transgressive gesture of all is the women's penetration of the soldiers' "tailes" with their own noses. Castrated and sodomized, the English soldiers are totally degraded and "unmanned."

The Welshwomen's violence in both play and chronicle accounts illustrates Phyllis Rackin's argument that, in early modern historiography, women "are typically defined as opponents and subverters of the historical and historiographic enterprise, in short, as antihistorians." In the patriarchal world of the Tudor chronicles, men construct nations and the canons of "civilization," while women, as the embodiments of a disorderly nature and sexual desire, invariably obstruct these projects.[64]

But the accounts of the atrocity also have more local resonances in that they point to specific anxieties aroused by Celtic, and especially Irish, women. In short, the accounts register the English impulse to imagine the threat from the borderlands in terms of the overthrow of a masculine identity through castration.[65]

Conceivably, Fleming/Shakespeare's interest in the Welshwomen's atrocities was informed by reports of similar outrages against English soldiers and settlers in Ireland. Bodily dismemberment and gagging were familiar elements in an imaginary repertoire of Gaelic violence constructed by the New English. In October 1598, for example, the Chief Justice of Munster, William Saxey, told Robert Cecil about the mutilations inflicted by the rebels on the English dead: "some with their tongues cut out of their heads, others with their noses cut off."[66] A decade earlier, the first Earl of Essex claimed it was rebel practice "to cut off their [English victims'] privy parts, set up their heads and put them in their mouths."[67] Such reports were more a reflection of English national prejudices and dark desires than an accurate record of actual events. After all, it was the New Englishman Barnabe Rich who urged the authorites to imitate the Egyptians in castrating their foes: "if this severity were used," he predicted, "the *Eunuches of Ireland*, would farre exceede in number over and above all the rest that were fit for propagation."[68]

Whatever the "fit" between the butcheries related by Fleming/Shakespeare and those supposedly committed in Ireland, reports about Irish atrocities do not identify them as the specific work of women. Yet women did figure prominently in other accounts of Irish rebellion and "barbarism" – a fact indicative of a broad drive to criminalize women both in the core and on the periphery of the English state.[69] As the Protestant forces of church and state redefined the patriarchal family as the central social institution in the latter sixteenth century, women who fell outside its confines or refused its dictates were stigmatized and persecuted: "The formation of the family within the absolutist state," Peter Stallybrass observes, "was staked out across the physical bodies of 'criminalised' women."[70] The process of criminalization and scapegoating was strongest on the margins of the nation-state, "where the call of the centre was weakest" and the "legitimacy [of the state] was most at peril." In both England and Scotland, witchcraft prosecutions, for example, were concentrated in border areas.[71]

In Ireland, New and Old English residents alike railed against the interference of Gaelic women with the spread of "civility." The body of the Gaelic woman with its nourishing and corrupting powers was a special site of English anxieties. According to Spenser and others, wet nurses communicated their "nature and disposition" to their English charges, thus perverting the child's entry into an English symbolic order.[72] Irish children were seen as escaping the techniques of bodily regulation, especially swaddling, to which their English counterparts of both sexes and all classes were subject. For Irish girls, this reprieve continued after childhood in the lack of straitlacing or corsetting. "The women generally," wrote Fynes Moryson, "are not straitlaced, perhaps for fear to hurt the sweetness of breath, and the greatest part are not laced at all." English observers saw the Irish female body as alarmingly liberated and free to grow to grotesque proportions: "[they] have very great duggs, some so big as they give their children suck over their shoulders." Growing without artificial restraint, Irishwomen were also perceived as unencumbered by the ideological constraints that corsetting symbolized.[73]

From a hostile English viewpoint, this physical laxity led inevitably to the vagrant-like mobility of female groups such as the "Mona-Shull" or "goyng women," the itinerant camp followers who serviced the rebels sexually. Thomas Smith described them as "great blasphemers of God . . . [who] rune from contry to contry, soynge sedicione amongst the people. They are comen to all men."[74] Just as Fleming/Shakespeare's Welshwomen gain their potency from the ease with which they traverse the geographical boundary between England and Wales, so the "Mona-Shull" derive their dynamism from a promiscuous movement among territories and also among men – a movement that is seen as not only outside male control, but as capable of degrading men to the women's level. English writers blamed Irish women in particular for preventing the establishment of a patriarchal and Godly society in the country. Contemplating "the cause and the very root of these [Irish] rebellions" in March 1596, Sir John Dowdall informed Burghley, that "in the tenth of Her Majesty's reign and since, they came very orderly to the church, but first their women grew weary of it, and that being unpunished their men left it." And in the same year William Lyon, Bishop of Cork and Ross, complained: "where I had a thousand or more in a church at sermon, I now have not five; and whereas I have seen 500 communicants or more, now are there not three; and not one woman either at Divine service or communion."[75] Through a kind of perverse agency, the English claimed, Irishwomen had led their men away from religion and into rebellion.

Other reports noted how Irishwomen, ignoring proscriptions that banned "civilized" women from war, participated directly in the rebellion. Shakespeare's reference to the Welshwomen's presence on the field of battle recalls English claims that Irishwomen of different social backgrounds played a crucial part in promoting rebellion.[76] Tyrone numbered among his neighbors and allies "O'Donnell's Ineen Duv – she whom the Four Masters describe as a woman 'like the mother of Machabees who joined a man's heart to a woman's thought'." Another Irish "Amazon" was Grace O'Malley, "a great feminine sea captain" of Connaught, as Sir Henry Sidney described her in 1583.[77] At times cooperating with the English, at times defying them, O'Malley was, according to Lord Justice Drury, "a woman that hath impudently passed the part of womanhood and been a great spoiler, and chief commander and director of thieves and murderers at sea," while in 1593 Sir Richard Bingham characterized her as that "notable traitoress and nurse to all rebellions in the province for forty years."[78] Rebel women also included "the witches of that country (which aboundeth with witches), [who] are all set on work to cross the [English] service by extraordinary unseasonable weather," as well as the "churls and 'Calliackes' [*cailleacha*, old women], or women who milked [the rebels'] 'Creates' [*creacha*, herds] and provided their victuals and other necessaries."[79] Fearful of these camp followers, Humphrey Gilbert argued that killing them "was the way to kill the men of war by famine."[80] Gilbert's discovery of a female infrastructure that sustained the rebels implicates the women in the economy of war and cancels any protection that enemy women (as non-combatants) were conventionally granted by the codes of warfare.

VII

In the early modern colonial imagination, sex and seduction were dangerous forces that imperilled English domination in Ireland. During the siege of an English stronghold, the Earl of Desmond attempted to "entrap" his opponents by sending "a fair young harlot as a present to the [English] constable, by whose means [Desmond] hoped to get the house." The ploy was discovered and the woman thrown "with a stone about her neck, into the river."[81] Narratives like this one about the vulnerability of Englishmen to sexualized Irishwomen play upon fears of symbolic castration, the same fears that Glendower's daughter arouses in *1 Henry IV*. Although this nameless, shadowy woman shares with her Welsh sisters the Amazonian desire to enter male space – "She'll be a soldier too, she'll to the wars" remarks Glendower (3.1.190) – her real transgressive power resides in her overcoming the great English warlord

Mortimer with her bewitching and unintelligible words and songs: "Charming your blood with pleasing heaviness" (3.1.212).

Shakespeare sets Mortimer's confinement in the enclosed vaginal space of Glendower's "bow'r" against Hotspur's earlier protestation that he will not be waylaid by similarly decadent and tempting surroundings: "I had rather live / With cheese and garlic in a windmill, far, / Than feed on cates and have [Glendower] talk to me / In any summer-house in Christendom" (3.1.156–59). As a dangerous space that the male hero must shun, the "bow'r" has its analogue in the "abode of sensual self-abandonment that Guyon must destroy in Book II of *The Faerie Queene*."[82] Here the Knight of Temperance discovers the witch Acrasia and her lover, "whom through sorceree / And witchcraft, she from farre did thither bring" (2.12.72). His "sleepie head" resting softly in the witch's "lap" (2.12.76), the man has been lured into the same symbolic pose of submission as Mortimer who reposes against his Welsh wife: "She bids you on the wanton rushes lay you down," remarks Glendower, "And rest your gentle head upon her lap, / And she will sing the song that pleaseth you" (3.1.208–10). This mysterious Welsh song (for which no text is provided) spellbinds Mortimer, transporting him into a liminal state "'twixt wake and sleep" and draining away his masculine volition (213).[83] As a rebel-song it serves not, like many bardic verses, to embolden one's own side but to subdue and enthrall an enemy.

In *1 Henry IV* the audience's encounters with Glendower's daughter and her castrating countrywomen could hardly be more fleeting and peripheral. While young Glendower communicates only through her father's translations (the stage directions indicate that she speaks in Welsh but her words are not printed), the Welshwomen are not allowed to represent themselves but are spoken about by men. Textually, the Welshwomen are twice removed or doubly mediated, since Westmorland's report of their atrocity is itself based on a prior report made to Westmorland by a "post from Wales" (1.1.37). The very brevity of Westmorland's report and the king's failure to respond seem calculated to minimize the transgressive nature of the incident. By omitting the gory details available in his source, Shakespeare sanitizes his own text, but thereby makes the incident more enigmatic and disturbing. Fleming, at least, gives the reader some interpretive help with understanding the Welshwomen's desecration of the soldiers' bodies by setting it in the context of other notorious acts of female cruelty; in the play, by contrast, the Welshwomen's actions are highlighted by their puzzling obscurity. Although the Welshwomen's gruesome deed seems to be raised only to be repressed and immediately forgotten, it turns out to be a defining moment in the play's imagining of nation and gender, and one that retains symbolic weight to the play's conclusion.

Responsibility for canceling the Welshwomen's violation and for repairing English masculinity falls to Prince Hal, whose suitability depends upon his conspicuous insulation from women in general. As Peter Erickson argues, the essential characteristic of the Englishman in such figures as Talbot and Henry V is an "approved image of manhood based on resistance to women and on allegiance to men." Hal's possession of a "self-contained masculine purity," effectively denies the determining and contaminating powers of women over men, the kind of powers associated with the nursing and fostering roles of Irishwomen.[84]

Hal's defeat of Hotspur at the battle of Shrewsbury is a pivotal moment in the play's rehearsal of the subversion and recovery of a masculine and militant English identity. Vernon's description of the armored prince endows Hal with a precocious sexual energy and presents his skill at horsemanship – he "vaulted with such ease into his seat" (4.1.108) – as a foreshadowing of the prince's "riding" of women. As the battle approaches, images of sexual vitality and erection turn into a kind of phallic competitiveness between Hal and Hotspur. Before the battle, Hotspur imagines their imminent encounter as a blend of homoerotic camaraderie and violence: "I will embrace him with a soldier's arm, / That he shall shrink under my courtesy"; but afterward it is Hal who proclaims victoriously over Hotspur's corpse: "how much art thou shrunk!" (5.2.73–74; 5.4.87).

In Glendower's absence from the battle of Shrewsbury, Hotspur takes the Welshman's place as the play's final attenuated version of Tyrone – a former loyalist turned rebel like Hotspur – and becomes the scapegoat who must bear off Tyrone's residual danger. Hal's showdown with Hotspur in the Welsh borderlands, moreover, recapitulates the earlier confrontation between Mortimer and Glendower,

> When on the gentle Severn's sedgy bank,
> In single opposition, hand to hand,
> He [Mortimer] did confound the best part of an hour
> In changing hardiment with great Glendower.
>
> (1.3.98–101).

The later fight enacts a substitution of one set of "valiant combatants" for another and projects onto Hotspur the oppositional energies earlier invested in Glendower. In killing Hotspur, Hal also captures and internalizes his rival's stock of personal chivalric capital, thus achieving a victory that helps to channel the mixed feelings of hatred and admiration toward Tyrone.[85]

In returning us to the same liminal space between two realms in which Mortimer is originally captured and the Welshwomen dismember the soldiers' corpses, Hal's climactic confrontation with Hotspur takes place in a highly charged symbolic zone. The battle occurs on the outskirts of Shrewsbury, a town situated on the margins of English territory in the Marches of Wales.[86] Forming a corridor of land on either side of the English–Welsh border, the marches had until early in the sixteenth century been divided into a series of miniature principalities, each governed by its own marcher lord. Equipped with private armies and observing only their local laws, these local magnates were synonymous with political autonomy and resistance to the crown. Only with the shiring of the marches and the introduction of English legal and administrative procedures in 1536 as part of the Act of Union did the crown finally curtail the powers of these magnates and take control of the region.[87] Yet long after this pacification and political incorporation, the Welsh borderlands retained in the English cultural memory a reputation for disorder and instability. Contemporary representations helped perpetuate the view of the marches as lawless territory. The play *1 Sir John Oldcastle* (1599), for example, opens with a bloody affray between the followers of Lords Herbert and Powis in the border town of Hereford.

English observers thus had no difficulty in comparing the Welsh marches to the territory of Gaelic Ireland that lay outside the "civilized" Pale around Dublin. The Pale itself was considered not so much a fixed physical area as "a moving 'colonial' frontier"; "by little and little to stretch the Pale further," so converting "formless" Gaelic march or borderland into productive shire ground, was a continuous goal of sixteenth-century English policy.[88] By the later 1590s, however, this was largely a forlorn objective as Tyrone's forces increasingly turned their weapons against the very "hart of the realme." According to Robert Bagot in 1597, the Pale, which had once measured thirty-six by thirty miles, was now shrunk to only twenty miles in each direction.[89]

Prince Hal's victory over the rebels near Shrewsbury, then, stages on closer and more familiar ground the kind of boundary-marking desired by the crown's forces in Ireland. Through Hal's ritual blood-letting, the nation's geographical and political center physically and symbolically reasserts control over its volatile and vulnerable borders. Furthermore, when Hal pronounces Hotspur's epitaph and observes the "fair rites of tenderness" (5.4.97) toward his rival's corpse, he reconstitutes a code of battlefield conduct that the Welshwomen had so outrageously overturned in this same territory through their acts of "illegitimate 'profane' violence."[90] In resecuring the border between England and Wales, Hal

enacts the metaphorical reintegration/remembering of the corpses of the
English soldiers, since – as anthropolgists recognize – across a range of
cultures "the body is a model which can stand for any bounded system.
Its boundaries can represent any boundaries which are threatened or
precarious."[91]

VIII

Writing from a position of relative English security in Ireland in the early
seventeenth century, Sir John Davies argued that the country's systemic
problems could be attributed to "the absence of our kings, three of them
only since the Norman conquest have made royal journeys into this
land." For Davies, Edward III's success in governing Ireland was due to
the "personal presence of the king's son as a concurrent cause of this
reformation, because the people of this land, both English and Irish, out
of a natural pride did ever love and desire to be governed by great
persons."[92] Through Hal's feats, *1 Henry IV* offers the fantasy-remedy
outlined by Davies of an activist male heir visiting the fringes of the
realm and virtually single-handedly thwarting rebellion. Hal's vanquishing of Hotspur triumphantly rewrites the torturously inconclusive
guerilla warfare of Ireland as a chivalrous conflict that is direct and
apparently final.

Hal's vigorous personal involvement in subduing rebellion also provides a happy contrast to the spectacle of an aging and incapacitated
Elizabeth – a ruler who, of course, had never set foot in her troubled
western colony. In the late 1590s, the queen's faltering body became a
focus of public comment: "when she rideth a mile or two in the park,
which now she seldom doth, she always complaineth of the uneasy going
of her horse; and when she is taken down her legs are so benumbed that
she is unable to stand."[93] If Hal is a version of the youthful male heir
that many in England craved (discussion of the succession was officially
prohibited), he is also conceived as an ideal successor to the long parade
of men appointed to govern Ireland. At a later stage in Hal's career,
Shakespeare explicitly likens him upon his victorious return from France
to Elizabeth's own "Generall" returning from Ireland with "Rebellion
broached on his Sword."[94] Although *1 Henry IV* dates from the time
when the young and charismatic Earl of Essex was first being linked with
the Irish post, we should not assume that Hal represents anything more
than a general pattern of the kind of decisive and single-minded
leadership that many sought in Ireland. Between 1597 and the spring of
1599 the Irish command was in a state of flux, with two lord deputies and
three interim justices in turn occupying the chief position. The arrival of

the aggressive Thomas, Lord Burgh, as deputy in May 1597 inspired confidence that Tyrone would soon be defeated, but less than five months later Burgh was dead of typhus. From Burgh's death in October 1597 to April 1599 when Essex arrived, the Irish government was effectively "in the hands of a committee, with the inevitable consequences of indecision and procrastination."[95]

IX

After Hal's victory over Hotspur – a triumphant alternative to an Irish war of attrition – the king announces with confidence and finality a sentiment that many English longed to pronounce about Ireland: "Thus ever did rebellion find rebuke" (5.5.1). And yet these moves toward resolution and closure are clouded by countercurrents. In his subsequent closing speech, Henry's rhetoric of victory falters as he reveals that the overall outcome of the rebellion is still undecided. As in Ireland, a single battle has settled nothing. While ordering Prince John and Westmorland to engage "Northumberland and the prelate Scrope," Henry announces his own intention to march with Hal "towards Wales, / To fight with Glendower and the Earl of March" (5.5.37–40). This sudden re-intrusion of Glendower and Mortimer transforms the effect of closure from a reassuring completion into a postponement, the deferral of a threat apparently dismissed earlier. Shakespeare had provoked contempt for Glendower through his absence at Shrewsbury; but now the play confuses audience responses by suddenly and un-expectedly reintroducing the Welshman, as if in recognition of the fact that Tyrone and his confederates were still loose and threatening beyond the Pale.

In *2 Henry IV*, we never see the king's promised attack upon "Glendower and the Earl of March"; in the sequel, Henry is preoccupied with other threats, and Shakespeare reduces Glendower to an elusive, insubstantial figure whom the English never directly confront. Whereas in the play's sources, the Welsh leader suffers a horrible, humiliating death – in Holinshed he starves after fleeing, defeated and abandoned, "into desert places and solitarie caves" (3:48) – Shakespeare says nothing of these circumstances. Instead, Warwick's claim to "have received / A certain instance that Glendower is dead" is all that we hear about the Welshman's purported demise (3.1.101–2).[96] Unlike that other stage rebel, *Stukeley*'s Shane O'Neill, Glendower is not emphatically dis-patched but allowed to linger ghost-like at the margins of the action, his death neither confirmed nor denied in a play that places considerable emphasis upon the danger of false report and rumor.[97] Far from offering consolation or reassurance about current tensions in Ireland, the two parts of *Henry IV* echo Gerald of Wales's sobering prediction that the "perfect or full conquest" of Ireland will be achieved "not much before dooms daie."[98]

5 "A softe kind of warre": Spenser and the female reformation of Ireland

On April 9, 1589, Lord Deputy Sir William Fitzwilliam informed Burghley about an unusual act of resistance among the Connaught rebels. Their leader, Sir Brian O'Rourke,

about two or three years since having found in a church or in some other place an image of a tall woman wrote upon the breast thereof QUEEN ELIZABETH, which done he presently fell with such spiteful and traitorous speeches to rail at it, and otherwise so filthily to use it ... During which time his barbarous gallowglasses standing by played their parts as fast, who with their gallowglass axes striking the image one while on the head, another while on the face, and sometimes stabbing it in the body, never ceased until with hacking, and mangling they had utterly defaced it. And being nevertheless not contented herewith they ... fastened a halter about the neck of the image, and tying it to a horse tail dragged it along upon the ground, and so beating it with their axes, and railing most despitefully at it they finished their traitorous pageant.[1]

Images of the queen had been targets for her enemies in the past, but never had an act of *lèse majesté* in Ireland been so spectacular or proven so fascinating to English observers. Indeed, O'Rourke's desecration of the queen's statue entered the collective memory both in and out of Ireland as a touchstone of native barbarism. In 1605 Sir John Harington referred to the Irishman who "trayld Queen Elisabeth's picture at his horse tayle," confident that his audience, Lord Mountjoy and Robert Cecil, would recognize the allusion.[2]

In Fitzwilliam's narrative, O'Rourke's assault on the statue is presented as an act of creative improvisation in which the anonymous "image of a tall woman" is appropriated as the centerpiece of an act of ritual iconoclasm. Here, the image-breaking energies of Protestant zealots are turned back against them by the Catholic Irish, in a reversal that draws attention to Elizabeth's own status as a kind of cult object. First verbally assaulted and "filthily" used by O'Rourke, the surrogate Elizabeth is then penetrated by repeated stabbings in a gang rape. What for O'Rourke and his men was an act of ritual catharsis in which the oppressor was symbolically obliterated becomes in Fitzwilliam's narrative an eloquent witness to alleged Irish barbarism.[3]

Clearly, Fitzwilliam's account is no bland, unadorned rendition of the "facts" written in the colorless prose of an official report, but a carefully wrought and rhetorically skillful textualization of an event that is recorded only in English documents. First, Fitzwilliam evokes the desecration of the statue in terms of assorted theatrical and oratorical practices. O'Rourke's ranting at the statue functions as a prologue to the entrance of the "barbarous gallowglasses" who then play their assigned "parts." The subsequent strangulation of the effigy replaces the image of the playhouse stage with the image of the gallows, and then with the spectacle of the "pageant." In the dragging of the statue behind a horse, Elizabeth suffers a final indignity – one that resonates as a parodic royal progress and as a reenactment of the fate of traitors conveyed to execution on a horse-drawn hurdle.[4]

O'Rourke's attack on the queen's statue is, as we would expect, strongly denounced in all the extant English accounts, but the denunciations veil more conflicted responses and impulses. Fitzwilliam's carefully honed description, in fact, bespeaks a level of imaginative investment indicating not a routine attention to the incident but an almost voyeuristic fascination. The attack proved so fascinating to English observers because it enacted the dark, unspeakable fantasies of rebellion and autonomy among Elizabeth's male officials in Ireland, one of whom, Sir John Perrot, was accused of collusion with O'Rourke and of complicity in the attack on the statue. As in his other alleged actions and statements, Perrot was seen as venting a "frustrated desire for mastery over" his female monarch.[5] "God's wounds, this it is to serve a base bastard piss-kitchin woman," was one of the "contemptuous speeches" attributed to Perrot at his trial, along with his claim to be "the fittest man in England to have the keeping of [the queen's] body" if she were ever "distressed."[6] Perrot's downfall was certainly the outcome of intense personal and factional rivalries in both countries, but in his arraignment for High Treason he also served as a scapegoat for the collective resentment and guilt of all those who chafed at their subordination to a woman ruler.[7]

I

Many of the officials, soldiers, and planters who ventured to Ireland during Elizabeth's reign were undoubtedly attracted by a perception that they were going to a place beyond the sway of the queen. Marginal to the female-dominated court at Whitehall, and lacking any similar "effeminizing" structure of its own, Ireland offered New English émigrés an arena conducive to the unfettered exhibition of male prowess – a space in which to establish a homosocial community outside of female control. Certainly, the arts most practiced in Ireland were the "masculine" ones of warfare and domination and, in the Irish, the English believed they faced "a nacion ever acquainted with warrs though but amongst them selves, and in theire owne kynde of militarie discipline trayned upp even from theire youthes."[8] As an extended war zone, Ireland was also constructed as a place unfit for English gentlewomen. Thus when Sir Henry Sidney's wife joined him in Ireland she soon "fell most greavously sick . . . and in that sicknes remayned ones in traunce above fifty-two houres!"[9] Sidney saw her as unsuited to the harsh reality of Ireland and quickly dispatched her back home. Barnabe Rich asserted more forthrightly the view of Ireland as an enclosure of English masculinity when he accused the "rampynge . . . ryotynge . . . [and] revelynge" wives of English servitors in Ireland of bankrupting both their husbands and their monarch. Rich turns to imperial Roman history for his model of a masculinized Ireland:

when [the Romans] used to send any offycers wyth authoryte into any of ther provynces, that wer farre dystant from Rome, they would in no wyse suffer them to carry ther wyves wyth them: A reason is rendered, bycause in the tyme of peace, women do alure & corupt the maners of men, by ther pryde & vanyte, and many tymes by ther intycynge provocatyons, the course of Justice is checked & perverted, and most injuryous wronges comytted and in the tyme of warre, they do hyndre the servyce by ther tymeryte & feare.[10]

Given the conviction that Ireland afforded a space for the free play of male power, the queen's ultimate control of Irish policy and her frequent restraints upon it generated both suppressed and overt frustration. In *1 Henry IV* resistance to English expansionism is figured in terms of a monstrous and emasculating Gaelic femininity; yet for many in the New English community a more potent female threat to their survival and success was the queen herself. This chapter explores the ways in which Elizabeth's imagined relationship to Ireland was discursively constructed and contested, especially in Spenser's later works – works that post-date his court visit of 1589–90, the composition of *Colin Clouts Come Home Againe*, and the publication of the first installment of *The Faerie Queene* in 1590. Intensely conscious of how the queen empowered and overshadowed New English endeavors in Ireland, Spenser was one of various agents and groups that participated in a "competition for representation" over Elizabeth's relation to Ireland. Irish rebels, and Old English malcontents, loyal Palesmen, and New English all entered this site of competition, imagining and defining the queen's posture toward Ireland in ways redolent of their own anxieties, desires, and agendas.[11] The queen's Old English subjects, for instance, finding themselves increasingly at odds with the New English administration in the later sixteenth century and wishing to bypass its authority by appealing directly to the queen, sought to portray her as their intimate confidante, the "Amor Hiberniae," as the Palesman, Sir Nicholas White, called her.[12] The New English, on the other hand, had a vested interest in presenting Elizabeth as the active scourge of Irish rebellion. Thus, Nicolas Dawtrey conjured an image of her in a Tamburlaine-like stance with a "foot [set] on [the rebels'] necks."[13]

II

Dawtrey's persona, however, was one that Elizabeth was reluctant to embrace. Even in the proclamation announcing the appointment of the Earl of Essex to lead a new offensive in 1599, Elizabeth's public rhetoric on Ireland remained palliative, conciliatory, even apologetic.[14] Unlike earlier proclamations about Ireland that employed an anonymous "collective" voice of authority – a voice that speaks for the queen – the 1599 document was framed as her personal statement, a rhetorical move designed to convey the impression of her direct concern with Irish matters.[15] Promulgated simultaneously in England and Ireland, the proclamation was aimed at an audience that included Irish rebels and skeptical Old English subjects, as well as domestic groups like the London authorities who partly financed the war, and the ordinary citizens who would fight it.[16] As a way of placating these diverse constituencies, the queen portrayed her inclinations as practically pacifist, claiming that she had always "preferred clemency before any other respect as a virtue both agreeable to our natural disposition, the sincerity of the religion which we profess, and always esteemed by us as the greatest surety to our royal state when our subjects' hearts are assured to us by the bond of love rather than by forced obedience."

Disclaiming any intention to reconquer Ireland – "the very name of conquest in this case seemeth so absurd" – the queen describes herself as "compelled" to exercise "an extraordinary power and force" as a last resort after all other "means" have been exhausted. She tries to understand and discriminate among the rebels: "the actors in this rebellion are not of one kind nor carried into it with one mind" – some, for example, have suffered mistreatment at the hands of her own officers, while others have been wrongly persuaded "that we intended an utter extirpation and rooting out of that nation." The queen is even willing to shift responsibility for the rebellion from the Irish themselves to "seditious priests and seminarians" who come from abroad to infect the natives with "superstitious impressions." Reluctantly, Elizabeth holds a sword above the heads of the rebels, but waits to strike, hopeful that some "with all expedition, penitence, and humility, [will] prostrate themselves to our mercy."

Spenser died in January 1599, before he could see the queen's proclamation or the dispatch of Essex – an intervention in the Irish crisis that Spenser would surely have judged as both overdue and inadequate. In neither conception nor execution did Essex's campaign come close to the radical proposals for total war followed by a sweeping reorganization of Gaelic society that he put forward in *A View of the Present State of Ireland*. The speakers in the dialogue, Irenius and Eudoxus, are preoccupied with the queen's ubiquitous imprimatur in the formulation and execution of Irish policy, and they repeatedly frame their questions and arguments around how best to serve her interests. These are overwhelmingly economic ones, and Irenius accordingly offers detailed plans for transforming Ireland from a drain on the royal exchequer into a source of revenue. But even as the economic discourse of *A View* reassures the queen and establishes her as the main implied reader, other parts of the text reveal her culpability for the mismanagement of Irish affairs.

Especially damaging to English objectives, *A View* argues, has been the queen's personal handling of Tyrone – her "greate faintnesse in . . . withstandinge [him]" in the past, resulting in his emergence as the "Arch Rebell" (145–46). Irenius' claim that the queen herself first "countenanced and strengthned" Tyrone, prompts us to see him not as the unfortunate product of a misconceived English policy but as Elizabeth's own creation (147). In place of "faintnesse" and vacillation, Irenius advocates the swift and violent suppression of the rebels by sword and famine (132–36). Responding to these draconian proposals with the skepticism befitting an English humanist gentleman, Eudoxus observes that when, after the mass starvation of the Irish,

the state of this miserie, and lamentable image of thinges shalbe told and felingelie presented to her sacred majestie, beinge by nature full of mercie, and clemencye, who is most inclynable to such pittyfull complaintes, and will not endure to heare such Tragedyes made of her people and poore subjectes, as some about her maie insynuate, then shee perhapps for verie compassion of such Calamities, will not onelie stopp the streame of such vyolence, and retourne to her wonnted myldnes, but also con them lyttle thankes which have bene the aucthors and Counsellors of such bloodye platformes. (136–37)

Here, the traits of mercy, clemency, compassion, and mildness that the queen embraces in her proclamation, become obstacles to a re-conquest of Ireland and weaknesses to be exploited by those dissuading her from action. Significantly, Irenius never answers Eudoxus' concern about Elizabeth's probably negative response; nor does Irenius offer a plan for winning over the queen to his project. The awkward silence produced by these unanswered questions suggests Spenser's discomfort at trying to persuade a ruler he knew was unlikely to favor his proposals.

If, as has long been thought, *A View* was suppressed by the government when it was submitted for publication in April, 1598, one obvious explanation was the work's insistence upon Elizabeth's mishandling of the Irish crisis – an insistence that represents *A View*'s most blatant contravention of "the codes governing sociopolitical communication" and something that was more likely to bother the censor than the work's attack on the Old English community or its critique of the Common Law as an instrument of reform.[17] But as Jean Brink has recently argued, the critical piece of evidence in support of the suppression theory – a marginal note next to the entry of *A View* in the Stationers' Register for April 14, 1598, requiring publisher Matthew Lownes to bring "further aucthoritie" – is far from conclusive. Since *A View* remained unpublished until 1633, the note of 1598 may indicate that "further aucthoritie" was sought but denied; it might also indicate, though, that such authority was never sought, or that authority was received and that Lownes then decided not to publish the work.[18] The entry of a work in the Stationers' Register did not necessarily imply an intention to publish; instead, the listing could be a way of staking a public claim to a work and of preventing others from publishing it.

In the case of *A View*, manuscript circulation offered Spenser a better medium than print for disseminating his controversial ideas. This was the sort of controlled, "semi-public" manuscript circulation of which the Earl of Essex took advantage when he advertised his belligerent anti-Spanish views in the manuscript *Apologie* of 1598. When the piece was later printed without Essex's approval, he blamed Fulke Greville for "the mistake of circulating this highly partisan and hitherto confidential document just a little too widely, thereby sparking the interest of printers eager for a scoop."[19] That Spenser never intended *A View* for publication is supported by the fact that the manuscript submitted by Lownes to the Stationers (Bodleian, MS Rawlinson B.478) lacks several textual features usually associated with an authorial intent to publish. Most striking is the lack of preliminary matter – the title page, dedications, dedicatory verses, and other pre-texts found in the only *published* treatise of the 1590s about Ireland that is comparable to Spenser's in scope and format: Richard Beacon's *Solon his Follie, or A Politique Discourse, Touching the Reformation of common-weales conquered, declined or corrupted* (Oxford, 1594). Also missing from *A View* but present in *Solon* and similar published tracts are "long diplomatic passages praising the queen."[20] *A View*, in fact, reserves its praise not for the queen but for her male deputies – especially the late Lord Grey, that "heroicke spirite" (140) whose patronage had established Spenser's career as an office- and land-owner in Ireland. Brink argues that these various "absences" in the manuscripts of *A View* are signs that the work is unfinished; but because *A View*'s undiplomatic tone seems a deliberate violation of convention, we can conclude that its "heddlesse" state was a way both of distancing the work from the queen-centered court and of keeping Spenser's patronage options open.[21]

Although the queen is the main implied reader of *A View*, then, she was not for Spenser the most important of the work's actual readers. These were men like Essex (who owned a copy), Sir Thomas Egerton (who added marginal annotations and an index in his copy), and other chief councilors of state – those "wise men," as Irenius calls them, who "have the handling" of Irish policy (219).[22] Essex, in fact, is the nominal hero of Spenser's *Prothalamion*, a work composed and published in 1596 – the same year in which the prose dialogue was probably completed. Here, as the narrator wanders through London, lamenting his "long fruitlesse stay / In Princes Court," (lines 6–7) Spenser revives the malcontented and vagrant persona of the Ormond sonnet and *Colin Clouts Come Home Againe*.[23] Despairing of further recognition from Elizabeth (his pension was awarded in February 1591) or of a "place" at the royal court, Spenser in *Prothalamion* looks toward Leicester House, once the home of his late patron Robert Dudley and now the dwelling of Essex (Dudley's political heir): "a noble Peer, / Great *Englands* glory and the Worlds wide wonder" (lines 145–46).[24] Essex, a popular hero after the Cadiz expedition in the summer of 1596, is invoked in similar terms in *A View* where Irenius calls for the appointment of "A Lord Lyveten-nant of some of the greatest personages of England (such an one I could name, upon whom the eye of all England is fixed and our last hopes now rest)" (217).[25] In late 1596, and certainly by April 1598 when *A View* was entered in the Stationers' Register, Spenser had good reason to look beyond the queen to Essex, who – if not an actual claimant to the throne – appeared set to play a crucial role in brokering the succession.[26]

Essex is only the most prominent of several militant male figures, the supporters of an activist English policy in Ireland, whose presence can be discerned behind the composition and early history of *A View*.[27] Another exemplary figure for Spenser, and one whom critics have omitted from "circles" of the poet's friends and associates, is the professional soldier and aggressive governor of Connaught, Sir Richard Bingham.[28] In bringing Spenser and Bingham together I want to refocus attention on the kind of extreme and masculinized policy in Ireland that *A View* and the second installment of *The Faerie Queene* endorse – a policy that implicates Spenser in the latent resentment of New Englishmen toward their sovereign.

III

Spenser and Bingham were almost exact contemporaries in Ireland with close ideological and factional allegiances. Bingham, like Spenser a protégé of the Earl of Leicester, arrived in Ireland in 1579, was present with Grey (and possibly Spenser) at Smerwick, became governor of Connaught in 1584, later sided with Essex against the Cecils, and died in January, 1599 – the same month as Spenser.[29] Although there is no direct evidence that the two men were acquainted, W. L. Renwick sees Bingham's hand in the details of *A View*'s military proposals: "Some of it certainly is the plan [Bingham] had developed, and he was the best qualified of them all to lay down the lines as is done here." A verbal echo of *A View* in a letter of Bingham's dated November 18, 1596, also indicates that he "had seen the *View* soon after its completion, if not before" (243).

In his brutal use of violence, martial law, and extra-legal methods, Bingham had no equal in early modern Ireland. At Ardnaree in 1586, for example, Bingham supervised the killing of three thousand men, "boyes, Woemen, Churles, and Children," while in the aftermath of the Armada he ordered the execution on a single day of three hundred shipwrecked Spaniards.[30] Bingham's methods alarmed his superiors in Dublin as well as the queen, who instructed him to treat the Irish more "temperately," and later suspended him from office in 1597.[31] But Bingham's tactics also found admirers, including Spenser's fellow-undertaker and the attorney general for Munster, Richard Beacon.[32] In *Solon his Follie*, Beacon extols "that famous knight Sir *R. Bingham* . . . as an other *Cesar*" whose "singuler art and skill in military discipline" had conquered "the rebelling *Gaules*" of Ireland (91).[33] Bingham is praised for appreciating – like Irenius – the limited use of Common Law procedures in Ireland: when "a general rebellion" was imminent, Bingham suspended the use of "lawfull inditement and other ceremonies" and immediately executed the imprisoned Burkes whom the rebels were planning to free. For Beacon, Bingham rightly understood that "*The times of warre and lawe are two thinges*" (16).

Just as Spenser accords Grey the status of exemplary commander in *A View*, so Beacon accords Bingham the same status in *Solon*. Beacon, moreover, describes Bingham as the successor to Grey, and as the custodian of Grey's legacy of "severe discipline" (8).[34] This same association beteen Bingham and Grey is also made by Fynes Moryson, who nominates the pair as the only "old Governors" able "to bridle [the Irish] at the point of the sword."[35] Moryson identifies Grey and Bingham as sharing similar fates: "[the] Complaynts [of the subdued Irish finding] such pittye in the Royall (may I with leave say womanly) breast of the late famous Queene, and such favour with the lordes of her Counsell . . . [that these] Magistrates [were] recalled into England, [and] reaped heavy reproofe for their merited reward."[36] Like Spenser in *A View*, Moryson locates responsibility for the protracted Irish crisis in the gendered "breast" of the queen. The result of this female control of Irish policy was, in Bingham's gender-inflected language, a "Lingring servyce [and] . . . softe kind of warre" – a phrase that marks out war as properly the space of an efficient and rigid masculinity. Given the tenor of Bingham's remark, it is revealing that he was one of the officers "reprimanded" for not reporting O'Rourke's notorious act of *lèse majesté*.[37] Although Bingham denied he had "misdemeaned her majestie" or attempted to conceal "this treason of the picture," his inexplicable "remissness" points none-the-less to darker, unspeakable motives, even, perhaps, to his tacit approval of the symbolic assault.[38]

Bingham's denigration of the feminine and implied exclusion of the female align him with a cult of militant masculinity whose symbols pervade his very portrait of c.1588 (figure 4).[39] In this head and torso composition, Bingham gazes resolutely, even defiantly, back at the viewer. He appears in soldierly fashion against a dark and smoky back-drop evocative of the battlefield, wearing a tight-fitting chain-mail tunic, and holding both hands close to the handles of weapons – a sign of his preparedness for action. His high lace neck-collar – like the small ruff sleeves, a hint of a more courtly identity – is dwarfed by and clearly subordinated to the imposing armored choker over it. Perhaps most suggestive of a militant masculinity, though, is the upper-body pose of arms akimbo with the right hand placed nonchalantly on the hip and the elbow thrust out firmly beyond the frame of the picture. In the icono-graphy of early modern portraiture this bodily gesture of the protruding male elbow is part of "an assertive body language . . . normally . . . associated with military power" and "indicative essentially of boldness or control – and therefore of the self-defined masculine role, at once protective and controlling."[40]

IV

Bingham's display of a militaristic masculinity is a familiar component of the chivalric ethos of late Elizabethan culture; as a set of cultural signs and practices, though, that ethos possessed a special intensity in Ireland,

4   Sir Richard Bingham. Artist unknown, c.1564.

providing New Englishmen with a way of expressing their collective identity and their muted hostility to the queen's interference in their affairs. Bingham's distinct cultural style has revealing implications for Book Five of *The Faerie Queene* – a book often interpreted as a kind of poetic translation of the cultural and military programs of *A View*. Bingham's own place in the book can be traced to a local, Irish-based level of allegory – a level often overlooked by modern readers because of the relative obscurity of topical details and of Spenser's technique of fragmenting and dispersing the material of contemporary history.[41] Yet

The Faerie Queene was a poem written largely in Ireland and was aimed in part at readers in Ireland. With their collective local knowledge, those readers could be expected by Spenser to know of Bingham's reputation and to hear an echo in Book Five between "the *Flail* of Connaught" – Bingham's sobriquet – and Artegall's assistant, Talus, "Who in his hand an yron *flale* did hould / With which he thresht out falshood, and did truth unfould" (5.1.12).[42] Although there is no consistent or sustained parallel between Talus' career in the poem and Bingham's in Ireland (Bingham's controversial reputation made a more transparent allegory dangerous for Spenser), some "informed" readers may have detected a provocative congruence between the "Flail of Connaught" and the flail-wielding Talus. Talus and Bingham seem most closely aligned in the book's final canto where, in a restaging of Grey's capture of the fort at Smerwick from a combined Irish, Spanish, and Italian garrison, Talus comes ashore like an amphibious force, "wading through the waves with stedfast sway" (5.12.5); Bingham's role at Smerwick had been amphibious, captaining a ship that bombarded the fort from off-shore.[43] More generally, Bingham's violent energy finds a surrogate in the pathological relentlessness that Talus demonstrates, for instance, in his pursuit and summary execution of the kern-like Malengin. Artegall and Arthur dispatch Talus after failing to capture this protean and elusive monster themselves:

> for he was swift in chace.
> He him pursewd, where ever that he went,
> Both over rockes, and hilles, and every place,
> Where so he fled, he followd him apace.
>
> (5.9.16)

Talus puts his "yron flayle" to characteristic use, "driv[ing] at [Malengin], with so huge might and maine, / That all his bones, as small as sandy grayle / He broke, and did his bowels disentrayle" (5.9.19).[44] Throughout Book Five Bingham's connection to Talus remains provisional and imprecise, relying more on a diffuse allusiveness than on the allegorical shadowing of particular historical events and details.

Whatever their nature and extent, the correspondences between Talus and Bingham are embedded in a less localized, more programmatic level of historical/Irish allegory that could be decoded by a wider audience in both Ireland and England. At this level, the always invulnerable and self-sufficient Talus – "Immoveable, resistlesse, without end" (5.1.12) – embodies the potent fantasy of immunity to both physical harm and to the threat of cultural "degeneration." Catering to New English aspirations, Talus functions as an imaginative stand-in for the colonists' military and security apparatuses. Michael West sees Talus as, by turns, Artegall's soldier, under-officer, sentry, spy, bodyguard, and – with his flail – a symbolic vehicle for the repertoire of colonial force in Ireland.[45] Talus is thus a potent alternative to what in reality was a poorly trained, ill-equipped, and badly disciplined English army consisting predomin- antly of Irish kerns and the "refuse people" of England: vagabonds, criminals, and other masterless types.[46] The queen's army was viewed as more of an impediment than an asset in the subjugation of Ireland, and many New English writers, including Spenser, made its reform a key priority.

English troops in Ireland were especially ill-prepared and equipped for the guerilla warfare of a rugged, boggy, and heavily wooded landscape.[47] In 1580, Sir Walter Ralegh wrote from the Irish wars that "many men had died of the heat in their ill-fitting armour," while other reports described armor-clad English soldiers being smothered, immobilized, or stuck in bogs where they were easily picked off by the lightly-clad and mobile rebels.[48] One proposed alternative to the cumbersome English armor of Ralegh's men was the Irish mantle.[49] In *The Faerie Queene*, Talus offers a different alternative to mantle-clad Englishmen: "made of yron mould," Talus is soldered into a seamless suit of armor – one that neither impedes his mobility nor ever needs removing. The special appeal of Talus' metal skin is illuminated by a contemporary genre of portrai- ture that depicts a gentleman-subject partly in and partly out of his armor. For example, in a composition by Nicholas Hilliard (c.1590–93), Sir Anthony Mildmay wears ornate upper-body armor, but his cuisses, helmet, and one gauntlet are casually strewn around the room, and his athletic legs are revealed in trunk-hose and slippers (figure 5).[50] The semiotics of the portrait obscure whether Mildmay is partly dressed or partly undressed, whether he is fitting or discarding armor. The indeter- minacy of Mildmay's posture captures a poise between two distinct but complementary selves: one active and militarily engaged, the other relaxed, courtly, or civic, that has abandoned or suspended the arts of war for those of diplomacy and love. Talus by contrast is never torn between these two selves, never in danger of exchanging a militarily engaged self for a less vigilant courtly one. Talus literally embodies a unitary and indivisible subjectivity: "Immoveable, resistlesse, without end." And in the world of the poem where courts and relaxation are usually associated with female wiles, Talus' monological, unswerving identity becomes the mark of an idealized and exclusive masculinity – the sort apparent in the portrait of Bingham.

In the *Argonautica* of Apollonious, Talus' prototype, Talos, is a man of bronze, fashioned by Vulcan, and given "to the wife of Minos, King of

5   Sir Anthony Mildmay by Nicholas Hilliard, c.1590–93.

Crete and famous law-giver, to guard the island."[51] This version of the Talos story combines the fantasy of an autonomous male procreative power and the myth of women's need for male protection. The account of Artegall's genesis in *The Faerie Queene*, by contrast, inverts that of Talos by granting creative power exclusively to women. As a child, Artegall was abducted by Astraea and "noursled" in her cave "till yeares he raught, / And all the discipline of justice there him taught" (5.1.6). Emerging from the womb-like cave, Artegall is literally reborn, his manly identity – symbolized by his "wreakfull hand" – fashioned by a woman (5.1.8).

As an important trope of the male will in Book Five, the "wreakfull hand" of Artegall like the "iron paw" (5.1.22) of Talos draws upon an emblematic and heraldic tradition of manual iconography in which hands – often clenched or grasping a weapon – signify as "explicit icons of power."[52] Yet while Artegall is constantly surrounded by such symbols of "manlinesse" (5.8.1), he is denied an autonomous or unfettered form of male power. Not only is he the product of Astraea's upbringing, but his actions in Book Five are framed and licensed by the female authority of the Fairy Queen; she bestows upon Artegall the task of rescuing Irena from the tyrant Grantorto in what is an allegory of England's mission to "free" Ireland from Spanish control (5.1.4).

V

Even as the careers of Artegall and Talos mirror New English aspirations in Ireland, Artegall's dependence upon a pair of powerful yet absent women resonates uneasily with the recognition that those aspirations were always subject to the whims of Elizabeth. If Talos represents a wish-fulfillment of English supremacy in Ireland, Artegall is the vehicle for Spenser's critique of what he saw as the queen's dilatory approach and failed policies in Ireland.[53] Fusing the ideal and the actual, then, Book Five mingles a prophecy of victory with a deep disaffection at the past and present conduct of Irish affairs, offering in effect a "satire of English maladministration."[54]

Spenser's frustration at the course of English policy is inscribed in a narrative structure that replicates a nightmarish inability to act directly, swiftly, or decisively. Aretegall's quest to rescue Irena from the giant Grantorto is cluttered with detours, interruptions, and postponements. To plot Artegall's route to Irena is symbolically to trace the swerving and uneven course of English policy in late sixteenth-century Ireland, where, as Spenser argues in *A View*, each new governor "will straight take a waye quite contrarie to the former," substituting leniency for rigor or vice-versa (119). Although Artegall and his companions score many victories, some against recognizably "Irish" enemies like Munera and Malengin, these "high" points, "uneven encounters," as Clarke Hulse calls them, "mythic exaggerations of the ability of the Elizabethans to extend their reach beyond the Pale, and denials of the formidable power of the Irish in resistance", are compromised by the dilatory and disrupted narrative in which they take place.[55]

Even as Artegall confronts allegorical replicas of Irish rebels, his primary task of rescuing Irena recedes ever further beyond the horizon. In 5.11, for example, the narrator finally seems confident that Artegall is poised to fulfill "his first quest," and, indeed, the knight comes "nigh unto the place" of Irena's island (5.11.36). But then Artegall meets Irena's ambassador, Sir Sergis, who upbraids him for failing to rendez-vous earlier. An ashamed Artegall first blames himself, then accuses the heavens for his delay, and finally renews his pledge to restore Irena. But this resolve is ironically undercut when Artegall is immediately deflected into another side-adventure. The re-conquest of Ireland – for Spenser, England's most urgent political and military objective – has again been postponed by the intrusion of another international crisis, this time the French wars of religion as represented in the Burbon episode. Artegall's charge that Burbon has temporized with his enemies is one that applies equally to Artegall's own failure to reach Irena, and by extension to the queen's war-effort in Ireland (5.11.57).

If Artegall at first appears loyal to the Fairy Queen as he pursues his assigned quest, a closer look shows him negotiating between compliance and resistance, maneuvering in subtle ways to escape the queen's control. Miming the halting course of Elizabeth's Irish policy, Artegall's detours can also be construed as intentional evasions of his original mission – a passive–aggressive means to obtain a degree of self-determination.[56] In a paradoxically stealthy bid for self-authorization, Artegall, and by impli-cation Spenser, unsettle the royalist ideology that posits the queen as the sole source of her subordinates' power and identity.

As Artegall moves farther away from the Fairy Queen's court, he forges relationships and alliances that threaten to displace his allegiance to her. At the court of Mercilla, for example, he briefly transfers his loyalty to a different sovereign. The convoluted detour that leads him here begins when he meets Samient, whose story of injustice rouses him and Arthur against the Souldan and Adicia; the knights reach Mercilla only after a further "straunge adventure" against Malengin (5.9.3–4). At Mercilla's court, Artegall and Arthur serve as judges in the trial of Duessa and, later, in a ritual that recapitulates and displaces those performed at the Fairy Queen's court, Arthur accepts from

Mercilla the task of rescuing the Lady Belge from oppression (5.9.37; 5.10.15–16).

Just as Artegall's "swervings" cast doubt upon his loyalty to the Fairy Queen, so they also render suspect his commitment to his Lady, Britomart. Artegall's quest to free Irena is, in fact, framed by a prior overarching quest to deliver Britomart's land from "The powre of forrein Paynims" – a task revealed in Merlin's prophecy and later confirmed at the Temple of Isis (3.3.27; 5.7.22–23). Artegall is as dilatory in trying to fulfill this female-directed mission as he is in Irena's. He misses a rendezvous with Britomart as a result of his enslavement to the Amazon queen Radigund, a lapse that leaves Britomart pining and uncertain of Artegall's fate (5.6.3). When Talus brings news of Artegall's "wretched bondage," Britomart expresses doubts about her betrothed, accusing him of courting "a straungers love," and of deceiving her (5.6.10, 12).[57] Later, after she rescues Artegall from Radigund – a double sign of the knight's dependence upon women – he abandons her again. Artegall resumes his "first adventure," more embarrassed by, than thankful for, Britomart's help, while she wanders away from the land of the Amazons and literally out of the poem, with the liberation of her homeland no nearer realization.

Artegall's troubling evasions of his obligations to women are counterbalanced by his attraction and loyalty to other men. Bonds with men offer Artegall a way of escaping his female-identified past and of asserting an autonomous male identity. After leaving Britomart at the end of 5.7, he unites with Arthur, forming with the "Briton prince" a homosocial union that pushes aside both knights' ostensible loyalties to women. This displacement of female by male ties is highlighted in Artegall's language of devotion to Arthur. Artegall, apologizing to Arthur for at first misrecognizing and attacking him, vows: "I will therefore / Yeeld for amends my selfe yours evermore" (5.8.13). The bodily entanglement of Artegall and Arthur in battle is now reenacted as a feudal ritual of blood brotherhood:

> Either embracing other lovingly,
> And swearing faith to either on his blade,
> Never thenceforth to nourish enmity,
> But either others cause to maintaine mutually.

(5.8.14)

Together, Artegall, Arthur, and Talus constitute a powerful triad, a miniature homosocial community acting ostensibly at the behest of and on behalf of women. But as Eve Sedgwick argues, homosocial ties among men actually depend upon excluding, marginalizing, and otherwise denying the presence of women. In homosocial systems like chivalry, women might appear to function as the objects of male veneration but women's deeper purpose is to unite men. While apparently dedicated to the service and protection of women, then, chivalric ideology is in fact grounded in and productive of misogyny.

The misogyny intrinsic to homosocial systems surfaces in Book Five – as elsewhere in the poem – in acts of violence against women. In an early episode with distinct Irish overtones, Talus chops off and nails in public view the hands and feet of the witch Munera before throwing her body from the battlements (5.2.25–27).[58] Munera and her tyrant-father Pollente, whom she assists with "wicked charmes," provide Artegall with an image of his own reliance upon powerful women and with an opportunity to vent his resentment (5.2.5). Having licenced Talus' dismemberment of Munera, Artegall himself decapitates Pollente and displays his head on a pole (5.2.19).

While Spenser has encoded his dismay at the course of Elizabeth's Irish policy through Artegall's various "swervings," male unions, and acts of aggression against power-wielding women, he ends Book Five with the spectacle of Artegall's recontainment by the Fairy Queen. Artegall finally rescues Irena and begins to reform the "salvage Iland," but any sense of triumph is quickly undercut by the knight's recall to the Fairy Queen's court (5.12.26–27). Instead of protesting his re-subjection to female control, Artegall returns without hesitation, his journey, unlike the protracted outward one, being swift and direct. Even when upbraided by the "ill favour'd Hags," Envie and Detraction, Artegall maintains his composure, restrains Talus, and "for nought would swerve / From his right course, but still the way did hold / To Faery court" (5.12.43). As a replaying of Grey's inglorious return from Ireland in 1582 and of the charges of misconduct against him, this final episode conveys through Artegall's stoical submission to royal fiat, Spenser's larger sense of the self-defeating, futile pattern underlying Elizabeth's approach to Ireland, an approach that, in Barnabe Rich's words, favored "*Parlies, Cessations, dayes of truce, Protectyons*, and . . . *Pardons*," over more decisive and punitive methods.[59]

VI

While Book Five ends in frustration at Artegall's truncated mission in the "salvage Iland," Book Six promises to point the way to the completion of Ireland's reformation. Calidore picks up Artegall's quest, reassuring his forerunner: "where ye ended have, now I begin / To tread an endlesse trace" (6.1.6) – a "trace," as Julia Lupton argues, "that passes through Ireland." "If Books V and VI are views of Ireland, Artegall executes Irenus' violent reformation through cutting off, while Book VI presents the milder uses of courtesy, 'friendly offices that bynde' (VI.x.23). Spenser's search for a pastoral Ireland in Book VI, far from signalling an escape from politics, in part strives to represent England's colonial activities in a milder light."[60]

Yet at the beginning of Calidore's career, "milder courses" seem little in evidence.[61] In his first adventure, he effectively combines the roles of Artegall and Talus when he storms Briana's castle, kills Malefort and the porter, and assaults the other occupants with the nonchalance of a horse brushing aside flies (6.1.23–24). At this point the killing temporarily stops. Briana, the Amazonian occupant of the castle, suffers a happier fate than Munera and Radigund, her counterparts in Book Five; whereas they are executed under Artegall's stern justice, Briana is forgiven and rehabilitated by the courteous Calidore.[62] Calidore's opening adventure, then, establishes a dialectic between coercive and conciliatory strategies – strategies that broadly correspond to the competing approaches of conquest and reformation in Ireland.[63]

One way in which Book Six tests the relative efficacy of these strategies is by placing in liminal and vulnerable positions symbolic figures of the queen herself. In Book One, Spenser introduces a recurrent topos of the woman among savages, in which Una, separated from the Red Cross Knight and threatened with rape by Sansloy, is saved by the providential intervention of "A rude, misshapen, monstrous rablement" of "*Faunes and Satyres*" (1.6.7–8).[64] This "salvage nation" that prostrates itself before Una and erects her as "th'Image of Idolatryes" (1.6.19), calls to mind English allegations that the Gaelic Irish "neyther love nor dredd God nor yet hate the Devell, they are superstycyous and worshippers of images and open idolaters."[65] Spenser makes the same charge in *A View* when Irenius describes the Irish as "papistes by theire profession, but in the same so blindelie and brutishelie enformed, for the most parte as that yow would rather thincke them *Athistes* or Infydells" (109). Irenius is pessimistic about the prospect of conversion; the few Protestant clergy in Ireland are "eyther unlearned or men of some badd note, for which they have forsaken England" (115). "Were all this redressed," he concludes, "yett what good shall anye Englishe minister doe amongst them, by preachinge or teaching, which eyther cannot understand him or will not heare him" (89).

Unlike Irenius' English minister, Una faces few problems of communication or resistance among her congregation; how the satyrs understand her is simply elided. As she gathers the satyrs "around" her for instruction (1.6.30), Una acts as surrogate for the Anglican church (the one true religion her name implies), and for its head, Queen Elizabeth.[66] Una's success in taming this "salvage nation" suggests Spenser's willingness to countenance the idea that the queen represented a special conduit of peaceful reformation in Ireland. Advocates of reform argued that even the most recalcitrant "subjects" could be brought within the pale of English civility through the spread of education and Protestantism. James Stanihurst, for example, urged "the erecting of Grammer Schooles, within every diocesse" in order "to breede in the rudest of our people, resolute English hearts," while Elizabeth herself licensed the translation of the Gospels and Prayer Book into Gaelic in order to expedite the missionary effort.[67]

The allegory of Una among the satyrs both rehearses the queen's influence in Ireland and tests the larger possibility that other godly Englishwomen could act as agents of reform and civility. Such an assumption was operating in 1591 when Tyrone married the English-woman Mabel Bagenal – an event, remarked Thomas Gainsford, that proved Tyrone "as brave and complete an *Amorist*, as the formallest Courtier in *England*."[68] But Sir Henry Bagenal, Mabel's custodian and Tyrone's long-standing adversary in Ulster, expressed horror that his family's blood should be "mingled with so traitorous a stock and kindred."[69] Tyrone defended the marriage, reassuring his friends at court that, "The gentlewoman was carried not into my country there to be abused," but had freely accompanied him to "an honest English gentle-man's house," where Tyrone "did not once touch her" until they were married by the Bishop of Meath.[70] Tyrone had married Mabel, he claimed, "chiefly to bring civility into my house, and among the country people, which I thank God by her good means is well begun, both in my house and in the country abroad."[71] In constructing Mabel as a reforming agent, a ministering angel in both home and region, Tyrone imagines her as a local surrogate or miniature version of Elizabeth, whose mission it was to bring reformation to the entire country. And by subtly equating his wife with the queen, Tyrone installed himself in an erotically charged imagined relationship with Elizabeth, a relationship he would seek to manipulate to his advantage in an ongoing struggle to retain the queen's favor. Thus, adopting the pose of an outcast Pet-rarchan lover, Tyrone protested that if the government would not relieve him of Henry Bagenal's oppression he would "come to Her Majesty and live there at her devotion."[72]

When, in later books of *The Faerie Queene*, Spenser rewrites the topos of the woman among savages, the resulting transformation in relations of gender and power suggests a greater unease with the kinds of assumptions about female efficacy underlying the narratives of Una and

Mabel. The topos appears next in Book Three, where the unchaste Hellenore is no Elizabeth surrogate or Godly Englishwoman. Having fled her husband, Malbecco, and the rapist, Paridell, Hellenore seeks refuge among a group of satyrs whose "shrieking Hububs" establish their affiliations with the Gaelic Irish (3.10.43). Unlike Una who educates her satyrs before leaving them, Hellenore submits to her satyrs' sexual desires and is permanently assimilated to their society. Her refusal to return home with Malbecco is framed as a rebellion against the domestic enclosure of women represented by their attachment to "bed and bord" (3.10.51). In Hellenore, Spenser adumbrates not woman's reforming potential but her susceptibility to the lure of Irish incivility – an incivility figured here as sexual license and an escape from patriarchal control.

In the second installment of *The Faerie Queene*, Spenser puts assumptions about female powers of reformation in Ireland under even greater pressure. Thomas Cain has argued that as the final books retreat from an "encomiastic program," so praise of Elizabeth is transferred to other, even rival, figures like Essex and Elizabeth Boyle.[73] In Book Six, the position reserved in each of the first three books for a royal type is usurped by Serena, whom Cain considers a patently unroyal figure. Judged by the poem's explicit criteria, Serena is not a royal type in the same way as Belphoebe or Mercilla. But Elizabeth's symbolic presence in the poem is not tied exclusively to these recognizable types; as a recurrent locus of meaning, the queen's presence is dispersed throughout the text and instantiated – often in elliptical and fragmentary form – in a range of female (and male) characters, some of whom represent "dark doubles" or demonized versions of Elizabeth.[74]

Serena's royal credentials are suggested by her close ties to Una, ties evident in the structural parallels between Books One and Six. Serena's fate insistently recalls Una's earlier predicament: both are separated from their male guardians and then captured by "salvage nations."[75] Unlike the pliable satyrs tamed by Una, however, Serena's satyrs are a fraternity of cannibals:[76]

> In these wylde deserts, where she now abode,
> There dwelt a salvage nation, which did live
> Of stealth and spoile, and making nightly rode
> Into their neighbours borders; ne did give
> Them selves to any trade, as for to drive
> The painefull plough, or cattell for to breed,
> Or by adventrous marchandize to thrive;
> But on the labours of poore men to feed,
> And serve their owne necessities with others need.

(6.8.35)

Once in the thrall of these Irish-like "savages," Serena is bereft of reforming agency and helpless to prevent her sacrifice in what Spenser presents as a demonic parody of the Catholic mass. The transformation of a proto-Elizabeth figure from powerful missionary (Una) to weak victim (Serena) can be seen in the way Spenser repeats but alters an image of encirclement: in Book One, the "salvage nation" encircles Una who holds it transfixed with her potent words; now, the "salvage nation" encircles the sleeping Serena in an act of enclosure anticipating her imminent consumption (1.6.30, 6.8.39). When Serena awakes, far from exercising the calming influence that her name suggests, she excites her assailants' barbarous instincts, the first glimpse of her face prompting them

> to devize what course to take:
> Whether to slay her there upon the place,
> Or suffer her out of her sleepe to wake,
> And then her eate attonce; or many meales to make.
>
> (6.8.37)

Like Sir William Fitzwilliam's description of O'Rourke's attack on the queen's image, Spenser's account of the cannibals' maltreatment of Serena is tinged with a prurient fascination that strains the bounds of decorum. In fact, the lingering, blazon-like itemizing of Serena's stripped body implicitly aligns the gaze of the (male) reader with that of the cannibals, thus implicating him voyeuristically in their "lustfull fantasyes" (6.8.41). Through Serena's plight Spenser vents subliminal hostility toward his queen while granting his male readers the vicarious pleasure of (visual) domination over her.[77]

A fate similar to Serena's befalls Pastorella, another shadowy and tantalizing figure of the queen or at least an attenuated re-embodiment of the nurturing and civilizing powers to which she laid claim.[78] Placed in a pastoral landscape that shares with Spenser's Munster a deceptively peaceful surface, Pastorella is kidnapped by "a lawlesse people, *Brigants* hight of yore" (6.10.39) – a version of *A View*'s "rebellious rout of loose people which eyther doe now stand out in open Armes or in wandringe Companies doe kepe the woodes spoylinge and infestinge the good subjecte" (124).[79] Pastorella's captivity by the brigants is both a timely warning about the intentions of Irish rebels and a reassuring portrait of their self-defeating divisiveness. Sparked by a competitive desire for her, the brigants' dissension escalates into civil war; as in *1 Henry VI* and *Captain Thomas Stukeley*, the internal collapse of a rebel confederacy lays the ground for the decisive intervention of "legitimate" English power.

That "legitimate" force finally arrives in the shape of Sir Calidore, who, like Calepine earlier, "thrusts into the thickest throng" of his enemies (6.8.49). The contest pits the single, self-sufficient male knight against a mass dehumanized enemy that swarms like "flies" – the same image used for Serena's captors, and for the Irish "routs" who oppose Artegall and Talus in Book Five (6.11.48, 6.8.40).[80] In vanquishing the brigants, Calidore exchanges his nominal role as the Knight of Courtesy for the "huge resistlesse might" of Talus (6.11.43). A resurgent Calidore, oblivious to his quest on behalf of the Fairy Queen, and piling up carcasses with his sword, is Spenser's final, unapologetic emblem of an unfettered male violence (6.11.45–51). To the putative Knight of Courtesy, "Bloud is no blemish" (6.1.26).

The complete dependency of Serena and Pastorella upon their male knights implicitly negates the kinds of reforming energies that Elizabeth claimed in her rhetoric about Ireland, and challenges her self-representation as an autonomous sovereign subject. Thus, as it is rewritten across the course of the poem, the topos of the woman among savages constitutes a revealing "darke conceit," an index to Spenser's increasing disaffection with Elizabeth's approach to the crisis in Ireland. Moreover, the transformation of the "salvage nation" from the innocent and libidinous satyrs who encounter Una and Hellenore to cannibals and brigants reveals Spenser's hardening opinion about the incorrigibly violent and uneducable nature of the Irish.

VII

Spenser's crisis of confidence in the queen receives its final airing in the Diana and Faunus episode in the first of the *Cantos of Mutabilitie*.[81] Invoking a legendary past in which Ireland was the most blessed of all "the *British* Islands" and the vicinity of his own Munster estate was the playground of the gods, Spenser constructs a myth of origins to explain the lapse of this same landscape into a barbarous wilderness (7.6.38). This "degeneration" begins when Diana, Ireland's animating deity, abandons the country after being seen naked by the wood god, Faunus. As critics have noted, the scenario suggests an allegory of Elizabeth's involvement in Ireland in which the Irish gaze threateningly from their wooded "fastnesses" upon a queen who was repeatedly styled a chaste Diana or Cynthia.[82] David Norbrook argues that Diana's flight represents "an image of the desolation caused in Ireland by an act of the royal will."[83] Yet Diana's acts can just as easily connote not a vindication of royal fiat but a failure of the royal will in Ireland. Faced with humiliation, Diana/Elizabeth vacillates and retreats: she, not Faunus, is the ultimate loser of their confrontation. In fact, Diana's power and resolve are in doubt throughout the scene: initially she is "powerless to protect her feminine space from violation by the male," and when she captures Faunus she seems unable to inflict upon him the extreme punishment accorded to Actaeon – Faunus's counterpart in the Ovidian source – who is torn to pieces by his own dogs.[84] In escaping Diana's dogs, Faunus evokes the elusiveness of the Irish rebels as well as the queen's failure to pursue them effectively.

Another topical construction of the Diana–Faunus encounter sees Diana as corresponding not to the queen but to the rebel Irish, while Faunus suggests the native spies employed by the government. In this scenario, Faunus's penetration of Diana's hiding place renders visible the stronghold of rebel leadership – a place hidden from the English authorities among the "over greate and thick [woods] serving for a covert unto rebells and theeves."[85] Faunus thus enacts a desire for colonial surveillance and knowledge, one also articulated in *A View*'s proposals for removing woodland (212), for a system of neighborhood surveillance (186), and for the repositioning of Ireland's chief governor from Dublin, "the owtest Corner in the Realme, and least neding the awe of his presence," to a more central geographical location, "whence he mighte easelye overlooke and sometymes overreach the Mores, The Butlers, the Dempses, the Ketins, the Connors Ocarrell Omoloy and all that heape of Irishe nations which there lye hudled togeather . . . for the Irisheman . . . feares the goverment noe longer then he is within sight or reach" (171).

The apparently unlikely allegory that identifies Diana with the native Irish is also suggested in Richard Beacon's *Solon his Folie*, which refers to Anglo-Irish relations under the guise of ancient Greece's relations with the colony of Salamina. Solon, the Greek politician and the main speaker, recounts a dream to his friend Epimenides in which Diana appears to him "with a beautiful Dove glistering like golde, placed upon her shoulder, slyding and wavering everywhere." When Solon extends his hand to control the bird, Diana, to his amazement, assumes "a sharpe and sowre countenaunce" and threatens to sever his hand (3). In response, Epimenides explains that

The people of *Salamina* [Ireland], is the threatening *Diana*, hating all reformation: the golden Dove, is the pleasaunt countrie of *Salamina*: the wavering of this Dove from place to place, is the frailty and mutability, whereunto this countrie of *Salamina* hath ever beene subject . . . the losse of hande threatened by *Diana*, is the difficulties and dangers, which shall from time to time, oppose themselves against you in this action of reformation. (4)

Epimenides' interpretation presents Diana and her entourage as an all-female version of the uncivil "salvage nations" that attack Serena and

Pastorella. The disturbing allegorical instability of Diana, her ability to represent simultaneously the queen and the queen's enemies creates a calculated confusion, a blurring of the distinction between the problem (the Irish rebels) and its ostensible solution (Elizabeth). In endowing Elizabeth with the same allegorical persona as her Irish enemies, Spenser, like Beacon, implies that she is no longer the solution, no longer a viable agent of reformation in Ireland, but an inextricable part of the problem itself.[86]

6   "If the Cause be not good": *Henry V* and Essex's Irish campaign

Sick Ireland is with a strange war possessed
Like to an ague, now raging, now at rest,
Which time will cure, yet it must do her good
If she were purged, and her head-vein let blood.

John Donne, Elegy 20

On August 14, 1598 at the battle of the Yellow Ford, Tyrone routed the English and captured the crucial strategic position of the Blackwater fort in Ulster. Then, in October, rebellion spread to Munster, supposedly the most "civil" and obedient area outside the Pale. "This rebellion," wrote an alarmed council in Dublin, "is now thoroughly sorted to an Irish war, whose drifts and pretences are, to shake off all English government, and subtract the kingdom from Her Majesty."[1] In response to what seemed like the imminent dissolution of English authority, Elizabeth – construing recent reversals as intolerable blows to her honor – at last seemed prepared to suspend her "wonnted myldnes."[2] Following the Blackwater debacle, she named Sir Richard Bingham Marshal of Ireland and dispatched him with reinforcements.[3] And, more important, after months of deliberation, she gave the long-vacant viceregency to the Earl of Essex. With what in retrospect seems a pointed irony, the first official confirmation of his appointment was made the day before Spenser's death in London on January 13, 1599.[4] During the Munster revolt the insurgents had burnt Spenser's home at Kilcolman, forcing him to flee with his family, first to Cork where he joined other displaced planters, and then to London where he was sent with letters from Sir Thomas Norris, the provincial president, to the English Privy Council.[5]

In *A View of the Present State of Ireland*, Spenser had urged the framers of Irish policy to allow Essex to operate from England as a kind of commander-in-chief, monitoring and directing the activities of the lord deputy on the ground in Ireland, and so avoiding the factional maneuvering against him at court that a protracted absence would entail. But Spenser's plan was not to be. Essex ended up negotiating the title of "Lieutenant-General and General Governor of Ireland," a status that carried more privileges than the more familiar one of lord deputy. He was to command the largest army ever to leave England: some sixteen thousand foot and thirteen hundred horse, with reinforcements of three thousand men to be sent out every two months.[6] With such a force, Essex allegedly boasted, he "mighte have gone thorowe all *Spayne*," while the Earl of Nottingham claimed that "with such an Army as the Earle had, the *French* King might be driven out of *France*, and *Spain* subdued."[7]

If the nature of Essex's appointment failed to realize Spenser's hopes, the earl's commission at least suggested to many in the New English community that the queen had finally licensed an aggressive masculine approach to the Irish "problem." In printed send-offs for Essex and his army, appeals to English masculinity were much in evidence. Thomas Churchyard claimed he had written "The Fortunate Farewell to the most forward and Noble Earle of Essex" in order "to stirre up a threefold manly courage to the mercenarie multitude of soldiers that follow this marshall-like Generall." Figuring Essex as a "Scipio" or a "Mars . . . with shining sword in hand," Churchyard imagines his hero in a kind of phallic one-on-one tussle with Tyrone, the "craven cock [who] . . . hangs down wing." "Wheel not about," Churchyard urges the English force, but "stand stiff like brazen wall."[8] Churchyard's put-down of Tyrone as flaccid and impotent works by contradicting the widespread English recognition of Tyrone's assertive virility.

Churchyard's "Farewell" was one of several hastily produced texts, including ballads and prayers, commemorating Essex's departure and forecasting his victory over the "TYERONishe Irishe Rebelles."[9] A massively more complex text was Shakespeare's *Henry V*, that – as the extraordinary allusion to Essex in the final Chorus reveals – was also written during (and possibly, in part, before) the earl's absence in Ireland and when the outcome of his mission hung in the balance.[10] The Folio version of the play, as critics have recognized, derives much of its energy and appeal from an acute public sensitivity to the fortunes of Essex in Ireland.[11] As the play most widely seen as being in dialogue with Anglo-Irish affairs, *Henry V* has been described by critics as a "fantasy of a successful Irish campaign," a "displaced, imaginary resolution of one of the state's most intractable problems."[12] It is this view and especially how it breaks down, that I want to pursue here. I will argue that although *Henry V* takes repeated steps to wish away the military and political emergency in Ireland, the play also begins forcefully to register Shakespeare's disillusioned ambivalence about the reasons behind and the consequences of English empire-building. In *Henry V*, Shakespeare's misgivings about Essex together with an awareness of burgeoning public alarm at the war in Ireland produce a skeptical counter-discourse about

English expansionism within the British Isles. Whereas for Churchyard, England's latest offensive in Ireland can ultimately be reduced to a simple quarrel between "Right [and] Wrong . . . Troeth [and] Falshed," for Shakespeare, the oppositions are far less clear cut.[13]

I

In *Henry V*, the prospect of a rousing foreign war finds its impetus both in the immediacy of Essex's Irish campaign and in England's position within the larger arena of European geopolitics. At the end of the sixteenth century, the nation's nervousness about Spanish aggression fostered a "perpetual militancy" and a "neurosis of invasion [that] made England something of a Troy, a nation ten years at war . . . besieged and paralyzed."[14] In the spring and early summer of 1599, the country was again on the alert and scrambling to repulse a feared Spanish invasion.[15] Writing from London on August 1, John Chamberlain described himself "in the middes of warres," and the city "in a hurle as though the ennemie were at our doores." In his reference to "a campe to be raysed at Tilbury" there were unmistakable echoes of the great Armada victory of 1588.[16]

Coinciding with this intensified sense of national vulnerability and confinement, *Henry V* offers audiences the vicarious release of strategically reversing the dynamics of England's habitual situation by showing an English monarch throwing off domestic concerns and directly confronting the enemy.[17] In *Henry V*, as the Dauphin's call for constant military readiness attests, the characteristic defensive posture of the English is transferred to the French:

> (Though War nor no knowne Quarrel were in question)
> But that Defences, Musters, Preparations,
> Should be maintain'd, assembled, and collected,
> As were a Warre in expectation.

> (TLN 905–8)[18]

For many theatergoers, the prospect of leaving behind the cramped confines of home and aggressively engaging the enemy on its own territory must have been irresistible. Essex had lately acted out such a prospect in his preemptive strikes against the Spanish at Cadiz and the Azores, but the "so much desired invasive war" championed by Essex, Bacon, and other members of the "war party" was still not official policy.[19]

As the summer of 1599 wore on, the anticipated Armada failed to appear and by early September the defensive troops were being demobilized; but the crisis in Ireland continued: "that ulcer of Ireland" – as Bacon put it – still "[ran] on and raged more."[20] Essex, dispatched finally to staunch that ulcer, left London on March 27, 1599, an event that John Stow recorded in the edition of his *Annales* published the following year:

> the right honorable Robert earl of Essex, lieutenant generall, lord high marshall, &c. departed from Seding lane, through Fenchurch streete, Grace streete, Corne-hill, Cheape, &c. towards Heldon, Highgate, and rode that night to S. Albons, towards Ireland, he had a great traine of Noble men, and gentlemen, on horsebacke before him, to accompany him on his journey, his coaches followed him.[21]

As a piece of civic theater designed to underscore Essex's authority and the gravity of his mission, his departure arrogated the symbolic language of the royal procession – a strategy Essex would be seen as deploying again when accused of going on "progress" through southern Ireland soon after assuming the sword of office.[22] Essex's ceremonial leave-taking from London was the latest initiative in a public relations campaign that drew him into a competition for popularity and legitimacy with the queen herself. Other gestures designed to shape public percep-tions of Essex included a series of portraits that figured him variously as court favorite, military hero, and sage counsellor. And in the "dangerous image" engraved by Thomas Cockson, Essex appeared as an imperial conqueror on horseback, with Ireland shown on the horizon, the next destination in the earl's heroic career.[23] Once there, Essex provocatively showed off his authority. On Saint George's Day, "he kept that feast in Dubline . . . with greate solemnitie and magnificence," but manipulated the celebrations to enhance his own stature, not the queen's. Essex was

> attended and wayted on by the cheife knightes and captaynes in that kingdom; eche man striving whoe should shewe hymselfe most forward to doe hym [Essex] honor by bringinge dishes to the table and doeing other services at the feastivall; insoemuch as it was conceived there was not greater state, plentie, and attendance used at that time in the Court of England on the Queene and all hir knightes of the Order.[24]

More dangerously still, Essex flouted the royal prerogative by bestowing knighthoods upon many of his officers in Ireland – an act expressly forbidden by the queen. The earl's munificence was a way of binding his followers to him, of initiating them fully into what Mervyn James calls a "distinctive social subculture" organized around the earl and defined by its emphasis upon militarism, the pursuit of honor, and the "mutual loyalty and support" of its members.[25]

In the spring and early summer of 1599, the Chorus's lines in *Henry V* reverberate as a glamorous evocation of the youthful "troupe of gallants," who shared Essex's honor-based ideology and flocked to join him in Ireland:[26]

> Now all the Youth of England are on fire,
> And silken Dalliance in the Wardrobe lyes:
> Now thrive the Armorers, and Honours thought
> Reignes solely in the breast of every man.
> They sell the Pasture now, to buy the Horse;
> Following the mirror of all Christian kings,
> With winged heeles, as English *Mercuries*.

(TLN 462–69)

While the account in Stow's *Annales* treats the impending campaign as the business of a leader and his elite entourage, Shakespeare's Chorus at least makes a bid for inclusiveness: "all the Youth of England," "every man." And yet, the apparent social breadth of the Chorus's vision is qualified by the fact that Henry's "followers" are either landowners ("They sell the Pasture now, to buy the Horse") or courtiers ("silken Dalliance in the Wardrobe lyes"). Neither Stow nor the Chorus adequately recognize the non-volunteer, rank-and-file soldiers who would fight and die in the ensuing campaigns in Ireland and France. Only in the later, 1615 edition of Stow's *Annales* as edited and enlarged by Edmund Howes, did this same passage finally register the presence of conscript soldiers, the "many others," in the train of Essex and his noble followers.[27] But if these "many others" are denied even a minimal recognition by the Chorus of *Henry V*, they are conspicuously present in the play in the figures of Pistol, Bardolph, and Nym: those members of the urban underclass whose first appearance offers a startling disjunction to the Chorus's preceding invocation of Henry's soldiers as "English *Mercuries*." As we shall see, such parodic undercurrents are characteristic of a play that both stages and resists the allure of militarism surrounding Essex and his Irish expedition, an allure that the Chorus shamelessly arouses.

The two slightly different accounts of Essex's departure in the 1600 and 1615 editions of Stow's *Annales* offer a suggestive parallel to *Henry V*'s ideological duality over English designs in Ireland. As well as adding that reference to "many others," the 1615 *Annales* also includes details about Essex's plain attire, and, most tellingly, about the crowds that "pressed exceedingly to beholde him, especially in the highwayes, for more than foure myles space crying and saying, God blesse your Lordship, God preserve your honour &c. and some followed him untill the evening, onely to behold him." When put alongside this portrait of a humble Essex who goes to Ireland with broad popular support, the earlier, 1600, version of the passage seems positively flat and unenthused about his great enterprise. There are no adoring crowds in this version, only a portentous thunderstorm to send Essex on his way. *Henry V*, in its complex and equivocal engagement with the latest, critical phase of England's crisis in Ireland, effectively enfolds the divergent perspectives offered by the two versions of Stow's passage.

II

The ordinary Londoners to whom Stow repeatedly refers elsewhere in the 1600 edition of the *Annales* as "pressed" and transported to Ireland in the later 1590s, faced there a host of enemies, not the least of which were hunger and malnutrition.[28] A representative report among the Irish State Papers from November, 1598, describes the current condition of the army: "It grieveth us not a little," wrote the Lords Justices Loftus and Gardener, "to see the nakedness of the soldiers for want of clothes, and their poverty for lack of their lendings, to buy them food; both which wants not only maketh many of them show like prisoners, half starved for want of cherishing, but also it dejecteth of them greatly in heart, insomuch as we look daily for some great mutiny and disbanding."[29] While all of Elizabeth's armies experienced provisioning problems, the unprecedented size of Essex's force made these problems particularly acute.[30] To ensure an adequate food supply, Essex demanded and was granted personal control of the victualling operation.[31] As John Chamberlain observed, even before Essex had received his appointment and with no new campaign imminent, the talk at court in December, 1598, was preoccupied with "provisions for Ireland."[32]

Against the backdrop of these conditions of extreme hardship in Ireland, the reiterated image in *Henry V* of an English army starving and sick in the field had an inescapable topical valence. After the siege of Harfleur, the Constable of France reports that the English soldiers are "sick, and famisht in their March" (TLN 1437), and Henry himself admits that his "people are with sicknesse much enfeebled . . . My Army, but a weake and sickly Guard" (TLN 1595, 1605). Later, on the eve of Agincourt, the French are reassured by news that "these English are shrowdly out of Beefe," and thus deprived of the "great Meales of Beefe, and Iron and Steele" that the French jokingly suspect are a source of the Englishman's ferocious strength (TLN 1781, 1779).[33] When the French nobility next gather, English hunger is again a source of consolation and mockery: "Shall we goe send them Dinners, and fresh sutes, / And give their fasting Horses Provender . . . ?" the Dauphin asks about the apparently moribund English force of "Iland Carrions" (TLN 2230–32, 2211).

Yet *Henry V* invites us to see the English soldiers' hunger as, not what it had become in Ireland, an impediment to victory, but as, paradoxically, a necessary condition for it. Whereas the French assume that empty stomachs will doom the English to defeat, Henry perversely redefines the stomach from the locus of debilitating needs to the seat of aggressive impulses: "he which hath no stomack to this fight, / Let him depart," Henry instructs Westmerland (TLN 2279–80). Hunger has become an empowering rather than a disabling condition. Deprived of food, then, Henry's army must look for other kinds and sources of sustenance. Echoing Essex's own determination to supervise the victualling of his forces, Henry takes on the role of feeder to his men: "Nor care I who doth feed upon my cost," he declares (TLN 2269). Proclaiming the need to be "spare in diet" (TLN 760) and upholding the virtues of early rising (TLN 1850–51), Henry embraces a new regimen for both himself and the nation.[34] The play's opening discussion between Canterbury and Ely has already established that the king's remarkable transformation from wayward heir to national leader has involved a change in his pattern of consumption, including the renunciation of "Ryots, Banquets, sports" (TLN 97). He has, as it were, heeded the advice of the Renaissance dietaries that sought to improve the health and increase the life-expectancy of members of the nation's governing elite. Works like *A Direction for the Health of Magistrates and Studentes* (translated 1574) exhorted present and future rulers to control their appetites and to accommodate themselves to a new regimen of work and rest, refreshment and exercise.[35] As an emblem of the degenerate gentry, the obese Falstaff, of course, continually flouts these imperatives in *Henry IV*. To "Do nothing but eat, and make good cheer" is the fit motto for this carnivalesque glutton (Part Two, 5.3.13). In *Henry V*, by contrast, the king seeks to rejuvenate both himself and the nation by replacing Falstaff's economy of unbridled consumption with a new regimen, one that would enforce the "permanent sovereignty of Lenten civil policy."[36] At the center of this new economy is war, which – as Francis Bacon argued – was a form of necessary exercise that "serveth to keep the body in health; for in slothful peace, both courages will effeminate and manners corrupt."[37]

Henry further "nourishes" his men by extending the promise of future bodily sustenance, a promise he makes in his vision of an annual commemorative feast. Foretelling how the survivor of the approaching battle "Will yeerely on the Vigil feast his neighbours / And say, to morrow is Saint *Crispian*" (TLN 2289–90), Henry revises the meaning of the banquet from the occasion for self-indulgence to a form of regulated communal feeding. Just as Bardolph assigns food a mediating function when he promises to "bestow a breakfast" upon Nym and Pistol as a way of reconciling them (TLN 515), so Henry sees the feast as a way of uniting and regenerating the nation. Yet, as well as relieving present scarcity by imagining the future satisfaction of physical appetite, Henry also "nourishes" his army metaphorically. On the eve of Agincourt, the Chorus describes Henry visiting his men

> With chearefull semblance, and sweet Majestie:
> That every Wretch, pining and pale before,
> Beholding him, plucks comfort from his Lookes.
> A Largesse universall, like the Sunne,
> His liberall Eye doth give to every one,
> Thawing cold feare, that meane and gentle all
> Behold, as may unworthinesse define.
> A little touch of *Harry* in the Night.
>
> (TLN 1829–36)

In the Chorus's utopian view, Henry's encompassing and unifying gaze radiates an inspirational sustenance, a "Largesse" that substitutes for actual victuals. And in providing his men with surrogate "nourishment," Henry appropriates the role of army victualler or "Sutler," a role that had originally been claimed by the rogue Pistol. Unlike the magnanimous Henry, however, Pistol's vision of this role is purely self-serving: "For I shal Sutler be unto the Campe," he declares, "and profits will accrue" (TLN 608–9). Although we never actually see Pistol discharging the duties of sutler, our impression of him as a self-seeking figure on the fringes of the army is fully consistent with the equivocal, indeterminate position – partly inside and partly outside the army structure – of his counterparts in Elizabeth's armed forces.[38]

In Pistol's final punishment and expulsion from the army, the role of sutler is momentarily displaced from Henry to the Welshman Fluellen. As requittal for an earlier insult, Fluellen cudgels Pistol and forces him to choke down a leek – the tuberous symbol of the Welshness that Pistol has continually ridiculed. Reducing Pistol to the ignominious passive status of the fed, Fluellen plays upon a widespread distrust of the army victualler, and provides a kind of catharsis for the resentments surrounding a figure who – in Ireland and other theaters of war – was often accused of cheating the troops with inflated prices and rotten fare. Even before arriving in Ireland, Essex complained that many of the government-appointed victuallers were untrustworthy, neglecting to dispatch provisions as agreed. He wanted offending suppliers punished with "extreme severity" since "there is not a more dangerous enemy than famine; and I would as soon execute him that should let in famine, or conspire with it against this army, as with (*sic*) him that should practice with Tyrone." The Privy Council promised "severity," but in practice the justice meted out to corrupt victuallers was usually spontaneous and unofficial. John Jolles, a London-based merchant and victualler to Essex's army complained "of divers intolerable violences and injuries, offered both by the Captains and other officers of bands . . . to such servants and inferior factors, as are necessarily employed by him."[39] At Ostend in 1588, one group of soldiers, fed up with their "rotten, unsavoury, and unwholesome victuals," caught a victualler's man, threw him from a bridge and stoned him when he came ashore.[40] Such violent attacks are both echoed and excused in the comic charivari to which Fluellen subjects Pistol – a charivari that seeks to restore both Fluellen's ethnic pride and a larger moral economy.[41]

Elsewhere in Shakespeare, the ability to survive without food that *Henry V* associates with the English army is represented "as a proof of aristocratic valor."[42] In *Coriolanus*, the hero's insensitivity to hunger in part defines his difference from the starving plebeians, while in *Antony and Cleopatra*, Caesar lauds Antony as one who

> fought'st against [famine],
> Though daintily brought up, with patience more
> Than savages could suffer. Thou didst drink
> The stale of horses and the gilded puddle
> Which beasts would cough at.
> . . .
> And all this – –
> . . .
> Was borne so like a soldier that thy cheek
> So much as lanked not.
>
> (1.4.60–72)[43]

But in *Henry V* the specter of hungry yet resolute Englishmen conjures up not so much the self-sustaining patrician body of Coriolanus or Antony as the Irish rebels' success at adapting their appetites to conditions of scarcity. According to a report of 1599, the English garrisons at Armagh and Blackwater had "put her Highness to most endless and exorbitant charges for the victualling and relieving of them," while the Irish, on the other hand, had survived on "their ordinary food . . . a kind of grass."[44] Tyrone himself was envied for his "strong body" that could "endure labour, watching, and hunger."[45] The assumption that strength and valor somehow depended upon the repression of bodily appetites was apparently not lost on Essex's successor Lord Mountjoy, who, upon assuming the deputyship, replaced his usual "nourishing brackefasts . . . [of] panadoes and broths" with the more meager fare of "a drie crust of bread" and "a cup of stale beere."[46]

The alleged resilience of the Irish in the face of hunger and other hardships was not, however, any real defense against English efforts to starve them into submission. Famine, having proven a brutally effective means of crushing the Munster rebellion of the early 1580s, was again proposed in 1599 as essential to English success: "Great force must be the instrument but famine must be the meane for till Ireland be famished it can not be subdued."[47] Famine is also one of the weapons that the Prologue to *Henry V* includes in the king's formidable arsenal:

> *and at his heeles*
> *(Leasht in, like Hounds) should Famine, Sword, and Fire*
> *Crouch for employment.*
>
> (TLN 6–8)

Yet, as the action unfolds, Henry and his men, rather than their enemy, find themselves famished, thus becoming the symbolic equivalent to the starving Irish. In this way, the play elaborates a fictional hybrid not of "the French-cum-Irish," as one critic has suggested, but of the English-cum-Irish.[48]

III

The paradoxical image of Henry's army empowered by its collective privation, grants to the English traits popularly associated with the "wild Irish." By coopting an elusive "Irishness" for the English, the play enacts the wish-fulfillment of seizing for "us" everything most feared yet envied about "them," and in so doing optimistically rehearses the success of Essex's forces in Ireland – a success that the earl recognized from the beginning would be as difficult to achieve as Henry V's against the French. The other element in the play's realignment of symbolic identities is the "Englishing" of the French who are shown in the nervous, defensive posture adopted by the English at the turn of the century. In their attitudes and behavior, moreover, the French are made to appear uncannily English. For example, when the Constable of France refers to the oncoming English as "a barbarous People," he speaks a discourse that generations of English had used to denigrate their Celtic neighbors (TLN 1383). Indeed, the whole French perspective on the English in the play recapitulates an English stance of cultural superiority toward the Irish.[49]

Yet if *Henry V* performs important cultural work through these imaginative displacements of national and ethnic categories, the play also tests the limits of its own wish-fulfillments by intimating the dangerous consequences that wars of conquest and the cultural logic of assimilation inevitably hold for unsuspecting empire-builders. To the Constable's charge that the English are "a barbarous People," the Dauphin adds an account of the origins of English racial identity: "Shall a few sprayes of us," he declares,

> The emptying of our Fathers Luxurie,
> Our Syens, put in wilde and savage Stock,
> Spirt up so suddenly into the Clouds,
> And over-looke their Grafters?
> *Brit.* Normans, but bastard Normans, Norman bastards.
>
> (TLN 1385–89)

To the French, the modern English race, a product of the mingling of civil Normans and savage Saxons, stands witness to the problem confronting all conquerors: of how to protect themselves and their imagined ethnic purity against contamination from the conquered. During Essex's campaign in Ireland, John Donne invoked the specter of degeneration when warning his friend Sir Henry Wotton (Essex's secretary) to beware "the Irish negligence" and "letargies" – ailments that Donne characterized only half playfully as more dangerous than "shott, and boggs, and skeines."[50] Yet, in *Henry V*, the Dauphin's contempt for "bastard Normans, Norman bastards," barely disguises the fact that the mingling of Norman and Saxon has produced not a degenerate race of weaklings but the resilient English whose characteristic "Mettell" suggests their peculiarly firm masculinity. "Our Madames mock at us," complains the Dauphin,

> and plainely say,
> Our Mettell is bred out, and they will give
> Their bodyes to the Lust of English Youth,
> To new-store France with Bastard Warriors.
>
> (TLN 1407–10)

Henry V's articulation of a eugenic fantasy in which the fusion of "civil" and "barbarous" peoples gives rise to a kind of masculine master-race reverses ubiquitous English fears of lapsing from disciplined "civility" into anarchic "barbarism" in Ireland.

In the play's final scene of Anglo-French diplomacy when a rhetoric of antagonism and difference gives way to one of brotherhood and sameness, the issue of national hybridization again looms large, only now with darker implications. Henry's betrothal to the French princess Catherine focuses anxieties about the intermarriage of newcomer and native and the dangers of miscegenation that were felt most acutely in Ireland.[51] Henry's French campaign began as a national crusade to highlight and differentiate an essential Englishness from its Others, but it ends in the blurring of identities whereby "English may as French, French Englishmen, / Receive each other" and with the prospect of the mongrel and weak Henry VI ascending the throne (TLN 3358–59). If the play celebrates an outstanding victory for the English at Agincourt, it is less confident that the English win the larger cultural war of which that battle is a part. Pistol's parting lament that "my *Doll* is dead i'th Spittle of a malady of France" represents one way in which the play ironically suggests (here through an image of a poisoned female sexuality) how an insidious form of defeat shadows even the "greatest" of conquests (TLN 2976–77).[52] Thus, even as the play provides imaginative reassurance to supporters of Essex and his Irish campaign, it asks audiences to question the very purpose of an expansionist war that inevitably results in the contamination of "Englishness" and in the acquisition of hostile and ungovernable territory. In marrying Catherine, Henry achieves, ironically, what had been on offer to him from near the beginning of the war (TLN 1073–74). His earlier refusal of Catherine (she is offered to him along with "Some petty and unprofitable Dukedomes") seems motivated not by loyalty to some worthier goal but by a blind determination to prosecute the war at any cost.

IV

The issues of hybridity and assimilation are explored most fully in the scene before Harfleur that brings together the four captains of England, Ireland, Scotland, and Wales (TLN 1192–1258). Specifically, the inclusion of the "Irish" Captain Mackmorrice in the "English" army reinscribes at an individual level the problem of assimilation broached in the play's "Irishing" of Henry's army. Critics have noted Mackmorrice's vexed and unstable ethnic and national identity – an identity that is powerfully yet obscurely at issue in Fluellen's remark, "Captaine *Mackmorrice*, I think, looke you, under your correction, there is not many of your Nation," and Mackmorrice's response, "Of my Nation? What ish my Nation? Ish a Villaine, and a Basterd, and a Knave, and a Rascall? What ish my Nation? Who talkes of my Nation?" (TLN 1237–42). Mackmorrice's sensitivity to the question of his "nation" originates in his descent from the Anglo-Norman conquerors of Ireland – many of whom had, since the twelfth century, changed their name's original prefix of "Fitz" to the Gaelic "Mac." As an Old English or Palesman, then, Mackmorrice encapsulates the insecurity of a group that had no place in dominant typologies of race and ethnicity – a group that in Ireland was seen by the New English as more Gaelic than English, and by the Gaels as more English than Gaelic, and that in England was treated as strangely indeterminate.[53]

Mackmorrice's short appearance is integral to the play's elaboration and interrogation of "an assimilationist mythology" – a phrase that Robert Stillman uses to characterize "the united action of Arthur (the emblem of English civility) and the Salvage Man" in Book Six of *The Faerie Queene*. That union of knight and Salvage, claims Stillman, constitutes a "mythic image of the salvageability of the old English settlers of Ireland and their potential aid to imperial British sovereignty."[54] In the encounter of the four captains of *Henry V*, the "mythology of assimilation" works to somewhat different ideological ends. By staging a confrontation between an "Irishman," a "Scot," and a "Welshman," the scene reworks the potential collusion of Celtic groups hostile to English rule in Ireland into an internal competition among reluctant allies over how best to advance the cause of an English king. While Mackmorrice yearns to return to the fighting and his mines, Fluellen engages him in theoretical arguments "concerning the disciplines of the Warre" (TLN 1214–15). The ensuing comic spectacle of intra-Celtic rivalry seems designed to massage away residual fears among an English audience of a hostile "pan-Celtic alliance."

The union of rebel Irish and Highland Scots – always the most troublesome component of this alliance from an official English view – was again drawing attention at the time of the Essex expedition. Now, however, not only were Scottish mercenaries assisting the Ulster rebels, but members of the Scottish nobility – even King James VI, it was rumored – were offering material and moral support to Tyrone's confederacy.[55] In *Henry V*, Mackmorrice's joint entrance with the Scots captain Jamy pinpoints the special and dangerous affinity between Ireland and Scotland; but Jamy's loyalty to the English cause in France soon soothes anxieties about him just as in Ireland the government's hiring of their own Scottish mercenaries calmed English nerves. Writing to Robert Cecil, Lord Justice Loftus recommended the use of "4,000 inland Scots . . . being a people for their nature fittest to deal with the northern [Irish] men, and for their hardness and neediness every way able to match them." But the English recruitment of Scots, like the recruitment of kerns, was always hazardous and needed careful handling: hence Loftus stipulated that only "inland Scots" should be used against Tyrone in the north since "the Irish Scots or islanders" were already fighting on Tyrone's side.[56]

For all the ways the encounter of the four captains works to alleviate English anxieties, the scene's tensions and simmering violence render this meeting of margins and center an unstable alliance at best, and only an unsettling emblem of what some critics see as the integration of the British nation-state. Mackmorrice's savage threats of violence (including decapitation) against Fluellen, rather than being safely assimilated by Henry or treated as an anomaly in the English economy of violence, actually come to define the king's own brand of warfare. Henry, in his war of aggression against the French, revives "the barbarous license" that he claimed to have sublimated since becoming king (TLN 421). In fact, the presentation of the English in the play as "a barbarous people" both lends them a reassuring "Irish" hardiness and fighting spirit, and implies their dependence upon a "savage" violence. Thus, when Henry addresses the defenders of Harfleur in a speech placed immediately after Mackmorrice's talk of scalping, the king picks up the Irishman's violent lexicon by threatening the French with horrifying atrocities. Henry's men are no longer the graceful "Grey-hounds in the slips" (TLN 1114) he had earlier imagined, but "flesh'd Souldier[s], rough and hard of heart" (TLN 1270), "savage" killers like the Irish kerns in John Derricke's *The Image of Irelande* or the Munster rebels of *The Supplication of the Blood of the English* (1598). In the latter work, the New English author appealed to the queen for help by cataloguing alleged atrocities against English settlers: "some smothered out of theire houses, others hewen to peeces . . . younge infants scarce yett seasoned with the ayre of the world, most lamentably brained: some dashed against the walles: others tombled from highe towers."[57] In *Henry V*, Shakespeare makes this kind of violence the work of the English themselves – a reminder that his countrymen's claim to a moral high-ground in Ireland was untenable; there, the English were as likely to merge with as to conquer a supposedly "barbarous" enemy, as likely to bring barbarism as to cleanse it.

If Mackmorrice is an ultimately discomforting, only partially assimilated figure, his Welsh antagonist Fluellen approximates the kind of fully assimilated Celt we find in works like Churchyard's *Worthines of Wales* – a work that participates in the discursive management of anxieties about the loyalties of the queen's Celtic subjects in general. As one of Wales's "Martiall Captaines" who had proved "serviceable" to "the imperiall Crowne of England" and its expansionist designs, Fluellen figures the colonial subject who has internalized English values and subordinated his own provincial loyalties to service to the English nation-state.[58] In terms of the dynamics of the second tetralogy, Shakespeare conceives Fluellen as the antithesis of Glendower whose rebellious energy is transformed in Fluellen's devoted service and unwittingly self-mocking humor. Meanwhile, Fluellen's name – an Anglicized form of Lluellen – sets him against another rebellious Welsh leader: Lluellen ap Gruffuth, the last native Prince of Wales who receives surprisingly sympathetic treatment in Peele's *Edward the First*.

The reinscription of Wales and the Welsh in *Henry V* as assimilated and "serviceable" to England is neatly encapsulated in the putative origins of the leek worn by Fluellen on Saint David's day. Fluellen traces the leek's significance back to Edward III's victory over the French at the battle of Crecy, when "the Welchmen did good service in a Garden where Leekes did grow, wearing Leekes in their *Monmouth* caps, which your Majesty know to this houre is an honourable badge of the service" (TLN 2628–31). The leek thus recalls an earlier act of sacrifice by the Welsh on behalf of their English masters. But this explanation of the origin of the leek's significance is not the only one available. In a different narrative, the leek was the special food of David, Patron Saint of Wales. According to Drayton's *Polyolbion*,

> That reverent British Saint in zealous ages past
> To contemplation lived; and did so truly fast,
> As he did only drinke what Crystall Hodney yields
> And fed upon the leeks he gathered in the fields.[59]

Saint David's association with leeks is elaborated in the preface to a seventeenth-century ballad, "The Welchmens Jubilee":

S. David when hee always went into the field, in Martiall exercise, he carried a Leek with him; and once being almost faint to death, he immediately remembered himself of the Leek, and by that means not onely preserved his life, but also became victorious: hence is the Mythologie of the Leek derived.[60]

Saint David's status as warrior serves as a bridge between this myth and another one that locates the leek's meaning in a sixth-century victory of ancient Britons over Saxons, the ancestors of the Welsh and English respectively. In at least one seventeenth-century account of this battle, David himself is present and instructs his (British/Welsh) soldiers to adopt leeks "for their military colours."[61]

Strikingly, both these explanations run counter to Fluellen's explanation in the play. For, through association with Saint David the leek figures an autonomous, never dependent or homogenized, Welsh culture. Furthermore, the leek's connection with David's feats in battle, especially the British defeat of the Saxons, commemorates native resistance to the English and their ancestors. In the explanation that Shakespeare gives to Fluellen, these alternative Welsh-centered traditions are suppressed in favor of an explanation that is possibly of Shakespeare's own devising, Fluellen's being the "earliest reference we have . . . to the Crecy tradition."[62] Shakespeare's version, then, empties the leek of all oppositional and anti-English significance and performs upon a powerful symbol of Welsh identity the same process of Anglicization embodied in Fluellen.

V

Fluellen's unswerving support for Henry may be amusing and reassuring, but it is also troubling in its single-minded intensity. In contrast to the Welshman's reflexive patriotism toward his king, Shakespeare delineates another, more complex and challenging relationship between soldier and ruler. At the opening of Act Four, the Chorus envisages Henry mingling openly with his men, inspiring and "nourishing" them for the approaching battle. Yet when we next see Henry he appears not as the Chorus's gallant leader, but as a disguised spy among his men who are disquietingly uninspired and argumentative. Considering that before Essex's Cadiz expedition of 1596, "a severe decree had prohibited soldiers from conversations like the one Bates and Williams are engaged in," the staging of a debate about the justice of war seems dangerously provocative.[63] Henry tries to win over Michael Williams, the most vocal and disgruntled of the common soldiers, but the king's answers prove unsatisfactory and the encounter ends with an exchange of gloves and a commitment to pursue the quarrel at a later date (TLN 2034–2072).[64] When Thomas Becon remarked about Henry VIII's invasion of France in 1543 that every man "is led even of nature with such an unspeakable loving affection toward his country . . . *Dulce et decorum est pro patria mori*," he was articulating an emergent, essentially Protestant, view of the relationship between the male subject and his *patria*, and of the duty of that subject to sacrifice himself for the national good. This is a sacrifice that Williams is loudly reluctant to make.[65]

After Agincourt, Henry tries to neutralize the memory of William's interrogation of the war and of royal authority by restaging their encounter with Fluellen acting unwittingly as the king's surrogate. By contriving a situation in which Williams will mistake Fluellen for the disguised antagonist of the night before, Henry attempts to displace a conflict between the top and bottom of the social hierarchy into rivalry between ethnic and class subgroups (TLN 2650–2769). What begins as a serious confrontation between king and commoner, Henry would rework as a comic showdown between English and Welsh soldiers. Ultimately, Henry's maneuver fails: Williams, when confronted with the royal identity of his rival, does not flinch or retract, but turns the fault back upon the king: "Your Majestie came not like your selfe: you appear'd to me but as a common man . . . and what your Highnesse suffer'd under that shape, I beseech you take it for your owne fault, and not mine: for had you beene as I tooke you for, I made no offence" (TLN 2767–2772). Henry offers no counter-argument to this confident self-defense but instead instructs Exeter to give Williams a glove of "Crownes." Henry's payment is at once a reward for the outspokenness of an inferior (a recognition of English "mettell") and an attempt to buy the soldier's conformity by exploiting his evident poverty, for, as Fluellen observes, Williams's shoes need repair – shoes being among the most valuable items in a soldier's kit.[66] Williams presumably accepts the king's money, but there is no indication that he finally takes Fluellen's "twelve-pence," despite the king's command that he and Fluellen "must needs be friends" (TLN 2780). There is in all this a sense of unfinished business and of lingering hostilities on all sides – Henry instructs Williams to wear his glove "for an Honor in thy Cappe / Till I doe challenge it," while Williams and Fluellen appear only to postpone their interrupted quarrel (TLN 2776–77). In his gruff stubbornness, unrepentant and unreconciled to the imperatives of expansionism, Williams throws new light on Fluellen, revealing the Welshman as not so much a loyal friend as a royal sycophant.[67]

That Williams's voice is not convincingly muted or discounted registers Shakespeare's increasingly equivocal attitude toward English militarism in Ireland. Even as *Henry V* deploys, like *1 Henry IV* before it, imaginative strategies designed to manage the collective pain associated with Ireland, those strategies are now forced up against deep misgivings about the necessity and value of English involvement across the Irish Sea. While *1 Henry IV* failed to achieve a satisfying sense of ideological closure – leaving the problem of Tyrone unresolved and pending – *Henry V* becomes an open site of struggle between conflicting impulses and explanations, an arena in which the ideology of benevolent colonialism begins to unravel even as it appears to be shored up.

Williams's deeply held concern lest "the Cause be not good" points outside the play to a subculture of dissent and resistance in early modern Britain – a subculture of diffuse and often silenced voices and texts that were suspicious of, if not downright hostile to, the imperatives of war-making and national expansion. Domestic unease at the latest offensive in Ireland is suggested by the fact that the government thought necessary to defend by proclamation the appointment of Essex at the head of a "royal army." Stressing "the justice of our cause" – the very concern that most troubles Williams – the queen claimed that she sought only to quell a rebellion among her own subjects and on her own sovereign territories.[68] These public assurances were matched by the private ones delivered to Essex by Bacon: "the goodness and justice [of your cause] is such as can hardly be matched in any example; it being no ambitious war against foreigners, but a recovery of subjects, and that after lenity of conditions often tried." Bacon adds other justifications, including the queen's right to reduce barbarians to civility, and the need to protect

England by keeping Ireland free from Spanish domination.[69] Yet despite the cumulative weight of English arguments, dissenting and oppositional voices can still be detected against the government's belligerent Irish policies. At a later stage in the long and inglorious history of English interference in Ireland, protesting voices would be more audible as a result of burgeoning literacy and the greater access of marginal political and religious groups to the printing press. Exactly fifty years after Essex's mission, Ireland was again the destination of a conquering English army led by Oliver Cromwell. His task of motivating an army in the summer of 1649, however, was no easy one. Some of the soldiers refused to fight because they had not been fully paid for past service; some argued against fighting in Ireland until domestic concerns had been resolved and, in particular, the army granted its full demands. But these objections became more potent when linked to the conviction of "a minority of soldiers and civilians . . . that the Irish expedition should be abandoned because it was morally wrong." "What have we to do with Ireland," protested the authors of *The Soldiers Demand* (1649), "to fight, to murder a people and nation . . . which have done us no harm . . . we have waded too far in that crimson stream (already) of innocent and Christian blood." At last imagining a reversal in the direction of colonial aggression – and thus taking a giant step forward in the ability to articulate the legitimacy of the Irish perspective – another dissenting tract asked "Whether the English would not do as the Irish have, if the Irish should dispossess and tyrannize over them [?]"[70]

Admittedly, as Norah Carlin argues, opposition to English interference in Ireland even in 1649 can be traced only to "a few 'left wing Levellers'" and not to the group's leadership. Nor can we say to what extent the unrest among English soldiers was motivated by a radical "political consciousness" of equality between nations and peoples as opposed to a vague indifference about the subjugation of Ireland. Yet the fact remains that in the late 1640s, despite the inflammatory effect of recently issued anti-Irish massacre literature, one could still set forth a "principled, radical opposition to English rule in Ireland," an opposition that invoked "typically Leveller ideas such as natural rights, freedom of conscience and the tyranny of rule by conquest."[71]

Although often submerged within or occluded by the larger discourses from which they emerge, the intellectual and social currents that informed the opposition to Cromwell's reconquest of Ireland reach back to Shakespeare's day and earlier. Both Christian scholastic thought and Reformation humanism argued against wars of conquest. "To make war on one's neighbours," wrote Augustine, "and from them to move on against the rest, crushing and subduing peoples who have given no offence, out of mere lust for dominion – what else can this be called except brigandage on a grand scale?"[72] The writings of Erasmus, although made to serve a range of ideological ends, could be construed as condemning all forms of warfare.[73] Even against the perceived threat from the infidel Turks, Erasmus rejected war, advocating that Europeans address their "enemy,"

not with threatening epistles or with books full of tyranny but with those which might show fatherly charity and resemble the very heart and mind of Peter and Paul ... undoubtedly [the Turks] also be men, neither their hearts be so iron adamant but that they may be mollified and won with benefits and kindness, wherewith even very wild beasts be waxen gentle and tame.[74]

How often the pacifist strands within Christian and Erasmian humanism helped to stimulate an interrogation of the Elizabethan conquest of Ireland is, of course, hard to determine. Yet even within the Anglican establishment, the source of many resounding defenses of state violence, the Irish wars became morally perplexing.[75] On August 9, 1600, Matthew Hutton, the Archbishop of York, shared his concerns with the Archbishop of Canterbury:

I take it to be against good policy for a great prince to keepe a longe and lingeringe warre with a subject nation, though the people be never so base; for it teacheth them to be skilfull, stout, and resolute, as appeareth by the Low Countries. God graunt it may not appeare by Ireland! The people there are growne verie valiant and desperate, and, being hable to abide all kind of hardines, take the benefite of the contrie, of woods and bogges, and are like to hould out a long time, without the losse of more noblemen and captaines then may be well spared in England. Besides that, manie of our English nation ... are verie unwilling to go thither; and many tall men at home, when they come there, prove cowards, and the verie contry consumeth them. Therefore (in myne opinion) it were not amisse for yow of hir Majestie's Counsell to thinke rather of an honorable peace, than to indainger so manie noblemen, valiant captaines, and dutifull subjects, and perhaps (in time) the losse of that kingdome. Yow and I are men of peace, and therefore I am bould to write unto yow, beinge nere to hir Majestie.[76]

Hutton's double view of the Irish as both base and admirable reflects a familiar English perspective; but his account of reluctance among Englishmen is remarkable for its non-censorious, understanding tone. For Hutton, the inevitably large loss of life means that war should be avoided – an imperative that, moreover, as a "man of peace" he seems to feel on moral as well as pragmatic grounds. Hutton still assumes that the "kingdome" of Ireland "belongs" to England, but unlike the scheming clergymen of *Henry V* who claim that France "belongs" to England, he refrains from urging "Bloods, and Sword and Fire, to win [England's] Right" (TLN 278).

If Anglicans like Hutton anguished about the Irish wars, so too did members of the mainland Catholic community. Although most stayed loyal to their Protestant monarch in their opposition to Hapsburg imperialism, they were not necessarily comfortable with the treatment of their co-religionists in Ireland, a discomfort that Tyrone sought to heighten by emphasizing the religious underpinnings of his struggle. Increasingly, in the later 1590s, Tyrone and his allies identified themselves as loyal Catholics fighting for freedom of conscience – a concept with which their English counterparts would have sympathized.[77] Misgivings among Catholics about Irish policy were also fuelled by recusant texts depicting the war as a conflict of faiths between beleaguered Catholics and cruel Protestants. For example, in Richard Verstegan's *Theatrum Crudelitatum Haereticorum Nostri Temporis* (Antwerp, 1588) – a Catholic response to Foxe's Protestant martyrology – an engraving shows English Calvinists in Ireland torturing and executing monks and priests (figure 6). The more committed recusants of England and Wales, as opposed to the outwardly conformist "church Catholics," were further alienated by punitive measures requiring them to raise money and horses for the queen's Irish campaigns.[78] But despite the risks and penalties involved, these determined non-conformists continued to monitor and support Irish resistance, leading one government informer in Lancashire in early 1599 to urge a "restraint on intercourse between England and Ireland, as at present the disaffected in both countries have free inter-course."[79] Shakespeare's own moral uncertainty at the latest English offensive in Ireland could only have been intensified if, as has been plausibly argued, he himself harbored recusant sympathies.[80]

Whatever the religious, moral, or intellectual grounds for skepticism about, or opposition to, English interference in Ireland, there were also important practical factors mentioned by Hutton discouraging broad domestic backing for the war. Economic burdens were critical in fomenting discontent among merchants, citizens, and other members of the prosperous "middling sort." As John Chamberlain explained in December 1598, "the greatest difficultie is mony which goes so lowe that for all the subsidies comming on, the privy seales that are past, and the loane of 20000 li the other day, the Quene is now in hand to borrow of the Citie 150000 li. more." But London's rulers were increasingly unenthusiastic about supporting the Irish wars with loans and subsidies: even if "they were willing," reflects Chamberlain, "I hardly thincke yt is to be had, for the citie is much decayed by reason theyre trafike is greatly impaired."[81]

Alarmed by the grumbling of Londoners against official policy in Ireland, the court issued an order in the summer of 1599, "forbidd[ing]

6 "Persecutiones adversus Catholicos à Protestantibus Calvinistis
excitae in Hibernia." An engraving from Richard Verstegan, *Theatrum
Crudelitatum Haereticorum Nostri Temporis* (Antwerp, 1588).

[anyone], on pain of death, to write or speak of Irish affairs; what is
brought by the post is known only to the Council."[82] The order (no
longer extant) was probably still in effect in late July, when the same
correspondent wrote, "I can send no news of the Irish wars, all advertise-
ments thence being prohibited, and such news as comes to Council
carefully concealed. I fear our part has had little success, lost many
captains and whole companies, and has little hopes of prevailing."[83] But
placing a blackout on Irish news could not guarantee, for instance, that
"when the vulgar sort / Sit on their ale-bench with cups and cans, /
Matters of state be not their common talk."[84] Nor could censorship
prevent members of "the vulgar sort" attending a play like *Henry V* from
recognizing the dramatization of their own exploitation by a war-
mongering state.

The scenes involving soldier Williams and his comrades in *Henry V* are
among several in contemporary plays that speak directly to the concerns
of potential recruits and conscripts for the Irish wars. In Thomas
Dekker's *The Shoemaker's Holiday* (1599) and the anonymous *Famous*

Victories of Henry the Fifth (published 1598), craftsmen and masterless men alike are unwillingly rounded up and shipped to France.[85] Such scenes, viewed in the context of well-known conditions and casualties in Ireland, would not "be matters of indifference" to audiences at the turn of the century.[86] In *The Shoemaker's Holiday*, the return from war of the reluctant soldier Rafe and his reunion with his wife constitute a much-needed "wish-fulfillment for a nation wearied and worried by war." And yet the play's idealizing strategies ultimately fail to mystify the domestic hardships imposed by war, including the separation of the newly married apprentice couple Rafe and Jane, Jane's despair at forged news of her husband's death, or the wound with which Rafe returns (1.1; 3.2.56–109; 4.1).[87] *The Shoemaker's Holiday* also links the injustices of war to the iniquities of social class. Thus, while the powerless Rafe is impressed against his will, his commanding officer, the aristocratic Rowland Lacy, is able to desert his position and, disguised, stay home to pursue his mistress (1.3).

In *Sir John Oldcastle* (1599), easy reassurances about the plight of demobilized soldiers are also little in evidence. The three maimed veterans who receive charity at Oldcastle's door, must first complain that "There be more stocks to set poor soldiers in / Than there be houses to relieve them at" – sentiments that condemn the Elizabethan state's punitive treatment of its neediest subjects (3.3–4). But in *Oldcastle* not only the common soldier suffers for his war service. The gentleman Sir Richard Lee returns from the Irish wars only to be murdered and robbed by his servant "MacChane of Ulster" – a stereotype of Irish ingratitude, duplicity, and viciousness (21.9). "The vulgar sort" who witnessed this spectacle of Irish treachery as well as other scenes featuring impressment, families broken by war, and injured soldiers, must have recoiled from a fate that possibly awaited them beyond the theater walls.[88]

By the time of *Henry V*, then, the mounting grievances of a range of social groups, together with a general awareness of English defeats and casualties, formed the basis for a reasoned critique of the English project in Ireland. Among the English forces there, critique frequently spilled over into protest and resistance to the "national" cause. Since most of the ordinary soldiers were disenfranchised and illiterate, their voices come down to us only muted and mediated through the reports of their officers and superiors.[89] In a typical report from early 1600, Thomas, Lord Burghley, wrote, "I never knew people more unwilling to go to a place reported by all that come thence as full of misery and poverty." They were men, he thought, who "ought rather to have two hearts put into them than one discouraged." The "greater discontent" that Burghley feared if relief were not forthcoming erupted repeatedly as conscripts rioted at the muster points and ports of embarkation, or sought passage back to England at the first opportunity.[90]

If, in *Henry V*, Fluellen's enthusiastic support of English militarism offsets and compensates for the rebelliousness of Elizabeth's Irish subjects, it also disguises the fact that resistance to service in Ireland was especially marked among the Welsh. "During Tyrone's rebellion," recalled Sir William Maurice of Caernarvonshire, "the people absented themselves from the musters, hiding in rocks and caves, some flying into foreign countries, so that . . . [I was] fain to hunt them by the pole like outlying deer."[91] Maurice and Sir John Wynn complained in 1596–97 that the Welsh "will venture any imprisonment rather than go for the Irish service," and, if forcibly sent, would return "to their own counties without pass-ports."[92] Some one thousand Welshmen are estimated to have died in Ireland every year over the course of the last eight years of Elizabeth's reign.[93] Official reports are naturally silent about the conscientious or political basis to soldiers' objections, portraying the men instead as either justly aggrieved yet loyal subjects or as undeserving "scum." Yet some of the Welsh who resisted conscription or deserted their posts once they shipped to Ireland can be counted among those "ideologically opposed to colonization."[94] Thus, when a constable tried to enlist the sons of David ap Roger of Montgomeryshire, the offical "was informed . . . in terse Welsh that in no conceivable circumstances would they fight for the Queen." The brothers refused, claims historian G. Dyfnallt Owen, out of religious and ideological opposition to the war.[95] In *Henry V*, Fluellen's enthusiastic support for the English war obfuscates the widespread intransigence of his compatriots who, rejecting the status of submissive colonial subjects, refused to fight in Ireland. After all, the common people of Wales had even less to gain from the subjugation of Ireland than did their English counterparts.

V

Welsh or English, the men sent to fight with Essex in Ireland were a source of constant shame to their commander. After a crushing defeat of English forces in the Curlew mountains of Munster in August, Essex decried the "baseness and cowardice most of these troops are grown unto," and urged that "these base clowns must be taught to fight again; else will Her Majesty's honour never be recovered, nor our nation valued, nor this kingdom reduced." Essex was caught in the contradiction of having to eradicate the "base" Irish rebels with his own "base" Englishmen. His fantasies of "sustaining" his army – fantasies that *Henry V* simultaneously fabricates and resists – and of achieving the reconquest of Ireland that had eluded so many of his predecessors (including his own father) were beginning to unravel. In the same letter to the Privy Council, Essex admitted: "I have sought by all the means that my industry and ability could compass, to put hope and spirit into this army, but it hath drooped every day."[96] Nor could he hope for the queen's encouragement. In a series of letters beginning in July, Elizabeth harshly criticized Essex's conduct, especially his distractions in Munster and his failure to engage Tyrone in the north.[97]

From the start, Essex knew that his leadership of the Irish campaign was a dangerous gamble that promised him either glory or disgrace. He accepted the commission in a bitter and fatalistic mood, uncertain of the queen's support and nervous that his enemies would undermine his success at every opportunity by withholding the "promised means" of men, equipment, and provisions.[98] Deprived of this support, Essex feared he would "be a martyr for" the queen whom he characterized as "a goddess not at leisure to hear prayers" – a remark that reveals his deep cynicism toward Elizabeth's own cults of divinity.[99]

But if Essex feared betrayal by the queen and privy council, they in turn had misgivings about his intentions in Ireland. Although Essex would not stage his ill-fated uprising until February, 1601, he had already excited suspicions before his departure. On the eve of accompanying Essex to Ireland, John Harington received a warning to:

Observe the man who commandeth, and yet is commanded himselfe; he goeth not forthe to serve the Queenes realme, but to humour his own revenge . . . If the Lord Deputy performs in the field what he hath promised in the council, all will be well; but, tho' the Queene hath graunted forgivenesse for [Essex's] late demeanor, in her presence, we know not what to think hereof . . . I know there are overlookers set on you all.[100]

Harington's correspondent was referring to an incident at court the previous summer in which Essex and the queen had argued over the Irish deputyship. In what is surely an exaggerated if not aprocryphal account of the encounter, Essex turned his back on Elizabeth who then struck him on the ear, provoking him to reach for his sword before leaving the court in disgrace. Whatever its veracity, the confrontation came to be seen as a turning point in an increasingly strained relationship. After this, Elizabeth ordered Essex to be watched for demonstrations of discontent, especially during his removal to Ireland where remoteness from court made him both more and less of a threat.[101]

As if assuming the role of "overlooker" himself, the Chorus to Act Five of *Henry V* compares the return of the king from France to both the return of Caesar from the wars and the impending return of Essex from Ireland. The Roman parallel consolidates the topicality around Essex, who, as Wayne A. Rebhorn observes, "was specifically connected with both Roman antiquity in general and Julius Caesar in particular." Elizabethans found much in the figure of Caesar that paralleled Essex: "both were self-publicizing, heroic warriors and conquerors; both successfully courted the common people and commanded powerful factions among the aristocracy; and both were seen as aspiring to kingship."[102]

> But now behold,
> In the quick Forge and working-house of Thought,
> How London doth powre out her Citizens,
> The Maior and all his Brethren in best sort,
> Like to the Senatours of th'antique Rome,
> With the Plebeians swarming at their heeles,
> Goe forth and fetch their Conqu'ring *Caesar* in:
> As by a lower, but by loving likelyhood,
> Were now the Generall of our gracious Empresse,
> As in good time he may, from Ireland comming,
> Bringing Rebellion broached on his Sword.

(TLN 2872–82)

The Chorus's syntactically ambivalent lines about Henry convey the exact sense of uncertainty, the mixture of danger and excitement surrounding Essex in Ireland. The image of the returning conqueror "Bringing Rebellion broached on his Sword" poises the figure of Essex, like the rebellion that he brings, between two contradictory constructions. From one perspective we see "the Generall" arriving home triumphantly with Irish rebellion metaphorically impaled and dead upon his sword, but from another (the plebeians'), we see "Conqu'ring *Caesar*" unleashing a new rebellion upon a "peacefull" London. Immediately after the Choric celebration of the victor's return and its ominous double meaning, the Chorus asks "How many would the peacefull Citie quit, / To welcome him?" Such a question can only be read as a nervous inquiry at a time of mounting political tension and uncertainty, a time at which Essex was believed to enjoy the broad backing of London's citizenry.

The Chorus's association of Essex and Caesar resonates with Shakespeare's *Tragedy of Julius Caesar*, a play written around the same time as *Henry V* and performed at the Globe on September 21, one week before Essex's unexpected return from Ireland.[103] In the opening scenes of *Julius Caesar*, Shakespeare furnishes an effective answer to the Chorus's dangerous question in *Henry V* of how many would welcome the returning Essex. For while *Henry V* anticipates the imminent return of Essex from Ireland, *Julius Caesar* opens with a victorious Caesar – fresh from his wars in Spain against the sons of Pompey – being acclaimed by the commons who throng "thick" in the streets to welcome him. Moving beyond the Chorus's moment of anticipation and into an imaginary future, *Julius Caesar* redefines and elaborates upon the threat to domestic peace that the popular "hero" brings with him from his overseas campaign. The threat Caesar embodies is not one of violent rebellion but of constitutional change: through his military victories and his subsequent popularity with the commons, he maneuvers to obtain the kingship, an office that at least the first half of the play presents as destructive both of the liberties guaranteed under the Republic and ultimately of civic and national stability. For Shakespeare, Caesar's foreign victory and his ensuing dominance at home represent a cautionary precedent as England awaited the return of Essex from Ireland and the resolution of his political ambitions.[104]

Yet Shakespeare lodges this warning about the possible dangers of Essex's desires, only to blur it, complicating the play's topical valencies by reorienting the audience's sympathies after the assassination of Caesar.[105] At Antony's hands, Caesar is transformed from would-be tyrant to martyred patriot; the republican alliance splits apart; and "Domestic fury and fierce civil strife" eventually "cumber all the parts of Italy" (3.1.263–64). *Julius Caesar*, then, connects with the contemporary political reality about Essex in provocative but ultimately elusive ways. And, lest Shakespeare and his company risk accusations of partisanship or meddling, the play includes a parable of the poet/playwright/intellectual's place in a dangerous political climate. In 4.2, as Brutus and Cassius are embroiled in an escalating argument, an unnamed poet unexpectedly forces his way into their company and urges the generals to "Love and be friends" (4.2.181). A representative of the artist/intellectual at a moment of historical crisis, the "poet" defines his role as that of peace-maker, mediator between conflicting positions. But even this modest claim to social relevance is rejected by Brutus and Cassius who laugh the "Saucy fellow" off the stage. "What should the wars do with these jigging fools?" exclaims Brutus. By equating writing and acting with both dancing and folly, Brutus subtly implies the artist/intellectual's powerlessness in shaping opinion, and more, compares the poet's arts with the martial arts, judging poetry useless. This apparently minor scene, by picturing the helplessness of a poet at the "front," disarms charges that Shakespeare and his collaborators were harming public confidence, let alone criticizing Essex, at a moment of acute political insecurity.[106]

Essex's overseas campaign, unlike those of Henry and Caesar, was unsuccessful, and his homecoming nothing like their public triumphs. After negotiating a truce with Tyrone in person, Essex set out for England, arriving unannounced at Nonsuch palace "upon *Michaelmas* Eve, about 10 a Clock in the Morning." "Full of Dirt and Mire" from riding, he went directly to "the Queens Bed Chamber, where he found the Queen newly up, the Hare about her Face." Essex's indecorous intrusion, his contamination of Elizabeth's most private of spaces, did not meet with immediate disapproval; only later was he confined to his chamber and placed under house arrest.[107] The queen wanted him punished not for his unauthorized, dishonorable negotiation with Tyrone but for his earlier rejection of her instructions, his profligate spending and creation of knighthoods, and returning without leave – a step that now left Ireland in a hazardous state of "no certainty."[108] On the contrary, the queen outwardly endorsed the treaty with Tyrone and worked to prolong it in the hope that the Irish warlord could even yet be recovered and made "a good subject."[109] But as Tyrone edged briefly back toward that position of "good subject," Essex moved toward Tyrone's own more familiar status of "arch-traitor."[110] Still under house arrest and denied access to the queen in June 1600, Essex was tried by his peers, stripped of his titles and offices but cleared of disloyalty.[111] Faced with a devastating loss of income, influence, and honor, and fearing the designs of his enemies Cecil, Cobham, and Ralegh, Essex resorted to desperate remedies. On February 8, 1601, he led his followers from Essex House through the city to the court in a bid to remove his rivals and to gain control of the queen.[112]

The failure of Essex's rebellion – "that dismal tumult, like the fit of Ephemera, or one-day's ague" as one observer called it – has often been retold.[113] What has not been noted is how immediately following the attempted rebellion, in Star Chamber speeches, in government-sponsored sermons, and at the trials of the earl's confederates, Essex and Tyrone, instead of changing places, came to occupy a single symbolic position. Whereas the ballads commemorating Essex's departure for and arrival in Ireland had constructed him as Tyrone's nemesis (with the two adversaries as the antithetical embodiments of loyalty and disloyalty, service and treason), the texts circulating after Essex's rebellion collapsed these boundaries, joining Essex and Tyrone as one composite rebel figure.[114] Central to this elision was the conviction that both earls were creatures of the queen, "the work of our own hands," in Elizabeth's words, and that their rebellions were thus acts of gross ingratitude against a generous maternal figure.[115] After Essex's uprising, a long-muted rumor could be publicly aired that Essex and Tyrone were secret friends and that Essex, as a clandestine Catholic, supported Tyrone's religious demands. News circulated that Essex's favor extended beyond Tyrone to the Irish people and that if Essex returned again to Ireland "he would wear the Irish *truses*" as a gesture of solidarity with them.[116] Allegations of sympathy and collusion between Essex and Tyrone reached an apotheosis in

Robert Cecil's claim that Essex had "conspired with Tyrone, that when he returned to England, and had removed some of the Queen's servants that watched him with eagle's eyes, and had governed the Queen a few months, Tyrone should land 8,000 men, the Queen be put aside, and all made a prey to Irish kerns." Essex was to be king of England, Tyrone king of Ireland.[117]

In raising the nightmare specter of an invasion by Gaelic forces under the control of a rebellious lord deputy, Cecil was also raising the ghost of Sir John Perrot and similar fears of his power. Cecil instructed London's preachers to disseminate the allegations against Essex from their pulpits in the hope of undermining whatever residual support the earl still enjoyed in the city.[118] But the possibility of a coup also cut other ways, even to the extent of reminding Londoners of how a threatened people like the Irish recoil from conquest. Meanwhile, the alignment of Essex and Tyrone also impressed upon observers the mutability of a culture in which the most civil of Englishmen and a former favorite of the queen could be suddenly tainted or "Irished" and in which, conversely, a low-born Irishman ("the generation of a blacksmith") could aspire to rule a nation and acquire the trappings of nobility.[119] In other words, the discordantly composite figure of Essex/Tyrone, an anomalous blend of the familiar and the strange, again disclosed the slippages and confusions of the very categories that supposedly defined and fixed the text of Ireland. As *Henry V* also intimates, the civil and the barbarous were not stable essences but alarmingly interchangable categories.

At the battle of Kinsale in September, 1601, Tyrone's challenge was finally ended by an English army under the command of Essex's successor, Lord Mountjoy. One English eye-witness described the victory against a combined Irish and Spanish force as an achievement comparable to Henry V's in France. Massively outnumbered by the enemy, Mountjoy's army was also "tyred and wearied out with the miserie of a long Winter's siege, our horses decayed, leane and very weake, our best meanes of victuals and forrage likely to be cut from us." Yet despite these overwhelming disadvantages, at the battle's end "there were (of the Irish Rebelles onely) found dead in the place, about twelve hundred bodies, and about eight hundred were hurt, whereof many dyed that night . . . On our side, onely one man was slaine."[120]

Militarily, at least, Ireland was subdued and the Nine Years War concluded. When Tyrone submitted to Mountjoy on March 30, 1603, the queen had been dead six days.[121] James's accession thus coincided with a watershed in Anglo-Irish relations; with organized resistance in Ireland at an end, English hegemony was to be secured by the planting of new colonies and the implementation of "juridical strategies . . . [designed] to lock a newly conquered country into permanent colonial dependence."[122] Upon the Stuart succession, wrote Thomas Dekker in *The Wonderful Yeare*, "two mighty nations were made one, [and] wild Ireland became tame on the sudden."[123]

Dekker's fantasy of an Anglo-Scottish union and Ireland's metamorphosis defiantly glosses over the troubled beginning of the new reign and its conflicted vision of nation and empire. James ordered Tyrone to the English court where the former "arch-rebel" was to be formally pardoned and reconfirmed as the primary power broker in the north of Ireland. Tyrone's visit vividly captured the schizophrenic English attitude toward the earl, who as both stranger and neighbor, outsider and insider, was both hated yet deemed indispensable by his adversaries. En route, Tyrone was accosted by English and Welshwomen "who had lost Husbands and Children in the Irish warres," and who now hurled "durt and stones at the Earle as he passed, and . . . revil[ed] him with bitter words."[124] At court, however, Tyrone was graciously received by the king, a scene of which a galled Sir John Harington complained:

I have lived to see that damnable rebel Tir-Owen broughte to Englande, curteouslie favourede, honourede, and well likede . . . How did I labour after that knave's destruction! I was callede from my home by hir Majesties commaund, adventurede perils by sea and lande, endurede toil, was near starvinge, eat horse-fleshe at Munster; and all to quell that man, who now smilethe in peace at those that did hazarde their lives to destroy him.[125]

Harington, having once reduced himself almost to the condition of an Irish kern, now witnessed the "great woodkerne" treated as a civil guest. Tyrone's rehabilitation as the friend of England would have been complete had he chosen, as Nicholas Canny thinks he might, to have "lived in splendid and luxurious retirement at court," perhaps serving as James's "adviser on Irish affairs."[126]

As circumstances in Ireland changed, however, Tyrone chose a different course, fleeing Ulster for the continent in September, 1607. Contemporaries and modern historians disagree about his motives although the erosion of his authority by the policies of Lord Deputy Sir Arthur Chichester and the Solicitor General Sir John Davies, seems to have been mainly responsible. Even in his absence, Tyrone's long shadow haunted Anglo-Irish affairs; rumors persisted until his death in 1616 that the earl would return to liberate Ireland at the head of a Catholic army.[127]

As Tyrone and his confederates vacated Ulster, new settlers, many from Scotland, descended upon the province. Thomas Dekker's sense of a providential coincidence between the pacification of Ireland and Anglo-Scottish union establishes the emergent framework of English discourse about Ireland in the early seventeenth century. The king's project of creating a unified Great Britain focused mainly upon Anglo-Scottish union, but it also called for the full incorporation of Ireland; indeed, the Ulster plantation that depended upon the resettlement of "inland" Scots as well as members of troublesome border families, had "been projected and prosecuted by the special direction and care of the king himself."[128] And yet Ireland was destined to be insecurely incorporated, a "younger sister to Great Britain" in Bacon's words, and never fully within what James called the "little World within itself" of England and Scotland – a mainland "intrenched and fortified round about with a naturall, and yet admirable strong pond or ditch." Ireland remained beyond the pale of an Anglo-Scottish core, whereas James imagined a seamless British nation in which Englishness, Scottishness, and Irishness were blended into a single homogeneous identity. English colonial policies, by perpetuating wrongs that led only to revenge and counter-revenge, proliferated national and ethnic differences, rivalries, and conflicts, that remain ingrained and raw even to this day.[129]

Notes

INTRODUCTION: ELIZABETH'S OTHER ISLE

1 *Calendar of State Papers, Domestic of the Reigns of Edward VI, Mary, Elizabeth, and James I,* ed. Robert Lemon and Mary Anne Everett Green (London, 1856–72), *1623–25,* 555.

2 Fynes Moryson, *Shakespeare's Europe: A Survey of the Condition of Europe at the End of the Sixteenth Century. Being Unpublished Chapters of Fynes Moryson's Itinerary (1617),* ed. Charles Hughes (New York: Benjamin Bloom, 1967), 194; henceforth, *Shakespeare's Europe.* While I refer in places to the cultural expressions of Gaelic writers, they remain outside the discourse of Ireland as I define it.

3 The withdrawal of Sir John Norris's troops from Brittany in February 1595, observes R. B. Wernham, "left not a single English soldier in the Queen's pay on French soil" (*The Return of the Armadas: The Last Years of the Elizabethan War Against Spain 1595–1603* (Oxford: Clarendon Press, 1994), 22.

4 J. J. N. McGurk, "Casualties and Welfare Measures for the Sick and Wounded of the Nine Year War in Ireland, 1593–1602," *Journal of the Society for Army Historical Research* 68 (1990): 22.

5 Wernham, *The Return of the Armadas,* 22–24, and *passim.* Also see William Palmer, *The Problem of Ireland in Tudor Foreign Policy 1485–1603* (Rochester, N.Y.: Boydell Press, 1994).

6 Richard Helgerson's impressive study of national self-fashioning in Renaissance England omits Ireland from the equation, as do books that focus on the encounter between English culture and alien Others (Richard Helgerson, *Forms of Nationhood: The Elizabethan Writing of England* [University of Chicago Press, 1992]; Emily C. Bartels, *Spectacles of Strangeness: Imperialism, Alienation, and Marlowe* [Philadelphia: University of Pennsylvania Press, 1993]).

For an excellent collection of essays that begins to rectify these deficiencies, see *Representing Ireland: Literature and the Origins of Conflict, 1534–1660,* ed. Brendan Bradshaw, Andrew Hadfield, and Willy Maley (Cambridge University Press, 1993).

7 Peter Stallybrass and Allon White, *The Politics and Poetics of Transgression* (Ithaca: Cornell University Press, 1986), 5.

8 For the wording of this Act and for related reports and legislation, see

Constantia Maxwell, *Irish History from Contemporary Sources (1509–1610)* (London: Allen and Unwin, 1923), 101–6. I have relied especially upon the following studies of Anglo-Irish relations: Steven G. Ellis, *Tudor Ireland: Crown, Community and the Conflict of Cultures, 1470–1603* (London: Longman, 1985), ch.5; Wallace T. MacCaffrey, *Elizabeth I: War and Politics, 1588–1603* (Princeton University Press, 1992), ch.16.

9 "Kingdom and Colony: Ireland in the Westward Enterprise 1536–1660," in *The Westward Enterprise: English Activities in Ireland, the Atlantic, and America, 1480–1650*, ed. K. R. Andrews, N. P. Canny, and P. E. H. Hair (Liverpool University Press, 1978), 54–64.

10 On strategies of national and ethnic authorization in early modern England, see Bartels, *Spectacles of Strangeness*, 4–5.

11 "State of Ireland, and Plan for its Reformation" (1515), quoted in Maxwell, *Irish History*, 79.

12 On Gerald's Irish ethnography and his indebtedness to classical ethnographic theories of "barbarism," see Robert Bartlett, *Gerald of Wales 1146–1223* (Oxford: Clarendon Press, 1982), chs.6–7.

13 R. R. Davies, "The Peoples of Britain and Ireland 1100–1400," *Transactions of the Royal Historical Society* 6th series 4 (1994): 6–7. Davies also observes that "the concept of *fir Erenn*, the men of Ireland, was a very old one; so was the notion that the story of the island had been that of the successive wars of the Irish against the foreigners" (19).

14 Lynda E. Boose argues persuasively that "for the English the group that was first to be shunted into [a position of] discursive derogation and thereafter invoked as almost a paradigm of inferiority was not the black 'race' – but the *Irish* race. . . the derogation of the Irish as 'a race apart' situates racial difference within cultural and religious categories rather than biologically empirical ones." " 'The Getting of a Lawfull Race': Racial Discourse in Early Modern England and the Unrepresentable Black Woman," in *Women, "Race," and Writing in the Early Modern Period*, ed. Margo Hendricks and Patricia Parker (London: Routledge, 1994), 36. Also see Margo Hendricks' thoughtful discussion of "the complexities of racial theorizing and racial consciousness in early modern English society." ("Managing the Barbarian: *The Tragedy of Dido, Queen of Carthage*," *Renaissance Drama* 23 [1992]: 165–88, esp. 183–85).

15 Bottigheimer, "Kingdom and Colony," 48–49.

16 Although I call these invaders "Anglo-Norman," I am aware that historians continue to disagree about the appropriate designation. According to J. R. S. Phillips, Anglo-Norman is a convenient but questionable term: "While it is true that many of the nobility came from England, they were not English either in racial origin or in speech; nor were they invariably Norman, although many had Norman ancestry and some still held land in Normandy when they first arrived in Ireland" ("The Anglo-Norman Nobility," in *The English in Medieval Ireland*, ed. James Lydon [Dublin: Royal Irish Academy, 1984], 88). John Gillingham prefers that we speak not of "the Norman invasion" of Ireland, but of the "English invasion," as a way of acknowledging that this episode be seen as integral to the history of English colonialism ("The English Invasion of Ireland," in *Representing Ireland*, ed. Bradshaw, Hadfield, and

Maley, 24–42). Also see Marie Therese Flanagan, *Irish Society, Anglo-Norman Settlers, Angevin Kingship: Interactions in Ireland in the Late Twelfth Century* (Oxford: Clarendon Press, 1989).

17 See Robin Frame, "'Les Engleys Nées en Irlande': The English Political Identity in Medieval Ireland," *Transactions of the Royal Historical Society*, 6th series 2 (1992): 83–102; and the same author's "England and Ireland, 1171–1399," in *England and Her Neighbours, 1066–1453*, ed. Michael Jones and Malcolm Vale (London: Hambledon Press, 1989), 139–55. For a slightly different reading of this group's identity, see James Lydon, "The Middle Nation," in *The English in Medieval Ireland*, ed. Lydon, 1–26.

18 Codified as the Statutes of Kilkenny (1366), one of the earliest attempts to discourage Gaelicization among the English settlers declared that: "Whereas at the conquest of the land of Ireland and for a long time afterwards the English of that land used the English tongue, manner of riding and dress, and were governed and ruled . . . by English law . . . now many English of that land, forsaking the English speech, outward appearance, manner of riding, laws and customs, live and conduct themselves according to the customs, appearance and tongue of the Irish enemies" (quoted in Frame, "'Les Engleys Nées en Irlande'," 84).

19 For a detailed account of Old English identity, traditions, and agendas, see Nicholas P. Canny, *The Formation of the Old English Elite in Ireland* (Dublin: The National University of Ireland, 1975).

20 Robin Frame points out that friction was already evident in the fourteenth century between "the English of Ireland" and newcomers from England ("England and Ireland," 151–52).

21 For a recent account of Spenser's radicalism before he embarked for Ireland, see Robert Lane, *Shepheards Devises: Edmund Spenser's "Shepheardes Calendar" and the Institutions of Elizabethan Society* (Athens: University of Georgia Press, 1993). For a related bid to rescue Spenser from the charge of political "toadyism," see Willy Maley, "How Milton and Some Contemporaries Read Spenser's *View*," in *Representing Ireland*, ed. Bradshaw, Hadfield, and Maley, 201–2.

22 Peter Erickson, "The Order of the Garter, the Cult of Elizabeth, and Class-Gender Tension in *The Merry Wives of Windsor*," in *Shakespeare Reproduced: The Text in History and Ideology*, ed. Jean E. Howard and Marion F. O'Connor (New York: Methuen, 1987), 133.

23 The Privy Council's words are from instructions to the Archbishop of Canterbury in 1587, ordering him to call in the second printing of Holinshed's *Chronicles*. Cited in Janet Clare, *"Art Made Tongue-tied by Authority": Elizabethan and Jacobean Dramatic Censorship* (Manchester University Press, 1990), 18.

24 I adopt Annabel Patterson's formulation of the relationship between writers and authorities in *Censorship and Interpretation: The Conditions of Writing and Reading in Early Modern England* (Madison: University of Wisconsin Press, 1984), esp. ch.2.

25 For an excellent account of the "license" of Renaissance theater, see Steven Mullaney, *The Place of the Stage: License, Play, and Power in Renaissance England* (University of Chicago Press, 1988), esp. ch.2.

26 *Shakespeare's Theatre* (London: Routledge and Kegan Paul, 1983), 66. For recent correctives to Thomson, see Michael Neill, "Broken English and Broken Irish: Nation, Language, and the Optic of Power in Shakespeare's Histories," *Shakespeare Quarterly* 45 (1994): 1–32, and Andrew Murphy, "Shakespeare's Irish History," *Literature and History* 5 (1996): 39–60. Both these essays draw upon my own published work.

27 *Teague, Shenkin and Sawney: Being an Historical Study of the Earliest Irish, Welsh, and Scottish Characters in English Plays* (Cork University Press, 1954), 99.

28 Patterson, *Censorship and Interpretation*, 53. Leah S. Marcus, *Puzzling Shakespeare: Local Reading and Its Discontents* (Berkeley: University of California Press, 1988), ch.1, 69–70.

29 On the "transcoding of alien territory," see Stallybrass and White, *The Politics and Poetics of Transgression*, 1–26.

30 For a discussion of the impact of Scottish affairs upon the English theater, see James Shapiro, "*The Scot's Tragedy* and the Politics of Popular Drama," *English Literary Renaissance* 23 (1993): 428–49.

31 The best-known analogy between New World Indians and native Irish appears in Thomas Hariot's *A Brief and True Report of the New Found Land of Virginia* (1590). For the tendency to flatten out the chronological and ideological contours of the "discourse of colonialism" and to lump Ireland and the New World together, see Paul Brown, "'This Thing of Darkness I Acknowledge Mine': *The Tempest* and the Discourse of Colonialism," in *Political Shakespeare: New Essays in Cultural Materialism*, ed. Jonathan Dollimore and Alan Sinfield (Ithaca: Cornell University Press, 1985), 48–71.

32 Meredith Anne Skura, "Discourse and the Individual: the Case of Colonialism in *The Tempest*," *Shakespeare Quarterly* 40 (1989): 42–69, esp. 51–57.

33 For Dee's interest in empire, see William H. Sherman, *John Dee: The Politics of Reading and Writing in the English Renaissance* (University of Massachusetts Press, 1995), ch.7. Dee is credited with coining the term, "British Empire." On the origins of this empire and the emphasis in sixteenth-century England upon trade routes rather than foreign colonies, see Kenneth R. Andrews, *Trade, Plunder, and Settlement: Maritime Enterprise and the Genesis of the British Empire, 1480–1630* (Cambridge University Press, 1984).

34 *A Discourse of Western Planting*, ed. David B. Quinn and Alison M. Quinn (London: The Hakluyt Society, 1993), 35. On English–Spanish rivalry in the New World, see David Read, "Ralegh's *Discoverie of Guiana* and the Elizabethan Model of Empire," in *The Work of Dissimilitude: Essays from the Sixth Citadel Conference on Medieval and Renaissance Literature*, ed. David G. Allen and Robert A. White (Newark: University of Delaware Press, 1992), 166–76.

35 See *Strangers Within the Realm: Cultural Margins of the First British Empire*, ed. Bernard Bailyn and Philip D. Morgan (Chapel Hill: University of North Carolina, 1991), 7–9; for the issue of national insecurity in post-Reformation England, see Carol Z. Wiener, "The Beleaguered Isle: a Study of Elizabethan and Jacobean Anti-Catholicism," *Past and Present* 51 (1971): 27–62.

36 Richard Strier, "Radical Donne: 'Satire III'," *ELH* 60 (1993), 283.

37 *Threshold of a Nation: A Study in English and Irish Drama* (Cambridge University Press, 1979), 78.

38 Bartlett, *Gerald of Wales*, 20–25. See the introduction to the standard modern edition of the *Expugnatio*: *Expugnatio Hibernica: The Conquest of Ireland by Giraldus Cambrensis*, ed. and tr. A. B. Scott and F. X. Martin (Dublin: Royal Irish Academy, 1978).

39 Previous English renderings included: a partial translation made in the fifteenth century for Old English readers; another partial translation, attributed to Richard Stanihurst, which appeared in the first edition of Holinshed (1577) (Bartlett, *Gerald of Wales*, 215, 178); a translated abridgement of the *Expugnatio* into one chapter of Campion's *Historie of Ireland* (1571) (ed. Rudolf B. Gottfried [New York: Scholars' Facsimiles and Reprints, 1940], "To the Loving Reader").

40 Quoted in Gerald of Wales, *The History and Topography of Ireland*, ed. and tr. John J. O'Meara (Harmondsworth: Penguin, 1982), 13.

41 "Rethinking Tudor Historiography," *South Atlantic Quarterly* 92 (1993): 196.

42 *A New Description of Ireland, Together with the Manners Customs, and Dispositions of the People* (1610), in *Elizabethan Ireland: A Selection of Writings by Elizabethan Writers on Ireland*, ed. James P. Myers (Archon Books, 1983), 126–27.

43 On Stanihurst, see Colm Lennon, *Richard Stanihurst the Dubliner, 1547–1618: A Biography with a Stanihurst Text, "On Ireland's Past"* (County Dublin: Irish Academic Press, 1981).

44 Hooker contributed an account of the Western Rebellion in Edward VI's reign to Foxe's *Acts and Monuments*. On Hooker, see *Dictionary of National Biography* (DNB), ed. Sidney Lee and Leslie Stephen. 63 vols. (New York: Macmillan, 1885–1900) 9:181–83; and Edward M. Hinton, *Ireland Through Tudor Eyes* (Philadelphia: University of Pennsylvania Press, 1935), 20–23.

45 Raphael Holinshed, *Chronicles of England, Scotland, and Ireland* (London, 1807–8), 6:14, 66–69. Henceforth, Holinshed, *Chronicles*.

46 *Ibid.*, 103.

47 *Ibid.*, 369.

48 *Ibid.*, 185–88, 221.

49 *Ibid.*, 149.

50 *Ibid.*, 109. Gerald is empowered in his treatment of England's rulers by his religious office and his conviction that the claims of the church outweigh those of the state. Thus, prefacing his description of Henry II, whom he served as chaplain, Gerald voices skepticism toward "the philosophers . . . opinion, that we ought to reverence so the higher powers in all maner of offices and dueties, as that we should not provoke nor moove them with anie sharpe speeches or disordered languages." In Gerald's portrait of Henry, praise of the king's physique and statecraft is offset by accusations of impiety and of shortcomings as a father (175–77).

51 *Ibid.*, 222.

52 *Ibid.*, 224, 118. Gerald's moral blurring of the Anglo-Irish mission in Ireland is more marked in later redactions of the *Expugnatio*, redactions that Gerald worked on while reconsidering his relationship to the English crown.

I   SPENSER'S IRISH COURTS

1 *The Collected Poems of Joseph Hall, Bishop of Exeter and Norwich*, ed. A. Davenport (Liverpool University Press, 1949), 66. It was precisely "undesirables" like Hall's "malecontent" whom the writers of tracts promoting English settlement in Ireland in the late sixteenth and early seventeenth century wanted to keep out. Thus, when Thomas Blenerhasset called for the repeopling of Ulster in 1610 with English subjects he warned the "poore indigent fellow [that] hast neither faculty nor money [to] goe not thither, for though there be plenty of all thinges, thou shalt starve there, Loyterers and lewd persons in this our new worlde, they will not be indured." Thomas Blenerhasset, *The Plantation in Ulster* (London, 1610), C4^v.

2 Quoted in Mark Eccles, "Barnabe Googe in England, Spain, and Ireland," *English Literary Renaissance* 15 (1985): 367–68.

3 *Ibid.*, 368.

4 For an outline of Spenser's professional career in Ireland including his offices and positions, see Willy Maley, *A Spenser Chronology* (London: Macmillan, 1994), 11–75.

5 Michael MacCarthy-Morrogh, *The Munster Plantation: English Migration to Southern Ireland, 1583–1641* (Oxford: Clarendon Press, 1986), 207.

6 *Ibid.*, 207–8. Ambitious New English settlers were not the only expatriates to benefit from less rigid social and legal codes. According to Fynes Moryson, many of the planters were "obstinate Papists" who had chosen "to leave their dwelling in England, where the severity of the lawes bridled them, and to remove into Ireland, where they might be more remote, and so have greater liberty" (*Shakespeare's Europe*, 209).

7 Arthur Marotti, "John Donne and the Rewards of Patronage," in *Patronage in the Renaissance*, ed. Guy Fitch Lytle and Stephen Orgel (Princeton University Press, 1981), 209–10.

8 *Spenser's Secret Career* (Cambridge University Press, 1993), 107.

9 See especially Julia Reinhard Lupton, "Home-Making in Ireland: Virgil's Eclogue I and Book VI of *The Faerie Queene*," *Spenser Studies* 8 (1990): 119–45; Richard A. McCabe, "Edmund Spenser, Poet of Exile," *Proceedings of the British Academy* 80 (1993): 73–103; and Andrew Hadfield, "'Who Knowes not Colin Clout?' The Permanent Exile of Edmund Spenser," chapter 6 of *Literature, Politics, and National Identity* (Cambridge University Press, 1994), 170–201.

10 "Political Women and Reform in Tudor Ireland," in *Women in Early Modern Ireland*, ed. Margaret MacCurtain and Mary O'Dowd (Edinburgh University Press, 1991), 82–83. The deputy's Kilmainham residence outside Dublin is described in a government work order as a "house of pleasure" although its precise function is unclear (*Calendar of State Papers Relating to Ireland, of the Reigns of Henry VIII, Edward VI, Mary, and Elizabeth*, ed. Hans Claude Hamilton *et al.* [London, 1860–1912] *1599–1600*, 240). Henceforth, *C.S.P. Ireland*. In his patriotic description of sixteenth-century Dublin, Palesman Richard Stanihurst relates that the "castell hath beene of late much beautified with sundrie and gorgious buildings in the time of sir Henrie Sidneie," but he

says nothing about cultural activities there (*A Description of Ireland* in Holinshed, *Chronicles*, 6:27).

11 For a plausible chronology of the poem's composition, see Josephine Waters Bennett, *The Evolution of "The Faerie Queene"* (New York: Burt Franklin, 1960), esp. ch.18.

12 "Spenser's Merlin," *Renaissance and Reformation* 4 (1980): 179.

13 It is interesting to note that in Malory's *Le Morte D'Arthur*, Ryence is ruler of north Wales and "of all Ireland." Ryence wears a mantle covered with the beards of the rulers who do him homage (ed. Janet Cowen, vol.1 [Harmondsworth: Penguin, 1969], 57–58).

14 All references to *The Faerie Queene* are to A. C. Hamilton's edition (New York: Longman, 1977).

15 Spenser arouses discomfort with Merlin not just by placing the genealogy/prophecy of the Tudors in the mouth of this dangerously double figure; the contents and structure of the genealogy/prophecy also problematize as much as they affirm the origins and self-evident legitimacy of Elizabeth's power. For further discussion of Merlin's genealogy/prophecy, see Howard Dobin, *Merlin's Disciples: Prophecy, Poetry, and Power in Renaissance England* (Stanford University Press, 1990), 105–6, 149–53, and Hadfield, *Literature, Politics*, 196–98.

16 Dobin, *Merlin's Disciples*, 1–8, 135–44. J. J. Scarisbrick, *The Reformation and the English People* (London: Blackwell, 1984), 178.

17 *Merlin's Disciples*, 4. The state's practice of coopting marginal forces is parodied near the end of *The Merry Wives of Windsor* where the "fairies" bestow their blessing upon Windsor castle (5.5.54–72).

18 Dobin sees Spenser's treatment of Merlin as uncomfortably double-edged: even as Spenser employs Merlin as a prophet of Tudor glory he must resort to narrative techniques that "contain" the disturbing associations of "a figure demonized, quite literally, as an agent of theological and civic subversion" (*Merlin's Disciples*, 144). For an excellent account of Dee's connections and utility to the Elizabethan political elite, see William H. Sherman, *John Dee: The Politics of Reading and Writing in the English Renaissance* (Amherst: University of Massachusetts Press, 1995).

19 "The Elizabethan Subject and the Spenserian Text," *Literary Theory / Renaissance Texts*, ed. Patricia Parker and David Quint (Baltimore: Johns Hopkins University Press, 1986), 323.

20 Geoffrey of Monmouth, *The History of the Kings of Britain*, ed. and tr. Lewis Thorpe (Harmondsworth: Penguin, 1966), 15, 21.

21 *Ibid.*, 196–98.

22 *Ibid.*, 221–22.

23 Holinshed, *Chronicles*, 6:223.

24 *Ibid.*, 222.

25 The dangerous marginality of Spenser's Merlin resonates with *Merlinus Calidonius*' condition as a wild man of the woods in the Marches of Scotland. See Gerald of Wales, *The Journey Through Wales and The Description of Wales*, ed. and tr. Lewis Thorpe (Harmondsworth: Penguin, 1978), 192–93.

26 Herbert F. Hore, "Irish Bardism in 1561," *The Ulster Journal of Archaeology* 1st series 6 (1858): 207.

27 *Two Histories of Ireland* (Dublin, 1633. Reprinted New York: Da Capo, 1971), 122.
28 *Essays and Introductions* (London: Macmillan, 1961), 372.
29 Annabel Patterson seems right in claiming that while Spenser might have endorsed the English policy of suppressing Gaelic culture, "it is a mistake to believe he was *comfortable* with this final solution" (*Reading Between the Lines* [Madison: University of Wisconsin Press, 1993], 110).
30 The justice of the peace and sheriff of Pembrokeshire, George Owen, was an avid supporter of the Welsh bardic tradition during Elizabeth's reign (*The Description of Pembrokeshire by George Owen of Henllys*, ed. Dillwyn Miles. The Welsh Classics [Dyfed, Wales: Gomer Press, 1994], lii-lv). Owen refers to Merlin as "the great prophet and chief bard of his time" (184).
31 Nerys Patterson makes the important qualification that "it cannot be safely assumed that [the brehons] shared the same views as the bards, for there are instances of the brehons co-operating in the political suppression of bardic families . . . The crown itself seems to have made this distinction, often omitting the brehons from sanctions, while singling out rhymers, bards, chroniclers, messengers and harpists" ("Gaelic Law and the Tudor Conquest of Ireland: the Social Background of the Sixteenth-Century Recensions of the Pseudo-Historical Prologue to the *Senchas már*," *Irish Historical Studies* 27 [1991]: 194).
32 E.C.S., *The Government of Ireland Under Sir John Perrot 1584–88* (London, 1626), C3v.
33 All references to *A View* are to W. L. Renwick's edition and appear parenthetically in the text (London: Scholartis Press, 1934. Republished 1971). Renwick's copy-text, Bodleian Rawlinson manuscript B478, was submitted for publication by Matthew Lownes in April 1598 and bears a note from Master Stationer Thomas Man instructing Lownes to bring "further aucthoritie" before printing can proceed. See Edward Arber, ed., *A Transcript of the Registers of the Company of Stationers of London 1554–1640* (London, 1875; reprinted Gloucester, Mass.: Peter Smith, 1967), 3:34. For a list and description of the different manuscripts of *A View*, see Gottfried's Variorum edition in Edwin Greenlaw, Charles Grosvenor Osgood, Frederick Morgan Padelford, and Ray Heffner, eds., *The Works of Edmund Spenser: A Variorum Edition* (Baltimore: Johns Hopkins University Press, 1932–49) 9:506–24; and Jean R. Brink, "Constructing the *View of the Present State of Ireland*," *Spenser Studies* 11 (1990): 203–28. In this provocative essay that focuses attention upon the various manuscripts of *A View*, Brink raises doubts about Spenser's authorship. *A View* was not firmly identified with Spenser until Sir James Ware first edited and published it in 1633. While I acknowledge the paucity of "bibliographical evidence" linking *A View* with Spenser and support the need for a thorough investigation of the manuscripts, I find persuasive internal evidence for Spenser's authorship. In particular, Irenius' powerful defense of Lord Grey and his self-characterization as "noe marshall man" who owes his knowledge of military matters to the ex-lord deputy are redolent of Spenser's own experience in Ireland, an experience that was closely tied early on to Grey's patronage and fortunes (*A View*, ed. Renwick, 154).
34 For a notable exception to the critical consensus on Spenser's relation to bardic culture, see McCabe, "Edmund Spenser, Poet of Exile."

35 The Variorum editor of *A View* notes that "Spenser [Irenius] shows an independent mind in defending Irish records with such persistence" (*The Works of Edmund Spenser*, ed. Greenlaw *et al.*, 9:311).
36 "The Irish Background of Spenser's *View*," *Journal of English and Germanic Philology* 42 (1943): 501n7.
37 "The Gaelic Response to Conquest and Colonisation: the Evidence of the Poetry," *Studia Hibernica* 20 (1980): 14.
38 *Ibid.*, 14–15. For a counter-argument to Dunne, see Brendan Bradshaw, "Native Reaction to the Westward Enterprise: a Case Study in Gaelic Ideology," in *The Westward Enterprise: English Activities in Ireland, the Atlantic, and America, 1480–1650*, ed. K. R. Andrews, N. P. Canny, and P. E. H. Hair (Liverpool University Press, 1978), 65–80. Bradshaw claims that bardic verse of the latter sixteenth century reflects "the first stages of development of a national political consciousness" – a consciousness that was strongly Gaelic.
39 Dunne, "The Gaelic Response," 12; on the Irish poet's office, see also Joseph Theodoor Leerssen, *Mere Irish and Fíor-Ghael: Studies in the Idea of Irish Nationality, its Development and Literary Expression Prior to the Nineteenth Century* (Philadelphia: John Benjamins, 1986), 177.
40 Quoted in David Beers Quinn, *The Elizabethans and the Irish* (Ithaca: Cornell University Press, 1966), 42. New English, Old English, and Gaelic authors of this period all acknowledge the (alleged) potency of bardic satire. According to Fynes Moryson, it wasn't only the leaders of Gaelic society who were wary of the bards: the Irish common soldiers were so "affected to vainglory as they nothing so much feared the Lord Deputy's anger as the least song or ballad these rascals [the bards] might make against them" (quoted in Quinn, 42).
41 Bardic poetry tended to treat the late sixteenth-century "invaders" of Ireland in the same way it had the Anglo-Norman newcomers of the twelfth: "as another element in the system of competing lordships, and . . . as potential patrons" (Dunne, "The Gaelic Response," 13). The encroachment of new-comers was typically dealt with in bardic poetry from the twelfth century onwards not as a national crisis requiring coordinated resistance but as just one threat among many to the chief's traditional privileges (Leerssen, *Mere Irish*; Dunne, "The Gaelic Response," 10).
42 See Katharine Simms, "Bards and Barons: the Anglo-Irish Aristocracy and the Native Culture," in *Medieval Frontier Societies*, ed. Robert Bartlett and Angus MacKay (Oxford: Clarendon Press, 1989), 177–97. Several of the bardic poems addressed to Ormond are discussed in Michelle Ó Riordan, *The Gaelic Mind and the Collapse of the Gaelic World* (Cork University Press, 1990), 141–50.
43 Richard Stanihurst, *A Description of Ireland* in Holinshed, *Chronicles*, 6:53.
    For Ormond's genealogy and his relation to the Boleyns, see *The Complete Peerage or a History of the House of Lords and all its Members from the Earliest Times*, ed. George Edward Cokayne, H. A. Doubleday, Geoffrey H. White, and Lord Howard de Walden (London: St. Catherine Press, 1945), 10:116–47.
    Nicholas Canny points out that Old English was "a nomenclature first employed by Edmund Spenser" in *A View* ("Identity Formation in Ireland:

The Emergence of the Anglo-Irish," in *Colonial Identity in the Atlantic World, 1500–1800*, ed. Nicholas Canny and Anthony Pagden [Princeton University Press, 1987], 160).

44 This information on Ormond is gleaned from *The Complete Peerage* ed. Cokayne *et al.*; *DNB* 3:531–33; Cyril Falls, "Black Tom of Ormonde," *The Irish Sword: The Journal of the Military History Society of Ireland* 5 (1961–62): 10–22; and Ciaran Brady, "Thomas Butler, Earl of Ormond (1531–1614) and Reform in Tudor Ireland," in *Worsted in the Game: Losers in Irish History*, ed. Ciaran Brady (Dublin: The Lilliput Press, 1989), 49–59.

45 Spenser's *View* is full of the evils associated with this ethnic group. According to Irenius most of the Old English families had cast off their English identity and allegiances in favor of Gaelic ones and in the process had developed an even stronger animosity toward English culture than had the Gaelic Irish. Many of the New English administrators in Ireland – including several lord deputies – automatically distrusted all Irish-born subjects, regardless of their particular lineage, upbringing, or declared loyalties.

46 The case against Ormond can be followed in *C.S.P. Ireland, 1598–99*, 361–75, and is also discussed in detail by Hiram Morgan, "Tom Lee: The Posing Peacemaker," in *Representing Ireland*, ed. Bradshaw, Hadfield, and Maley, 132–65.

47 Donald Jackson, "The Irish Language and Tudor Government," *Eire–Ireland* 8:1 (1973): 26.

48 *Poems on the Butlers of Ormond, Cahir, and Dunboyne (A.D. 1400–1650)* (Dublin Institute for Advanced Studies, 1945), 136.

49 "Spenser, Holinshed, and the *Leabhar Gabhála*," *Journal of English and Germanic Philology* 43 (1944): 400–1n55. An even more intriguing suggestion – and one that sits uneasily with *A View*'s ultimately anti-bardic sentiments – is that Spenser may have had a native guide to Irish poetry in the person of Teig Olyve, the bard of his hostile Old English neighbor in Munster, Lord Roche. Pauline Henley points to "the ancient bardic custom [in which] an Irish poet's house . . . was open to all literati, and not for one night only, but for as long as they wished to partake of his hospitality" (*Spenser in Ireland* [New York: Longmans Green, 1928], 66, 103).

50 Frederic Ives Carpenter, *A Reference Guide to Edmund Spenser* (New York: Kraus Reprint, 1969), 33.

51 Carpenter, *A Reference Guide*, 40; Raymond Jenkins, "Spenser and the Clerkship in Munster," *PMLA* 47 (1932), 109–21; *The Complete Peerage*, ed. Cokayne *et al.*, 10:146.

52 MacCarthy-Morrogh, *The Munster Plantation*, 104.

53 I quote from the sonnets as they appear in an appendix to A. C. Hamilton, ed., *The Faerie Queene*, 741–43. The sonnet to Ormond is one of four addressed to men whom Spenser knew through his Irish service: Lord Grey of Wilton, Sir Walter Ralegh, Sir John Norris (the Lord President of Munster). Other sonnets were dedicated to individuals with more oblique connections to Ireland: Christopher Hatton was one of the original undertakers along with Spenser in Munster although he remained an absentee landlord; Francis Walsingham's cousin, Sir Edward Denney, was another undertaker; Charles Howard, the Earl of Nottingham, had married his daughter Frances to Henry

Fitzgerald, the twelfth Earl of Kildare; and Mary Sidney, Countess of Pembroke, whose father, Sir Henry Sidney, had served as lord deputy, was related through marriage to Sir William Herbert, another undertaker in the Munster plantation and the author of a tract about the colony. As a distinct subgroup within the collection of dedicatory sonnets, the ones to Ormond, Grey, Ralegh, and Norris, work together to establish the Irish origins of the first installment of *The Faerie Queene*.

For the view that Spenser offers qualified praise of Ormond in *A View*, see David Baker, "Off the Map: Charting Uncertainty in Renaissance Ireland," in *Representing Ireland*, ed. Bradshaw, Hadfield, and Maley, 86–89.

54 Leerssen, *Mere Irish*, 208.
55 For a brief account of Churchyard's life and writings, see Edward M. Hinton, *Ireland Through Tudor Eyes* (Philadelphia: University of Pennsylvania Press, 1935), 29–32.
56 Quoted in Raymond Jenkins, "Spenser with Lord Grey in Ireland," *PMLA* 52 (1937), 342–43.
57 Bernadette Cunningham, "Women and Gaelic Literature, 1500–1800," in *Women in Early Modern Ireland*, ed. Margaret MacCurtain and Mary O'Dowd (Edinburgh University Press, 1991), 149–52. Carney, *Poems on the Butlers*, 137. Carney also makes the interesting observation that "Dermitius Meara, who describes himself as a native of Ormond and an alumnus of Oxford, published in 1615 a heroic Latin poem in five books (in all about 4000 lines) on Thomas, 10th Earl of Ormond" (173).

The active role taken by the wives of Gaelic and Old English lords in the patronage system dovetails with Spenser's practice of dedicating many of his poems to noble English women. Several poems in the *Complaints* volume, as well as *Daphnaida*, the *Fowre Hymnes*, and *Prothalamion* are dedicated to noble English women.

58 All references to Spenser's shorter poems (excluding the dedicatory sonnets to *The Faerie Queene*) are to *The Yale Edition of the Shorter Poems of Edmund Spenser*, ed. William A. Oram, Einar Bjorvand, Ronald Bond, Thomas H. Cain, Alexander Dunlop, and Richard Schell (New Haven: Yale University Press, 1989).
59 See A. L. Beier, *Masterless Men: The Vagrancy Problem in England, 1560–1640* (London: Methuen, 1985), ch. 1.
60 In his helpful introduction to the poem, William Oram notes that "Spenser's myth laments a civilization in which the ruling class has abandoned its cultural mission" (265).
61 *A View*, ed. Renwick, 70.
62 Quoted in Anne Laurence, "The Cradle to the Grave: English Observation of Irish Social Customs in the Seventeenth Century," *The Seventeenth Century* 3 (1988): 79. In *A View*, Irenius notes besides war cries, "other sortes of cryes all so used amongst the Irishe, which savoure greatlie of *Scithian*: barbarisme, as theire Lamentacions at theire burialls, with disparefull outcryes, and ymoderate waylinges." Like many of the Gaelic customs he records, this one is seen by Irenius as linking the Irish with "Pagans, and *Infidells*" (72–73). However, unlike other New and Old English writers, Spenser does not connect the custom specifically with women.

63 For an account of the Munster rebellion of 1598, see Anthony J. Sheehan, "The Overthrow of the Plantation of Munster in October 1598," *The Irish Sword* 15 (1982): 11–22.

64 "Thomas Butler, Earl of Ormond," 56.

65 Brian De Breffny and Rosemary Ffolliott, *The Houses of Ireland: Domestic Architecture from the Medieval Castle to the Edwardian Villa* (New York: Viking Press, 1975), 25.

66 The deer park attached to Ormond's Kilkenny estate is a further indication of the earl's cultivation of the dual persona of English gentleman/Irish chief. See Falls, "Black Tom," 14.

67 Brady, "Political Women," 82–83.

68 Although not published until 1606, Bryskett's work was probably written in the early to mid-1580s. See Henry R. Plomer and Tom Peete Cross, eds., *The Life and Correspondence of Lodowick Bryskett* (University of Chicago Press, 1927), 78–83.

69 *The Works of Lodowick Bryskett*, ed. J. H. P. Pafford (Gregg International, 1972), 3.

70 *Ibid.*, 5–6. The guest list included: "Doctor *Long* Primate of *Ardmagh*, Sir *Robert Dillon* Knight, M. *Dormer* the Queenes Sollicitor, Capt. *Christopher Carleil*, Capt. *Thomas Norreis*, Capt. *Warham*, *St Leger*, Capt. *Nicolas Dawtrey* . . . & *Th. Smith* Apothecary" (6).

71 Bryskett's text observes the convention of spreading the discussion over several days; in this case the three days correspond to the three dialogues of Cinthio's text (91–92). On the second and third days – also following convention – the guests move out (temporarily) into the host's garden. Valerie Wayne discusses the "textual geography" of the symposium genre. See *"The Flower of Friendship." A Renaissance Dialogue Contesting Marriage by Edmund Tilney*, ed. Valerie Wayne (Ithaca: Cornell University Press, 1992), 71.

72 After Sidney's death, his sister Mary functioned as a virtual surrogate for him in Spenser's verse. Named as *"Urania"* in *Colin Clout* (line 487), she is addressed in one of *The Faerie Queene*'s dedicatory sonnets as "Remembraunce of that most Heroike spirit."

73 See Sam Meyer, *An Interpretation of Edmund Spenser's "Colin Clout"* (Cork University Press, 1969), 145–47; Steven W. May, *The Elizabethan Courtier Poets: The Poems and their Contexts* (Columbia: University of Missouri Press, 1991), 123.

74 For details about the composition, registration, and publication of the poem, see Sam Meyer, "Spenser's *Colin Clout*: The Poem and the Book," *The Papers of the Bibliographical Society of America* 56 (1962): 397–413.

75 Spenser also uses Colin Clout as his persona in *The Ruines of Time* – a *Complaints* poem that belongs to the same period as *Colin Clout* (225).

Patricia Coughlan offers a complementary analysis to my own when she argues that "Spenser, who would be regarded as the agent of civility, in a sense places in the position of wild men – severe critics of the court, church and state establishment – some of the most forceful among his personae both prose and poetic. Colin Clout brought to Ireland becomes as a native" (70). Coughlan shows that in *A View*, Spenser characterizes Irenius as rough and impetuous in contrast to the more controlled and moderate Eudoxus. She explores as a subtext to *A View*, Lucian's *Toxaris*, a dialogue about friendship in which the interlocutors are a Scythian (Toxaris) and a Greek (Mnesippus). Spenser positions his interlocutors in a similar relationship with Irenius exhibiting features of the "quasi-barbarian Scythian" and Eudoxus those of a "sane, centrist Greek." "'Some Secret Scourge Which Shall by Her Come unto England': Ireland and Incivility in Spenser," in *Spenser and Ireland: An Interdisciplinary Perspective*, ed. Patricia Coughlan (Cork University Press, 1989), 46–74.

76 For Smith, see Hore, "Irish Bardism," 206; Douglas Hyde, *A Literary History of Ireland: From Earliest Times to the Present Day* (London: T. Fisher Unwin, 1920), 496–97.

77 It is only during Colin's initial encounter with the "Shepheard of the Ocean" that the bardic division of roles makes itself felt. In an image designed to evoke the intimacy between Spenser and his patron Ralegh, the two men are shown alternately accompanying each other on the pipe: "He pip'd, I sung; and when he sung, I piped, / By chaunge of turnes, each making other mery, / Neither envying other, nor envied, / So piped we, untill we both were weary" (lines 76–79).

78 *Shorter Poems of Edmund Spenser*, ed. Oram, *et al.*, 527.

79 As Mary Claire Randolph observes, "the *Brehon Laws* [the ancient tribal laws of Gaelic Ireland] and minor legal tracts clearly show that the [Irish] folk attached a dread significance to words, any words apparently, in a recognizable order, repeated a specific number of times; to special words; to the chiming repetition of a victim's name . . . ; and to the recurrence of verbal echoes and interlocking rhymes (some rhymes were so deadly as to have been absolutely forbidden by law)." Randolph further claims that "The Celtic satirist was frankly out for actual blood or 'word-death.' In many instances he meant to destroy his victim, flesh, bone, nerve, and sinew; his victim's hounds, cattle, horses, pigs, wife, and children . . . In other cases, he meant to mutilate the victim's face so shamefully that, if it were a man, he could hold no high tribal office" ("The Medical Concept in English Renaissance Satiric Theory: Its Possible Relationships and Implications," *Studies in Philology* 38 [1941]: 132, 129).

80 Forrest G. Robinson, ed., *Sir Philip Sidney's An Apology for Poetry* (Indianapolis: Bobbs-Merrill, 1970), 89. Modern critics assume that Sidney must have had in mind the Irish bards' reputation for being able to rhyme rats to death. But there is enough evidence to show that the bards also claimed power over the life and death of their human subjects. The seventeenth-century Gaelic chroniclers known as the Four Masters asserted that the English deputy John Stanley had been rhymed to death by the bards as a punishment for his harsh treatment of the native intelligentsia (Randolph, "The Medical Concept," 139–40).

81 See Herbert Berry and E. K. Timings, "Spenser's Pension," *Review of English Studies* 11 (1960): 254–59.

82 Robert Payne, *A Briefe description of Ireland: Made in this yeare, 1589* (reprinted 1594), The English Experience 548 (New York: Da Capo Press, 1973), 10.

83 Rambuss, *Spenser's Secret Career*, 61. The idea that *The Faerie Queene* might serve as a vehicle for ingratiating Spenser with the court elite is articulated in one of the epic's commendatory verses. Rehearsing Spenser's transition from pastoral to epic, the verse, signed by "Hobynoll" (Harvey?), explains: "So moughtst thou now in these refyned layes, / delight the dainty eares of higher powers. / And so mought they in their deepe skanning skill / Alow and grace our Collyns flowing quill" (*The Faerie Queene*, ed. Hamilton, 739).

The kinds of worldly ambitions that were virtually axiomatic for the educated humanist like Spenser are cogently articulated in Bryskett's *Discourse* (*Works of Lodowick Bryskett*, 8–9).

84 Catherine Bates, *The Rhetoric of Courtship in Elizabethan Language and Literature* (Cambridge University Press, 1992), 132. Bates argues that Spenser's attitude to the patronage system involved "conflicting impulses toward gratitude and toward grievance" (137). She sees Spenser offering in Book Six of *The Faerie Queene* "a sustained meditation on the relations between a poet and his patron, one which manages to celebrate the patronage system while simultaneously and subtly reviling it" (138).

85 In *A View*, the Irish Carrowes are described as "a kynde of people that wander upp and downe gentlemens howses lyvinge onelye upon Cardes and dyce" (98–99). Earlier in *Colin Clout*, Colin refers to his responsibility "to warne yong shepheards wandring wit" (line 684).

86 See Henley, *Spenser in Ireland*, 103. A recurring theme of the contemporaneous *Complaints* volume is the low esteem in which poetry and poets are held in the modern world. Also, compare Geoffrey Hiller's remarks about Drayton and the bards: "What perhaps appealed to Drayton most of all in his reading about bards and Druids was the profound respect they enjoyed in the British community. Drayton had lamented bitterly and often the neglect and scorn he believed to be the lot of the poet in his own time" (" 'Sacred Bards' and 'Wise Druides': Drayton and his Archetype of the Poet," *ELH* 51 [1984]: 8–9).

87 Rambuss, *Spenser's Secret Career*, 61.

88 See Pádraig A. Breatnach, "The Chief's Poet," *Royal Irish Academy Proceedings* 83,C,3 (1983): esp. 55–60. Breatnach also usefully explains the different titles applied to various kinds of bards (37–38).

89 C. S. Lewis describes *The Faerie Queene* as the "work of one who is turning into an Irishman" (quoted in Anne Fogarty, "The Colonization of Language: Narrative Strategies in *A View of the Present State of Ireland* and *The Faerie Queene*, Book VI," in Coughlan, ed., *Spenser and Ireland*, 76).

90 *The Works of Lodowick Bryskett*, 28.

91 See W. L. Renwick ed., *"Daphnaida" and Other Poems by Edmund Spenser* (London: Scholartis Press, 1929), 182–84; Meyer, *Spenser's "Colin Clout"*, 165–66.

On Harvey's relationship with Spenser, see Muriel Bradbrook, "No Room at the Top: Spenser's Pursuit of Fame," *Elizabethan Poetry*, Stratford-Upon-Avon Studies 2 (New York: St. Martin's Press, 1960), 91–109. From Dublin in 1586, Spenser addressed a sonnet to Harvey, signing it "Your devoted frend, during life, Edmund Spencer" (*Shorter Poems of Edmund Spenser*, ed. Oram *et al.*, 773).

92 MacCarthy-Morrogh, *The Munster Plantation*, 70–106.

93 Quoted in *ibid.*, 96.
94 *C.S.P. Ireland 1588–92*, 62. For a detailed summary and examination of Herbert's colonial tract in relation to Spenser's *View*, see Brendan Bradshaw, "Robe and Sword in the Conquest of Ireland," in *Law and Government Under the Tudors*, ed. Claire Cross, David Loades, and J. J. Scarisbrick (Cambridge University Press, 1988), 139–62.
95 According to Nicholas Canny, the New English settlers in sixteenth-century Ireland "came to see themselves as a distinct people engaged in a special mission barely understood by those resident in England" ("Identity Formation," 176). While I am indebted to Canny's work on the emergence of a New English communal identity in Ireland, I emphasize more the diversity and divisions within this group. Brendan Bradshaw is right to doubt the "existence of a colonial consensus among the New English of Elizabethan Ireland." He highlights instead "the tensions within the colonial ethos" ("Robe and Sword," 162). Michael MacCarthy-Morrogh also debunks "the image of a monolithic new order in Munster" (*The Munster Plantation*, 92).
   The phrase "imagined community" is taken from Benedict Anderson, *Imagined Communities: Reflections on the Origin and Spread of Nationalism* (London: Verso, 1983).
96 See *DNB*, 10:5; and Kathy Lynn Emerson, *Wives and Daughters: The Women of Sixteenth Century England* (Troy, New York: Whitston, 1984), 118.
97 See Lupton for an extended discussion of Spenser's home-making project in Ireland ("Home-Making in Ireland," 119–45).
98 *The Arte of English Poesie* (Kent, Ohio: Kent State University Press, 1970), 22.
99 See Hore, "Irish Bardism," 167, 207–10; Ó Riordan, *The Gaelic Mind*, 1–2; J. E. Caerwyn Williams, *The Court Poet in Medieval Society* (London: Oxford University Press, 1971), 14–17.
   The continuing connection between seer and bard in the sixteenth century is suggested by Thomas Churchyard's remark that "certain blind prophesiers called rhymers" were sacked, whipped, and banished by the English at Kilkenny (quoted in Quinn, *The Elizabethans and the Irish*, 126–27).
   Herbert F. Hore, the editor of Thomas Smith's 1561 tract about the bards, notes that "The 'Ollav Filea' was the poet, and an eminent man. The 'Bard' was merely a versifier, or 'rhymer'. This inferior class were scoffed at by the Fileas as 'prattling Bards'" ("Irish Bardism," 207).
100 Cf. Rambuss's view that Spenser "fashions a counter to the court that has no place for him by exerting a nearly occult centripetal force to establish himself as the poem's center . . . Colin, so to speak, himself *holds court*" (*Spenser's Secret Career*, 99).
101 Sir William Herbert, *Croftus Sive De Hibernia Liber*, ed. and tr. Arthur Keaveney and John A. Madden (Irish Manuscripts Commission, 1992), 113–15.
102 Quoted in Henley, *Spenser in Ireland*, 106. On the Articles of Plantation and their early violation, see MacCarthy-Morrogh, *The Munster Plantation*, 30–45.

103 See Nicholas P. Canny, *The Upstart Earl: A Study of the Social and Mental World of Richard Boyle, First Earl of Cork, 1566–1643* (Cambridge University Press, 1982), 196n22, 127.

A similar fantasy is elaborated at the conclusion of Ben Jonson's *Irish Masque at Court* (1612) – a text produced at a later moment of tension in English–Irish relations – where the introduction of an Irish bard who sings to the accompaniment of two harps, signifies the harmonious union of England and Ireland. Paradoxically, the triumphal appearance of "the immortal bard" signals the subordination of Irish to English values, barbarism to civility, as first the rude Irish servants who form the anti-masque are silenced and then their Irish masters are magically transformed into elegantly attired court masquers (*Ben Jonson: The Complete Masques*, ed. Stephen Orgel [New Haven: Yale University Press, 1969], 211). The bard's praise of King James and his demand that James's Irish subjects show obedience, transform this threatening figure – who stands as a synecdoche for everything the English feared about Ireland – into a reassuring voice of loyalty (David Lindley, "Embarrassing Ben: The Masques for Frances Howard," *English Literary Renaissance* 16 [1986]: 354–55). For related discussions of the masque and the English appropriation of the Irish bard, see Ann Rosalind Jones and Peter Stallybrass, "Dismantling Irena: The Sexualizing of Ireland in Early Modern England," in *Nationalisms and Sexualities*, ed. Andrew Parker, Mary Russo, Doris Sommer, and Patricia Yaeger (New York: Routledge, 1992), 167–68, and Lisa Jardine, "Encountering Ireland: Gabriel Harvey, Edmund Spenser, and English Colonial Ventures," in *Representing Ireland*, ed. Bradshaw, Hadfield, and Maley, 60–61.

104 Thomas H. Cain, *Praise in "The Faerie Queene"* (Lincoln: University of Nebraska Press, 1978), 131.

105 *Shorter Poems of Edmund Spenser*, ed. Oram *et al.*, 523; Rambuss, *Spenser's Secret Career*, 99–100.

106 David Norbrook, *Poetry and Politics in the English Renaissance* (London: Routledge and Kegan Paul, 1984), 152. For Spenser's use of the Stesichorus and Helen legend in the "April" eclogue of *The Shepheardes Calender*, see Lane, *Shepheards Devises*, 20–21.

107 Barnabe Rich claimed that during the Tyrone rebellion, "it myght have byne called, a choyce & a specyal company, that had not thre *Iryshe* for one *Englyshe*: then was ther agayne wholl companyes of the *Iryshe* that wer raysed at hys Majesties charge" (Edward M. Hinton, "Rych's *Anothomy of Ireland*, with an Account of the Author," *PMLA* 55 (1940): 96). Also see G. A. Hayes-McCoy, "Strategy and Tactics in Irish Warfare, 1593–1601," *Irish Historical Studies* 2 (1940–41): 259–60.

108 The use of bards could sometimes become an issue of contention among the English administrators themselves. Even that ostensible enemy of bards, Sir John Perrot, was accused by his enemies on the Irish council of having bards sing his own praises (Pauline Henley, "The Treason of Sir John Perrot," *Studies: An Irish Quarterly* 21 (1932): 408, 411). Also see *The Works of Edmund Spenser*, ed. Greenlaw *et al.*, 9:360.

109 Quoted in Brian Ó Cuiv, "The Irish Language in the Early Modern Period,"

in *A New History of Ireland*, ed. T. W. Moody, F. X. Martin, and F. J. Byrne (Oxford: Clarendon Press, 1976), 3:521.

110 Randolph, "The Medical Concept," 140. This same incident is also discussed by Ó Riordan, *The Gaelic Mind*, 207, and by Jackson, "The Irish Language," 28.

111 For charges of disloyalty against bards supposedly in the service of the English, see Anne O'Sullivan, "Tadhg O'Daly and Sir George Carew," *Eigse* 14 (1971), 32.

2 REVERSING THE CONQUEST: DEPUTIES, REBELS, AND SHAKESPEARE'S "2 HENRY VI"

1 Unless otherwise stated, quotations from *1* and *2 Henry VI* are from Michael Hattaway's editions which are based on the Folio text (Cambridge University Press, 1991, 1992).

2 *Puzzling Shakespeare: Local Reading and Its Discontents* (Berkeley: University of California Press), ch.2.

3 The Treaty of Cateau-Cambresis required that France return Calais to English control after eight years of forfeit 500,000 crowns. But as historians point out, the English apparently realised in 1559 that this agreement would never be honored and that Calais had been permanently lost.

4 Holinshed, *Chronicles*, 6:152.

5 Sir D. Plunket Barton, *Links Between Ireland and Shakespeare* (London: Maunsel, 1919), 137–39. Art Cosgrove, "Principal Officers of the Central Government in Ireland, 1172–1922," *A New History of Ireland*, ed. Moody, Martin, and Byrne, 9:476–77.

6 According to Spenser's Munster neighbor, William Herbert, "When England was ablaze with civil wars, the Irish, given the opportunity, turned everything into confusion and in their savagery and fury destroyed civil law and society" (*Croftus Sive De Hibernia Liber*, ed. and tr. Arthur Keaveney and John A. Madden [Irish Manuscripts Commission, 1992], 83).

7 *The Itinerary of Fynes Moryson* (Glasgow: MacLehose, 1907–8), 2:169.

8 Thomas Wilson, *The State of England, Anno Dom. 1600*, ed F. J. Fisher, Camden Miscellany 16 (London, 1936), 42. On the operation of faction in Ireland, see Ciaran Brady, "Court, Castle and Country: the Framework of Government in Tudor Ireland," in *Natives and Newcomers: Essays on the Making of Irish Colonial Society 1534–1641*, ed. Ciaran Brady and Raymond Gillespie (Dublin: Irish Academic Press, 1986), esp. 41–49.

9 Quoted in Nicholas Canny, "Ireland as *Terra Florida*," in *Kingdom and Colony: Ireland in the Atlantic World, 1560–1800* (Baltimore: The Johns Hopkins University Press, 1988), 27.

10 In the quarto version of *2 Henry VI*, published in 1594 with the title "The First part of the Contention betwixt the two famous Houses of Yorke and Lancaster," the equivalent passage reads, "The wilde Onele my Lords, is up in Armes, / With troupes of Irish Kernes that uncontrold, / Doth plant themselves within the English pale" (*Shakespeare's Plays in Quarto*, ed. Michael J. B. Allen and Kenneth Muir [Berkeley: University of California Press, 1981], 59). The quarto's anachronistic reference to "Onele" helps to

accentuate the immediacy of the rebellion; in 1594, the name had multiple connotations: on one level it evoked any Gaelic chief, but more specifically it revived memories of Shane O'Neill, Elizabeth's great adversary earlier in the reign, and suggested the rising star of the moment in Gaelic Ireland – Hugh O'Neill, Earl of Tyrone. Fynes Moryson, following Camden, mentions that "from the first Conquest of Ireland, to the following warres betweene the Houses of Yorke and Lancaster in England, I find small or no mention of the Oneals greatnesse among the Irish Lords" (*Itinerary*, 2:168).

The quarto further heightens the urgency of the situation by referring specifically to a rebel incursion within "the English pale." Ironically, the rebels "plant themselves" in the Pale, thus displacing the English settlers who had undertaken to "plant" the country by cultivating the confiscated and supposedly "barren" land of the rebels and reclaiming it for "civilization."

All quarto references are to the Allen and Muir volume.

11 Edward Hall describes the Duke of York as being "in pryson (as the kynges deputie) in ye Realm of Irelande" (*The Union of the Two Noble and Illustre Families of Lancastre and Yorke* (1548), reprinted as *Hall's Chronicle; Containing the History of England, During the Reign of Henry the Fourth, and the Succeeding Monarchs, to the End of the Reign of Henry the Eighth* (London, 1809), 219.

12 Ireland is similarly construed in Marlowe's contemporaneous *Edward II* (c.1593). The enemies of Edward's lover, Gaveston, initially welcome his departure for Ireland as a banishment, only to realize how exile could easily be turned into a dangerous opportunity. "Know you not," says Mortimer junior, "Gaveston hath store of gold / Which may in Ireland purchase him such friends / As he will front the mightiest of us all" (*Edward II*, ed. W. Moelwyn Merchant [New York: W. W. Norton, 1967], 1.4.258–60). Edward sees Ireland as a safe-haven, first for Gaveston and later for himself (1.4.125–26; 4.5.3).

13 London and Dublin were, for most of the century, in touch only via slow and unreliable lines of communication, with news taking up to three weeks to travel from court to colony. For example, reports of Edward VI's death took nineteen days to reach Kilkenny. Elizabeth later complained about the lack of regular and reliable news from Ireland, but she refused to maintain royal posts between London and the points of embarkation for Ireland except in times of extreme crisis. Not until late 1598 was "a regular postal service" established (Cyril Bentham Falls, *Elizabeth's Irish Wars* [London: Methuen, 1950], 228; Mark Brayshay, "Royal Post-Horse Routes in England and Wales: the Evolution of the Network in the Later-Sixteenth and Early-Seventeenth Century," *Journal of Historical Geography* 17 [1991]: 384–85).

14 *Shakespeare's Europe*, 187–88; also see Ciaran Brady, "Court, Castle and Country," 41. On Moryson's career in Ireland, see Constantia Maxwell, *The Stranger in Ireland from the Reign of Elizabeth to the Great Famine* (London: Jonathan Cape, 1954), 68–77.

15 *Shakespeare's Europe*, 189–90.

16 On the identity of Derricke and his possible employment by Sir Henry Sidney, see John Derricke, *The Image of Irelande with a Discoverie of Woodkarne*, ed. David B. Quinn (Blackstaff Press, 1985), ix–xx. Other works defending the ex-

deputy included Sir Philip's manuscript tract on Ireland (of which only a fragment survives), and Edward Molyneux's note on Sir Henry's career in Holinshed's *Chronicles*. Philip's tract is reprinted in *Sir Philip Sidney: The Defence of Poetry, Political Discourses, Correspondence, Translations*, ed. Albert Feuillerat (Cambridge University Press, 1923), 46–50, and helpfully discussed in Katherine Duncan-Jones, *Sir Philip Sidney: Courtier Poet* (New Haven: Yale University Press, 1991), 135–37.

17 *The Image of Irelande*, 199.

18 *C.S.P. Ireland 1599–1600*, 362–63. My discussion of *The Image of Irelande* and the implicit competition it sets up between Sidney and his queen draws upon the remarks of Andrew Hadfield and Willy Maley in their introduction to *Representing Ireland: Literature and the Origins of Conflict, 1534–1660* (Cambridge University Press, 1993), 13–14, 195–96.

19 *The Image of Irelande*, 196–97.

20 Sidney's memoir in the State Papers Domestic is dated March 1, 1583.

21 "Sir Henry Sidney's Memoir of His Government in Ireland, 1583," ed. Herbert F. Hore, *The Ulster Journal of Archaeology*, 1st series, 8 (1860): 194; 3 (1856): 37–38, 87.

22 *Ibid.*, 8 (1860): 194.

23 *Ibid.*, 189–90.

24 *Ibid.*, 192, 194. Recognizing his dangerous position, Sidney confides after an especially painful recollection of his betrayal by former allies: "These things . . . had well nere broken my heart; and left the sword I would, and gone over without leave, though I had adventured the getting of the Queen's displeasure, and losse of myne owne lief, had not an obscure and base varlett called Rorie oge O'Moore stirred" (184).

25 *Hall's Chronicle*, 225–27, 232–33; Holinshed, *Chronicles*, 3:229–30.

26 Morris Palmer Tilley, *A Dictionary of the Proverbs in England in the Sixteenth and Seventeenth Centuries* (Ann Arbor: University of Michigan Press, 1950), 188.

27 Penry Williams, *The Tudor Regime* (Oxford: Clarendon Press, 1979), 338–45.

28 On French and Spanish interest in Ireland, see David Potter, "French Intrigue in Ireland During the Reign of Henri II, 1547–1559," *The International History Review* 5 (1983), 167; Jane E. A. Dawson, "William Cecil and the British Dimension of Early Elizabethan Foreign Policy," *History: The Journal of the Historical Association* 74 (1989), 202; Niall Fallon, *The Armada in Ireland* (Middletown, Connecticut: Wesleyan University Press, 1978), 2–8.

29 Shakespeare tropes to comic effect upon this image of Ireland as England's postern in *The Comedy of Errors*, where Dromio of Syracuse literally maps the female body of the kitchen maid, Nell. To the question "In what part of her body stands Ireland?" Dromio replies, "Marry, sir, in her buttocks. I found it out by the bogs" (3.2.116–18).

30 Although the quarto text is more specific and evocative than the Folio in its account of the uprising in Ireland, it makes no mention in either stage direction or dialogue of York's Irish army; York's later speech about Cade's Irish service is also missing from the quarto and the general emphasis placed by the Folio upon the importance of Ireland as a catalyst of the Cade/York

rebellion is removed. These particular absences may be the result of outside censorship or of self-censorship on the part of Shakespeare and his company, who may have thought it prudent to tone down the Irish overtones in the first published version of the play. Although not published until 1623, the Folio text, because it appears to be based on the author's original manuscripts, is generally seen as the basis of the 1594 quarto.

31 On Irish vagabonds in England and Wales, also see A. L. Beier, *Masterless Men: The Vagrancy Problem in England, 1560–1640* (London: Methuen, 1985), 10–11, 62–65.

32 Quoted in David Beers Quinn, *The Elizabethans and the Irish* (Ithaca: Cornell University Press, 1966), 144; Richard Carew, *The Survey of Cornwall*, ed. F. E. Halliday (London: Melrose, 1953), 139.

33 Quoted in Constantia Maxwell, *Irish History from Contemporary Sources (1509–1610)* (London: Allen and Unwin, 1923), 171–72.

34 For the oral traditions preserved in ballads and other ephemeral texts, see Edward D. Snyder, "The Wild Irish: a Study of Some English Satires Against the Irish, Scots, and Welsh," *Modern Philology* 17 (1919–20), 147–85.

35 The text of *Macbeth* leaves open the possibility that the kerns and gallow-glasses actually appear on stage. Thomas Hughes's *The Misfortunes of Arthur* (1587) also features a long-haired kern in a dumb show. As Kathleen Rabl writes of this play, "The allegorical pantomime of the dumbshow is drama-tized in the succeeding act by an Irish king, whose name [Gillamor] is taken from one of the drama's historical sources. His treacherous alliance with Mordred against the absent Arthur would certainly have recalled the con-temporary Irish situation" ("Taming the 'Wild Irish' in English Renaissance Drama," *National Images and Stereotypes*, ed. Wolfgang Zach and Heinz Kosok [Tubingen: G. Narr, 1987], 49).

36 *The Tragedy of Macbeth*, ed. Nicholas Brooke (Oxford University Press, 1990), 1.2.12–13, 1.2.30, 5.7.18–19.

37 See Spenser's remarks on the kern and gallowglass in *A View*, ed. Renwick, 93. Spenser's description follows closely John Hooker's comments in his edition of Gerald's *Expugnatio Hibernica* (Holinshed, *Chronicles*, 6:132).

38 Holinshed, *Chronicles*, 6:314–15. On Henry VIII's employment of Irish soldiers in his military campaigns, see Dean Gunter White, "Henry VIII's Irish Kerne in France and Scotland," *The Irish Sword* 3 (1957–58), 217–19.

39 *A View*, ed. Renwick, 92; Holinshed, *Chronicles*, 6:132.

40 Shannon Miller, "Coming Home to the New World: the Ralegh Circle in Ireland," unpublished manuscript. Also see Andrew Murphy, "Shakespeare's Irish History," *Literature and History* 5 (1996), 41.

41 See Marilynne S. Robinson's comments, cited in *The Second Part of Henry VI*, ed. Michael Hattaway (Cambridge University Press, 1991), 23n10.

42 Holinshed, *Chronicles*, 6:445–46.

43 Maxwell, *Irish History*, 219n1.

44 Edward H. Sugden, *A Topographical Dictionary to the Works of Shakespeare and his Fellow Dramatists* (Manchester University Press, 1925), 271.

45 See Gerald of Wales for this same trope (Holinshed, *Chronicles*, 6:230).

46 *Ibid.*, 3:220. John Stow also refers to "John Cade borne in Ireland" (*The Annales of England* [London, 1615], 391).

47 Hall, *Hall's Chronicle*, 429, 489.
48 R. B. Outhwaite writes, "the policy of mutual devastation of the Irish countryside began well before the era of Mountjoy, with whose campaigns such policies are usually associated," "Dearth, the English Crown, and the 'Crisis of the 1590s'," in *The European Crisis of the 1590s: Essays in Comparative History*, ed. Peter Clark (London: Allen and Unwin, 1985), 31.
49 *A View*, ed. Renwick, 135.
50 Richard Wilson, *Will Power: Essays on Shakespearean Authority* (Detroit: Wayne State University Press, 1993), 27.
51 "History and Ideology, Masculinity and Miscegenation: The Instance of *Henry V*," (written with Jonathan Dollimore) in Alan Sinfield, *Faultlines: Cultural Materialism and the Politics of Dissident Reading* (Berkeley: University of California Press, 1992), 125.
52 *Lanthorne and Candle-light, or the Bell-mans Seconnd Nights Walke* (London, 1608), in *Thomas Dekker: Selected Writings*, ed. E. D. Pendry, The Stratford-Upon-Avon Library 4 (Cambridge, Mass.: Harvard University Press, 1968), 287.
53 *The Mirror for Magistrates*, ed. Lily B. Campbell (Cambridge University Press, 1938), 171–81.
54 *The Image of Irelande*, 200.
55 *Ibid.*, 207.
56 *Ibid.*, half-title page, 210–11, 213–16.
57 *Ibid.*, 213.
58 Nicholas Canny, "The Ideology of English Colonization: From Ireland to America," *William and Mary Quarterly* 3rd series 30 (1973): 581–82.
59 *The Image of Irelande*, title page.
60 *Fragmenta Regalia: or Observations on Queen Elizabeth, Her Times and Favorites*, ed. John S. Cerovski (London: Associated University Presses, 1985), 65.
    Before serving as deputy, Perrot had been President of Munster under Sir Henry Sidney. In his Memoir, Sidney describes Perrot as "the most complete and best humoured man to deale with that nation that I know lyving" ("Sir Henry Sidney's Memoir," ed. Hore, *The Ulster Journal of Archaeology* 3 [1856]: 352).
61 E. C. S., *The Government of Ireland Under Sir John Perrot 1584–1588* (London, 1626). Allegedly, Perrot was known affectionately among the natives as "a *Righ*," the Gaelic term for chieftain ("Sir Henry Sidney's Memoir," ed. Hore, 3 [1856]: 356n81).
62 *A View*, ed. Renwick, 141.
63 Naunton, *Fragmenta Regalia*, 65; E.C.S., *The Government of Ireland*, 5, 60, 72, Preface 7.
64 E. M. Tenison, *Elizabethan England: Being a History of this Country in Relation to all Foreign Princes. From Original Manuscripts, many hitherto unpublished; co-ordinated with XVIth Century Printed Matter Ranging from Royal Proclamations to Broadside Ballads* (Royal Leamington Spa, 1950), 9:78. On Perrot's arrest and trial, see Hiram Morgan, "The Fall of Sir John Perrot," in *The Reign of Elizabeth I: Court and Culture in the Last Decade*, ed. John Guy (Cambridge University Press, 1995), 109–25.
65 *A Complete Collection of State Trials and Proceedings for High Treason and*

Other Crimes and Misdemeanors from the Earliest Period to the Year 1783, ed. T. B. Howell (London, 1816), 1:1316 (henceforth, *State Trials*); Pauline Henley, "The Treason of Sir John Perrot," *Studies: An Irish Quarterly* 5 (1932): 416.

66 *State Trials*, ed. Howell, 1:1325.

67 The consensus is that Shakespeare was working on *2 Henry VI* in the spring of 1592. Even if he finished it earlier, he is likely to have known of Perrot's predicament and the charges facing him. On the dating of the play, see H. R. Born, "The Date of *2, 3 Henry VI*," *Shakespeare Quarterly* 25 (1974): 323–24; Annabel Patterson, *Shakespeare and the Popular Voice* (Oxford: Basil Blackwell, 1989), 36.

68 When suspected of referring sympathetically to the downfall of the Earl of Essex in his play *Philotas* (1605), Samuel Daniel defended himself by pointing out, in Janet Clare's words, that "since history is repetitive, correspondences are inevitable and inadvertent" (*"Art Made Tongue-tied by Authority": Elizabethan and Jacobean Dramatic Censorship* [Manchester University Press, 1990], 127–28).

69 *The Life, Deedes, and death of Sir John Perrot, the Author Unknown*, ed. Richard Rawlinson (London, 1728), 309–10; *State Trials*, ed. Howell, 1:1317, 1324–25.

70 For a detailed study of the "intimately connected" cases of Perrot and O'Rourke, see Hiram Morgan, "Extradition and Treason-Trial of a Gaelic Lord: the Case of Brian O'Rourke," *The Irish Jurist* 22 (1987): 285–301.

71 *The Annales of England* (London, 1592), 1291–94.

72 Stow, *Annales* (1592), 1294. J. A. Sharpe notes that some "obdurate" criminals refused to make penitent speeches but instead railed at the injustice of their accusers and the legal system. I suspect there were actually more "obdurate" criminals than Sharpe (whose main source of evidence is the popular pamphlet and ballad accounts) allows (" 'Last Dying Speeches': Religion, Ideology, and Public Execution in Seventeenth-Century England," *Past and Present* 107 [1985]: 154–55).

73 D. Allen Carroll, "Rich and Greene: Elizabethan Beast Fables and Ireland," *Eire–Ireland* 25 (1990): 106–13. The pamphlet in which Greene defends Perrot is the same one in which he notoriously condemns Shakespeare as "an upstart Crow . . . with his *Tygers hart wrapt in a Players hyde*" – a phrase Greene adapts from a line in *3 Henry VI* (*The Second Part of King Henry VI*, ed. Andrew S. Cairncross [London: Methuen, 1962], xv). Was Greene's defense of Perrot and his characterization of Shakespeare as deceptively cruel in some way related to what Greene may have taken to be Shakespeare's unjust insinuations about Perrot's loyalty in *2 Henry VI*? The pamphlet was entered at the Stationers' Register on September 20, 1592.

74 For details of Rich's conflict with Loftus, see "Greene's Ghost in Ireland," in Edward M. Hinton, *Ireland Through Tudor Eyes* (Philadelphia: University of Pennsylvania Press, 1935), 86–91.

75 *State Trials*, ed. Howell, 1:1316, 1318.

76 *Fragmenta Regalia*, 67. Hiram Morgan confirms that Perrot "was deliberately and systematically framed," principally by his successor in Ireland Sir William Fitzwilliam, and Fitzwilliam's patron, Lord Burghley ("The Fall of Sir John Perrot," 109, 124–25).

77 Lacey Baldwin Smith, *Treason in Tudor England: Politics and Paranoia* (Princeton University Press, 1986). My discussion of treason draws upon Curt Breight's fine essay " 'Treason Doth Never Prosper': *The Tempest* and the Discourse of Treason," *Shakespeare Quarterly* 41 (1990): 1–28. Breight notes the Tudor regime's readiness to "create aristocratic scapegoats when such a move was necessary or advantageous" (17).

78 *State Trials*, ed. Howell, 1:1331.

79 For evidence of the state-manufactured Jesuit scare of the early 1590s, see the proclamation, "Establishing Commissions against Seminary Priests and Jesuits," in Paul L. Hughes and James F. Larkin, *Tudor Royal Proclamations* (New Haven: Yale University Press, 1969), 3:86–93. Jesuits were described as a "concealed infection, in the entrails of the kingdom" (*C.S.P. Domestic 1591–94*, 114). Penry Williams discusses the extension of the treason statutes in the 1580s to cover Jesuits and seminary priests: "For the first time no overt action or speech was required to incur condemnation for treason: merely *being* a Jesuit or seminarist was enough" (*The Tudor Regime*, 376).

80 *An Humble Supplication to Her Majestie*, ed. R. C. Bald (Cambridge University Press, 1953), 22.

81 Leaving the play politically "open" in this way was a strategy that evidently did Shakespeare no harm with the powerful men like the Lord Chancellor, Sir Christopher Hatton, and the Lord Chamberlain, Lord Hunsdon, who were both instrumental in Perrot's downfall. These were men whom the players might look to to help protect their interests at a time when the Lord Mayor and aldermen of the city were becoming increasingly hostile toward the public theater. Hunsdon, himself a deputy of sorts as Lord Warden General of the Marches of Scotland, was the chief commissioner at the trial. Some two years later, Shakespeare – now a member of the recently formed Lord Chamberlain's Men – was wearing Hunsdon's livery.

82 *Fragmenta Regalia*, 43.

83 *Elizabeth of England: Certain Observations Concerning the Life and Reign of Queen Elizabeth by John Clapham*, ed. Evelyn Plummer Read and Conyers Read (Philadelphia: University of Pennsylvania Press, 1951), 87.

84 The first quarto of *Richard II* was published in 1597 after its entry in the Stationers' Register on August 29. On the play's compositional time-frame, see *King Richard II*, ed. Peter Ure (London: Routledge, 1956), xxix–xxx. All references are to this edition.

85 *King Richard II*, 39–40; Phyllis Rackin, *Stages of History: Shakespeare's English Chronicles* (Ithaca: Cornell University Press, 1990), 100.

86 *Henry IV, Part 1*, ed. David Bevington (Oxford: Clarendon Press, 1987), 5.1.53. Peter Ure mentions the possibility of parallels being drawn "between Richard's and Elizabeth's management of Irish affairs" (*King Richard II*, lvii). Lily B. Campbell shows that the Elizabeth/Richard parallel was in circulation long before the Essex uprising and the queen's subsequent remark likening herself to Richard ("The Use of Historical Patterns in the Reign of Eliza-beth," *The Huntington Library Quarterly* 2 [1938]: 135–67).

87 *The First and Second Parts of John Hayward's The Life and Raigne of King Henrie IIII*, ed. John J. Manning. Camden 4th series. Vol. 42 (London: Royal Historical Society, 1991). Hayward explained that the Romans – his model

colonizers – prevented their governors from establishing an independent sovereignty by changing them every year (109–110).

88 Ireland – "the lowly west" – is the grave in which Richard's "sun sets weeping" (2.4.21). When he hears that the Welsh troops are gone, Richard says "Have I not reason to look pale and dead?" (3.2.79).

89 *Chronicles*, 6:259. Shakespeare would have also known from Holinshed that Richard had paid an earlier visit to Ireland in 1394 as a way of occupying himself after the death of his wife, Anne.

3   IRELAND, WALES, AND THE REPRESENTATION OF ENGLAND'S
    BORDERLANDS

1 See Edward H. Sugden, *A Topographical Dictionary to the Works of Shakespeare and his Fellow Dramatists* (Manchester University Press, 1925), 269–73; J. O. Bartley, *Teague, Shenkin and Sawney*: (Cork University Press, 1954); and Kathleen Rabl, "Taming the 'Wild Irish'" in *National Images and Stereotypes*, ed. Wolfgang Zach and Heinz Kosok (Tubingen: G. Narr, 1987). The essays by Michael Neill ("Broken English and Broken Irish: Nation, Language, and the Optic of Power in Shakespeare's Histories," *Shakespeare Quarterly* 45 [1994]: 1–32) and Andrew Murphy ("Shakespeare's Irish History," *Literature and History* 5 [1996]: 39–60) are notable exceptions.

2 For the regulation of drama, see Richard Dutton, *Mastering the Revels: The Regulation and Censorship of English Renaissance Drama* (University of Iowa Press, 1991); Janet Clare, *"Art Made Tongue-tied by Authority": Elizabethan and Jacobean Dramatic Censorship* (Manchester University Press, 1990). For a broader attempt to theorize censorship in early modern English culture, see Annabel Patterson, *Censorship and Interpretation: The Conditions of Writing and Reading in Early Modern England* (Madison: University of Wisconsin Press, 1984).

3 I borrow the term "faultlines" from Alan Sinfield's book of the same title. My thinking in general has been greatly influenced by Sinfield's highly nuanced writings on political and ideological processes in early modern Britain.

4 *The Description of Britain* in Holinshed, *Chronicles*, 1:10.

5 Quoted in James Lydon, "The Middle Nation," in James Lydon ed., *The English in Medieval Ireland* (Dublin: Royal Irish Academy, 1984), 26.

6 "The Beginnings of English Imperialism," *The Journal of Historical Sociology* 5 (1992): 406, 397–98. Also see W. R. Jones, "England Against the Celtic Fringe: A Study in Cultural Stereotypes," *Cahiers d'Histoire Mondiale* 13 (1971): 155–71; and R. R. Davies, *Domination and Conquest: The Experience of Ireland, Scotland and Wales 100–1300* (Cambridge University Press, 1990), 20–24.

7 Patrick Collinson, "The Elizabethan Church and the New Religion," in *The Reign of Elizabeth I*, ed. Christopher Haigh (Athens: University of Georgia Press, 1985), 181. According to recent reassessments, the spread of Protestantism even in England was slower, more uneven, and encountered more resistance from the local population than has traditionally been acknowledged. "The English Reformation," writes Christopher Haigh, "was not a joyous national rejection of outmoded superstition: it was a long drawn-out struggle between reformist minorities and a reluctant majority, and the

victory of the reformers was late and limited" ("Conclusion," in *The English Reformation Revised*, ed. Christopher Haigh [Cambridge University Press, 1987], 209).

8 John Penry, *Three Treatises Concerning Wales*, ed. David Williams (Cardiff: University of Wales Press, 1960), 28.

9 For the activities of the Council in the Marches against recusancy and superstition, see Penry Williams, *The Council in the Marches of Wales Under Elizabeth I* (Cardiff: University of Wales Press, 1958), ch.4.

10 Roger A. Mason, "Scotching the Brut: Politics, History, and National Myth in Sixteenth Century Britain," in *Scotland and England 1286–1815*, ed. Roger A. Mason (Edinburgh: John Donald, 1987), 71; Keith Brown, "The Price of Friendship: the 'Well Affected' and English Economic Clientage in Scotland before 1603," in *Scotland and England 1286–1815*, ed. Mason, 139–62.

11 R. R. Davies, *Domination and Conquest*, 86.

12 The last English assault against Scotland during Henry VIII's reign was meant to secure the marriage of the king's heir, Prince Edward, to the Scottish Princess, Mary Stuart. For more on the so-called "rough wooing," see Mason, "Scotching the Brut," 67.

13 Issued after the Scottish Wars of Independence in 1320, the Declaration of Arbroath affirmed the "unity of the nation of the Scots across the ages and of their distinctiveness as a people . . . it was their right to be a people and to enjoy the freedom to be such." Quoted in R. R. Davies, "The Peoples of Britain and Ireland 1100–1400," *Transactions of the Royal Historical Society*, 6th series 4 (1994), 19.

14 Ivor Bowen ed., *The Statutes of Wales* (London, 1908), 3.

15 R. R. Davies, "The Peoples of Britain," 19. Peter R. Roberts, "The 'Act of Union' in Welsh History," *The Transactions of the Honourable Society of Cymmrodorion* (1974): 49–72.

16 *C.S.P. Ireland 1598–99*, 440. When quoting the Irish state papers I have mostly relied on the printed calendar, although in some instances I have consulted the original manuscripts in the Public Record Office, London (P.R.O.). From 1585 on, as Cyril Falls notes, the calendars are virtually complete transcriptions of the originals (*Elizabeth's Irish Wars* [London: Methuen, 1950], 347–48).

17 Quoted in Penry Williams, "The Welsh Borderland Under Queen Elizabeth," *Welsh History Review* 1 (1960): 31. Also see Nicholas Canny, *The Elizabethan Conquest of Ireland: A Pattern Established, 1565–76* (Hassocks: Harvester, 1976), 97–99, on "the example of Wales" and Sir Henry Sidney's policy of establishing Welsh-style provincial presidencies in Ireland.

18 On Wynn and Owen, see chapter 6 of R. Ian Jack, *Medieval Wales* (Ithaca: Cornell University Press, 1972).

19 Bowen, ed., *The Statutes of Wales*, 75. Retrospectively invested by English and patriotic Welsh authors with a virtually magical power, the Act of Union demonstrated a remarkable historical tenacity. Witness Edmund Burke's comment in 1775 that: "As from that moment, as by a charm, the tumults subsided; obedience was restored; peace, order and civilization followed in the train of liberty. When the day-star of the English constitution had arisen in their hearts, all was harmony within and without" (quoted in Roberts, "The 'Act of Union'," 55).

20 Bowen, ed., *The Statutes of Wales*, 75–76. On laws against the Welsh language, see Roberts, "The 'Act of Union'," 54, 58. Also see Rees Davies, "Race Relations in Post-Conquest Wales: Confrontation and Compromise," *Transactions of the Honourable Society of Cymmrodorion* (1974–75), 34–35.

21 Quoted in Canny, *Elizabethan Conquest*, 97.

22 All parenthetical references to *Worthines* are to the reprint of 1876 (London: The Spenser Society). Churchyard writes about Ireland in *A generall rehearsall of warres* (1579); *The Miserie of Flaunders . . . Unquietnes of Ireland* (1579); and *A scourge for rebels: wherin are many notable services truly set out, touching the troubles of Ireland* (1584). There are also references to his Irish service in *A Pleasant Discourse of Court and Wars* (1596). For more on Churchyard's Irish canon, see Edward M. Hinton, *Ireland Through Tudor Eyes* (Philadelphia: University of Pennsylvania Press, 1935), 32.

23 One of Churchyard's immediate political objectives in *Worthines* is to clear Wales from the stain of treason after the recent prosecution of certain Welsh conspirators for their alleged involvement in a plot to kill the queen. One of the men, William Parry, was so reviled by "the common people [that they] would have torne [him] in peeces if the lawe had not proceeded" (6). Maurice Kyffin's *The Blessednes of Brytaine, or a Celebration of the Queenes Holyday* was another apology for Wales following Welsh participation in the Babington plot of 1586–87 (*DNB* 31:352–53; Roberts, "The 'Act of Union'," 67).

24 Parenthetical references to *The Historie* are to the facsimile in The English Experience series 163 (New York: Da Capo Press, 1969). Powel was also the first to publish Gerald's two Welsh works, *Descriptio Cambriae* and *Itinerarium Cambriae* in a Latin volume of 1585.

25 Two manuscripts of Geoffrey of Monmouth's *The History of the Kings of Britain*, include the following *explicit*: "The task of describing [the Welsh] kings, who succeeded from that moment onwards in Wales, I leave to my contemporary Caradoc of Llancarfan" (ed. and tr. Lewis Thorpe [Harmondsworth: Penguin, 1966], 284).

26 *DNB* 16:238.

27 Holinshed, *Chronicles*, 6:369.

28 *Ibid.*, 6:224–25.

29 *Ibid.*, 6:227.

30 On theories of resistance to established religious and secular power in early modern England, see the essays by Donald R. Kelley and Richard Strier in *The Historical Renaissance: New Essays on Tudor and Stuart Literature and Culture*, ed. Heather Dubrow and Richard Strier (Chicago University Press, 1988), and Richard Holmes, *Resistance and Compromise: The Political Thought of the Elizabethan Catholics* (Cambridge University Press, 1982), 134.

31 On Philip Sidney's ambitions in Ireland, see Katherine Duncan-Jones, *Sir Philip Sidney: Courtier Poet* (New Haven: Yale, 1991), 225.

32 *Henslowe's Diary*, ed. R. A. Foakes and R. T. Rickert (Cambridge University Press, 1961), 88.

33 Gerald of Wales, *The Journey Through Wales and The Description of Wales*, ed. and tr. Lewis Thorpe (Harmondsworth: Penguin, 1978), 162. On Gruffud ap Cynan, see R. R. Davies, *Conquest, Coexistence and Change: Wales*

1063–1415 (Oxford University Press, 1987), 43–45. Also from a modern perspective, see R. R. Davies, "Henry I and Wales," *Studies in Medieval History Presented to R. H. C. Davis*, ed. Henry Mayr-Harting and R. I. Moore (London: Hambledon Press, 1985), 133–47.

34 I use the term "English" loosely here to cover a broader and evolving range of identities including Norman, Anglo-Norman, and English proper.

35 R. R. Davies, "In Praise of British History," in *The British Isles 1100–1500: Comparisons, Contrasts and Connections*, ed. R. R. Davies (Edinburgh: John Donald, 1988), 22.

36 Quoted in Constantia Maxwell, *Irish History from Contemporary Sources (1509–1610)* (London: Allen and Unwin, 1923), 220.

37 All parenthetical references to *Edward I* are to page numbers in Frank S. Hook's edition. See his introduction for discussion of the play's date, text, sources, and analogues. *The Dramatic Works of George Peele*, ed. Frank S. Hook. Vol.2 of *The Life and Works of George Peele*, ed. Charles Tyler Prouty (New Haven: Yale University Press, 1961).

38 Hook ed., *George Peele*, 18; William Tydeman, "Peele's *Edward I* and the Elizabethan View of Wales," in *The Welsh Connection*, ed. William Tydeman (Llandysul, Dyfed: Gomer Press, 1986), 29–30.

39 In Anne Barton's influential formulation, Shakespeare's "tragical history" is distinguished from and ranked above the "comical history" of his contemporaries ("The King Disguised: Shakespeare's *Henry V* and the Comical History," in *The Triple Bond: Plays, Mainly Shakespearean, in Performance*, ed. Joseph G. Price [London: Penn. State University Press, 1975], 92–117). Recent critics, though, have questioned these designations and their political ramifications – especially their complicity in maintaining a restricted canon and securing a hierarchy of dramatic genres. Daryl W. Palmer argues that the prevailing strictures of classification governing Renaissance comedy tend to exclude a whole assortment of plays from the canon and hence from critical consideration. Drawing on the work of Franco Moretti, Palmer critiques the ways in which generic hierarchies of Renaissance plays are constructed and maintained – ways which inevitably marginalize "plays devoted to the practices of the lower orders and to multiplicity and open-endedness" (*Hospitable Performances: Dramatic Genre and Cultural Practices in Early Modern England* [West Lafayette: Purdue University Press, 1992], 39).

Richard Helgerson also sees that the effect of Barton's value-laden categories is to denigrate non-Shakespearean histories – plays that "represent a very different understanding of English history and the English polity than do Shakespeare's." Part of that "understanding" is the substitution of Shakespeare's "obsessive and compelling focus on the ruler" and questions of a ruler's legitimacy for an alternative focus on the common people of Britain and the problems of subjecthood. While Helgerson's characterization of the history plays performed by the Henslowe companies is persuasive, I am less convinced by his reductive view of Shakespeare as a rigidly establishment, pro-monarchical playwright (*Forms of Nationhood: The Elizabethan Writing of England* [University of Chicago Press, 1992], 230–31, 239).

40 Simon Shepherd, *Marlowe and the Politics of Elizabethan Theatre* (Brighton: Harvester, 1986), 49–51.

41 Clare, *"Art Made Tongue-tied"*, 55. "Peele's reluctance to offer any detailed account of the English campaign against the Welsh" is not, as Frank S. Hook argues, a sign of Peele's political naiveté but another example of "diffusion" or indirection designed to get the play past the censor (*George Peele*, 15).

42 "Peele's *Edward I*," 34.

43 On this episode, also see A. R. Braunmuller, *George Peele* (Boston: Twayne, 1983), 98–99.

44 Peele elsewhere exploits the shock value of the on-stage display of graphic bodily violence. "In the plot of the Admiral's *Battle of Alcazar* three characters are executed and disembowelled on stage" (Andrew Gurr, *The Shakespearean Stage, 1574–1642* [Cambridge University Press, 1992], 182). On this point, also see Braunmuller, *George Peele*, 98–99, and Shepherd, *Marlowe*, 62.

45 Hook ed., *George Peele*, 7; also see Braunmuller, *George Peele*, 87–88.

46 David Wiles, *The Early Plays of Robin Hood* (Cambridge: D. S. Brewer, 1981), 1.

47 See, for example, Edwin Greenlaw, Charles Grosvenor Osgood, Frederick Morgan Padelford, and Ray Heffner eds., *The Works of Edmund Spenser: A Variorum Edition* (Baltimore: John Hopkins University Press, 1932–49), 9:412–13; and *C.S.P. Ireland, 1598–99*, 255.

48 This encounter contradicts Anne Barton's argument about the outcome and function of "disguised ruler scenes" in non-Shakespearean "comical histories." Barton claims that in these plays, the ruler, after revealing his true identity, is reconciled to his previously disgruntled subject(s). But there is no reconciliation in *Edward I*. Lluellen's momentary admiration for Edward is one-sided; and Edward reiterates his "deadly hatred . . . to that notorious rebell" (Hook ed., *George Peele*, 141).

49 See *A View*, ed. Renwick, where the mantle serves, among other things, as a disguise-cum-portable domicile-cum-shield-cum-baby cradle (65–69). The Irish mantle has also proven a compelling object to modern critics. For one of the best discussions, see Anne Rosalind Jones and Peter Stallybrass, "Dismantling Irena: The Sexualizing of Ireland in Early Modern England," in *Nationalisms and Sexualities*, ed. Andrew Parker, Mary Russo, Doris Sommer, Patricia Yaeger (New York: Routledge, 1992), 165–66.

50 *Historical Journal* 21 (1978): 475–502.

51 Michael MacCarthy-Morrogh, *The Munster Plantation: English Migration to Southern Ireland, 1583–1641* (Oxford: Clarendon Press, 1986), 339–41; Hiram Morgan, *Tyrone's Rebellion: The Outbreak of the Nine Years War in Tudor Ireland* (Woodbridge, Suffolk: The Boydell Press. The Royal Historical Society, 1993), ch.1.

52 "The Road to the *View*: on the Decline of Reform Thought in Tudor Ireland," in Patricia Coughlan ed., *Spenser and Ireland: An Interdisciplinary Perspective* (Cork University Press, 1989), 25–45.

53 *C.S.P. Ireland, 1588–92*, 225.

54 Hook ed., *George Peele*, 204–5, 37.

55 Braunmuller, *George Peele*, 94; also see Shepherd, *Marlowe*, 53–54.

56 Stephen Orgel, "The Authentic Shakespeare," *Representations* 21 (1988):24. Also see Margreta De Grazia and Peter Stallybrass on the myth of the unitary and stable dramatic work, "The Materiality of the Shakespearean Text," *Shakespeare Quarterly* 44 (1993): 257–62.

4   THE TYRONE REBELLION AND THE GENDERING OF COLONIAL
    RESISTANCE IN "I HENRY IV"

1 John Gillingham, "Images of Ireland 1170–1600: the Origins of English
  Imperialism," *History Today* 37 (1987): 21.
2 *The Oxford Illustrated History of Ireland*, ed. R. F. Foster (Oxford University
  Press, 1991), 83.
      On the trend among historians to place English history in the broader
  context of British concerns, see Steven Ellis, "'Not Mere English': the British
  Perspective, 1400–1650," *History Today* 38 (1988): 41–48. Ellis insists on the
  interconnectedness of early modern England's borderlands: "the far north of
  England, the Welsh marches, and the Irish lordships . . . [posed] common
  problems . . . to English government . . . [while] Gaelic Scotland and Gaelic
  Ireland formed a single cultural entity" (43). My concern in this chapter is
  with the symbolic dimension of these connections.
      The Cornish could also be numbered among these suspect "outlandish
  peoples." Richard Carew observed in his description of Cornwall that "the
  western people . . . together with the Welsh, their ancient countrymen" still
  fostered "a fresh memory of their expulsion [from England] long ago by the
  English." As well as "bitter[ly] repining" at their past subjugation and
  marginalization by the English, "the worst sort" among the Cornish continued to resist the English by "combining against and working them all the
  shrewd turns which with hope of impunity they can devise" (*The Survey of
  Cornwall*, ed. F. E. Halliday [London: Melrose, 1953], 139).
3 Glanmor Williams, *Recovery, Reorientation, and Reformation: Wales
  c.1415–1642* (Oxford: Clarendon Press, 1987), 16.
4 Quoted in Penry Williams, *The Council in the Marches of Wales under
  Elizabeth I* (Cardiff: University of Wales Press, 1958), 99; Joel Hurstfield, *The
  Elizabethan Nation* (London: British Broadcasting Corporation, 1964), 78. At
  the trial of Sir John Perrot, it was alleged that the traitor Sir William Stanley
  had said that if the Spanish wanted to invade England they should choose
  Milford Haven as a landing place because "they should find better friends in
  Wales than the queen had, and some of them were near the queen" (*State
  Trials*, ed. Howell, 1:1326).
5 *C.S.P. Ireland 1598–99*, 461–62.
6 John J. Manning ed., Camden 4th series, Vol. 42 (London: Royal Historical
  Society, 1991). The Authorities who questioned Hayward and his publisher
  saw the work as alluding to the management of the current Irish crisis (29,
  109–10, 190–95).
7 In his edition of the play, David Bevington argues for late 1597 as the most
  likely date of composition. See *Henry IV, Part 1* (Oxford: Clarendon Press,
  1987), 8–9. All references are to this edition.
8 *C.S.P. Ireland 1596–97*, 233.
9 *Ibid.*, 116–117. For the development of a news service in Elizabethan
  England, see H. S. Bennett, *English Books and Readers, 1558–1603: Being a
  Study in the History of the Book Trade in the Reign of Elizabeth I* (Cambridge
  University Press, 1965), 220–47.
10 On the Munster rebellion, see Nicholas Canny, *The Elizabethan Conquest of
   Ireland: A Pattern Established, 1565–76* (Hassocks: Harvester, 1976).

11 G. A. Hayes-McCoy, "The Completion of the Tudor Conquest and the Advance of the Counter-Reformation, 1571–1603," in *A New History of Ireland*, ed. T. W. Moody, F. X. Martin, and F. J. Byrne (Oxford: Clarendon Press, 1976), 3:112.

12 *Ibid.*, 117–23.

13 G. A. Hayes-McCoy, "The Army of Ulster, 1593–1601," *The Irish Sword* 1 (1949/1953): 105–117.

14 Quoted in Sir Robert Naunton, *Fragmenta Regalia: or Observations on Queen Elizabeth, Her Times and Favorites*, ed. John S. Cerovski (London: Associated University Presses, 1985), 102 n111. The proclamation declaring Tyrone a traitor is reprinted in Constantia Maxwell, *Irish History from Contemporary Sources (1509–1610)* (London: Allen and Unwin, 1923), 175.

The period between June 1595 and June 1598, when concerted hostilities resumed, was generally one of sporadic fighting, treaties, pardons, and duplicities on both sides. The first major battle of the rebellion was fought at the Yellow Ford in August 1598, where the English were routed (Hayes-McCoy, "The Completion of the Tudor Conquest," 124–25; Cyril Bentham Falls, *Elizabeth's Irish Wars* [London: Methuen, 1950], chs. 13–15). On the chronology of Tyrone's rebellious career, also see Steven Ellis, *Tudor Ireland: Crown, Community and the Conflict of Cultures, 1470–1603* (London: Longman, 1985), 298–312, esp. 303–7, for Tyrone and a nationalist confederacy; and Hiram Morgan, *Tyrone's Rebellion: The Outbreak of the Nine Years War in Tudor Ireland* (Woodbridge, Suffolk: The Boydell Press. The Royal Historical Society, 1993).

15 Hayes-McCoy, "The Completion of the Tudor Conquest," 118.

16 *A View*, ed. Renwick, 113.

17 *The Description of Ireland, and the State thereof as it is at this Present in Anno 1598*, ed. Edmund Hogan (London, 1878), 33.

18 *C.S.P. Ireland 1596–97*, 487–90.

19 The Percys' reputation as "overmighty subjects" continued into Elizabeth's reign. In 1572 Thomas Percy, seventh Earl of Northumberland, was executed for his leading part in the Northern Rebellion that aimed to restore Catholicism and establish Mary Stuart as Elizabeth's successor. And in 1585 Thomas's brother Henry died in the Tower where he was imprisoned on suspicion of aiding Catholic malcontents (*DNB* 15: 409–11).

20 Quoted in Nicholas Canny, "The Ideology of English Colonization: from Ireland to America," *William and Mary Quarterly* 3rd series 30 (1973): 591.

21 See James Lydon, "The Middle Nation," in *The English in Medieval Ireland*, ed. James Lydon (Dublin: Royal Irish Academy, 1984), on early attempts at preventing the so-called "English of Ireland" from assimilating themselves to Gaelic culture (13–18).

22 *A View*, ed. Renwick, 62, 84, 86.

23 Quoted in Hayes-McCoy, "The Completion of the Tudor Conquest," 123; also see Ellis, *Tudor Ireland*, 303.

24 Nicholas Canny, "The Permissive Frontier: Social Control in English Settlements in Ireland and Virginia, 1550–1650," in *The Westward Enterprise: English Activities in Ireland, the Atlantic, and America, 1480–1650*, ed. K. R. Andrews, N. P. Canny, and P. E. H. Hair (Liverpool University Press, 1978), 23–24; also see, A. L. Rowse, *The Expansion of Elizabethan England* (London: Macmillan, 1955), 417, 420–21.

25 *A View*, ed. Renwick, 196.
26 The most detailed account of Lee's career, writings, and cultural identity is Hiram Morgan's "Tom Lee: The Posing Peacemaker," in *Representing Ireland: Literature and the Origins of Conflict, 1534–1660*, ed. Brendan Bradshaw, Andrew Hadfield, and Willy Maley (Cambridge University Press, 1993), 132–65. Also see E. K. Chambers, *Sir Henry Lee: An Elizabethan Portrait* (Oxford: Clarendon Press, 1936), 185–203, esp. 190–91.
27 Nicholas Canny, "Early Modern Ireland c.1500–1700," in *The Oxford Illustrated History of Ireland*, ed. Foster, 126.
28 Quoted in Chambers, *Sir Henry Lee*, 194. Richard Bagwell, *Ireland Under the Tudors* (London: Holland Press, 1963), 3:238; *DNB* 32:382.
29 Throughout this section I have found helpful Patrick Brantlinger's treatment of "going native" (or "backsliding") in Victorian Africa. The fact that this cultural trope persisted across several centuries indicates the extent to which colonizing societies felt constantly insecure about the integrity of their missions ("Victorians and Africans: the Genealogy of the Myth of the Dark Continent," in *"Race," Writing, and Difference*, ed. Henry Louis Gates, Jr. [University of Chicago Press, 1986], 213–17).
30 Quoted in Falls, *Elizabeth's Irish Wars*, 198.
31 *C.S.P. Ireland 1596–97*, 41.
32 *Ibid.*, 86–87.
33 Quoted in Paul A. Jorgensen, "The 'Dastardly Treachery' of Prince John of Lancaster," *PMLA* 76 (1961): 490.
34 See Sean O'Faolain, *The Great O'Neill: A Biography of Hugh O'Neill, Earl of Tyrone, 1550–1616* (New York: Duell, Sloan, and Pearce, 1942), 245.
    Burgh's colorful rhetoric was not well received by Robert Cecil who replied that "your style to the rebel is held too curious . . . you do in all your writings a little too much imitate the succinctness of Tacitus, which for a man to write to a Council is not held so proper" (*C.S.P. Ireland 1596–97*, 320, xxiii). On the political implications of the Tacitean style which was later associated with the Essex circle, see Mervyn James, *Society, Politics and Culture: Studies in Early Modern England* (Cambridge University Press, 1986), 418–19.
35 Quoted in O'Faolain, *The Great O'Neill*, 234. Also compare "the great Devil of the North" (*C.S.P. Ireland 1598–99*, 505). At 2.4.357, Falstaff refers to "that devil Glendower."
36 *Chronicles*, 3:22.
37 For discussions of a general English ambivalence toward Ireland which oscillates between revulsion and admiration, see Patricia Fumerton, "Exchanging Gifts: the Elizabethan Currency of Children and Poetry," *ELH* 53 (1986): 256, and David Quinn, *The Elizabethans and the Irish* (Ithaca: Cornell University Press, 1966), 61.
38 *The Description of Ireland*, ed. Hogan, 33. Although Hiram Morgan argues that modern historians are wrong in thinking that Tyrone was educated in England, many contemporary observers evidently believed he was (*Tyrone's Rebellion*, 11–12). The French ambassador De Maisse wrote in 1597 that Tyrone "was brought up at the English court," while Thomas Gainsford opined in his 1619 biography that "in his yonger time he trooped in the streets of *London* with sufficient equipage, and orderly respect." See *A Journal of all*

that was Accomplished by Monsieur De Maisse Ambassador in England from King Henri IV to Queen Elizabeth Anno Domini 1597, ed. G. B. Harrison (London: Nonesuch Press, 1931), 49; *The True Exemplary, and Remarkable History of the Earle of Tirone* (London, 1619), 14.

39 On Glendower's training and service in England, see Herbert V. Fackler, "Shakespeare's 'Irregular and Wild' Glendower: the Dramatic Use of Source Materials," *Discourse: A Review of the Liberal Arts* 13 (1970): 311–12, and J. E. Lloyd, *Owen Glendower* (Oxford: Clarendon Press, 1931).

40 *C.S.P. Ireland 1599–1600*, 223.

41 *The Letters and Epigrams of Sir John Harington, Together with "The Prayse of Private Life"*, ed. Norman Egbert McClure (Philadelphia: University of Pennsylvania Press, 1930), 77–78; Gainsford, *History of the Earle of Tirone*, 16. For further discussion of the "transgressive and hybrid figure" of Tyrone, see Andrew Hadfield and John McVeagh, eds., *Strangers to that Land: British Perceptions of Ireland from the Reformation to the Famine* (Ulster Editions and Monographs 5. Gerrards Cross: Colin Smythe, 1994), 88–96.

42 On Glendower's son, see Holinshed, *Chronicles*, 3:21, 34.

43 *C.S.P Ireland 1592–96*, 231.

44 *The Itinerary of Fynes Moryson* (Glasgow: MacLehose, 1907–8), 2:178.

45 *A View*, ed. Renwick, 93–94.

46 Holinshed, *Chronicles*, 6:68. On the three-tier organization of the Irish soldiery also see John Dymmok's account in Maxwell, *Irish History*, 221–22.

47 Quoted in D. L. W. Tough, *The Last Years of a Frontier: A History of the Borders During the Reign of Elizabeth* (Oxford: Clarendon Press, 1928), 34.

48 *The Shoole of Abuse, Conteining a Plesaunt invective against Poets, Pipers, Plaiers, Jesters, and such like Caterpillers of a Commonwelth* (London, 1579), 24.

49 This is a phrase Jean E. Howard uses in her helpful overview of the methodologies and practices of New Historicist Renaissance critics ("The New Historicism in Renaissance Studies," *English Literary Renaissance* 16 [1986]: 35).

50 See S. P. Zitner, "Staging the Occult in *1 Henry IV*," in *Mirror up to Shakespeare: Essays in Honour of G. R. Hibbard*, ed. J. C. Gray (Toronto University Press, 1984), 145.

51 *Calender of the Carew Manuscripts Preserved in the Archiepiscopal Library at Lambeth, 1515–1624*, ed. J. S. Brewer and William Bullen (London: 1867–73), *1575–88*, 573. Behind Glendower's preoccupation with prophecies and astrological signs is perhaps more disdain for the superstitions that Protestant Englishmen associated with the popular Catholicism of their western neighbors.

52 *C.S.P. Ireland, 1598–99*, 169.

53 Henslowe identified *stewtley* as a new play in December 1596. The play was performed ten times between then and June 1597, although it was not entered in the Stationers' Register until August 1600. On the vexed question of the relationship between the play as performed and the published text, see Judith C. Levinson, ed., *The Famous History of Captain Thomas Stukeley 1605*, The Malone Society Reprints (Oxford University Press, 1970 [1975]), vii–xix; and

E. K. Chambers, *The Elizabethan Stage* (Oxford: Clarendon Press, 1923), 4:47. All references are to Levinson's edition.

Also see Joseph Candido, "Captain Thomas Stukeley: the Man, the Theatrical Record, and the Origins of Tudor 'Biographical Drama'," *Anglia* 105 (1987): 50–68.

54 Since few records survive about *Stukeley*'s performance and none about its reception and possible censorship, we do not know whether the printed version of the play reflects what was actually seen on stage. That the play was performed and printed at all, though, should make us wary of accepting too monolithic and inflexible a view of dramatic censorship in the late sixteenth century.

55 Before the reopening of the indoor "private" theaters at the turn of the century, Inns of Court members mingled with citizens, laborers, and others at public amphitheaters like the Rose (Andrew Gurr, *Playgoing in Shakespeare's London* [Cambridge University Press, 1988], 67–69). On Donne and Ireland, see R. C. Bald, *John Donne: A Life* (Oxford University Press, 1970), 160–61, and Andrew Murphy, "Gold Lace and a Frozen Snake: Donne, Wotton, and the Nine Years War," *Irish Studies Review* 8 (1994): 9–11.

56 For the textual problems in these scenes, see Levinson's edition, vi–vii, xix; and J. O. Bartley, *Teague, Shenkin and Sawney: Being an Historical Study of the Earliest Irish, Welsh and Scottish Characters in English Plays* (Cork University Press, 1954), 14, 42, 272.

57 Joseph Leerssen, *Mere Irish and Fior-Ghael: Studies in the Idea of Irish Nationality, its Development and Literary Expression Prior to the Nineteenth Century* (Philadelphia: John Benjamins, 1986), 93.

58 In Peele's *The Battle of Alcazar* (c.1588–89), the Tamburlaine-like Stukeley boasts: "I am the marques now of Ireland made, / And will be shortly king of Ireland" (quoted in Candido, "Captain Thomas Stukeley," 56).

If Stukeley were an ambiguous hero on the public stage and in popular ballads, he was remembered in official circles as the worst sort of traitor and fugitive: "the rakehell" as Burghley called him, the leader of "certain savage rebels ... given to bestiality" in the queen's words (quoted in *The School of Shakspere*, ed. Richard Simpson [London: Chatto and Windus, 1878], 1:41, 85).

59 A marginal gloss attributes the passage to Abraham Fleming who derives it from Thomas Walsingham's *Hypodigme*. As co-editor of the second edition of the *Chronicles*, Fleming was responsible for various changes and additions to the first edition of 1577. Hereafter, page references to the *Chronicles* appear parenthetically

60 Citing the work of Mary Douglas, Louis Adrian Montrose describes the human body "as the primary symbolic medium for the articulation of social relations" ("'Shaping Fantasies': Figurations of Gender and Power in Elizabethan Culture," *Representations* 2 [1983]: 91n31).

61 Peter Stallybrass and Allon White discuss these two models of the body and note the special attachment of colonized peoples to carnivalesque and grotesque forms (*The Politics and Poetics of Transgression* [Ithaca: Cornell University Press, 1986], 11–12).

62 See Richard Halpern, "Puritanism and Maenadism in *A Mask*," in *Rewriting the Renaissance: The Discourses of Sexual Difference in Early Modern Europe*,

ed. Margaret W. Ferguson, Maureen Quilligan, and Nancy J. Vickers (University of Chicago Press, 1986), 94–95.

63 English attitudes toward, and legislation regarding, the Welsh and Irish languages are complex and often contradictory. On English efforts to preserve the Irish language and the queen's own interest in learning it, see Brian Ó Cuiv, "The Irish Language in the Early Modern Period," in *A New History of Ireland*, ed. Moody *et al.*, 3:511–13.

64 *Stages of History: Shakespeare's English Chronicles* (Ithaca: Cornell University Press, 1990), 148.

65 In *The Faerie Queene*, Spenser uses "degendered" as a synonym for degenerated – the former word implying both general moral decay and sexual impairment (*The Faerie Queene*, ed. Hamilton, 527).

66 *C.S.P. Ireland 1598–99*, 300.

67 Quoted in Canny, *Elizabethan Conquest*, 139.

68 *A New Description of Ireland* (London, 1610), 23.

69 Gayle Whittier points out that "By attributing the bestial action to Welsh-women only . . . Shakespeare selectively heightens a cultural prejudice [against Celtic societies], vividly associating the female sex with an act of mutilation destructive of male identity" ("Falstaff as a Welshwoman: Uncomic Androgyny," *Ball State University Forum* 20 [1979]: 25).

70 "Rethinking Text and History," *Literature Teaching Politics* 2 (1983): 103. David Underdown claims that around 1600 there was a heightened awareness bordering on moral panic of the increasing numbers of masterless women in the realm and especially around London (*Revel, Riot, and Rebellion: Popular Politics and Culture in England, 1603–1660* [Oxford University Press, 1986], 37–38).

71 Christina Larner, *Enemies of God: The Witch-Hunt in Scotland* (London: Chatto, 1981), 199.

72 *A View*, ed. Renwick, 67–68. Stephen Greenblatt also notes that Englishmen felt "threatened in Ireland by the native women" (*Renaissance Self-Fashioning: From More to Shakespeare* [University of Chicago Press, 1980], 185).

73 Quoted in *Illustrations of Irish History and Topography, Mainly of the Seventeenth Century*, ed. C. Litton Falkiner (London: Longmans, 1904), 315. Ralph A. Houlbrooke discusses the practices of swaddling and corsetting in England. Swaddling was thought necessary to prevent the child from "going down on all fours like an animal" (*The English Family, 1450–1700* [London: Longman, 1984], 132). Also see Anne Laurence, "The Cradle to the Grave: English Observation of Irish Social Customs in the Seventeenth Century," *The Seventeenth Century* 3 (1988): 63–84.

74 Quoted in Herbert Hore, "Irish Bardism in 1561," *The Ulster Journal of Archaeology* 1st series 6 (1858): 167, 210–11. For the claim that the women acted as spies for the Irish rebels, see Hore, 211, and *A View*, ed. Renwick, 69–70. Also see Peter Stallybrass, "Time, Space, and Unity: the Symbolic Discourse of *The Faerie Queene*," in *Patriotism: The Making and Unmaking of British National Identity*, ed. Raphael Samuel (London: Routledge, 1989), 3:206. I have benefited from all of Stallybrass's work on the construction of national identities in early modern Britain.

75 *C.S.P. Ireland 1592–96*, 487; *C.S.P. Ireland 1596–97*, 14.

76 See William Palmer, "Gender, Violence, and Rebellion in Tudor and early Stuart Ireland," *Sixteenth Century Journal* 23 (1992): 700–1.

77 O'Faolain, *The Great O'Neill*, 121; quoted in Mona L. Schwind, "'Nurse to all Rebellions': Grace O'Malley and Sixteenth-Century Connacht," *Eire–Ireland* 13 (1978): 45.

78 Quoted in Anne Chambers, *Granuaile: The Life and Times of Grace O'Malley, c.1530–1603* (Dublin: Wolfhound, 1979), 93; also see Schwind, "'Nurse to all Rebellions'," 43.

79 Geoffrey Fenton quoted in Rowse, *The Expansion of Elizabethan England*, 417.

80 Quoted in Quinn, *The Elizabethans and the Irish*, 127.

81 Quoted in *The Works of Edmund Spenser: A Variorum Edition*, ed. Edwin Greenlaw, Charles Grosvenor Osgood, Frederick Morgan Padelford, and Ray Heffner (Baltimore: Johns Hopkins University Press, 1932–49), 3:174.

82 Matthew Wikander as quoted in Rackin, *Stages of History*, 172. On this episode, also see Greenblatt, *Renaissance Self-Fashioning*, ch.4.

83 Linda Austern observes that "the female musician came to personify sensual intoxication, inspiring either pure spiritual ecstasy or destructive physical passion . . . Both music and feminine beauty were considered intense inflamers of the passions, and, when used together, resulted in an uncontrollable sensual experience for the masculine listener" ("'Sing Againe Syren': the Female Musician and Sexual Enchantment in Elizabethan Life and Literature," *Renaissance Quarterly* 42 [1989]: 420, 447).

84 "Fathers, Sons, and Brothers in *Henry V*," in *William Shakespeare's Henry V*, ed. Harold Bloom (New York: Chelsea, 1988), 124–25.

85 Numerous critics have remarked on the dynamics of appropriation and transference between Hotspur and Hal; see, for example, Derek Cohen, "The Rite of Violence in *1 Henry IV*," *Shakespeare Survey* 38 (1985): 83.

86 The importance of Shrewsbury is suggested by the full title of the play as it appeared in the Stationers' Register: "The historye of Henry iiijth with his battaile of Shrewsburye against Henry Hottspurre of the Northe with the conceipted mirthe of Sir John ffalstof" (Chambers, *The Elizabethan Stage*, 3:484–85).

87 See Penry Williams, "The Welsh Borderland under Queen Elizabeth," *Welsh History Review* 1 (1960): 20–21; Glanmor Williams, *Recovery, Reorientation*, ch.11.

88 J. H. Andrews, "Geography and Government in Elizabethan Ireland," in *Irish Geographical Studies*, ed. Nicholas Stephens and Robin E. Glasscock (Queen's University, Belfast, 1970), 182; Sir William Gerard as quoted in Hayes-McCoy, "The Completion of the Tudor Conquest," 103.

89 *Acts of the Privy Council 1596–97*, 418; *Historical Manuscripts Commission, 4th Report*, 337. For further details, see the section, "State of the Pale under Elizabeth," in Maxwell, *Irish History*, 388–89.

90 Graham Holderness, Nick Potter, and John Turner, *Shakespeare: The Play of History* (London: Macmillan, 1988), 59.

91 Mary Douglas, *Purity and Danger: An Analysis of the Concepts of Pollution and Taboo* (London: Ark, 1985), 115. For an excellent discussion of the analogy between the borders of the realm and the borders of the royal female

body, see Peter Stallybrass, "Patriarchal Territories: the Body Enclosed," in *Rewriting the Renaissance*, ed. Ferguson, Quilligan, and Vickers, 129.

92 *A Discovery of the True Causes Why Ireland Was Never Entirely Subdued*, ed. James P. Myers, Jr. (Washington D. C.: The Catholic University of America, 1988), 190.

93 Quoted in Joel Hurstfield, "The Succession Struggle in Late Elizabethan England," in *Elizabethan Government and Society: Essays Presented to Sir John Neale*, ed. S. T. Bindoff, J. Hurstfield, and C. H. Williams (University of London Press, 1961), 370. Richard McCoy discusses "the decline of the cult of Elizabeth" in the last years of her reign and the queen's ever more desperate attempts to shore it up. See "'Thou Idol Ceremony': Elizabeth I, *The Henriad*, and the Rites of the English Monarchy," in *Urban Life in the Renaissance*, ed. Susan Zimmerman and Ronald F. E. Weissman (Associated University Presses, 1989), 259–60; and "Lord of Liberty: Francis Davison and the Cult of Elizabeth," in *The Reign of Elizabeth I: Court and Culture in the Last Decade*, ed. John Guy (Cambridge University Press, 1995), 212–28.

94 *Henry V*, in *The First Folio of Shakespeare*, prepared by Charlton Hinman (New York: W. W. Norton, 1968), TLN 2882.

95 Hayes-McCoy, "The Completion of the Tudor Conquest," 124; also see *Historical Manuscripts Commission, 4th Report*, 337; and Falls, *Elizabeth's Irish Wars*, 224.

96 References are to Giorgio Melchiori's edition, *The Second Part of King Henry IV* (Cambridge University Press, 1989). Melchiori conjectures that in an earlier form the two parts of *Henry IV* existed as a single play, "the ur-*Henry IV*" (9–15).

97 For suggestive comments on the relevance of the Irish wars to *2 Henry IV*, see Jorgensen, "'Dastardly Treachery'," 488–92. Jorgensen likens Henry IV's "interminable series of battles" to England's wars in Ireland and also argues that John of Lancaster's act of grand deception at Gaultree Forest is indicative of the increasingly "treacherous" tactics (including the Smerwick massacre) employed by crown forces against the Irish (490–91).

98 Holinshed, *Chronicles*, 6:222.

5   "A SOFTE KIND OF WARRE": SPENSER AND THE FEMALE
    REFORMATION OF IRELAND

1 *C.S.P. Ireland 1588–92*, 142–43. The episode and its aftermath are also discussed on 141, 273, and 336 of the same volume.

2 *A Short View of the State of Ireland*, ed. W. Dunn MacRay. *Anecdota Bodleiana*, vol. 1 (Oxford and London: James Parker, 1879), 16. Hiram Morgan offers the most recent and detailed account of the incident: "Extradition and Treason – Trial of a Gaelic Lord: the Case of Brian O'Rourke," *The Irish Jurist* 22 (1987): 293–94. He sees the sudden "discovery" of the incident so long after it purportedly occurred as motivated by the need to justify a government assault upon O'Rourke. Also see Hiram Morgan, "The Fall of Sir John Perrot," in John Guy, ed., *The Reign of Elizabeth I: Court and Culture in the Last Decade* (Cambridge University Press, 1995), 118–20.

3 Roy Strong includes this incident among the various attempts that were made

to injure the queen "by stabbing, burning, or otherwise destroying her image." The attempts share a common assumption about the magical properties of the royal image and a belief that "it partook in some mysterious way of the nature of the sitter" (*Portraits of Queen Elizabeth I* [Oxford: Clarendon Press, 1963], 40).

4 John Bellamy, *The Tudor Law of Treason: An Introduction* (London: Routledge, 1979), 187.

5 Louis Adrian Montrose, "The Elizabethan Subject and the Spenserian Text," in *Literary Theory/Renaissance Texts*, ed. Patricia Parker and David Quint (Baltimore: Johns Hopkins University Press, 1986), 326.

6 *State Trials*, ed. Howell, 1:1321, 1319. "Piss-kitchin" is probably an English rendering of the Gaelic word *phiseogach*, meaning sorceress or charm-worker. Another epithet of abuse for the queen was "Caliaghe" [*cailleach*], which literally meant an old woman or hag, but was a culturally charged word with connotations of magic (See *Foclóir Gaeilge-Béarla*, ed. Niall Ó Dónaill [Richview: Browne and Nolan, 1977] 172. I am grateful to Terry Odlin for assistance with translations).

7 On the factionalism surrounding Perrot, see Morgan, "The Fall of Sir John Perrot."

8 Spenser, *A View*, ed. Renwick, 7. Hereafter, page references to *A View* will appear parenthetically.

9 "Sir Henry Sidney's Memoir of his Government in Ireland, 1853," ed. Herbert F. Hore, *The Ulster Journal of Archaeology* 1st series 3 (1856): 44.

10 Edward M. Hinton, "Rych's *Anothomy of Ireland*, with an Account of the Author," *PMLA* 55 (1940): 88–89.

11 Breaking with the notion that the "cult of Elizabeth" was a monolithic set of cultural images and practices controlled by and serving the queen, Susan Frye argues that Elizabeth's image was always a locus of contestation among various factions, individuals, and interest groups. "In the 1590s," Frye writes, "Elizabeth worked to create herself as powerful, remote, divinely approved, and magical in her physical location in the privy chamber, as well as in her lyric poetry, speeches, spectacles, and portraiture . . . But as an aging unmarried woman, the queen was vulnerable to the redefinition of her represented powers" (*Elizabeth I: The Competition for Representation* [Oxford University Press, 1993], 20).

12 Quoted in Edwin Greenlaw, Charles Grosvenor Osgood, Frederick Morgan Padelford, and Ray Heffner, eds., *The Works of Edmund Spenser: A Variorum Edition* (Baltimore: Johns Hopkins University Press, 1932–49) 5:318.

13 Quoted in David Quinn, *The Elizabethans and the Irish* (Ithaca: Cornell University Press, 1966), 37.

14 Paul L. Hughes and James F. Larkin, eds., *Tudor Royal Proclamations* (New Haven: Yale University Press, 1969), 3:200–2. All quotations are from this version. A different version appears as a "Declaration by the Queen regarding the Irish Rebellion" in *C.S.P. Ireland 1601–03*, 608–9. Although the proclamation is ostensibly the queen's own composition, the note added in one version by the editor of the printed State Papers – "with alterations and additions in Sir Robert Cecil's hand" – shows it to be a collaborative production (*C.S.P. Ireland 1598–99*, 468).

15 The impersonal voice is used, for example, in the proclamation of 1595 declaring Tyrone a traitor. The effect is slightly to distance Elizabeth from Tyrone whom she had originally "advanced," and thus to insulate her from the responsibility for his disobedience (see Constantia Maxwell, *Irish History from Contemporary Sources (1509–1610)* (London: Allen and Unwin, 1923), 175).

16 *C.S.P. Ireland 1599–1600*, 6, 18.

17 Annabel Patterson, *Censorship and Interpretation: The Conditions of Writing and Reading in Early Modern England* (Madison: University of Wisconsin Press, 1984), 53. Critics have found no shortage of offensive passages and arguments in *A View* to support their suppression theory. Also see David J. Baker, "'Some Quirk, Some Subtle Evasion': Legal Subversion in Spenser's *A View of the Present State of Ireland*," *Spenser Studies* 6 (1986): 147–63; and Clark Hulse, "Spenser, Bacon, and the Myth of Power," in *The Historical Renaissance: New Essays on Tudor and Stuart Literature and Culture*, ed. Heather Dubrow and Richard Strier (University of Chicago Press, 1988), 329–30.

18 Crucially, the note does not tell us what sort of authority was required. Brink observes that "the cautionary note in the entry for the *View* could just as well signal a disagreement over publication rights as government censorship." When the *View* was entered, Ponsonby was still Spenser's "recognized publisher" ("Constructing the *View of the Present State of Ireland*," *Spenser Studies* 11 [1990]: 207).

19 Paul E. J. Hammer, "The Earl of Essex, Fulke Greville, and the Employment of Scholars," *Studies in Philology* 41 (1994): 174; "The Uses of Scholarship: the Secretariat of Robert Devereux, Second Earl of Essex, c.1585–1601," *English Historical Review* 109 (1994): 38.

20 Brink, "Constructing the *View*," 213.

21 The term "heddlesse" is from a letter written by the licencer Samuel Harsnett about his handling of John Hayward's *Henry the Fourth*. Harsnett was explaining to the Privy Council how the manuscript of Hayward's work that he had been asked to license, had been "heddlesse without epistle, preface, or dedication at all" (quoted in W. W. Greg, "Samuel Harsnett and Hayward's *Henry IV*," *The Library* 5th series 11 [1956], 4).

22 Ray Heffner claims that "in 1601, when Essex's secretary, Green, made copies for preservation of the Earl's most important papers, Spenser's *View* was among them" ("Spenser's *View of Ireland*: Some Observations," *Modern Language Quarterly* 3 [1942]: 509).

23 Spenser dedicated his *Fowre Hymnes* from "Greenwich this first of September. 1596" (p. 690).

24 *Prothalamion* announces itself as Spenserian autobiography in its reference to "London, my most kyndly Nurse, / That to me gave this Lifes first native sourse: / Though from another place I take my name, / An house of auncient fame" (lines 128–31).

25 R. B. Gottfried, "Spenser's *View* and Essex," *PMLA* 52 (1937): 645–51.
   Spenser does not wish the lord lieutenant to replace the lord deputy in Ireland but to act as the latter's superior and defender back at the English court. Such a proposal would have allowed Essex to control Irish policy without running the risks that a prolonged absence from court entailed. In the

event, Essex's sojourn in Ireland gave rival court factions the opportunity to maneuver against him. See Josephine Waters Bennett, "The Allegory of Sir Artegall in *The Faerie Queene*, V, xi-xii," *Studies in Philology* 37 (1940): 182.

26 See Richard C. McCoy, *The Rites of Knighthood: The Literature and Politics of Elizabethan Chivalry* (Berkeley: University of California Press, 1989), 100–101.

27 Essex's signature appears on a Privy Council letter recommending Spenser's appointment as Sheriff of Cork in 1598. The letter described Spenser as "a man endowed with good knowledge in learning, and not unskillful or without experience in the service of the warrs" (quoted in Frederick Ives Carpenter, *A Reference Guide to Edmund Spenser* [New York: Kraus Reprint, 1969], 67).

28 See the "circles" drawn up by Carpenter, *A Reference Guide*, 84–94; and Willy Maley, *A Spenser Chronology* (London: Macmillan, 1994), 85–108.

29 My information on Bingham comes from the *DNB*, and Wallace T. MacCaffrey, *Elizabeth I: War and Politics, 1588–1603* (Princeton University Press, 1992), 354–55 and passim.

30 "Docwra's Relation of the Service Done in Ireland," *Miscellany of the Celtic Society*, ed. John O'Donovan (Dublin, 1849), 211–12. Dowcra was Bingham's officer and apologist; Niall Fallon, *The Armada in Ireland* (Middletown, Connecticut: Wesleyan University Press, 1978), 54. Philip O'Sullivan Beare, an Irish nationalist, recalled how "the heretic" Bingham, "After he had established a great reputation for kindness and goodness . . . broke out into more than Phalaric cruelty, greedily spilling the blood of Catholics" (*Ireland Under Elizabeth*, tr. Matthew J. Byrne [Dublin, 1903], 38).

31 *The Chronicle of Ireland 1584–1608. By Sir James Perrot*, ed. Herbert Wood (Dublin: Irish Manuscripts Commission, 1933), 60.

32 For Bingham's conflict with Perrot and other deputies, see MacCaffrey, *Elizabeth I: War and Politics*, 358ff.

33 Beacon's interest in Bingham is also discussed in Nicholas Canny, "Identity Formation in Ireland: the Emergence of the Anglo-Irish," in Nicholas Canny and Anthony Pagden ed., *Colonial Identity in the Atlantic World, 1560–1800* (Princeton University Press, 1987), 171–72.

34 Grey is mentioned a second time when he is complimented along with a later lord deputy, Sir William Russell (44).

35 *Shakespeare's Europe: A Survey of the Condition of Europe at the End of the Sixteenth Century*, ed. Charles Hughes (New York: Benjamin Bloom, 1967), 2nd edition, 259.

36 *Ibid.*, 260.

37 "Docwra's Relation," 200; *C.S.P. Ireland 1588–92*, 432.

38 Quoted in Morgan, "Extradition and Treason – Trial," 299.

39 For a general discussion of Spenser's relation to "an ideology of masculinity as aggression," see Gary Waller, *Edmund Spenser: A Literary Life* (New York: St. Martin's Press, 1994), 26–37.

40 Joaneath Spicer, "The Renaissance Elbow," in *A Cultural History of Gesture*, ed. Jan Bremmer and Herman Roodenburg (Ithaca: Cornell University Press, 1992), 90, 85.

41 Seventeenth-century readers apparently had more success at constructing local patterns of signification in the poem. See, for example, Walter Oakeshott, "Carew Ralegh's Copy of Spenser," *The Library* 26 (1971): 1–21,

and Anon., "Ms Notes to Spenser's *Faerie Queene*," *Notes and Queries* (December, 1957): 509–15.

42 Fallon, *The Armada in Ireland*, 243. My emphasis.

43 Holinshed, *Chronicles*, 6:437.

44 Spenser's portrait of Malengin is characteristic of how Gaelicized figures in the poem are shrouded by an aura of mythical and archetypal significance. To avoid capture, Malengin undergoes a series of metamorphoses that transform him at one point into a stone, an "it." Thus dehumanized through his own ingenuity, Malengin is drained of any vestigial sympathy that Talus' destruction of him may provoke.

Sir William Herbert remarked of the Irish mantle that it served the rebels "as to a hedgehog his skin or to a snail her shell for a garment by day or a house by night" (quoted in Quinn, *The Elizabethans and the Irish*, 97). At one point, Malengin transforms himself into a "Hedgehogge" to escape from Artegall's grasp (5.9.18).

45 "Spenser's Art of War: Chivalric Allegory, Military Technology, and the Elizabethan Mock-Heroic Sensibility," *Renaissance Quarterly* 41 (1988): 665.

46 See C. G. Cruickshank, *Elizabeth's Army* (Oxford: Clarendon Press, 2nd edition, 1966); Hiram Morgan, *Tyrone's Rebellion: The Outbreak of the Nine Years War in Tudor Ireland* (Woodbridge, Suffolk: The Boydell Press. The Royal Historical Society, 1993), 179–84; and for contemporary documents, Maxwell, *Irish History*, 212–16.

The fantasy of a well-disciplined English army in Ireland appears in the woodcuts to Derricke's *The Image of Irelande* where the soldiers are presented as virtually indistinguishable in dress, weaponry, and appearance. The ideals of uniformity and regimentation – signs of an obedient and homogeneous fighting force – were a far cry from the brutal realities.

47 Sean O Domhnaill, "Warfare in Sixteenth-Century Ireland," *Irish Historical Studies* 5 (1946–47): 39–42.

48 Norman Lloyd Williams, *Sir Walter Raleigh* (London: Cassell, 1988), 27; Holinshed, *Chronicles*, 6:435; *C.S.P. Ireland 1599–1600*, 42–43.

49 Maxwell, *Irish History*, 215. Although the recommendation for mantles was never adopted, some nominal Englishmen like Thomas Lee and George Bourchier believed that only by becoming like the rebels could one defeat them. John Hooker writes of Captain Bourchier: "If he served upon foot, he was apparelled in the manner of a Kerne and a foot souldior, and was so light of foot as no Kerne swifter: for he would persue them in bogs, in thickets, in woods, in passes, and in streicts whatsoever; and never leave them, untill he did performe the charge and service committed unto him."

However effective Bourchier's methods, his imitation of the enemy had disquieting implications. Such boundary-crossing radiates an anxious irony in the way it makes a mockery of official emphasis on the relation between dress and civility in Ireland. Hooker's account of Bourchier, in fact, follows a discussion of government efforts to reform the Irish through regulating their appearance and apparel, "suffering no glibes nor like usages of the Irishrie to be used among the men, nor the Egyptiacall rolles upon womens heads to be worn" (Holinshed, *Chronicles*, 6:370).

50 Roy Strong, *Artists of the Tudor Court: The Portrait Miniature Rediscovered 1520–1620* (London: Victoria and Albert Museum, 1983), 156–58.

204   Notes to pages 123–28

51 *The Faerie Queene*, ed. Hamilton, 532.
52 *Ibid.*, 537. On the iconography of the dismembered martial hand, see Katherine A. Rowe, "Dismembering and Forgetting in *Titus Andronicus*," *Shakespeare Quarterly* 45 (1994): 287.
53 At various moments in Book Five, Artegall shadows particular historical figures like Grey, Essex, and Sir John Norris, yet he always retains his general significance as the representative of the New English mission in Ireland.
54 Kenneth Borris, *Spenser's Poetics of Prophecy in "The Faerie Queene" V*, English Literary Studies Monograph Series no.52 (Victoria, Canada: University of Victoria, 1991), 64.
55 "Spenser, Bacon, and the Myth of Power," 329.
56 Artegall's subordination of the Fairy Queen's quest to multiple self-chosen adventures prefigures Calidore's complete abandonment of his primary quest in Book Six.
57 There is in Britomart's encounter with "the bad newes-man" Talus – whom she spies from a window "that opened West" – a distinct ring of Elizabeth's own reactions to bad news from Ireland (5.6.11, 7). The queen's anger and impatience echo throughout the letters she wrote to her ministers; for an example, see Maxwell, *Irish History*, 185.
58 For the scene's Irish resonances, see *The Works of Edmund Spenser*, Greenlaw *et al.*, eds., 5:17.
59 Hinton, "Rych's *Anothomy of Ireland*," 95.
60 "Home-Making in Ireland: Virgil's Eclogue I and Book VI of *The Faerie Queene*," *Spenser Studies* 8 (1990): 131–32.
61 David Norbrook, *Poetry and Politics in the English Renaissance* (London: Routledge and Kegan Paul, 1984), 143–44.
62 *The Faerie Queene*, ed. Hamilton, 628.
63 See Brendan Bradshaw, "Sword, Word and Strategy in the Reformation in Ireland," *Historical Journal* 21 (1978): 475–502.
64 See John N. King, *Spenser's Poetry and the Reformation Tradition* (Princeton University Press, 1990), 89–90, for further discussion of this episode. On this episode, also see Lisa Jardine, "Encountering Ireland: Gabriel Harvey, Edmund Spenser, and English Colonial Ventures," in *Representing Ireland: Literature and the Origins of Conflict, 1534–1660*, ed. Bradshaw, Hadfield and Maley (Cambridge University Press, 1993), 69–70; and Patricia Coughlan, "'Some Secret Scourge which shall by Her come unto England': Ireland and Incivility in Spenser," in Coughlan, ed., *Spenser and Ireland: An Interdisciplinary Perspective* (Cork University Press, 1989), 51.
65 Quoted in Nicholas Canny, "The Ideology of English Colonization: from Ireland to America," *William and Mary Quarterly* 3rd series 30 (1973), 584.
66 On Una and Elizabeth, see Richard A. McCabe, "The Masks of Duessa: Spenser, Mary Queen of Scots, and James VI," *English Literary Renaissance* 17 (1987): 227n11, 229; and Frances A. Yates, *Astraea: The Imperial Theme in the Sixteenth Century* (London: Routledge and Kegan Paul, 1975), 69–74.
67 Stanihurst is quoted in Edmund Campion, *A Historie of Ireland* (1571), ed. Rudolf B. Gottfried (New York: Scholars' Facsimiles and Reprints, 1940), 132.
   In 1571 there appeared from a Dublin press an "Alphabet of the Irish Language and Catechism – for anyone who would be obedient to – the Queen

of this Kingdom, translated from Latin and to Irish by JOHN O'KEARNEY." The translated *New Testament* finally appeared in 1602 followed in 1608 by the *Book of Common Prayer*. See William K. Sessions, *The Spread of British Printing 1557 to 1695* (York, England: The Ebor Press, 1988), 155–56, and Bruce Dickins, "The Irish Broadside of 1571 and Queen Elizabeth's Types," *Transactions of the Cambridge Bibliographical Society* 1 (1949): 48–60.

68 *History of the Earle of Tirone*, 16.

69 Quoted in Richard Bagwell, *Ireland Under the Tudors* (London: Holland Press, 1963), 3:224.

70 *C.S.P. Ireland 1588–92*, 435–36.

71 *Ibid.*, 565.

72 *Ibid.*, 436. Many Irish suitors actually made the trip to London. On Elizabeth's complaints against them, see Quinn, *The Elizabethans and the Irish*, 155–56.

73 Thomas H. Cain, *Praise in "The Faerie Queene"* (Lincoln, Nebraska: University of Nebraska Press, 1978), 136, 156, 161–64. Cain notes that "Spenser salutes [Essex] in terms that ignore his total dependence on the queen" (163).

The pessimistic, even satirical, tone of the second half of the poem has been widely recognized. See, for example, McCoy, *The Rites of Knighthood*, ch.6, and Richard Helgerson, *Forms of Nationhood: The Elizabethan Writing of England* (University of Chicago Press, 1992), 40–59.

74 King, *Spenser's Poetry*, 114–20.

75 Cain, *Praise in "The Faerie Queene"*, 135–36; also see Norbrook, *Poetry and Politics*, 144–45.

76 For claims of Irish cannibalism, see Robert E. Stillman, "Spenserian Autonomy and the Trial of the New Historicism: Book Six of *The Faerie Queene*," *English Literary Renaissance* 22 (1992): 309–10; and Norbrook, *Poetry and Politics*, 142.

77 For related readings of the scene, see Theresa M. Krier, *Gazing on Secret Sights: Spenser, Classical Imitation, and the Decorums of Vision* (Ithaca: Cornell University Press, 1990), 115, and Norbrook, *Poetry and Politics*, 152.

78 Pastorella's rose-shaped birthmark connects her with the House of Tudor (6.12.18–19).

79 On the Irish overtones of the brigants, see the entry in *The Spenser Encyclopedia* ed. A. C. Hamilton *et al.* (London: Routledge, 1990), as well as Lupton, "Home-Making in Ireland," 132–38; and Stillman, "Spenserian Autonomy," 312–13.

Since, according to Thomas Cooper, the Brigantes were an "auncient people in the North part of Englande," Spenser's use of the name for this Irish-like people suggests the kind of correspondences made among the Irish and other outlandish, border-dwelling peoples in the British Isles (*Thesaurus Linguae Romanae et Britannicae* [London, 1565] S. V. Brigantes). The Briganti, in fact, were a specifically Celtic tribe.

80 For a valuable discussion of Spenser's rhetoric of violence in *The Faerie Queene* and *A View*, see Richard A. McCabe, "The Fate of Irena: Spenser and Political Violence," in *Spenser and Ireland*, ed. Coughlan, 121–22.

81 Constituting a fragmentary seventh book of the poem, the *Cantos of Mutabilitie* were first published in the 1609 Folio edition. For their disputed date of composition, see the entry in *The Spenser Encyclopedia*.

82 John N. King, "Queen Elizabeth I: Representations of the Virgin Queen," *Renaissance Quarterly* 43 (1990): 58–65. Also see Andrew Hadfield, "Spenser, Ireland, and Sixteenth-Century Political Theory," *Modern Language Notes* 89 (1994), 13–18.

83 Norbrook, *Poetry and Politics*, 152.

84 Philippa Berry, *Of Chastity and Power: Elizabethan Literature and the Unmarried Queen* (London: Routledge, 1989), 164.

85 Quoted in R. A. Butlin, "Land and People, c.1600," in *A New History of Ireland*, ed. T. W. Moody, F. X. Martin, and F. J. Byrne (Oxford: Clarendon Press, 1976), 3:143.

86 For a further insightful analysis of the dream in terms of the queen's policies in Ireland, see Clare Carroll, "Representations of Women in Some Early Modern English Tracts on the Colonization of Ireland," *Albion* 25 (1993): 388–93.

6 "IF THE CAUSE BE NOT GOOD": "HENRY V" AND ESSEX'S IRISH CAMPAIGN

1 *C.S.P. Ireland 1598–99*, 305.

2 *A View*, ed. Renwick, 137.

3 *C.S.P. Ireland 1598–99*, 257–59.

4 *Acts of the Privy Council 1598–99*, 464.

5 Willy Maley, *A Spenser Chronology* (London: Macmillan, 1994), 72–76. Also see Anthony J. Sheehan, "The Overthrow of the Plantation of Munster in October 1598," *The Irish Sword* 15 (1982): 11–22. On the circumstances of Spenser's death and funeral, see *The Works of Edmund Spenser: A Variorum Edition*, Edwin Greenlaw, Charles Grosvenor Osgood, Frederick Morgan Padelford, and Ray Heffner eds. (Baltimore: Johns Hopkins University Press, 1932–49), 5:324.

6 Laura Hanes Cadwallader, *The Career of the Earl of Essex: From the Islands Voyage of 1597 to His Execution in 1601* (Philadelphia: University of Pennsylvania Press, 1923), 31.

7 *Sidney Papers (Letters and Memorials of State)*, ed. Arthur Collins (London, 1746), 2:148, 139; L. W. Henry, "The Earl of Essex and Ireland, 1599," *Bulletin of the Institute of Historical Research* 32 (1959): 4–5.

8 John Nichols, *The Progresses and Public Processions of Queen Elizabeth* (London, 1823), 3:433–37.

9 Edward Arber, ed., *A Transcript of the Registers of the Company of Stationers of London: 1554–1640* (London, 1875), 3:49, 50b. John Norden, "A Prayer for the Prosperous Proceedings and Good Successe of the Earle of Essex and his companies, in their present expedition in Ireland against Tyrone and his adherents, Rebels there. Fit to be used of all loyall subjects, as well in that Countrie, as in England" (London: Edward Allde, 1599). Norden urged prayer not only upon those "in the daunger of the battell, but of such also as are secure at home in their houses, who if they neglect the cause of God and their countrie, God will holde them not onely unprofitable droanes, but reprobates." Norden here addresses the same stay-at-homes implicitly invoked and put to shame in the Chorus's admonition in *Henry V* to: "Follow, follow: / Grapple your minds to sternage of this Navie, / And leave

your England as dead Mid-night, still, / Guarded with Grandsires, Babyes, and old Women, / Eyther past, or not arriv'd to pyth and puissance: / For who is he, whose Chin is but enricht / With one appearing Hayre, that will not follow / These cull'd and choyse-drawne Cavaliers to France?" (TLN 1061–68). As Joel B. Altman astutely points out, these stay-at-homes included the actual audience members watching the play in the spring of 1599 ("'Vile Participation': the Amplification of Violence in the Theater of *Henry V*," *Shakespeare Quarterly* 42 [1991]: 13–14, 17).

10 On the date of composition, see *Henry V*, ed. Gary Taylor (Oxford University Press, 1982), 3–8.

11 See especially, Altman, " 'Vile Participation'."

12 Alan Sinfield, *Faultlines: Cultural Materialism and the Politics of Dissident Reading* (Berkeley: University of California Press, 1992), 125–26.

13 Nichols, *Progresses*, 3:434.

14 Eric S. Mallin, "Emulous Factions and the Collapse of Chivalry: *Troilus and Cressida*," *Representations* 29 (1990): 146.

15 James Shapiro discusses the impact on the play of these invasion fears. "Revisiting *Tamburlaine*: *Henry V* as Shakespeare's Belated Armada Play," *Criticism* 31 (1989): 351–66.

16 *The Letters of John Chamberlain*, ed. Norman Egbert McClure (Philadelphia: The American Philosophical Society, 1939), 1:78.

17 Focusing on the Chorus's reference to the anticipated successful return of Essex from Ireland, most commentators have preferred a completion date of early in the summer which would place the play before the renewal of invasion fears. Citing Chamberlain's letters, however, Keith Brown has shown that Shakespeare would still have had reasonable grounds for expecting an Essex victory as late as August ("Historical Context and *Henry V*," *Cahiers Elisabethains* 29 [1986]: 77–78).

18 All references are to the Folio edition of *Henry V* in the Norton Facsimilie, *The First Folio of Shakespeare*, prepared by Charlton Hinman (New York: W. W. Norton, 1968).

19 *The Letters and the Life of Francis Bacon*, ed. James Spedding, vol. 2:89. Vol. 9 of *The Works of Francis Bacon*, ed. James Spedding, Robert Leslie Ellis, and Douglas Denon Heath (London: Longman, 1862); Mallin, "Emulous Factions," 146.

20 Shapiro, "Revisiting *Tamburlaine*," 358; *The Letters and the Life of Francis Bacon*, ed. Spedding, 2:88.

21 *The Annales of England, Faithfully collected out of the most authenticall Authors, Records, and other Monuments of Antiquitie, lately corrected, encreased, and continued, from the first inhabitation untill this present yeere 1600* (London: Ralfe Newberry, 1600), 1304.

22 Henry, "Essex and Ireland," 10.

23 Roy Strong observes that Gheeraerts's full-length portrait of Essex painted after his raid on Cadiz was "designed for mass production" (*Artists of the Tudor Court: The Portrait Miniature Rediscovered 1520–1620* [London: Victoria and Albert Museum, 1983], 105–6; *The Cult of Elizabeth: Elizabethan Portraiture and Pageantry* [Berkeley: University of California Press, 1977], 64–68). On the Cockson engraving and Essex's image generally, see Richard

C. McCoy, *The Rites of Knighthood: The Literature and Politics of Elizabethan Chivalry* (Berkeley: University of California Press, 1989), ch.4.

24 Herbert Wood, ed., *The Chronicle of Ireland 1584–1608. By Sir James Perrot* (Dublin: Irish Manuscripts Commission, 1933), 161–62. The 1615 edition of Stow's *Annales* remarks pointedly that when Lord Mountjoy, Essex's successor in Ireland, left from London, he was "in all points very honourably accompanied and attended: though not in such magnificence as was the Earle of Essex" (789).

25 *Society, Politics and Culture: Studies in Early Modern England* (Cambridge University Press, 1986), 429, 434.

26 Chamberlain, *Letters*, 1:62; James, *Society, Politics*, 428n43.

27 *The Annales or Generall Chronicle of England, begun first by Maister John Stow, and after him continued and augmented with matters forreyne, and domestique, auncient and moderne, unto the ende of this present yeare 1614* (London: Thomas Adams, 1615), 787–88.

28 See, for example, 1299, 1303, 1308.

29 *C.S.P. Ireland 1598–99*, 357.

30 See C. G. Cruickshank, *Elizabeth's Army*, 2nd edition (Oxford: Clarendon Press, 1966), esp. ch.5.

31 *C.S.P. Domestic 1598–1601*, 172. On preparations and negotiations for the campaign, see Chamberlain, *Letters*, 1:55–72; Cadwallader, *Earl of Essex*, 30–37, and Henry, "Earl of Essex." On victualling problems, also see Ciaran Brady, "Spenser's Irish Crisis: Humanism and Experience in the 1590s," *Past and Present* 111 (1986): 48n, and *A View*, ed. Renwick, 129.

32 *Letters*, 1:55.

33 Theories relating national identity to diet were common in the Renaissance. In his comparative ethnography of England and France, John Aylmer let his readers draw their own conclusions from the two countries' respective diets: the French "eat hearbes: and thou Beefe and Mutton. Thei rotes: and thou butter, chese, and egges . . . Thei go from the market with a sallet: and thou with good fleshe fill thy wallet" (*An harborowe for faithfull and trewe subjectes, agaynst the late blowne blaste concerninge the government of wemen* [London, 1559], 62).

34 As Bryan S. Turner explains, "the term 'diet' comes from the Greek '*diaita*,' meaning a mode of life. As a regulation of life, it has the more specific medical meaning of eating according to prescribed rules. There is a second meaning of 'diet' which is a political assembly of princes for the purpose of legislation and administration. This second meaning comes from the French word '*dies*' or 'day,' because political diets met on specified days and were thus regulated by a calendar. Diet is either a regulation of the individual body or a regulation of the body politic. The term 'regimen' also has this double implication. It is derived from '*regere*' or 'rule' and, as a medical term, means a therapeutic system, typically involving diet, but regimen is also a system of government as in 'regimentation' or 'regime.' We can see, therefore, that 'diet' and 'regimen' both apply to the government of the body and the government of citizens" (*The Body and Society: Explorations in Social Theory* [Oxford: Basil Blackwell, 1984], 165–66).

35 Turner, *The Body and Society*, 167. Also see Edward Jeninges, *A Briefe*

Discovery of the Damages that Happen to this Realme by Disordered and Unlawful Diet (London, 1593).

36 Michael Bristol, *Carnival and Theater: Plebeian Culture and the Structure of Authority in Renaissance England* (New York: Methuen, 1985), 206.

37 "Of the True Greatness of Kingdoms and Estates," in *Francis Bacon: The Essays*, ed. John Pitcher (Harmondsworth: Penguin, 1985), 153.

38 Paul A. Jorgensen, *Shakespeare's Military World* (Berkeley: University of California Press, 1956), 83–84.

39 *C.S.P. Ireland 1599–1600*, 9–10, 35–36.

40 Quoted in Jorgensen, *Shakespeare's Military World*, 84.

41 In making Fluellen the means of Pistol's exclusion, Shakespeare revises the contemporary reputation of the army captain; it was the captain more than any other officer who was considered responsible for the general disarray of the troops in Ireland and the Low Countries and for the specific complaint that pay, clothes, and food were not being properly distributed to the ordinary soldier (Constantia Maxwell, *Irish History from Contemporary Sources (1509–1610)* [London: Allen and Unwin, 1923], 212–13).

42 Phyllis Rackin, *Stages of History: Shakespeare's English Chronicles* (Ithaca: Cornell University Press, 1990), 213n18; also see 211–12.

43 References are to the edition of the play in David Bevington ed., *The Complete Works of Shakespeare*, 4th edition (New York: HarperCollins, 1992).

44 Maxwell, *Irish History*, 219–20.

45 William Camden as quoted in Alexander C. Judson, *The Life of Edmund Spenser* (Baltimore: Johns Hopkins University Press, 1945), 159.

46 Fynes Moryson, *Itinerary* (Glasgow: MacLehose, 1907–8), 2:262–63.

47 *The Works of Edmund Spenser*, ed. Greenlaw *et al.*, 9:244. Also see *The Spenser Encyclopedia* ed. A. C. Hamilton *et al.* (London: Routledge, 1990), 111–12.

48 Altman, "'Vile Participation,'" 19.

49 Also see Michael Neill, "Broken English and Broken Irish: Nation, Language, and the Optic of Power in Shakespeare's Histories," *Shakespeare Quarterly* 45 (1994) 20ff. The Constable's description of England and its inhabitants is also reminiscent of English estimates of the Irish climate, diet, and character (TLN 1395–1405).

50 "H. W. in Hiber. Belligeranti," in *The Satires, Epigrams, and Verse Letters*, ed. W. Milgate (Oxford: Clarendon Press, 1967), 74–75; on Donne and Ireland, see R. C. Bald, *John Donne: A Life* (Oxford University Press, 1970), 104, 160–1; and Andrew Murphy, "Gold Lace and a Frozen Snake: Donne, Wotton, and the Nine Years War," *Irish Studies Review* 8 (1994): 9–11.

51 Sinfield, *Faultlines*, 142–43.

52 For a useful discussion of the social significance of Pistol and his companions, see Robert Lane, "'When Blood is their Argument': Class, Character, and Historymaking in Shakespeare's and Branagh's *Henry V*," *ELH* 61 (1994): 32–36.

53 Sir D. Plunket Barton, *Links Between Ireland and Shakespeare* (Dublin: Maunsel, 1919), 114–36. For recent discussions of Mackmorrice, see David J. Baker, "'*Wildehirisshman*': Colonialist Representation in Shakespeare's

Henry V," *English Literary Renaissance* 22 (1992): 37–61; Neill, "Broken English and Broken Irish," 18–19; Willy Maley, "Review of David Cairns and Shaun Richards, *Writing Ireland*," *Textual Practice* 3 (1989): 293–94; Andrew Murphy, "Shakespeare's Irish History," *Literature and History* 5 (1996): 52–55.

54 "Spenserian Autonomy and the Trial of the New Historicism: Book Six of *The Faerie Queene*," *English Literary Renaissance* 22 (1992): 308–9. Stillman continues: "With typical Spenserian doubleness, the Salvage Man represents salvageable natural power (his name suggests specifically *Irish* power), which, disciplined by English civility, can be turned against the unreformable savagery of a Turpine . . . Typical of Spenser, the Salvage Man's progress toward civilization is represented as a recuperation of 'his gentle blood'; the move forward is accomplished by moving backward, as one more mythic image of the salvageability of the old English settlers of Ireland and their potential aid to imperial British sovereignty (5.2.5)."

55 *C.S.P. Ireland 1599–1600*, 464–65.

56 *Ibid.*, 409–11.

57 *The Supplication of the Blood of the English Most Lamentably Murdered in Ireland, Cryeng out of the Yearth for Revenge (1598)*, ed. Willy Maley, *Analecta Hibernica* (Irish Manuscripts Commission) 36 (1994): 20.

58 William Camden, *Remains Concerning Britain*, ed. R. D. Dunn (University of Toronto Press, 1984), 14–15.

59 Quoted in Arthur E. Hughes, "The Welsh National Emblem: Leek or Daffodil?" *Y Cymmrodor* (1916): 176.

60 T. Morgan, "The Welchmens Jubilee to the Honour of St. David" (London, 1642), A3^r.

61 Hughes, "Welsh National Emblem," 179; Taylor ed., *Henry V*, 248n.

62 Hughes, "Welsh National Emblem," 166.

63 Jorgensen, *Shakespeare's Military World*, 164.

64 *Henry V*, ed. Andrew Gurr (Cambridge University Press, 1992), 64–65. Williams is never actually named in the text, but the Folio speech-prefixes refer to him as Williams and Will. In *Shakespeare and the Popular Voice* (Oxford: Basil Blackwell, 1989), Annabel Patterson suggests that "Will" is Shakespeare's own signature (88–89).

65 Quoted in Patrick Collinson, *The Birthpangs of Protestant England: Religious and Cultural Change in the Sixteenth and Seventeenth Centuries* (London: Macmillan, 1988), 8.

  In his account of the genealogy and ideology of nationalism, Benedict Anderson claims that it is the felt apprehension of the nation as "a deep, horizontal comradeship" or "fraternity" that makes people willing to die for it (*Imagined Communities: Reflections on the Origin and Spread of Nationalism* [London: Verso, 1983], 16).

66 A report of 1596 observed how some soldiers' "feet and legs rotted off for want of shoes" (*C.S.P. Ireland 1596–97*, 195).

67 See Anne Barton on the different, harmonious outcomes of similar encounters between monarch and subject in other popular plays ("The King Disguised: Shakespeare's *Henry V* and the Comical History," in *The Triple Bond: Plays, Mainly Shakespearean, in Performance*, ed. Joseph G. Price [London: Penn. State University Press, 1975], 92–117).

Neill suggests that "in the quarrel between [Williams] . . . with his oddly Welsh-sounding name, and the loyal Welsh-Englishman Fluellen, the play comes close to restaging the crisis of nationality provoked by Macmorris" ("Broken English and Broken Irish," 32).

68 Paul L. Hughes and James F. Larkin, eds., *Tudor Royal Proclamations* (New Haven: Yale University Press, 1969), 3:200–1.

In a list of demands issued in late 1599, Tyrone and his supporters rejected the *a priori* assumption that they were the queen's subjects. The document in which Tyrone set forth his vision of a semi-autonomous "Republic" of Ireland was endorsed "Ewtopia" by Robert Cecil (*C.S.P. Ireland 1599–1600*, 279–80).

69 *The Letters and the Life of Francis Bacon*, ed. Spedding, 2:130–31.

70 Chris Durston, " 'Let Ireland be Quiet': Opposition in England to the Cromwellian Conquest of Ireland," *History Workshop Journal* 21 (1986): 109–110.

71 "The Levellers and the Conquest of Ireland in 1649," *The Historical Journal* 30 (1987): 288, 280–83, 271.

Unlike the extant text of *The Soldiers Demand*, other works denouncing the English conquest of Ireland survive only as "transcripts" in anti-Irish polemics. One of these, *Certain Queries propounded to the consideration of those who are intended for the service of Ireland*, which appears only in a pro-Cromwellian publication, asks provocatively: "Whether Julius Caesar, Alexander the Great, William Duke of Normandie, or anie other the great Conquerors of the world, were anie other then so manie great and lawless thievs; And whether it be not as unjust to take our neighbor Nations Lands, and liberties from them, as our neighbor's goods of our own Nation?" (271).

Yet even if works like *Certain Queries* had no independent existence but were produced only to be refuted and their alleged authors and sympathizers discredited, their "publication," as well as implying that a "radical" message was already thinkable, helped, ironically, to disseminate that message to a wider audience.

72 Quoted in Andrew Gurr, "*Henry V* and the Bees' Commonwealth," *Shakespeare Survey* 30 (1977), 62. For a survey of legal arguments about the justice of different kinds of war, see Theodor Meron, *Henry's Wars and Shakespeare's Laws: Perspectives on the Law of War in the Later Middle Ages* (Oxford: Clarendon Press, 1993), esp. ch.3.

73 Bruce Mansfield, *Phoenix of His Age: Interpretations of Erasmus c.1550–1570* (University of Toronto Press, 1979).

74 *The Manual of the Christian Knight* (English translation 1518), quoted in Brendan Bradshaw, "Sword, Word and Strategy in the Reformation in Ireland," *Historical Journal* 21 (1978): 500.

On Shakespeare's participation in "a genuine pacifist culture," see Steven Marx, "Shakespeare's Pacifism," *Renaissance Quarterly* 45 (1992): 49–95, esp.62. Also see Janet M. Spencer, "Princes, Pirates, and Pigs: Criminalizing Wars of Conquest in *Henry V*," *Shakespeare Quarterly* 47 (1996): 160–77. On the roots and forms of early Tudor pacifism, also see Ben Lowe, "Peace Discourse and Mid-Tudor Foreign Policy," in *Political Thought and the Tudor Commonwealth: Deep Structure, Discourse, and Disguise*, ed. Paul A. Fideler and T. F. Mayer (London: Routledge, 1992), 108–39.

75 J. R. Hale, "Incitement to Violence? English Divines on the Theme of War, 1578–1631," in *Renaissance War Studies* (London: Hambledon Press, 1983), 487–517.

76 *The Correspondence of Dr. Matthew Hutton, Archbishop of York* (London: Surtees Society, 1843), 154–55.

77 On the influence of the Counter-Reformation upon the Tyrone confederacy, see Hiram Morgan, *Tyrone's Rebellion: The Outbreak of the Nine Years War in Tudor Ireland* (Woodbridge, Suffolk: The Boydell Press. The Royal Historical Society, 1993), 198–99.

78 *C.S.P. Ireland, 1598–99*, 211, 221; *Acts of the Privy Council 1598–99*, 131. Also see, Bald, *John Donne*, 23. On the Catholic community under Elizabeth, see Gillian E. Brennan, "Papists and Patriotism in Elizabethan England," *Recusant History* 19 (1988): 1–15, and Arnold Pritchard, *Catholic Loyalism in Elizabethan England* (Chapel Hill: University of North Carolina Press, 1979).

79 HMC, *Salisbury* MS. 9:18–19.

80 Focusing on *1 Henry IV*'s satire of the Protestant martyr Sir John Oldcastle (the original name for Falstaff), Gary Taylor has argued for a "papist" Shakespeare in "The Fortunes of Oldcastle," *Shakespeare Survey* 38 (1985): 98–100, and "Forms of Opposition: Shakespeare and Middleton," *English Literary Renaissance* 24 (1994): 283–314. On Shakespeare's possible recusant ties, also see E. A. J. Honigmann, *Shakespeare: The "Lost Years"* (Manchester University Press, 1985), 114–25.

81 *Letters*, 1:56. Also see the account in Altman of the war's financial burdens and of public apathy, ambivalence, and hostility toward the war ("'Vile Participation'," 8–16).

82 Following Essex's return to England in September, the Privy Council complained of "many falce and slaunderous Speeches ageinste her Majestie and Councell, conserning the Marshallinge of the Affayres and State of Ireland . . . [and] many scandelous Libells in the Courte, Cittie, and Countrey" (Collins, ed., *Sidney Papers*, 2:147).

83 *C.S.P. Domestic 1598–1601*, 225, 251.

84 *Sir John Oldcastle, Part 1*, in *The Oldcastle Controversy: Sir John Oldcastle, Part 1 and The Famous Victories of Henry V*, ed. Peter Corbin and Douglas Sedge (Manchester University Press, 1991), 1.120–23.

85 See the edition of *Famous Victories* in Corbin and Sedge, eds., *The Oldcastle Controversy*, 178–80. Dekker's *Old Fortunatus* (1599) also treats with sympathy the plight of impoverished, begging soldiers (1.2).

Shakespeare's best-known recruitment scene is exhaustively examined in Charles Whitney, "Festivity and Topicality in the Coventry Scene of *1 Henry IV*," *English Literary Renaissance* 24 (1994): 410–48. Insisting upon the "plurality of responses" generated by such scenes, Whitney scrutinizes the class, economic, and ideological factors determining the reactions of various social groups (411). Whitney's analysis also applies to Falstaff's recruitment scene in *2 Henry IV*.

86 David Scott Kastan, "Workshop and/as Playhouse: Comedy and Commerce in *The Shoemaker's Holiday*," *Studies in Philology* 84 (1987): 329.

87 *Ibid.*, 330.

88 For the presence of the lower orders at London's public theaters, see Andrew Gurr, *Playgoing in Shakespeare's London* (Cambridge University Press, 1987), ch.3.

89 Robert Lane discusses ballads as a form of popular cultural discourse that was capable of contesting dominant constructions of the real. Printers of ballads often evaded the licensing requirements for texts (*Shepheards Devises: Edmund Spenser's "Shepheardes Calender" and the Institutions of Elizabethan Society* [Athens: University of Georgia Press, 1993], 52).

90 *C.S.P. Domestic 1598–1601*, 403. Inadequate clothing was a constant source of complaint and animosity among the recruits. When a contingent of men from Angelsey arrived for embarkation at Chester "very well apparelled with caps, cassocks, doublets, breeches, netherstocks, shoes and shirts," the Mayor reported that it "gave great discontentment to the residue of the soldiers which had no apparel, and to us some trouble for their pacification" (quoted in G. Dyfnallt Owen, *Elizabethan Wales: The Social Scene* [Cardiff: University of Wales Press, 1962], 236n177).

91 *Calendar of Wynn (of Gwydir) Papers, 1515–1690*, ed. John Ballinger (Aberystwyth: National Library of Wales, 1926), item 710.

92 *Ibid.*, items 174, 181; also see HMC, *Salisbury* MSS. 11:460, 498–99.

93 A. H. Dodd, *Studies in Stuart Wales* (Cardiff: University of Wales Press, 1952), 79. Penry Williams points out that "Wales provided the most convenient recruiting ground for Ireland and a useful base of operations" (*The Council in the Marches of Wales under Elizabeth I* [Cardiff: University of Wales Press, 1958], 115–16). He also gives estimates for selected years of the number of Welsh recruits sent to Ireland (117).

94 Nicholas Canny, "The Permissive Frontier: Social Control in English Settlements in Ireland and Virginia, 1550–1650," in K. R. Andrews, N. P. Canny, and P. E. H. Hair, eds., *The Westward Enterprise: English Activities in Ireland, the Atlantic, and America, 1480–1650* (Liverpool University Press, 1978), 19.

95 *Elizabethan Wales*, 74.

96 *C.S.P. Ireland 1599–1600*, 124.

97 *Ibid.*, 106. Also see Henry, "Essex and Ireland," 15–17.

98 Henry, "Essex and Ireland," 21. For Cecil's interference with Essex's mission and for evidence of disagreement among Essex and his officers, see L. W. Henry, "Contemporary Sources for Essex's Lieutenancy in Ireland, 1599," *Irish Historical Studies* 11 (1958), 8–17.

99 *C.S.P. Ireland 1599–1600*, 4–6.

100 Sir John Harington, *Nugae Antiquae: Being a Miscellaneous Collection of Original Papers*, ed. Thomas Park (London, 1804), 1:240–42.

101 James, *Society, Politics*, 444–45; Cadwallader, *Earl of Essex*, 27–33.

102 "The Crisis of the Aristocracy in *Julius Caesar*," *Renaissance Quarterly* 43 (1990): 102–3.

103 *Julius Caesar*, ed. A. R. Humphreys (Oxford University Press, 1984), 1.

104 Wayne A. Rebhorn discusses the influence of Essex on the factional struggles of *Julius Caesar* in "The Crisis of the Aristocracy," 100–6. At his trial, Essex was accused by Coke of seeking to become "Robert the first" of England (*State Trials*, ed. Howell, 1:1339). Richard McCoy argues that Essex's

ambitions were more limited to "broker[ing] the succession" (*The Rites of Knighthood*, 100).

105 Rebhorn, "The Crisis of the Aristocracy," 106–7.

106 In an earlier but related scene, Cinna the poet meets a street-mob that has been enraged by Antony's oration. When the plebeians mistake Cinna for one of the conspirators, he assures them "I am Cinna the poet!" Again suggesting the powerlessness of the intellectual, Cinna's self-defense proves futile and only hastens his demise: "Tear him for his bad verses, tear him for his bad verses" (3.3). For further discussion of the two poet scenes in *Julius Caesar*, see Gary Taylor, "Bardicide," in *Shakespeare and Cultural Traditions: The Selected Proceedings of the International Shakespearean Association: World Congress, Tokyo, 1991*, ed. Tetsuo Kishi, Roger Pringle, and Stanley Wells (London: Associated University Presses, 1994): 333–49.

107 Collins, ed., *Sidney Papers*, 2:127; Cadwallader, *Earl of Essex*, 57–58.

108 *C.S.P. Ireland 1599–1600*, 217.

109 *Ibid.*, 177.

110 In a letter of November 6, 1600, to Geoffrey Fenton, the queen, again hopeful of pardoning Tyrone, dropped her usual terms for him of rebel and traitor, referring to him instead by his lapsed English title (*ibid.*, 227–29).

111 Cadwallader, *Earl of Essex*, 69–70.

112 James, *Society, Politics*, 448–53.

113 *C.S.P. Domestic 1598–1601*, 550.

114 *The Shirburn Ballads 1585–1616*, ed. Andrew Clark (Oxford: Clarendon Press, 1907), 321–26.

115 *C.S.P. Ireland 1599–1600*, 178.

116 *C.S.P. Domestic 1598–1601*, 570.

117 *Ibid.*, 554.

118 See the directions for preachers in *ibid.*, 565–68, 589. In relaying the allegations against Essex, London's preachers proved less cooperative than Cecil would have liked. As Vincent Hussey remarked, the preachers, "from malice or desire to please, amplified [the charges] beyond all probability. On the one side they cry 'Crucify'; on the other there is such a jealousy of light and bad fellows, that it is rumoured the preachers of London will rise and deliver [Essex] out of the Tower" (584).

119 *C.S.P. Ireland 1599–1600*, 223.

120 Arthur F. Kinney ed., *Elizabethan Backgrounds: Historical Documents of the Age of Elizabeth I* (Archon Books, 1975), 346, 351.

121 Cyril Bentham Falls, *Mountjoy: Elizabethan General* (London: Odhams, 1955), 198–202.

122 Hans S. Pawlisch, *Sir John Davies and the Conquest of Ireland: A Study in Legal Imperialism* (Cambridge University Press, 1985), 4.

123 *Thomas Dekker: Selected Writings*, ed. E. D. Pendry, The Stratford-Upon-Avon Library 4 (Cambridge, Mass.: Harvard University Press, 1968), 39.

124 Moryson, *Itinerary*, 3:336; Thomas Gainsford, *The History of the Earle of Tirone* (London, 1619), 46–47.

125 *The Letters and Epigrams of Sir John Harington, Together with "The Prayse of Private Life"*, ed. Norman Egbert McClure (Philadelphia: University of Pennsylvania Press, 1930), 107; also see Philip S. Robinson, *The Plantation*

of Ulster: British Settlement in an Irish Landscape, 1600–1670 (New York: St. Martin's Press, 1984), 38.

126 "The Flight of the Earls, 1607," *Irish Historical Studies* 17 (1971): 391.

127 See Maxwell, *Irish History* 150–51, 292; and 203–5.

128 Sir John Davies, *A Discovery of the True Causes Why Ireland Was Never Entirely Subdued*, ed. James P. Myers, Jr. (Washington D.C.: Catholic University of America, 1988), 221; also see David Harris Willson, *King James VI and I* (London: Jonathan Cape, 1956), 326.

129 Bacon is quoted in Maxwell, *Irish History*, 274; for James's first speech to the English parliament, see Charles Howard McIlwain, ed., *The Political Works of James I* (Cambridge, Mass.: Harvard University Press, 1918), 272. Also see Willy Maley, "'Another Britain'?: Bacon's *Certain Considerations Touching the Plantation in Ireland* (1609)," *Prose Studies* 18 (1995): 1–18.

Works cited

Acts of the Privy Council of England, ed. J. R. Dasent. 32 vols. (London, 1890–1907).

Albright, Evelyn May. "The Folio Version of *Henry V* in Relation to Shakespeare's Times," *PMLA* 43 (1928): 722–56.

Allen, Michael J. B. and Kenneth Muir, eds. *Shakespeare's Plays in Quarto* (Berkeley: University of California Press, 1981).

Altman, Joel B. "'Vile Participation': the Amplification of Violence in the Theater of *Henry V*," *Shakespeare Quarterly* 42 (1991): 1–32.

Amussen, Susan. *An Ordered Society: Gender and Class in Early Modern England* (Oxford: Blackwell, 1988).

Anderson, Benedict. *Imagined Communities: Reflections on the Origin and Spread of Nationalism* (London: Verso, 1983).

Andrews, J. H. "Geography and Government in Elizabethan Ireland," in *Irish Geographical Studies*, ed. Nicholas Stephens and Robin E. Glasscock (Queen's University, Belfast, 1970), 178–91.

Andrews, K. R., N. P. Canny, and P. E. H. Hair, eds. *The Westward Enterprise: English Activities in Ireland, the Atlantic, and America, 1480–1650* (Liverpool University Press, 1978).

Andrews, Kenneth R. *Trade, Plunder, and Settlement: Maritime Enterprise and the Genesis of the British Empire, 1480–1630* (Cambridge University Press, 1984).

Anon. "Ms Notes to Spenser's *Faerie Queene*," *Notes and Queries* (December, 1957): 509–15.

Arber, Edward, ed. *A Transcript of the Registers of the Company of Stationers of London 1554–1640*, 5 vols. (London, 1875–77; reprinted Gloucester, Mass.: Peter Smith, 1967).

Austern, Linda Phyllis. "'Sing Againe Syren': the Female Musician and Sexual Enchantment in Elizabethan Life and Literature," *Renaissance Quarterly* 42 (1989): 420–48.

Aylmer, John. *An harborowe for faithfull and trewe subjectes, agaynst the late blowne blaste concerninge the governmet of wemen* (London, 1559).

Bacon, Francis. *The Essays*, ed. John Pitcher (Harmondsworth: Penguin, 1985).

Bagwell, Richard. *Ireland Under the Tudors*. 3 vols. (London: Holland Press, 1963).

Bailyn, Bernard and Philip D. Morgan, eds. *Strangers Within the Realm: Cultural Margins of the First British Empire* (Chapel Hill: University of North Carolina Press, 1991).

Baker, David J. "'Some Quirk, Some Subtle Evasion': Legal Subversion in Spenser's *A View of the Present State of Ireland*," *Spenser Studies* 6 (1986): 147–63.

"'*Wildehirissheman*': Colonialist Representation in Shakespeare's *Henry V*," *English Literary Renaissance* 22 (1992): 37–61.

"Off the Map: Charting Uncertainty in Renaissance Ireland," in Bradshaw, Hadfield, and Maley, eds., *Representing Ireland*, 76–92.

Bald, R. C. *John Donne: A Life* (Oxford University Press, 1970).

Baldo, Jonathan. "Wars of Memory in *Henry V*," *Shakespeare Quarterly* 47 (1996): 132–59.

Bartels, Emily C. *Spectacles of Strangeness: Imperialism, Alienation, and Marlowe* (Philadelphia: University of Pennsylvania Press, 1993).

Bartlett, Robert. *Gerald of Wales 1146–1223* (Oxford: Clarendon Press, 1982).

Bartley, J. O. *Teague, Shenkin and Sawney: Being an Historical Study of the Earliest Irish, Welsh, and Scottish Characters in English Plays* (Cork University Press, 1954).

Barton, Anne. "The King Disguised: Shakespeare's *Henry V* and the Comical History," in *The Triple Bond: Plays, Mainly Shakespearean, in Performance*, ed. Joseph G. Price (London: Penn. State University Press, 1975), 92–117.

Barton, Sir D. Plunket. *Links Between Ireland and Shakespeare* (Dublin: Maunsel, 1919).

Bates, Catherine. *The Rhetoric of Courtship in Elizabethan Language and Literature* (Cambridge University Press, 1992).

Beacon, Thomas. *Solon His Follie, or A Politique Discourse, Touching the Reformation of Common-Weales Conquered, Declined or Corrupted* (Oxford, 1594).

Bednarz, James P. "Ralegh in Spenser's Historical Allegory," *Spenser Studies* 4 (1983): 49–70.

Beier, A. L. *Masterless Men: The Vagrancy Problem in England, 1560–1640* (London: Methuen, 1985).

Bellamy, John. *The Tudor Law of Treason: An Introduction* (London: Routledge, 1979).

Belsey, Catherine. "The Illusion of Empire: Elizabethan Expansionism and Shakespeare's Second Tetralogy," *Literature and History* 1 (1990): 13–21.

Bennett, H. S. *English Books and Readers, 1558–1603: Being a Study in the History of the Book Trade in the Reign of Elizabeth I* (Cambridge University Press, 1965).

Bennett, Josephine Waters. "The Allegory of Sir Artegall in *F.Q.* V, xi–xii," *Studies in Philology* 37 (1940): 177–200.

The Evolution of "The Faerie Queene" (New York: Burt Franklin, 1960).

Berleth, Richard. *The Twilight Lords: An Irish Chronicle* (New York: Alfred A. Knopf, 1978).

Berry, Herbert and E. K. Timings. "Spenser's Pension," *Review of English Studies* 11 (1960): 254–59.

Berry, Philippa. *Of Chastity and Power: Elizabethan Literature and the Unmarried Queen* (London: Routledge, 1989).

Bevington, David. *Tudor Drama and Politics: A Critical Approach to Topical Meaning* (Cambridge, Mass.: Harvard University Press, 1968).

Bevington, David, ed. *Henry IV, Part 1* (Oxford: Clarendon Press, 1987).
   The Complete Works of Shakespeare, 4th edition (New York: Harper Collins, 1992).
Bindoff, S. T., J. Hurstfield, and C. H. Williams, eds. *Elizabethan Government and Society: Essays Presented to Sir John Neale* (University of London Press, 1961).
Blackburn, William. "Spenser's Merlin," *Renaissance and Reformation* 4 (1980): 179–98.
Blenerhasset, Thomas. *The Plantation in Ulster* (London, 1610).
Boose, Lynda E. " 'The Getting of a Lawfull Race': Racial Discourse in Early Modern England and the Unrepresentable Black Woman," in Hendricks and Parker, eds., *Women, "Race," and Writing*, 35–54.
Born, H. R. "The Date of *2, 3 Henry VI*," *Shakespeare Quarterly* 25 (1974): 323–34.
Borris, Kenneth. *Spenser's Poetics of Prophecy in "The Faerie Queene" V* English Literary Studies Monograph Series no. 52. (Victoria, B.C., Canada: University of Victoria, 1991).
Bottigheimer, Karl S. "Kingdom and Colony: Ireland in the Westward Enterprise 1536–1660," in Andrews, Canny, and Hair, eds., *The Westward Enterprise*, 45–64.
Bowen, Ivor, ed. *The Statutes of Wales* (London, 1908).
Bradbrook, Muriel. "No Room at the Top: Spenser's Pursuit of Fame," *Elizabethan Poetry*, Stratford-Upon-Avon Studies 2 (New York: St. Martin's Press, 1960).
Bradshaw, Brendan. "Native Reaction to the Westward Enterprise: a Case-Study in Gaelic Ideology," in Andrews, Canny, and Hair, eds., *The Westward Enterprise*, 65–80.
   "Sword, Word and Strategy in the Reformation in Ireland," *Historical Journal* 21 (1978): 475–502.
   "Robe and Sword in the Conquest of Ireland," in *Law and Government Under the Tudors*, ed. Claire Cross, David Loades, and J. J. Scarisbrick (Cambridge University Press, 1988), 139–62.
   "Geoffrey Keating: Apologist of Irish Ireland," in Bradshaw, Hadfield, and Maley, eds., *Representing Ireland*, 166–90.
Bradshaw, Brendan, Andrew Hadfield, and Willy Maley, eds. *Representing Ireland: Literature and the Origins of Conflict, 1534–1660* (Cambridge University Press, 1993).
Brady, Ciaran. "Spenser's Irish Crisis: Humanism and Experience in the 1590s," *Past and Present* 111 (1986): 17–49.
   "Court, Castle and Country: the Framework of Government in Tudor Ireland," in Brady and Gillespie, eds., *Natives and Newcomers*, 22–49.
   "Thomas Butler, Earl of Ormond (1531–1614) and Reform in Tudor Ireland," in *Worsted in the Game: Losers in Irish History*, ed. Ciaran Brady (Dublin: The Lilliput Press, 1989), 49–59.
   "The Road to the *View*: on the Decline of Reform Thought in Tudor Ireland," in Coughlan, ed., *Spenser and Ireland*, 25–45.
   "Political Women and Reform in Tudor Ireland," in MacCurtain and O'Dowd, eds., *Women in Early Modern Ireland*, 69–90.

Brady, Ciaran, and Raymond Gillespie, eds. *Natives and Newcomers: Essays on the Making of Irish Colonial Society 1534–1641* (Dublin: Irish Academic Press, 1986).

Brantlinger, Patrick. "Victorians and Africans: The Genealogy of the Myth of the Dark Continent," in *"Race," Writing, and Difference*, ed. Henry Louis Gates, Jr. (University of Chicago Press, 1986), 185–222.

Braunmuller, A. R. *George Peele* (Boston: Twayne, 1983).

Brayshay, Mark. "Royal Post-Horse Routes in England and Wales: the Evolution of the Network in the Later-Sixteenth and Early-Seventeenth Century," *Journal of Historical Geography* 17 (1991): 373–89.

Breatnach, Pádraig A. "The Chief's Poet," *Royal Irish Academy Proceedings* 83, C, 3 (1983): 37–79.

Breight, Curt. "'Treason Doth Never Prosper': *The Tempest* and the Discourse of Treason," *Shakespeare Quarterly* 41 (1990): 1–28.

Brennan, Gillian E. "Papists and Patriotism in Elizabethan England," *Recusant History: A Journal of Research in Post- Reformation Catholic History in the British Isles* 19 (1988): 1–15.

Brink, Jean R. "Who Fashioned Edmund Spenser?: The Textual History of *Complaints*," *Studies in Philology* 88 (1991): 153–68.

"Constructing the *View of the Present State of Ireland*," *Spenser Studies* 11 (1990): 203–28.

Bristol, Michael. *Carnival and Theater: Plebeian Culture and the Structure of Authority in Renaissance England* (New York: Methuen, 1985).

Brooke, Nicholas, ed. *The Tragedy of Macbeth* (Oxford University Press, 1990).

Brown, Keith. "Historical Context and *Henry V*," *Cahiers Elisabethains* 29 (1986): 77–81.

"The Price of Friendship: the 'Well Affected' and English Economic Clientage in Scotland before 1603," in *Scotland and England 1286–1815*, ed. Mason, 139–62.

Brown, Paul. "'This Thing of Darkness I Acknowledge Mine': *The Tempest* and the Discourse of Colonialism," in *Political Shakespeare: New Essays in Cultural Materialism*, ed. Jonathan Dollimore and Alan Sinfield (Ithaca: Cornell University Press, 1985), 48–71.

Bryskett, Lodowick. *The Works of Lodowick Bryskett*, ed. J. H. P. Pafford (England: Gregg International, 1972).

Butlin, R. A. "Land and People, c.1600," in Moody, Martin, and Byrne, eds., *A New History of Ireland*, 3: 142–86.

Cadwallader, Laura Hanes. *The Career of the Earl of Essex: From the Islands Voyage of 1597 to His Execution in 1601* (Philadelphia: University of Pennsylvania Press, 1923).

Cain, Thomas H. *Praise in "The Faerie Queene"* (Lincoln: University of Nebraska Press, 1978).

Cairncross, Andrew S., ed. *The Second Part of King Henry VI* (London: Methuen, 1962).

Cairns, David, and Shaun Richards. *Writing Ireland: Colonialism, Nationalism, and Culture* (Manchester University Press, 1988).

Calendar of the Carew Manuscripts Preserved in the Archiepiscopal Library at

Lambeth, 1515–1624, ed. J. S. Brewer and William Bullen. 6 vols. (London: 1867–73).

Calendar of State Papers, Domestic of the Reigns of Edward VI, Mary, Elizabeth, and James I, ed. Robert Lemon and Mary Anne Everett Green. 12 vols. (London, 1856–72).

Calendar of State Papers Relating to Ireland, of the Reigns of Henry VIII, Edward VI, Mary, and Elizabeth, ed. Hans Claude Hamilton *et al.* 11 vols. (London, 1860–1912).

Calendar of Wynn (of Gwydir) Papers, 1515–1690, ed. John Ballinger (Aberystwyth: National Library of Wales, 1926).

Camden, William. *The History of the Most Renowned and Victorious Princess Elizabeth Late Queen of England (Selected Chapters),* ed. Wallace T. MacCaffrey (University of Chicago Press, 1970).

Remains Concerning Britain, ed. R. D. Dunn (University of Toronto Press, 1984).

Campbell, Lily B. "The Use of Historical Patterns in the Reign of Elizabeth," *The Huntington Library Quarterly* 2 (1938): 135–67.

Campbell, Lily B., ed. *The Mirror for Magistrates* (Cambridge University Press, 1938).

Campion, Edmund. *Historie of Ireland,* ed. Rudolf B. Gottfried (New York: Scholars' Facsimiles and Reprints, 1940).

Candido, Joseph. "Captain Thomas Stukeley: the Man, the Theatrical Record, and the Origins of Tudor 'Biographical Drama,'" *Anglia* 105 (1987): 50–68.

Canny, Nicholas. "The Flight of the Earls, 1607," *Irish Historical Studies* 17 (1971): 380–99.

"The Ideology of English Colonization: from Ireland to America," *William and Mary Quarterly* 3rd series, 30 (1973): 574–98.

The Formation of the Old English Elite in Ireland (Dublin: National University of Ireland, 1975).

The Elizabethan Conquest of Ireland: A Pattern Established, 1565–76 (Hassocks: Harvester, 1976).

"The Permissive Frontier: Social Control in English Settlements in Ireland and Virginia, 1550–1650," in Andrews, Canny, and Hair, eds., *The Westward Enterprise,* 17–44.

The Upstart Earl: A Study of the Social and Mental World of Richard Boyle, First Earl of Cork, 1566–1643 (Cambridge University Press, 1982).

"The Formation of the Irish Mind: Religion, Politics and Gaelic Irish Literature 1580–1750," *Past and Present* 95 (1982): 91–116.

"Identity Formation in Ireland: the Emergence of the Anglo-Irish," in *Colonial Identity in the Atlantic World, 1500–1800,* ed. Nicholas Canny and Anthony Pagden (Princeton University Press, 1987), 159–212.

Kingdom and Colony: Ireland in the Atlantic World, 1560–1800 (Baltimore: Johns Hopkins University Press, 1988).

"Debate: Spenser's Irish Crisis: Humanism and Experience in the 1590s," *Past and Present* 120 (1988): 201–9.

"Early Modern Ireland c. 1500–1700" in *The Oxford Illustrated History of Ireland,* ed. R. F. Foster (Oxford University Press, 1989), 104–60.

Carew, Richard. *The Survey of Cornwall*, ed. F. E. Halliday (London: Melrose, 1953).

Carlin, Norah. "The Levellers and the Conquest of Ireland in 1649," *The Historical Journal* 30 (1987): 269–88.

Carney, James, ed. *Poems on the Butlers of Ormond, Cahir, and Dunboyne (A.D. 1400–1650)* (Dublin Institute for Advanced Studies, 1945).

Carpenter, Frederic Ives. "Spenser in Ireland," *Modern Philology* 19 (1921–22): 405–19.

A Reference Guide to Edmund Spenser (New York: Kraus Reprint, 1969).

Carroll, Clare. "The Construction of Gender and the Cultural and Political Other in *The Faerie Qveene 5* and *A View of the Present State of Ireland*: the Critics, the Context, and the Case of Radigund," *Criticism* 32 (1990): 163–91.

"Representations of Women in Some Early Modern English Tracts on the Colonization of Ireland," *Albion* 25 (1993): 379–93.

Carroll, D. Allen. "Rich and Greene: Elizabethan Beast Fables and Ireland," *Eire–Ireland* 25 (1990): 106–13.

Chamberlain, John. *The Letters of John Chamberlain*, ed. Norman Egbert McClure (Philadelphia: The American Philosophical Society, 1939). 2 vols.

Chambers, Anne. *Granuaile: The Life and Times of Grace O'Malley, c.1530–1603* (Dublin: Wolfhound, 1979).

Chambers, E. K. *Sir Henry Lee: An Elizabethan Portrait* (Oxford: Clarendon Press, 1936).

The Elizabethan Stage. 4 vols. (Oxford: Clarendon Press, 1923).

Churchyard, Thomas. *The Worthines of Wales* (Manchester: The Spenser Society, 1876).

Clapham, John. *Elizabeth of England: Certain Observations Concerning the Life and Reign of Queen Elizabeth*, ed. Evelyn Plummer Read and Conyers Read (Philadelphia: University of Pennsylvania Press, 1951).

Clare, Janet. *"Art Made Tongue-tied by Authority": Elizabethan and Jacobean Dramatic Censorship* (Manchester University Press, 1990).

Clark, Andrew, ed. *The Shirburn Ballads 1585–1616* (Oxford: Clarendon Press, 1907).

Cohen, Derek. "The Rite of Violence in *1 Henry IV*," *Shakespeare Survey* 38 (1985): 77–84.

Colley, Linda. "Britishness and Otherness: An Argument," *Journal of British Studies* 31 (1992): 309–29.

Collinson, Patrick. "The Elizabethan Church and the New Religion," in Haigh, ed., *The Reign of Elizabeth*, 169–94.

The Birthpangs of Protestant England: Religious and Cultural Change in the Sixteenth and Seventeenth Centuries (London: Macmillan, 1988).

The Complete Peerage or a History of the House of Lords and all its Members from the Earliest Times, ed. George Edward Cokayne, H. A. Doubleday, Geoffrey H. White, and Lord Howard de Walden (London: St. Catherine Press, 1945). Vol. 10.

Cooper, Thomas. *Thesaurus Linguae Romanae et Britannicae* (London, 1565).

Corbin, Peter and Douglas Sedge. *The Oldcastle Controversy: Sir John Oldcastle,*

Part 1 and The Famous Victories of Henry V, The Revels Plays Companion Library (Manchester University Press, 1991).

Cosgrove, Art. "Principal Officers of the Central Government in Ireland, 1172–1922," in *A New History of Ireland*, ed. Moody, Martin, and Byrne, 9:476–77.

Coughlan, Patricia. "'Some Secret Scourge Which Shall by Her Come unto England': Ireland and Incivility in Spenser," in Coughlan, ed., *Spenser and Ireland*, 46–74.

Couglan, Patricia, ed. *Spenser and Ireland: An Interdisciplinary Perspective* (Cork University Press, 1989).

Coulomb, Charles A. *The Administration of the English Borders During the Reign of Elizabeth* (Philadelphia: University of Pennsylvania Press, 1911).

Cressy, David. *Bonfires and Bells: National Memory and the Protestant Calendar in Elizabethan and Stuart England* (London: Weidenfeld and Nicolson, 1989).

Cruickshank, C. G. *Elizabeth's Army*, 2nd edition (Oxford: Clarendon Press, 1966).

Cummings, R. M. *Spenser: The Critical Heritage* (New York: Barnes and Noble, 1971).

Cunningham, Bernadette. "Women and Gaelic Literature, 1500–1800," in Mac-Curtain and O'Dowd, eds., *Women in Early Modern Ireland*, 147–59.

Davies, Sir John. *A Discovery of the True Causes Why Ireland Was Never Entirely Subdued*, ed. James P. Myers, Jr. (Washington D.C.: Catholic University of America, 1988).

Davies, Rees. "Race Relations in Post-Conquest Wales: Confrontation and Compromise," *Transactions of the Honourable Society of Cymmrodorion* (1975–75).

Davies, R. R. "English Synopsis: The Manners and Morals of the Welsh," *Welsh History Review* 12 (1984): 174–79.

"Henry I and Wales," in *Studies in Medieval History Presented to R. H. C. Davis*, ed. Henry Mayr-Harting and R. I. Moore (London: Hambledon Press, 1985), 133–47.

Conquest, Coexistence and Change: Wales 1063–1415 (Oxford University Press, 1987).

"In Praise of British History," in *The British Isles 1100–1500: Comparisons, Contrasts and Connections*, ed. R. R. Davies (Edinburgh: John Donald, 1988), 9–26.

Domination and Conquest: The Experience of Ireland, Scotland and Wales 100–1300 (Cambridge University Press, 1990).

"The Peoples of Britain and Ireland 1100–1400," *Transactions of the Royal Historical Society* 6th series 4 (1994): 1–20.

Dawson, Jane E. A. "William Cecil and the British Dimension of Early Elizabethan Foreign Policy," *History: The Journal of the Historical Association* 74 (1989): 196–216.

De Breffny, Brian and Rosemary Ffolliott. *The Houses of Ireland: Domestic Architecture from the Medieval Castle to the Edwardian Villa* (New York: Viking Press, 1975).

De Grazia, Margreta, and Peter Stallybrass. "The Materiality of the Shake-spearean Text," *Shakespeare Quarterly* 44 (1993): 255–83.

Dekker, Thomas. *Thomas Dekker: Selected Writings*, ed. E. D. Pendry. The Stratford-Upon-Avon Library 4 (Cambridge, Mass.: Harvard University Press, 1968).

De Maisse. *A Journal of all that was Accomplished by Monsieur De Maisse Ambassador in England from King Henri IV to Queen Elizabeth Anno Domini 1597*, ed. G. B. Harrison (London: Nonesuch Press, 1931).

Derricke, John. *The Image of Irelande with a Discoverie of Woodkarne*, ed. David B. Quinn (Blackstaff Press, 1985).

Dickins, Bruce. "The Irish Broadside of 1571 and Queen Elizabeth's Types," *Transactions of the Cambridge Bibliographical Society* 1 (1949): 48–60.

Dictionary of National Biography (DNB), ed. Sidney Lee and Leslie Stephen. 63 vols. (New York: Macmillan, 1885–1900).

Doan, James E. "The Ó'Dálaigh Family of Bardic Poets, 1139–1691," *Eire-Ireland* 20 (1985): 19–31.

Dobin, Howard. *Merlin's Disciples: Prophecy, Poetry, and Power in Renaissance England* (Stanford University Press, 1990).

Dodd, A. H. *Studies in Stuart Wales* (Cardiff: University of Wales Press, 1952).

Donne, John. *The Satires, Epigrams and Verse Letters*, ed. W. Milgate (Oxford: Clarendon Press, 1967).

The Complete English Poems, ed. A. J. Smith (Harmondsworth: Penguin, 1978).

Douglas, Mary. *Purity and Danger: An Analysis of the Concepts of Pollution and Taboo* (London: Ark, 1985).

Dubrow, Heather, and Richard Strier, eds. *The Historical Renaissance: New Essays on Tudor and Stuart Literature and Culture* (University of Chicago Press, 1988).

Duncan-Jones, Katherine. *Sir Philip Sidney: Courtier Poet* (New Haven: Yale University Press, 1991).

Dunne, T. J. "The Gaelic Response to Conquest and Colonisation: the Evidence of the Poetry," *Studia Hibernica* 20 (1980): 7–30.

Durston, Chris. "'Let Ireland be Quiet': Opposition in England to the Cromwellian Conquest of Ireland," *History Workshop Journal* 21 (1986): 105–13.

Dutton, Richard. *Mastering the Revels: The Regulation and Censorship of English Renaissance Drama* (University of Iowa Press, 1991).

Eccles, Mark. "Barnabe Googe in England, Spain, and Ireland," *English Literary Renaissance* 15 (1985): 353–70.

E.C.S. *The Government of Ireland Under Sir John Perrot 1584–1588* (London, 1626).

Edwards, Philip. *Threshold of a Nation: A Study in English and Irish Drama* (Cambridge University Press, 1979).

Edwards, R. Dudley. "Ireland, Elizabeth I, and the Counter-Reformation," in Bindoff, Hurstfield, and Williams, eds., *Elizabethan Government and Society*, 315–339.

Edwards, R. W. Dudley, and Mary O'Dowd. *Sources for Early Modern Irish History, 1534–1641* (Cambridge University Press, 1985).

Ellis, Steven G. *Tudor Ireland: Crown, Community and the Conflict of Cultures, 1470–1603* (London: Longman, 1985).

"'Not Mere English': the British Perspective, 1400–1650," *History Today* 38 (1988): 41–48.

Emerson, Kathy Lynn. *Wives and Daughters: The Women of Sixteenth Century England* (Troy, New York: Whitston, 1984).

Erickson, Peter. "Fathers, Sons, and Brothers in *Henry V*," in *William Shakespeare's "Henry V"*, ed. Harold Bloom (New York: Chelsea, 1988), 111–33.

"The Order of the Garter, the Cult of Elizabeth, and Class–Gender Tension in *The Merry Wives of Windsor*," in Howard and O'Connor, eds., *Shakespeare Reproduced*, 116–140.

Fackler, Herbert V. "Shakespeare's 'Irregular and Wild' Glendower: the Dramatic Use of Source Materials," *Discourse: A Review of the Liberal Arts* 13 (1970): 306–14.

Falkiner, C. Litton, ed. *Illustrations of Irish History and Topography, Mainly of the Seventeenth Century* (London: Longmans, 1904).

Fallon, Niall. *The Armada in Ireland* (Middletown, Conn.: Wesleyan University Press, 1978).

Falls, Cyril Bentham. *Elizabeth's Irish Wars* (London: Methuen, 1950).

Mountjoy: Elizabethan General (London: Odhams, 1955).

"Black Tom of Ormonde," *The Irish Sword: The Journal of the Military History Society of Ireland* 5 (1961–62): 10–22.

Ferguson, Margaret W., Maureen Quilligan, and Nancy J. Vickers, eds. *Rewriting the Renaissance: The Discourses of Sexual Difference in Early Modern Europe* (University of Chicago Press, 1986).

Feuillerat, Albert, ed. *Sir Philip Sidney: The Defence of Poetry, Political Discourses, Correspondence, Translations* (Cambridge University Press, 1923).

Flanagan, Marie Therese. *Irish Society, Anglo-Norman Settlers, Angevin Kingship: Interactions in Ireland in the Late Twelfth Century* (Oxford: Clarendon Press, 1989).

Fleming, Juliet. "The Ladies' Man and the Age of Elizabeth," in *Sexuality and Gender in Early Modern Europe: Institutions, Texts, Images*, ed. James Grantham Turner (Cambridge University Press, 1993), 158–81.

Foakes, R. A., and R. T. Rickert, eds. *Henslowe's Diary* (Cambridge University Press, 1961).

Fogarty, Anne. "The Colonization of Language: Narrative Strategies in *A View of the Present State of Ireland* and *The Faerie Queene*, Book VI," in Coughlan, ed. *Spenser and Ireland*, 75–108.

Ford, Alan. *The Protestant Reformation in Ireland, 1590–1641* (New York: Lang, 1987).

Foster, R. F., ed. *The Oxford Illustrated History of Ireland* (Oxford University Press, 1991).

Frame, Robin. "England and Ireland, 1171–1399," in *England and her Neighbours, 1066–1453*, ed. Michael Jones and Malcolm Vale (London: Hambledon Press, 1989), 139–55.

"'Les Engleys Nées en Irlande': the English Political Identity in Medieval Ireland," *Transactions of the Royal Historical Society* 6th series 2 (1992): 83–102.

Frye, Susan. *Elizabeth I: The Competition for Representation* (Oxford University Press, 1993).

Fumerton, Patricia. "Exchanging Gifts: the Elizabethan Currency of Children and Poetry," *ELH* 53 (1986): 241–78.

Gainsford, Thomas. *The True Exemplary, and Remarkable History of the Earle of Tirone* (London, 1619). The English Experience 25 (New York: Da Capo Press, 1968).

Galloway, Bruce. *The Union of England and Scotland, 1603–1608* (Edinburgh: John Donald, 1986).

Geoffrey of Monmouth. *The History of the Kings of Britain*, ed. and tr. Lewis Thorpe (Harmondsworth: Penguin, 1966).

Gerald of Wales. *The History and Topography of Ireland*, ed. and tr. John J. O'Meara (Harmondsworth: Penguin, 1982).

The Journey through Wales and The Description of Wales, ed. and tr. Lewis Thorpe (Harmondsworth: Penguin, 1978).

Gillingham, John. "Images of Ireland 1170–1600: The Origins of English Imperialism," *History Today* 37 (1987): 16–22.

"The Beginnings of English Imperialism," *The Journal of Historical Sociology* 5 (1992): 392–409.

"The English Invasion of Ireland," in Bradshaw, Hadfield, and Maley, eds., *Representing Ireland*, 24–42.

Gosson, Stephen. *The Schoole of Abuse, Conteining a Plesaunt invective against Poets, Pipers, Plaiers, Jesters, and such like Caterpillers of a Commonwealth* (London, 1579).

Gottfried, Rudolf B. "Spenser's *View* and Essex," *PMLA* 52 (1937): 645–51.

"The Early Development of the Section on Ireland in Camden's *Britannia*," *ELH* 10 (1943): 117–30.

Gray, M. M. "The Influence of Spenser's Irish Experience on *The Faerie Queene*," *Review of English Studies* 6 (1930): 413–28.

Greenblatt, Stephen. *Renaissance Self-Fashioning: From More to Shakespeare* (University of Chicago Press, 1980).

"Learning to Curse: Aspects of Linguistic Colonialism in the Sixteenth Century." Ch.2, *Learning to Curse: Essays in Early Modern Culture* (New York: Routledge, 1990).

Greenlaw, Edwin, Charles Grosvenor Osgood, Frederick Morgan Padelford, and Ray Heffner, eds. *The Works of Edmund Spenser: A Variorum Edition.* 10 vols. (Baltimore: Johns Hopkins University Press, 1932–49).

Greg, W. W. "Samuel Harsnett and Hayward's *Henry IV*," *The Library* 5th series 11 (1956): 1–10.

Gurr, Andrew. "*Henry V* and the Bees' Commonwealth," *Shakespeare Survey* 30 (1977): 61–72.

Playgoing in Shakespeare's London (Cambridge University Press, 1988).

The Shakespearean Stage, 1574–1642, 3rd edition (Cambridge University Press, 1992).

Gurr, Andrew, ed. *King Henry V* (Cambridge University Press, 1992).

Guy, John. *Tudor England* (Oxford University Press, 1988).

Guy, John, ed. *The Reign of Elizabeth I: Court and Culture in the Last Decade* (Cambridge University Press, 1995).

Hadfield, Andrew. "Briton and Scythian: Tudor Representations of Irish Origins," *Irish Historical Studies* 28 (1993): 390–408.

"Spenser, Ireland, and Sixteenth-Century Political Theory," *Modern Language Notes* 89 (1994): 1–18.

Literature, Politics, and National Identity (Cambridge University Press, 1994).

Hadfield, Andrew, and John McVeagh, eds. *Strangers to that Land: British Perceptions of Ireland from the Reformation to the Famine*, Ulster Editions and Monographs 5 (Gerrards Cross: Colin Smythe, 1994).

Haigh, Christopher. "The Church of England, the Catholics and the People," in Haigh, ed., *Reign of Elizabeth*, 195–219.

"The Governance of the Realm: Bureaucracy and Aristocracy," in *Queen Elizabeth I: Most Politick Princess*, ed. Simon Adams (London: History Today, nd.).

Haigh, Christopher, ed. *The Reign of Elizabeth I* (Athens: University of Georgia Press, 1985).

The English Reformation Revised (Cambridge University Press, 1987).

Hakluyt, Richard. *A Discourse of Western Planting*, ed. David B. Quinn and Alison M. Quinn (London: The Hakluyt Society, 1993).

Hale, J. R. "Incitement to Violence: English Divines on the Theme of War, 1578–1631" in *Renaissance War Studies* (London: Hambledon Press, 1983), 487–517.

Hall, Edward. *The Union of the Two Noble and Illustre Families of Lancastre and Yorke* (1548). Reprinted as *Hall's Chronicle; Containing the History of England, During the Reign of Henry the Fourth, and the Succeeding Monarchs, to the End of the Reign of Henry the Eighth* (London, 1809).

Hall, Joseph. *The Collected Poems of Joseph Hall*, ed. A. Davenport (Liverpool University Press, 1949).

Halpern, Richard. "Puritanism and Maenadism in *A Mask*," in Ferguson, Quilligan, and Vickers, eds., *Rewriting the Renaissance*, 88–105.

Hamilton, A. C., ed. *The Faerie Queene* (New York: Longman, 1977).

Hammer, Paul E. J. "The Earl of Essex, Fulke Greville, and the Employment of Scholars," *Studies in Philology* 41 (1994): 167–76.

"The Uses of Scholarship: the Secretariat of Robert Devereux, Second Earl of Essex, c.1585–1601," *English Historical Review* 109 (1994): 26–51.

Harington, Sir John. *Nugae Antiquae: Being a Miscellaneous Collection of Original Papers*, ed. Thomas Park (London, 1804). 2 vols.

A Short View of the State of Ireland, ed. W. Dunn MacRay, in *Anecdota Bodleiana*, vol.1 (Oxford and London: James Parker, 1879).

The Letters and Epigrams of Sir John Harington, Together with "The Prayse of Private Life", ed. Norman Egbert McClure (Philadelphia: University of Pennsylvania Press, 1930).

Harrington, John P. "A Tudor Writer's Tracts on Ireland, His Rhetoric," *Eire-Ireland* 17 (1982): 92–103.

Hattaway, Michael, ed. *The First Part of King Henry VI* (Cambridge University Press, 1990).

The Second Part of King Henry VI (Cambridge University Press, 1991).

Hayes-McCoy, G. A. "The Completion of the Tudor Conquest and the Advance of the Counter-Reformation, 1571–1603," in Moody, Martin, and Byrne, eds., *A New History of Ireland*, 3:142–86.

"Strategy and Tactics in Irish Warfare, 1593–1601," *Irish Historical Studies* 2 (1940–41): 258–60.

"The Army of Ulster, 1593–1601," *The Irish Sword* 1 (1949/1953): 105–17.

Hayward, John. *The First and Second Parts of John Hayward's The Life and Raigne of King Henrie IIII*, ed. John J. Manning. Camden 4th series vol. 42 (London: Royal Historical Society, 1991).

Heffner, Ray. "Spenser's *View of Ireland*: Some Observations," *Modern Language Quarterly* 3 (1942): 507–15.

Helgerson, Richard. *Self-Crowned Laureates: Spenser, Jonson, Milton and the Literary System* (Berkeley: University of California Press, 1983).

Forms of Nationhood: The Elizabethan Writing of England (University of Chicago Press, 1992).

Hendricks, Margo, and Patricia Parker, eds. *Women, "Race," and Writing in the Early Modern Period* (London: Routledge, 1994).

Hendricks, Margo. "Managing the Barbarian: *the Tragedy of Dido, Queen of Carthage*," *Renaissance Drama* 23 (1992): 165–88.

Heninger, S. K., Jr. "Spenser and Sidney at Leicester House," *Spenser Studies* 8 (1987): 239–49.

Henley, Pauline. *Spenser in Ireland* (New York: Longmans Green, 1928).

"The Treason of Sir John Perrot," *Studies: An Irish Quarterly* 21 (1932): 404–22.

Henry, L. W. "Contemporary Sources for Essex's Lieutenancy in Ireland, 1599," *Irish Historical Studies* 11 (1958): 8–17.

"The Earl of Essex and Ireland, 1599," *Bulletin of the Institute of Historical Research* 32 (1959): 1–23.

Herbert, Sir William. *Croftus Sive De Hibernia Liber*, ed. and tr. Arthur Keaveney and John A. Madden (Dublin: Irish Manuscripts Commission, 1992).

Hiller, Geoffrey G. "'Sacred Bards' and 'Wise Druides': Drayton and his Archetype of the Poet," *ELH* 51 (1984): 1–15.

Hinman, Charlton, ed. *The First Folio of Shakespeare: The Norton Facsimile* (New York: Norton, 1968).

Hinton, Edward M. *Ireland Through Tudor Eyes* (Philadelphia: University of Pennsylvania Press, 1935).

Hinton, Edward M., ed. "Rych's *Anothomy of Ireland*, with an Account of the Author," *PMLA* 55 (1940): 73–101.

Historical Manuscripts Commission Reports (HMC).

Hogan, Edmund, ed. *The Description of Ireland, and the State thereof as it is at this Present in Anno 1598* (London, 1878).

Holderness, Graham. *Shakespeare's History* (New York: St. Martin's Press, 1985).

Holderness, Graham, Nick Potter, and John Turner. *Shakespeare: The Play of History* (London: Macmillan, 1988).

Holinshed, Raphael. *Holinshed's Chronicles of England, Scotland, and Ireland (1587)* (Reprinted London, 1807–8, 6 vols.).

Holmes, Richard. *Resistance and Compromise: The Political Thought of the Elizabethan Catholics* (Cambridge University Press, 1982).

Honigmann, E. A. J. *Shakespeare: The "Lost Years"* (Manchester University Press, 1985).

Hore, Herbert F. "Irish Bardism in 1561," *The Ulster Journal of Archaeology* 1st series 6 (1858): 165–67, 202–12.

Hore, Herbert F., ed. "Sir Henry Sidney's Memoir of his Government in Ireland, 1583," *The Ulster Journal of Archaeology* 1st series 3 (1856): 33–52, 85–109, 336–57; 5 (1857): 299–323; 8 (1860): 179–195.

Houlbrooke, Ralph. *The English Family, 1450–1700* (London: Longman, 1984).

Howard, Jean E. "The New Historicism in Renaissance Studies," *English Literary Renaissance* 16 (1986): 13–43.

The Stage and Social Struggle in Early Modern London (London: Routledge, 1994).

Howard, Jean E., and Marion F. O'Connor, eds. *Shakespeare Reproduced: The Text in History and Ideology* (New York: Methuen, 1987).

Howell, T. B., ed. *A Complete Collection of State Trials and Proceedings for High Treason and Other Crimes and Misdemeanors from the Earliest Period to the Year 1783*, vol. 1 (London, 1816). 21 vols.

Howells, Brian, ed. *Elizabethan Pembrokeshire: The Evidence of George Owen* (Pembrokeshire Record Society, 1973).

Hughes, Arthur E. "The Welsh National Emblem: Leek or Daffodil?" *Y Cymmrodor* 26 (1916): 147–90.

Hughes, Paul L., and James F. Larkin, eds. *The Later Tudors (1588–1603)* (New Haven: Yale University Press, 1969), vol. 3 of *Tudor Royal Proclamations*. 3 vols.

Hulse, Clark. "Spenser, Bacon, and the Myth of Power," in Dubrow and Strier eds., *The Historical Renaissance*, 315–46.

Humphreys, A. R., ed. *The Second Part of King Henry IV* (London: Methuen, 1966).

Julius Caesar (Oxford University Press, 1984).

Hurstfield, Joel. *The Elizabethan Nation* (London: British Broadcasting Corporation, 1964).

"The Succession Struggle in Late Elizabethan England," in Bindoff, Hurstfield, and Williams eds., *Elizabethan Government and Society*, 369–96.

Hutton, Matthew. *The Correspondence of Dr. Matthew Hutton, Archbishop of York* (London: Surtees Society, 1843).

Hyde, Douglas. *A Literary History of Ireland From Earliest Times to the Present Day* (London: T. Fisher Unwin, 1920).

Jack, R. Ian. *Medieval Wales* (Ithaca: Cornell University Press, 1972).

Jackson, Donald. "The Irish Language and Tudor Government," *Eire–Ireland* 8 (1973): 21–29.

James, Mervyn. *Society, Politics and Culture: Studies in Early Modern England* (Cambridge University Press, 1986).

Jardine, Lisa. "Encountering Ireland: Gabriel Harvey, Edmund Spenser, and English Colonial Ventures," in Bradshaw, Hadfield, and Maley eds., *Representing Ireland*, 60–75.

Jeninges, Edward. *A Briefe Discovery of the Damages that Happen to this Realme by Disordered and Unlawful Diet* (London, 1593)

Jenkins, Raymond. "Spenser and the Clerkship in Munster," *PMLA* 47 (1932): 109–21.

"Spenser with Lord Grey in Ireland," *PMLA* 52 (1937): 338– 53.

"Spenser: the Uncertain Years 1584–1589," *PMLA* 53 (1938): 350–62.

Jones, Ann Rosalind. "Italians and Others: Venice and the Irish in *Coryat's Crudities* and *The White Devil*," *Renaissance Drama* 18 (1987): 101–19.

Jones, Anne Rosalind, and Peter Stallybrass. "Dismantling Irena: the Sexualizing of Ireland in Early Modern England," in *Nationalisms and Sexualities*, ed. Andrew Parker, Mary Russo, Doris Sommer, Patricia Yaeger (New York: Routledge, 1992), 157–71.

Jones, W. R. "England Against the Celtic Fringe: a Study in Cultural Stereotypes," *Cahiers d'Histoire Mondiale* 13 (1971): 155–71.

"*Giraldus Redivivus* – English Historians, Irish Apologists, and the Works of Gerald of Wales," *Eire–Ireland* 9 (1974): 3–20.

Jorgensen, Paul A. *Shakespeare's Military World* (Berkeley: University of California Press, 1956).

"The 'Dastardly Treachery' of Prince John of Lancaster," *PMLA* 76 (1961): 488–92.

Judson, Alexander C. *The Life of Edmund Spenser* (Baltimore: Johns Hopkins University Press, 1945), vol. 9 of Greenlaw, Osgood, Padelford, and Heffner, eds., *The Complete Works of Edmund Spenser*.

"Spenser and the Munster Officials," *Studies in Philology* 44 (1947): 157–73.

Kastan, David Scott. "Workshop and/as Playhouse: Comedy and Commerce in *The Shoemaker's Holiday*," *Studies in Philology* 84 (1987): 324–37.

Kelley, Donald R. "Ideas of Resistance Before Elizabeth," in Dubrow and Strier, eds., *The Historical Renaissance*, 48–76.

Kendrick, T. D. *British Antiquity* (London: Methuen, 1950).

King, John N. *Spenser's Poetry and the Reformation Tradition* (Princeton University Press, 1990).

"Queen Elizabeth I: Representations of the Virgin Queen," *Renaissance Quarterly* 43 (1990): 30–74.

Kinney, Arthur F. *Elizabethan Backgrounds: Historical Documents of the Age of Elizabeth I* (Archon Books, 1975).

Krier, Theresa M. *Gazing on Secret Sights: Spenser, Classical Imitation, and the Decorums of Vision* (Ithaca: Cornell University Press, 1990).

Lacey, Robert. *Robert, Earl of Essex* (New York: Athenaeum, 1971).

Lane, Robert. *Shepheards Devises: Edmund Spenser's "Shepheardes Calender" and the Institutions of Elizabethan Society* (Athens: University of Georgia Press, 1993).

"'When Blood is their Argument': Class, Character, and Historymaking in Shakespeare's and Branagh's *Henry V*," *ELH* 61 (1994): 27–52.

Larner, Christina. *Enemies of God: The Witch-Hunt in Scotland* (London: Chatto, 1981).

Laurence, Anne. "The Cradle to the Grave: English Observation of Irish Social Customs in the Seventeenth Century," *The Seventeenth Century* 3 (1988): 63–84.

Leerssen, Joseph Theodoor. *Mere Irish and Fior-Ghael: Studies in the Idea of Irish Nationality, its Development and Literary Expression Prior to the Nineteenth Century* (Philadelphia: John Benjamins, 1986).

Lennon, Colm. "Richard Stanihurst (1547–1618) and Old English Identity," *Irish Historical Studies* 21 (1978): 121–43.

Richard Stanihurst the Dubliner, 1547–1618: A Biography with a Stanihurst Text, "On Ireland's Past" (County Dublin: Irish Academic Press, 1981).

Levinson, Judith C., ed. *The Famous History of Captain Thomas Stukeley 1605*, The Malone Society Reprints (Oxford University Press, 1970 [1975]).

Levy, F. J. *Tudor Historical Thought* (San Marino: The Huntington Library, 1967).

Lindley, David. "Embarrassing Ben: the Masques For Frances Howard," *English Literary Renaissance* 16 (1986): 343–59.

Lloyd, J. E. *Owen Glendower* (Oxford: Clarendon Press, 1931).

Lowe, Ben. "Peace Discourse and Mid-Tudor Foreign Policy," in *Political Thought and the Tudor Commonwealth: Deep Structure, Discourse, and Disguise*, ed. Paul A. Fideler and T. F. Mayer (London: Routledge, 1992), 108–39.

Lupton, Julia Reinhard. "Home-Making in Ireland: Virgil's Eclogue I and Book VI of *The Faerie Queene*," *Spenser Studies* 8 (1990): 119–45.

Lydon, James ed. *The English in Medieval Ireland* (Dublin: Royal Irish Academy, 1984).

"The Middle Nation," in Lydon ed., *The English in Medieval Ireland*, 1–26.

Maley, Willy. Review of David Cairns and Shaun Richards, *Writing Ireland*. *Textual Practice* 3 (1989): 291–98.

"How Milton and Some Contemporaries Read Spenser's *View*," in Bradshaw, Hadfield, and Maley, eds., *Representing Ireland*, 191– 208.

A Spenser Chronology (London: Macmillan, 1994).

"'Another Britain'? Bacon's *Certain Considerations Touching the Plantation in Ireland* (1609)," *Prose Studies* 18 (1995): 1–18.

Maley, Willy, ed. *The Supplication of the Blood of the English Most Lamentably Murdered in Ireland, Cryeng out of the Yearth for Revenge (1598)*, in *Analecta Hibernica* (Irish Manuscripts Commission) 36 (1994): 1–90.

Mallin, Eric S. "Emulous Factions and the Collapse of Chivalry: *Troilus and Cressida*," *Representations* 29 (1990): 145–79.

Malory, Sir Thomas. *Le Morte D'Arthur*, ed. Janet Cowen, vol. 1 (Harmondsworth: Penguin, 1969). 2 vols.

Mansfield, Bruce. *Phoenix of His Age: Interpretations of Erasmus c.1550–1570* (University of Toronto Press, 1979).

Marcus, Leah S. *Puzzling Shakespeare: Local Reading and Its Discontents* (Berkeley: University of California Press, 1988).

Marotti, Arthur F. "John Donne and the Rewards of Patronage," in *Patronage in the Renaissance*, ed. Guy Fitch Lytle and Stephen Orgel (Princeton University Press, 1981), 207–35.

Martin, Colin and Geoffrey Parker. *The Spanish Armada* (London: Hamilton, 1988).

Marx, Steven. "Shakespeare's Pacificism," *Renaissance Quarterly* 45 (1992): 49–95.

Mason, Roger A. "Scotching the Brut: Politics, History, and National Myth in Sixteenth-Century Britain," in *Scotland and England 1286–1815*, ed. Mason, 60–84.

Mason, Roger A., ed. *Scotland and England 1286–1815* (Edinburgh: John Donald, 1987).

Maxwell, Constantia. *Irish History from Contemporary Sources (1509–1610)* (London: Allen and Unwin, 1923).

The Stranger in Ireland from the Reign of Elizabeth to the Great Famine (London: Jonathan Cape, 1954).

May, Steven W. *The Elizabethan Courtier Poets: The Poems and their Contexts* (Columbia: University of Missouri Press, 1991).

MacCaffrey, Wallace T. *Queen Elizabeth and the Making of Policy, 1572–1588* (Princeton University Press, 1981).

Elizabeth I: War and Politics, 1588–1603 (Princeton University Press, 1992).

MacCarthy-Morrogh, Michael. *The Munster Plantation: English Migration to Southern Ireland, 1583–1641* (Oxford: Clarendon Press, 1986).

McCabe, Richard A. "The Masks of Duessa: Spenser, Mary Queen of Scots, and James VI," *English Literary Renaissance* 17 (1987): 224–42.

"The Fate of Irena: Spenser and Political Violence," in Coughlan, ed., *Spenser and Ireland*, 109–25.

"Edmund Spenser, Poet of Exile," *Proceedings of the British Academy* 80 (1993): 73–103.

McCoy, Richard C. *The Rites of Knighthood: The Literature and Politics of Elizabethan Chivalry* (Berkeley: University of California Press, 1989).

"'Thou Idol Ceremony:' Elizabeth I, *The Henriad*, and the Rites of the English Monarchy," in *Urban Life in the Renaissance*, ed. Susan Zimmerman and Ronald F. E. Weissman (Associated University Presses, 1989), 240–66.

"Lord of Liberty: Francis Davison and the Cult of Elizabeth," in Guy, ed., *The Reign of Elizabeth I*, 212–28.

MacCurtain, Margaret. "Women, Education and Learning in Early Modern Ireland," in MacCurtain and O'Dowd, eds., *Women in Early Modern Ireland*, 160–78.

MacCurtain, Margaret and Mary O'Dowd, eds. *Women in Early Modern Ireland* (Edinburgh University Press, 1991).

McGurk, J. J. N. "Casualties and Welfare Measures for the Sick and Wounded of the Nine Year War in Ireland, 1592–1602," *Journal of the Society for Army Historical Research* 68 (1990): 22–35, 188–204.

McIlwain, Charles Howard, ed. *The Political Works of James I* (Cambridge, Mass.: Harvard University Press, 1918).

Melchiori, Giorgio, ed. *The Second Part of King Henry IV* (Cambridge University Press, 1989).

Merchant, W. Moelwyn, ed. *Edward II* (New York: W. W. Norton, 1967).

Meron, Theodor, *Henry's Wars and Shakespeare's Laws: Perspectives on the Law of War in the Later Middle Ages* (Oxford: Clarendon Press, 1993).

Meyer, Sam. "Spenser's *Colin Clout*: the Poem and the Book," *The Papers of the Bibliographical Society of America* 56 (1962): 397–413.

An Interpretation of Edmund Spenser's "Colin Clout" (Cork University Press, 1969).

Miller, David Lee. *The Poem's Two Bodies: The Poetics of the 1590 "Faerie Queene"* (Princeton University Press, 1988).

Miller, Shannon. "Coming Home to the New World: the Ralegh Circle in Ireland," unpublished manuscript.

Montrose, Louis Adrian. "'Shaping Fantasies': Figurations of Gender and Power in Elizabethan Culture," *Representations* 2 (1983): 61–94.

"The Elizabethan Subject and the Spenserian Text," in *Literary Theory / Renaissance Texts* ed. Patricia Parker and David Quint (Baltimore: Johns Hopkins University Press, 1986), 303–40.

"The Work of Gender in the Discourse of Discovery," *Representations* 33 (1991): 1–41.

Moody, T. W., F. X. Martin, and F. J. Byrne, eds. *A New History of Ireland.* 9 vols. (Oxford: Clarendon Press, 1976–84).

Morgan, Hiram. "Extradition and Treason-Trial of a Gaelic Lord: the Case of Brian O'Rourke," *The Irish Jurist* 22 (1987): 285–301.

"Tom Lee: The Posing Peacemaker," in Bradshaw, Hadfield, and Maley, eds., *Representing Ireland*, 132–65.

Tyrone's Rebellion: The Outbreak of the Nine Years War in Tudor Ireland (Woodbridge, Suffolk: Boydell Press. Royal Historical Society, 1993).

"The Fall of Sir John Perrot," in Guy, ed., *The Reign of Elizabeth I*, 109–25.

Morgan, T. "The Welchmens Jubilee to the Honour of St. David" (London, 1642).

Moryson, Fynes. *The Itinerary of Fynes Moryson.* 4 vols. (Glasgow: MacLehose, 1907–8).

Shakespeare's Europe: A Survey of the Condition of Europe at the End of the Sixteenth Century. Being Unpublished Chapters of Fynes Moryson's Itinerary (1617), ed. Charles Hughes (New York: Benjamin Bloom, 1967). 2nd edition.

Mullaney, Steven. *The Place of the Stage: License, Play, and Power in Renaissance England* (University of Chicago Press, 1988).

Murphy, Andrew. "Gold Lace and a Frozen Snake: Donne, Wotton, and the Nine Years War," *Irish Studies Review* 8 (1994): 9–11.

"Shakespeare's Irish History," *Literature and History* 5 (1996): 39–60.

Myers, James P., ed., *Elizabethan Ireland: A Selection of Writings by Elizabethan Writers on Ireland* (Archon Books, 1983).

Naunton, Sir Robert. *Fragmenta Regalia: or Observations on Queen Elizabeth, Her Times and Favorites*, ed. John S. Cerovski (London: Associated University Presses, 1985).

Neale, J. E. *Elizabeth I and Her Parliaments, 1584–1601* (London: Jonathan Cape, 1957).

Queen Elizabeth I (New York: Doubleday-Anchor, 1957).

Neill, Michael. "Broken English and Broken Irish: Nation, Language, and the Optic of Power in Shakespeare's Histories," *Shakespeare Quarterly* 45 (1994): 1–32.

Newman, Karen. *Fashioning Femininity and English Renaissance Drama* (University of Chicago Press, 1991).

Nichols, John, ed. *The Progresses and Public Processions of Queen Elizabeth.* 3 vols. (London, 1823).

Nohrnberg, James. *The Analogy of "The Faerie Queene"* (Princeton University Press, 1976).

Norbrook, David. *Poetry and Politics in the English Renaissance* (London: Routledge and Kegan Paul, 1984).

Norden, John. "A Prayer for the Prosperous Proceedings and Good Successe of the Earle of Essex and his companies, in their present expedition in Ireland against Tyrone and his adherents, Rebels there. Fit to be used of all loyall subjects, as well in that Countrie, as in England" (London: Edward Allde, 1599).

Oakeshott, Walter. "Carew Ralegh's Copy of Spenser," *The Library* 26 (1971): 1–21.

Ó Cuiv, Brian. "The Irish Language in the Early Modern Period," in Moody, Martin, and Byrne, eds., *A New History of Ireland*, 3: 509–45.

Ó Domhnaill, Sean. "Warfare in Sixteenth-Century Ireland," *Irish Historical Studies* 5 (1946–47): 29–54.

Ó Dónaill, Niall. *Foclóir Gaeilge-Béarla* (Richview: Borwn and Nolan, 1977).

O'Donovan, John, ed. "Docwra's Relation of the Service Done in Ireland," in *Miscellany of the Celtic Society* (Dublin, 1849), 189–229.

O'Faolain, Sean. *The Great O'Neill: A Biography of Hugh O'Neill, Earl of Tyrone, 1550–1616* (New York: Duell, Sloan, and Pearce, 1942).

Oram, William A., Einar Bjorvand, Ronald Bond, Thomas H. Cain, Alexander Dunlop, and Richard Schell, eds. *The Yale Edition of the Shorter Poems of Edmund Spenser* (New Haven: Yale University Press, 1989).

Orgel, Stephen. *Ben Jonson: The Complete Masques* (New Haven: Yale University Press, 1969).

"The Authentic Shakespeare," *Representations* 21 (1988): 1– 26.

Ó Riordan, Michelle. *The Gaelic Mind and the Collapse of the Gaelic World* (Cork University Press, 1990).

Osborne, Francis. *The Works of Francis Osborne*. 8th edition (London, 1682).

O'Sullivan, Anne. "Tadhg O'Daly and Sir George Carew," *Eigse* 14 (1971): 27–38.

O'Sullivan Beare, Don Philip. *Ireland Under Elizabeth*, ed. and tr. Matthew J. Byrne (Dublin, 1903).

Outhwaite, R. B. "Dearth, the English Crown and the 'Crisis of the 1590s,'" in *The European Crisis of the 1590s: Essays in Comparative History*, ed. Peter Clark (London: Allen and Unwin, 1985), 23–43.

Owen, G. Dyfnallt. *Elizabethan Wales: The Social Scene* (Cardiff: University of Wales Press, 1962).

Owen, George. *The Description of Pembrokeshire by George Owen of Henllys*, ed. Dillwyn Miles. The Welsh Classics (Dyfed, Wales: Gomer Press, 1994).

Palmer, Daryl W. *Hospitable Performances: Dramatic Genre and Cultural Practices in Early Modern England* (West Lafayette: Purdue University Press, 1992).

Palmer, William. *The Problem of Ireland in Tudor Foreign Policy, 1485–1603* (Rochester, N.Y.: Boydell Press, 1994).

"Gender, Violence, and Rebellion in Tudor and Early Stuart Ireland," *Sixteenth Century Journal* 23 (1992): 699–712.

Patterson, Annabel. *Censorship and Interpretation: The Conditions of Writing and Reading in Early Modern England* (Madison: University of Wisconsin Press, 1984).

Shakespeare and the Popular Voice (Oxford: Basil Blackwell, 1989).

"Rethinking Tudor Historiography," *The South Atlantic Quarterly* 92 (1993): 185–208.

Reading Between the Lines (Madison: University of Wisconsin Press, 1993).

Reading Holinshed's "Chronicles" (University of Chicago Press, 1994).

Patterson, Nerys. "Gaelic Law and the Tudor Conquest of Ireland: the Social Background of the Sixteenth-Century Recensions of the Pseudo-Historical Prologue to the *Senchas mar*," *Irish Historical Studies* 27 (1991): 193–215.

Pawlisch, Hans S. *Sir John Davies and the Conquest of Ireland: A Study in Legal Imperialism* (Cambridge University Press, 1985).

Payne, Robert. *A Briefe description of Ireland: Made in this yeare, 1589.* The English Experience 548 (New York: Da Capo Press, 1973).

Peele, George. *Edward I. The Dramatic Works of George Peele*, ed. Frank S. Hook. Vol.2 of *The Life and Works of George Peele*, ed. Charles Tyler Prouty (New Haven: Yale University Press, 1961).

Penry, John. *Three Treatises Concerning Wales*, ed. David Williams (Cardiff: University of Wales Press, 1960).

Phillips, J. R. S. "The Anglo-Norman Nobility," in Lydon, ed., *The English in Medieval Ireland*, 87–104.

Plomer, Henry R. and Tom Peete Cross. *The Life and Correspondence of Lodowick Bryskett* (University of Chicago Press, 1927).

Potter, David. "French Intrigue in Ireland During the Reign of Henri II, 1547–1559," *The International History Review* 5 (1983): 159–80.

Powel, David. *The Historie of Cambria now called Wales* (London, 1584) The English Experience 163 (New York: Da Capo Press, 1969).

Pritchard, Arnold. *Catholic Loyalism in Elizabethan England* (Chapel Hill: University of North Carolina Press, 1979).

Puttenham, George. *The Arte of English Poesie* (Kent, Ohio: Kent State University Press, 1970).

Quinn, David Beers. *The Elizabethans and the Irish* (Ithaca: Cornell University Press, 1966).

Rabl, Kathleen. "Taming the 'Wild Irish' in English Renaissance Drama," in *National Images and Stereotypes*, ed. Wolfgang Zach and Heinz Kosok (Tubingen: G. Narr, 1987), 47–59. Vol. 3. of *Literary Interrelations: Ireland, England and the World*. 3 vols.

Rackin, Phyllis. *Stages of History: Shakespeare's English Chronicles* (Ithaca: Cornell University Press, 1990).

Rambuss, Richard. *Spenser's Secret Career* (Cambridge University Press, 1993).

"Spenser's Lives, Spenser's Careers," unpublished manuscript.

Randolph, Mary Claire. "The Medical Concept in English Renaissance Satiric Theory: its Possible Relationships and Implications," *Studies in Philology* 38 (1941): 125–57.

Rawlinson, Richard, ed. *The Life, Deedes and death of Sir John Perrot, the Author Unknown* (London, 1728).

Read, Conyers. *Lord Burghley and Queen Elizabeth* (New York: Alfred A. Knopf, 1960).

Read, David, "Ralegh's *Discoverie of Guiana* and the Elizabethan Model of Empire," in *The Work of Dissimilitude: Essays from the Sixth Citadel Conference on Medieval and Renaissance Literature*, ed. David G. Allen and Robert A. White (Newark: University of Delaware Press, 1992), 166–76.

Rebhorn, Wayne A. "The Crisis of the Aristocracy in *Julius Caesar*," *Renaissance Quarterly* 43 (1990): 75–111.

Renwick, W. L., ed. *"Daphnaida" and Other Poems by Edmund Spenser* (London: Scholartis Press, 1929).

  ed. *A View of the Present State of Ireland* (London: Scholartis Press, 1934 [republished 1971]).

Ribner, Irving. *The English History Play in the Age of Shakespeare* (New York: Octagon Books, 1979).

Rich, Barnabe. *A New Description of Ireland* (London, 1610).

The Irish Hubub (London, 1619).

Roberts, Peter R. "The 'Act of Union' in Welsh History," *Transactions of the Honourable Society of Cymmrodorion* (1974): 49–72.

Robinson, Forrest G., ed. *Sir Philip Sidney's An Apology for Poetry* (Indianapolis: Bobbs-Merrill, 1970).

Robinson, Philip S. *The Plantation of Ulster: British Settlement in an Irish Landscape, 1600–1670* (New York: St. Martin's Press, 1984).

Rosenberg, Eleanor. *Leicester: Patron of Letters* (New York: Columbia University Press, 1955).

Rowe, Katherine A. "Dismembering and Forgetting in *Titus Andronicus*," *Shakespeare Quarterly* 45 (1994): 279–303.

Rowse, A. L. *The Expansion of Elizabethan England* (London: Macmillan, 1955).

Ryan, Michael T. "Assimilating New Worlds in the Sixteenth and Seventeenth Centuries," *Comparative Studies in Society and History* 23 (1981): 519–38.

Samuel, Raphael, ed. *Patriotism: The Making and Unmaking of British National Identity*. 3 vols. (London: Routledge, 1989).

Scarisbrick, J. J. *The Reformation and the English People* (Oxford: Blackwell, 1984).

Schoenbaum, Samuel. *William Shakespeare: A Compact Documentary Life* (Oxford University Press, 1977).

Schwind, Mona L. "'Nurse to All Rebellions': Grace O'Malley and Sixteenth-Century Connacht," *Eire–Ireland* 13 (1978): 40–61.

Scott, A. B. and F. X. Martin eds. and trs. *Expugnatio Hibernica: The Conquest of Ireland by Giraldus Cambrensis* (Dublin: Royal Irish Academy, 1978).

Sedgwick, Eve Kosofsky. *Between Men: English Literature and male Homosocial Bonding* (New York: Columbia University Press, 1985).

Sessions, William. *The Spread of British Printing 1557 to 1695* (York, England: Ebor Press, 1988).

Shapiro, James. "Revisiting *Tamburlaine*: *Henry V* as Shakespeare's Belated Armada Play," *Criticism* 31 (1989): 351–66.

  "*The Scot's Tragedy* and the Politics of Popular Drama," *English Literary Renaissance* 23 (1993): 428–49.

Sharpe, J. A. "'Last Dying Speeches': Religion, Ideology and Public Execution in Seventeenth-Century England," *Past and Present* 107 (1985): 144–67.

Sharpe, Robert Boies. *The Real War of the Theaters: Shakespeare's Fellows in Rivalry with the Admiral's Men, 1594–1603. Repertories, Devices, and Types* (London: Oxford University Press, 1935).

Sheehan, Anthony J. "The Overthrow of the Plantation of Munster in October 1598," *The Irish Sword* 15 (1982): 11–22.

Shepherd, Simon. *Marlowe and the Politics of Elizabethan Theatre* (Brighton: Harvester, 1986).

Spenser. Harvester New Readings (New York: Harvester Wheatsheaf, 1989).

Sherman, William H. *John Dee: The Politics of Reading and Writing in the English Renaissance* (Amherst: University of Massachusetts Press, 1995).

Shire, Helena. *A Preface to Spenser* (London: Longman, 1978).

Sidney Papers (Letters and Memorials of State), ed. Arthur Collins, vol. 2 (London, 1746). 2 vols.

Simms, Katharine. "Bards and Barons: the Anglo-Irish Aristocracy and the Native Culture," in *Medieval Frontier Societies*, ed. Robert Bartlett and Angus MacKay (Oxford: Clarendon Press, 1989), 177–97.

Simpson, Richard, ed. *The School of Shakspere*, vol. 1 (London: Chatto and Windus, 1878). 2 vols.

Sinfield, Alan. *Faultlines: Cultural Materialism and the Politics of Dissident Reading* (Berkeley: University of California Press, 1992).

Skura, Meredith Ann. "Discourse and the Individual: the Case of Colonialism in *The Tempest*," *Shakespeare Quarterly* 40 (1989): 42–69.

Smith, Lacey Baldwin. *Treason in Tudor England: Politics and Paranoia* (Princeton University Press, 1986).

Smith, Roland M. "The Irish Background of Spenser's *View*," *Journal of English and Germanic Philology* 42 (1943): 499– 515.

"Spenser, Holinshed, and the *Leabhar Gabhála*," *Journal of English and Germanic Philology* 43 (1944): 390–401.

"A Further Note on Una and Duessa," *PMLA* 61 (1946): 592– 96.

"Irish Names in *The Faerie Queene*," *Modern Language Notes* 61 (1946): 27–38.

Snyder, Edward D. "The Wild Irish: a Study of Some English Satires Against the Irish, Scots, and Welsh," *Modern Philology* 17 (1919–20): 147–85.

Southwell, Robert. *An Humble Supplication to Her Majestie*, ed. R. C. Bald (Cambridge University Press, 1953).

Spedding, James, ed. *The Letters and the Life of Francis Bacon*, vol. 2 (London: Longman, 1862). Vol. 9 of *The Works of Francis Bacon*, ed. James Spedding, Robert Leslie Ellis, and Douglas Denon Heath.

Spencer, Janet M. "Princes, Pirates, and Pigs: Criminalizing Wars of Conquest in *Henry V*," *Shakespeare Quarterly* 47 (1996): 160–77.

The Spenser Encyclopedia, ed. A. C. Hamilton *et al.* (London: Routledge, 1990).

Spicer, Joaneath. "The Renaissance Elbow," in *A Cultural History of Gesture*, ed. Jan Bremmer and Herman Roodenburg (Ithaca: Cornell University Press, 1992), 84–128.

Stallybrass, Peter. "Rethinking Text and History," *LTP: Journal of Literature Teaching Politics* 2 (1983): 96–107.

"Patriarchal Territories: the Body Enclosed," in Ferguson, Quilligan, and Vickers, eds., *Rewriting the Renaissance*, 123–42.

"Time, Space, and Unity: the Symbolic Discourse of *The Faerie Queene*," in Samuel, ed., *Patriotism*, 3: 199–214.

Stallybrass, Peter, and Allon White. *The Politics and Poetics of Transgression* (Ithaca: Cornell University Press, 1986).

Stillman, Robert E. "Spenserian Autonomy and the Trial of the New Historicism: Book Six of *The Faerie Queene*," *English Literary Renaissance* 22 (1992): 299–314.

Stone, Lawrence. *The Family, Sex, and Marriage in England, 1500–1800* (London: Weidenfeld and Nicolson, 1977).

Stow, John. *The Annales of England* (London, 1592, 1600, 1615).

Strier, Richard. "Radical Donne: 'Satire III'," *ELH* 60 (1993), 283–322.

Strong, Roy. *Portraits of Queen Elizabeth I* (Oxford: Clarendon Press, 1963).

The Cult of Elizabeth: Elizabethan Portraiture and Pageantry (Berkeley: University of California Press, 1977).

Artists of the Tudor Court: The Portrait Miniature Rediscovered 1520–1620 (London: Victoria and Albert Museum, 1983).

Sugden, Edward H. *A Topographical Dictionary to the Works of Shakespeare and his Fellow Dramatists* (Manchester University Press, 1925).

Taylor, Gary, ed. *Henry V* (Oxford: Clarendon Press, 1982).

"The Fortunes of Oldcastle," *Shakespeare Survey* 38 (1985): 85–100.

"Bardicide," in *Shakespeare and Cultural traditions: The Selected Proceedings of the International Shakespearean Association: World Congress, Tokyo, 1991*, ed. Tetsuo Kishi, Roger Pringle, and Stanley Wells (London: Associated University Presses, 1994): 333–49.

"Forms of Opposition: Shakespeare and Middleton," *English Literary Renaissance* 24 (1994): 283–314.

Tenison, E. M. *Elizabethan England: Being a History of this Country in Relation to all Foreign Princes. From Original Manuscripts, many hitherto unpublished; co-ordinated with XVIth Century Printed Matter Ranging from Royal Proclamations to Broadside Ballads*, vol. 9 (Royal Leamington Spa, 1950). 12 vols.

Tennenhouse, Leonard. *Power on Display: The Politics of Shakespeare's Genres* (New York: Methuen, 1986).

Thomson, Peter. *Shakespeare's Theatre* (London: Routledge and Kegan Paul, 1983).

Tilley, Morris Palmer. *A Dictionary of the Proverbs in England in the Sixteenth and Seventeenth Centuries* (Ann Arbor: University of Michigan Press, 1950).

Tough, D. L. W. *The Last Years of a Frontier: A History of the Borders During the Reign of Elizabeth* (Oxford: Clarendon Press, 1928).

Turner, Bryan S. *The Body and Society: Explorations in Social Theory* (Oxford: Basil Blackwell, 1984).

Tydeman, William. "Peele's *Edward I* and the Elizabethan View of Wales," in *The Welsh Connection*, ed. William Tydeman (Llandysul, Dyfed: Gomer Press, 1986), 24–53.

Tylus, Jane. "Orpheus in the Shade: Spenser's pastoral Communities," in *Writing and Vulnerability in the Late Renaissance* (Stanford University Press, 1993), 113–43.

Underdown, David. "The Taming of the Scold: The Enforcement of Patriarchal Authority in Early Modern England," in *Order and Disorder in Early*

Modern England, ed. Anthony Fletcher and John Stevenson (Cambridge University Press, 1985), 116–36.

Revel, Riot, and Rebellion: Popular Politics and Culture in England, 1603–1660 (Oxford University Press, 1986).

Ure, Peter, ed. *King Richard II* (London: Routledge, 1956).

Urkowitz, Steven. "Good News about 'Bad' Quartos," in *"Bad" Shakespeare: Revaluations of the Shakespeare Canon*, ed. Maurice Charney (Associated University Presses, 1988), 189– 206.

"'If I Mistake in Those Foundations Which I Build Upon': Peter Alexander's Textual Analysis of *Henry VI Parts 2 and 3*," *English Literary Renaissance* 18 (1988): 230–56.

Verstegan, Richard. *Theatrum Crudelitatum Haereticorum Nostri Temporis* (Antwerp, 1588).

An Advertisement Written to a Secretarie of my L. Treasurers of Ingland (Antwerp, 1592).

Waller, Gary. *Edmund Spenser: A Literary Life* (New York: St. Martin's Press, 1994).

Ware, James. *Two Histories of Ireland* (Dublin, 1633). The English Experience 421 (New York: Da Capo Press, 1971).

Wayne, Valerie, ed. *The Flower of Friendship: A Renaissance Dialogue Contesting Marriage by Edmund Tilney* (Ithaca: Cornell University Press, 1992).

Wernham, R. B. *The Return of the Armadas: The Last Years of the Elizabethan War Against Spain 1595–1603* (Oxford: Clarendon Press, 1994).

West, Michael. "Spenser's Art of War: Chivalric Allegory, Military Technology, and the Elizabethan Mock-Heroic Sensibility," *Renaissance Quarterly* 41 (1988): 654–704.

White, Dean Gunter. "Henry VIII's Irish Kerne in France and Scotland," *The Irish Sword* 3 (1957–58): 213–25.

Whitney, Charles. "Festivity and Topicality in the Coventry Scene of *1 Henry IV*," *English Literary Renaissance* 24 (1994): 410–48.

Whittier, Gayle. "Falstaff as a Welshwoman: Uncomic Androgyny," *Ball State University Forum* 20 (1979): 23–35.

Wiener, Carol Z. "The Beleaguered Isle: a Study of Elizabethan and Jacobean Anti-Catholicism," *Past and Present* 51 (1971): 27– 62.

Wikander, Matthew H. *The Play of Truth and State: Historical Drama from Shakespeare to Brecht* (Baltimore: Johns Hopkins University Press, 1986).

Wiles, David. *The Early Plays of Robin Hood* (Cambridge: D. S. Brewer, 1981).

Williams, Glanmor. *Recovery, Reorientation, and Reformation: Wales, c.1415–1642* (Oxford: Clarendon Press, 1987).

Williams, J. E. Caerwyn. *The Court Poet in Medieval Society* (London: Oxford University Press, 1971).

Williams, Norman Lloyd. *Sir Walter Raleigh* (London: Cassell, 1988).

Williams, Penry. *The Council in the Marches of Wales Under Elizabeth I* (Cardiff: University of Wales Press, 1958).

"The Welsh Borderland under Queen Elizabeth," *Welsh History Review* 1 (1960): 19–36.

The Tudor Regime (Oxford: Clarendon Press, 1979).

"The Crown and the Counties," in Haigh, ed., *The Reign of Elizabeth*, 125–46.

Willson, David Harris. *King James VI and I* (London: Jonathan Cape, 1956).

Wilson, Richard. *Will Power: Essays on Shakespearean Authority* (Detroit: Wayne State University Press, 1993).

Wilson, Thomas. *The State of England, Anno Dom. 1600*, ed. F. J. Fisher, Camden Miscellany 16 (London, 1936).

Wood, Herbert, ed. *The Chronicle of Ireland 1584–1608. By Sir James Perrot* (Dublin: Irish Manuscripts Commission, 1933).

Yates, Frances A. *Astraea: The Imperial Theme in the Sixteenth Century* (London: Routledge and Kegan Paul, 1975).

Yeats, W. B. *Essays and Introductions* (London: Macmillan, 1961).

Zitner, S. P. "Staging the Occult in *1 Henry IV*," in *Mirror up to Shakespeare: Essays in Honour of G. R. Hibbard*, ed. J. C. Gray (University of Toronto Press, 1984), 138–48.

Index

Cambridge Studies in Renaissance Literature and Culture

General editor
STEPHEN ORGEL
Jackson Eli Reynolds Professor of Humanities, Stanford University